Students' Identities and Literacy Learning

Sarah J. McCarthey
University of Illinois at Urbana-Champaign
Champaign, Illinois, USA

INTERNATIONAL
**Reading
Association**

800 Barksdale Road,
PO Box 8139
Newark, Delaware 19714-8139, USA
www.reading.org

National Reading Conference

National Reading Conference
122 South Michigan Avenue
Suite 1100
Chicago, Illinois 60603, USA

Director of Publications   Joan M. Irwin
Editorial Director, Books and Special Projects   Matthew W. Baker
Senior Editor, Books and Special Projects   Tori Mello Bachman
Permissions Editor   Janet S. Parrack
Production Editor   Shannon Benner
Assistant Editor   Corinne M. Mooney
Editorial Assistant   Tyanna L. Collins
Publications Manager   Beth Doughty
Production Department Manager   Iona Sauscermen
Supervisor, Electronic Publishing   Anette Schütz
Senior Electronic Publishing Specialist   Cheryl J. Strum
Electronic Publishing Specialist   R. Lynn Harrison
Proofreader   Charlene M. Nichols

Project Editor   Janet S. Parrack

Library of Congress Cataloging-in-Publication Data

McCarthey, Sarah J., 1955-
    Students' identities and literacy learning/Sarah J. McCarthey.
      p. cm.— (Literacy studies series)
  Includes bibliographical references (p.) and index.
    ISBN 0-87207-446-3 (alk. paper)
  1. Language arts (Elementary)—United States—Case studies. 2. Multicultural education—United States—Case studies. 3. Identity (Psychology)—United States—Case studies.
  I. Title. II. Series.
    LB1576 .M249 2002
    372.6—dc21

                        2002002344

In memory of my mother

and to my son...

may the power of story continue to connect us.

Contents

Note From the Series Editors

Few topics are as important as the development of identity and the role of literacy in this process. In this eighth book in the Literacy Studies Series, Sarah J. McCarthey synthesizes a powerful body of ethnographic case study research conducted across three diverse sites. Through a qualitative lens, the children and teachers in these classes come alive, displaying varying degrees of alliance or resistance within the prescribed literacy curricula. We see the payoff and price of "doing school" in students' willingness to conform or resist practices that influence their in- and out-of-school identity construction.

Managerial and curricular practices that have their origins in business spill over into classroom settings with varying consequences for students (Chouliaraki & Fairclough, 2001). These practices collide with the postmodern reality that

> identity can no longer be written through the lens of cultural uniformity or enforced through the discourse of assimilation—rather, students bring to the classroom not some unified grand narrative but multiple narratives representing diverse immigration and language and cultural experiences. (Giroux, 2000, p. 190)

The case studies presented here move our debates and discussions well beyond the bounds of method into a challenging consideration of how curriculum interacts with students' identity construction. Issues of power and positioning underpin much of this work, illustrating the complex forces that cause children to weigh the costs and benefits of classroom conformity. Consistent with a growing body of work on identity construction, Sarah McCarthey's classroom research challenges past views of literacy curriculum as a kind of neutral zone, devoid of asymmetrical power struggles.

Students' Identities and Literacy Learning offers a carefully researched window on children and teachers as social actors, making thoughtful judgments about how to proceed in enacting their literate selves. We hope this work will challenge us to pay attention to how our curriculum decisions in literacy help or hinder students' identities in various social contexts.

Thomas W. Bean
University of Nevada, Las Vegas
Las Vegas, Nevada, USA

Lisa Patel Stevens
State Department of Education
Honolulu, Hawaii, USA

Series Editors

References

Chouliaraki, L., & Fairclough, N. (2001). *Discourse in late Modernity: Rethinking critical discourse analysis*. Edinburgh: Edinburgh University Press.

Giroux, H.A. (2000). Postmodern education and disposable youth. In P.P. Trifonas (Ed.), *Revolutionary pedagogies: Cultural politics, institutional education, and the discourses of theory* (pp. 174–195). New York: Routledge Falmer.

Review Board

Marjorie Siegel
Columbia University Teachers College
New York, New York

Margaret M. Smith
Clark County School District
Las Vegas, Nevada

Sharon Vaughn
University of Texas at Austin
Austin, Texas

Josephine Peyton Young
Arizona State University
Tempe, Arizona

Acknowledgments

I wish to thank the many teachers who offered me the opportunity to spend significant amounts of time in their classrooms. Their efforts to change classroom instruction and to teach against the grain are valiant. I also want to thank the many wonderful students who have touched my life by offering their writing and their voices to me during interviews and observations. Parents have contributed their ideas, attitudes, and in many cases their home to me. Without these many participants, I could not have written this book—thank you.

I also wish to thank graduate students who helped in data collection and analysis, especially Jung-ah Choi and Ana Herrera from the University of Illinois at Urbana-Champaign. Many colleagues from several institutions have supported my work, and I wish to acknowledge them. I particularly appreciate the insights of my husband, colleague, and friend, Mark Dressman. Anonymous reviewers of this book also provided encouragement and helpful critiques.

Some funding throughout the years provided by the National Center for Research on Teacher Education at Michigan State University, the Spencer Postdoctoral Program from the Spencer Foundation, The University of Texas Summer Grants, and the University of Illinois Research Board have helped with data collection and analysis.

Introduction

Who are we? How did we become who we are? These compelling questions have been asked for decades by people in the Western world. However, the most recent theories about identity require that these questions be reframed: How do our social worlds construct who we are? In what contexts do we enact certain aspects of our identities? These questions reflect the shift from viewing identity as a unitary, fixed essence within the individual to viewing it as a multidimensional, fluid process that depends on social context.

At the same time these shifts in theories about identity were occurring, conceptions of literacy and their implications for changing classroom practices were evolving as well. For example, process approaches to writing have reflected a change in focus from the written *product* to a focus on *process*, and moved from considering writing as an individual endeavor to also considering the social functions and contexts of writing. Shifts from believing that meaning resides in the text to considering the interaction of reader and text within social contexts have paralleled the changes in theories about writing. In the 1980s and 1990s, some classrooms began to reflect these changes by incorporating writing process and literature-based instruction in order to provide students with more opportunities to explore their identities as readers and writers within supportive contexts. These classrooms placed the student at the center of the learning process, while the teacher acted as a scaffold, understanding students' needs and providing support for the next steps in the learning process. Writing workshops offered opportunities for students to choose topics of importance to them and to communicate with real audiences for authentic purposes. Using authentic children's literature to learn skills

1

within the context of meaningful reading material and purposeful activities has been the focus of literature-based classrooms.

The Influence of Contexts on Students' Identities

This book highlights the influences of school contexts, and to some extent home contexts, on students' identities as readers and writers by presenting data collected from school sites in which teachers implemented writing workshop and literature-based instruction. The three sites where I collected data from 1990 to 1999 had much in common: The students were from diverse cultural and social backgrounds, and the teachers, who were white and middle class, had extensive workshops or preservice education in writing workshop or literature-based instruction. In addition, the teachers held strong views about how to support children's reading and writing and, in many ways, were adventurers attempting to make changes in their classrooms and in their schools by introducing innovative instruction to their students and other teachers.

The primary focus in this book is on the students, but in providing information about the contexts in which they read and wrote, I also demonstrate the power of the teacher-student relationship, the importance of the classroom curriculum, and the influence of parents and peers on students. As I recount students' stories, several important issues are acknowledged about my relationships with them: First, the students and I came from different cultural and linguistic backgrounds, and although I may not have presented their stories in the same way as a researcher who shared their backgrounds would have, I learned much from trying to understand their worlds. Second, I developed significant relationships with many of the students, and therefore I may reveal some bias toward the students' points of view over those of the teachers. For example, in the case of Anita in Chapter 2, I provide examples of the teacher-student writing conference and suggest that the teacher was imposing her view of good writing on the student. Although the teacher's explanation is presented, I interpreted the interaction from the point of view of the student. Third, I constructed narratives about the students based on my interviews with them, my interpretations of their writing, and my observations of them in different contexts; however, they did not have the opportunity to read my interpretations or respond to my characterizations of them. With this in mind, I present snapshots of nine students from diverse linguistic and cultural backgrounds, who taught me lessons about what it means to learn to read and write in U.S. classrooms. Their stories illustrate the dynamic relationship between identity and context and the value of understanding individual children in relation to their home and school cultures.

Organization of the Book

In Chapter 1, I outline the theoretical foundations of the constructs of identity and briefly review the literature relevant to current literacy practices; provide an overview of the methods used in each of the three studies from which I draw; and define the frames used for analysis such as appropriation, resistance, and transformation. Subsequent chapters are organized according to three features: (1) presenting the data in chronological order of its collection, (2) presenting data that captures an evolving sense of the various contexts that shape and are shaped by students' identities, and (3) selecting cases that represent the concepts I wished to explore.

The site of the first study was a combination fifth/sixth-grade classroom in New York City in the fall of 1990. I collected data for 5 weeks on students' views about writing and their interactions with the teacher. The site of the second study was a third/fourth-grade classroom in central Texas during the 1994–1995 school year, where I expanded my understanding of the contexts that influenced students' literacy learning. I made home visits and asked students to talk more about their home literacy learning. These data helped me to focus more on issues of identity and the ways that various contexts influence students' views of reading and writing. For the third study conducted in the spring of 1999, I collected data at another central Texas site to incorporate in the studies not only information about home and school settings, but also about peers. I was particularly interested in the constructed nature of identity and how others' perceptions (teachers, parents, and peers) of a student might influence a particular student's views of literacy tasks. Although I interviewed and gathered data from parents in the latter two studies, I found the data collected in the classrooms to be the most informative about students'

3

school literacy learning. Therefore, I organized this book by study (or site), selecting three cases from each study to illustrate the range of ways in which students shape their identities in relation to classroom settings. In each chapter, the following case studies are presented: one involving a student who appropriates the classroom norms by conforming to the rules, one involving a student who resists the classroom expectations by avoiding or challenging norms, and one involving a student who transforms the expectations to create alternative spaces for literacy learning.

In Chapter 2, I analyze the data collected from the New York City site in which students participated in a writing workshop. The three case studies used demonstrate the variations in students' understanding of the purposes of writing and their responses to classroom norms. Miguel conformed to the classroom norms and saw writing as an important tool for learning and fulfilling classroom assignments. In contrast, Anita resisted the teacher's expectations and saw writing as a dialogue with herself to be done outside of school. Ella saw writing as a creative process done for an audience and was able to transform the classroom norms to maintain her identity as a fiction writer. These cases highlight the importance of the teacher-student relationship in developing students' identities as writers.

In Chapter 3, I analyze the data collected from the first central Texas classroom site, which included interviews with teachers and parents. Three cases demonstrate the variations in students' identities as readers and writers and the contexts that influenced them. Rita, who was in the process of appropriating classroom expectations, viewed writing as a form of social connection to assist her in understanding these expectations. Greg felt oppressed by the classroom structures. He resisted through his antisocial behavior, but maintained his journal writing as an important means of self-expression. Mandy also saw writing as a form of self-expression, but she questioned the classroom norms and found many ways to communicate with audiences through different genres. These cases illustrate how teachers' implicit values affect students' views of themselves as readers and writers.

In Chapter 4, I focus on data from a fifth-grade classroom at another central Texas site, in which students participated in a literature-based curriculum, writing workshop, and a schoolwide computerized reading program (Accelerated Reader Program). Interviews with the teacher, parents, students, and peers revealed that students defined themselves in relation to various features of the school curriculum, as well as their home literacy experiences. Jennifer conformed to the expectations implicit in all three classroom routines and was well accepted by her teacher and peers. Lucas was not successful in the Accelerated Reader Program and resisted school-related reading and writing tasks. Daniel excelled in all areas of the language arts curriculum and was able to integrate his home and school writings to transform his strong feelings about race relations from one context to another. The public nature of the Accelerated Reader Program highlighted students' success or lack thereof in reading and had a strong influence on their self-perceptions as readers. These cases demonstrate the ways in which students negotiated their literate identities within classroom and larger institutional norms.

In Chapter 5, I use cross-case analyses from the three studies to draw conclusions about the relationships between student identity and home and classroom contexts. The discussion focuses on the comparisons among students who appropriated classroom norms, resisted expectations, and transformed classroom norms in some way, and contextualizes students' identities in terms of the teacher-student relationship and classroom curriculum. Implications for practice focus on (1) the need for teachers to examine their assumptions about literacy, curriculum, and the students they teach; (2) the need to understand students' backgrounds and provide relevant curriculum; (3) the importance of students having purposes for literacy experiences and audiences beyond the classroom; and (4) the need for explicit discussions about identity.

Throughout the book, I highlight the teacher-student relationship and demonstrate the ways in which the teacher's authority influenced students' literacy learning. Those students who appropriated the classroom norms tended to have their work valued in the classroom at the same time that home and school values were shared. Students who resisted classroom norms found their classrooms oppressive because their interactions with their teachers were negative and, more often than not, there was a lack of communication between parents and the teachers. Students who resisted classroom norms but who transformed their identities had found ways to interact positively with their teachers and peers. For some students, the curricular contexts such

5

as writing workshop or literature response allowed opportunities to excel and enact features of their identities, while for other students, the same curriculum posed dilemmas and challenges. The cases display the multiple ways in which students make sense of, interact with, and enact particular features of literacy curriculum. Although each chapter portrays individual students and their teachers within particular settings, the book as a whole emphasizes the importance of understanding students within multiple, layered contexts in order to promote the continual process of identity construction.

Considerations for the Reader

Readers of this book should consider their own literacy backgrounds, teaching experiences, and beliefs about language and learning, because the cases are intended not only to inform our instruction but also to connect to our own experiences of learning and teaching. Readers should suspend their judgments about the teachers in the studies because, as one reviewer stated, "These stories, these teachers, could be any one of us at any given time." These stories are not about bad teaching, but are examples of real-life teachers and students who interact in complex ways that are informed by social and cultural influences. The teachers worked within larger institutional norms: Some had the full support of their administrators to undertake the kinds of "adventurous teaching" (Cohen, 1988, p. 58) they were attempting, while others were rather constrained by forces such as statewide testing in Texas or schoolwide reading programs. Still others were influenced by the norms implicit in programs such as writing workshop in which certain practices were expected. All the teachers operated within their own cultural milieus and brought with them their expectations about students and literacy. As Aronowitz and Giroux (1991) point out, "teachers exist within social, political, and cultural boundaries, which are both multiple and historical in nature" (p. 130). These boundaries clearly influenced the teachers I studied.

An appreciation of the social and cultural influences that affected teachers and students can offer readers the opportunity to use this book in different ways. Teachers might see students in their own classrooms who remind them of Ella, for whom writing fictional stories was a pleasure; of Greg, who always seemed to be doing something other

6

than what the teachers hoped; or of Lucas, who struggled to read. Or, teachers might relate to some of the dilemmas faced by the teachers in these studies and use the cases to reconsider their own instruction. Teacher educators may wish to use the book with preservice and practicing teachers to illuminate some of the conflicts that arise when implementing writing workshop or literature-based instruction. As the book suggests, although there is a wealth of models and strategies that we think will reach all learners, the truth is that teaching is situated and no single method can meet all students' needs. New researchers may see their own dilemmas reflected in my struggles to create relationships with teachers and students, and to find my voice in representing their stories. The studies in this book can raise questions about how to establish, maintain, and represent our relationships with those about whom or with whom we conduct research. I hope that this book offers all readers an opportunity to consider the multiple, dynamic identities of the students we teach, and to consider the ways in which we all are created by our social and cultural settings.

CHAPTER 1

Situating Identity in Theory, Research, and Practice

Picture this classroom setting:

Forty-nine third and fourth graders are seated on the carpet listening to music and imagining a scene from *Pedro's Journal* (Conrad, 1991). One teacher, Ms. Martin, reads aloud a chapter from the book and asks students to write a response in their logs. After 5 minutes of intense writing, students are called on to share their work. A second teacher, Ms. Allen, writes examples of descriptive language from the students' logs on a chart. Both teachers respond to students after volunteers have read their work aloud.

David reads from the perspective of Pedro saying the cannons on the Santa Maria went "boom boom."

[Ms. Martin writes *boom boom* on the chart.]

Ms. Martin:	Very nice. I certainly do like the way David started his passage with the sound of the cannons. What were the cannons doing, David?
David:	They were shooting to make the rest of the Santa Maria…[go down?]
Ms. Martin:	So what did they do? They went, and they got everything they possibly could use from the Santa Maria to build this new fort. There wasn't ready-made lumber there on the island, was there? So they used the timbers from the Santa Maria to build a fort. And then I can just see it out in the distance, can't you? The cannon's going to sink the rest of it. Very nice description. Emily.

Emily reads from the perspective of Pedro about being glad to leave, being "homeward bound" yet still keeping "adventure and my dream."

Ms. Martin: But I will still keep what?
Emily: "my adventure and my dream."

[Ms. Martin writes *homeward bound*. Ms. Allen calls on Nina.] Nina reads softly, almost inaudibly.

Ms. Martin: OK, Thomas. I really like the way most of you are sitting and listening for those juicy words. From the expressions on your face, I can tell that those words delight you too. I kind of pick up from your reactions to what people are reading. I want to thank those of you who are listening. Thomas.

Thomas reads from the perspective of Pedro, "I am worried the Santa Maria will come back and haunt me in my dreams."
[Ms. Martin writes *haunted* on the chart.]

Ms. Martin: Right. Geoffrey.

Geoffrey reads about Alonzo being "full of excuses" and getting a "taste of his own medicine."

Ms. Allen: Oooh—A taste of his own medicine. I love that. That would serve him right for leaving.

[Ms. Martin writes *a taste of his own medicine* and *full of excuses* on the chart, then calls on Rachel.]
Rachel reads about bumping into the other ship, "What will become of us?"
[Ms. Martin writes *What will become of us?* on the chart.]

Ms. Allen: What will become of us? Good. I love questions at the end. Ana.

Ana reads so softly, she is inaudible.
Ms. Allen tells Ana the class could not hear her, and asks her to take her tissue away from her face.
Ana reads again.

Ms. Martin: It reminds you of the journal you kept while read-
                ing the story. That is a nice reflection of your per-
                sonal experience. Mandy.

Mandy reads from the perspective of Pedro, describing the scene.

Ms. Allen: Good.

[Ms. Martin writes down three of the words Mandy uses—*spied,
thousands*, and *decided*.]

During this teaching session, the teachers' comments were filled
with praise and encouragement; they pointed out specific features of students' language, wrote down students' words, and commented orally.
However, certain students' comments (e.g., David, Emily, Geoffrey,
Rachel's) were extended and valued, while others (e.g., Nina's) were not.
The teachers tended to implicitly value students who used descriptive
or metaphorical language or asked questions at the end. The teachers' differential responses to students reflected their implicit assumptions about
what constituted an ideal student response. However, some students who
were not accustomed to using colorful language may have found it difficult to write in a way that matched the teachers' implicit expectations
(Michaels, 1987). Those students' responses did not fit the cultural
model of what the teachers had defined as "normal and natural" for that
classroom (Gee, 2001, p. 720). This, in turn, may have influenced how
students constructed their literate identities in the classroom setting.

In the following chapters, I draw from classroom data to explore
the impact of classroom practices on students' identities as literacy
learners. The next section situates literate practices, like those described in the previous scene, within larger discussions about the nature of identity, the role of language in identity, and the relationship
between power and knowledge.

Reconsidering Identity

Tensions between conceptualizing identity as a process rather than
as a category have provoked extended discussions in the literature
(e.g., Yon, 2000). Traditional views have focused on identity as a uni-
fied, cohesive essence belonging to an individual whose core unfolds
or develops in stages (Erikson, 1968). In contrast, social constructivist

and postmodern perspectives have emphasized the constructed and dynamic nature of identity. Mead (1934) recognized the self as the result of symbolic interaction with significant others. Postmodernists have taken the perspective that identity is less coherent than social interactionists proposed, and have theorized that identity is multiple, fragmentary, and contradictory (Yon, 2000).

Sarup (1996) defines identity as "a construction, a consequence of interaction between people, institutions, and practices" (p. 11). Mishler (1999) suggests that identity is relational, that is, individuals make claims about who they are by aligning or contrasting themselves with others. Identity, then, can be viewed as a process that is constructed in relation to others' perceptions (Tatum, 1997). Anzaldúa (1999) stated this view quite cogently, "We are clusters of stories we tell ourselves and others tell about us."

Aronowitz and Giroux (1991) maintain that aspects of identity such as race, social class, and gender that previously were considered more essentialist in nature can be considered partial, local, and contingent on the situation. Egan-Robertson (1998) extends this view to define identity as "the intersection of a myriad of complex sociological factors (e.g., race, class, gender)" within the historical moment (p. 455). In his study of Canadian urban youth, Yon (2000) found that students constructed their identities "in relation, and often in opposition, to the constraints imposed by gender, race, and culture" (p. 122). In her study of 30 working-class young women of Latina, African American, and European American descent at an alternative high school, Weiler (2000) established that the identities of young women from particular social class or racial and ethnic groups were far from unitary or homogeneous. She found that gender identity was fluid in that young women placed different values on schooling, future employment, marriage, and children; and that there were differential effects of schooling processes on their identity construction.

Because identity is the intersection of features at any given moment, our selves may be inconsistent or even in contradiction with one another (Belsey, 1980). We can take on different identities depending on the social setting, yet there are relationships among our different selves (Gee & Crawford, 1998). Bakhtin (1981) suggests that we engage in internal dialogues that are the result of the many voices we have encountered in the past. These internal dialogues are often sites of struggle, and through these dialogues we are able to construct and reconstruct ourselves. Sarup

(1996) echoes this view by defining identity as "a multidimensional space in which a variety of writings blend and clash" (p. 25).

The Role of Language

Language plays a key role in the process of identity construction. Belsey (1980) argues, "It is through language that people constitute themselves" (p. 59). Because language and identity are linked, Gee (1990) explains that language is more than a set of rules for communication; it is an "identity kit" that signals membership in particular groups. He suggests that "Discourses" include "ways of being in the world, or forms of life which integrate words, acts, beliefs, attitudes, social identities, as well as gestures, glances, body positions and clothes" (p. 142). Primary discourses are learned initially within the home and family, while secondary discourses are learned from being apprenticed to many groups and institutions. Discourses are communities of practice, and cultural models within a community define what counts as normal and what is considered deviant (Gee, 2001).

Bakhtin (1981, 1986) theorizes that inner speech is modeled on social discourse; inner speech consists of dialogues conducted with imagined audiences drawn from the many voices a person has encountered. An utterance is always responding to preceding utterances and anticipating succeeding ones, even if the speakers are temporally, spatially, or socially distant. The utterance focuses on concrete action within a particular context, yet is shaped by national languages, social languages, or speech genres (Wertsch, 1991). Bakhtin (1986) suggests,

> The unique speech experience of each individual is shaped and developed in continuous and constant interaction with others' individual utterances. This experience can be characterized to some degree as the process of *assimilation*—more or less creative—of others' words.... Our speech, that is, all our utterances (including creative works), is filled with others' words, varying degrees of otherness or varying degrees of "our-own-ness," varying degrees of awareness and detachment. These words of others carry with them their own expression, their own evaluative tone, which we assimilate, rework, and re-accentuate. (p. 89)

Bakhtin (1981) describes two ways of assimilating social discourse by the individual: (1) "reciting by heart" and (2) "retelling in one's own words" (p. 341). Reciting by heart involves using another's words in the form of models, rules, and directions. This is an inflexible kind of assimilation fused with authority that is transmitted not transformed, thus it is called "authoritative discourse" (p. 342). Retelling in one's own words is more flexible and responsive, making it possible to originate an idea (Emerson, 1983). Intellectual growth in the form of "internally persuasive discourse" results from the struggle between these two forms of assimilation (Bakhtin, 1981, p. 342). The internally persuasive word is "half-ours and half-someone else's" (p. 345), yet it is not static and isolated, but rather a part of a creative process that can be applied to new situations. Bakhtin further describes "single-voiced" discourse as direct, unmediated, and imitative, whereas "double-voiced" discourse (p. 65) is filled with words of others, but speakers use the others' discourse for their own purposes (Morson & Emerson, 1990).

Because the word is "half-ours and half-someone else's" (Bakhtin, 1981), a concept referred to as "ventriloquation" (Holquist, 1990; Wertsch, 1991, p. 59) and is continually shaped by interactions with others, issues of power and authority come into play. Social structures that give order are enduring and invisible in the normal course of life and control to a great extent what individuals can and cannot do (Lemert, 1997). School, as a significant social structure, serves to sort students in ways that reproduce existing inequities. Bourdieu (1977, p. 19) theorizes that "cultural capital" serves as symbolic credit in which one learns to enact signs of social standing and thus provides some students with higher social standing than others. Exams, rewards, and disciplinary procedures act to ensure success for those who already possess capital, resulting in cultural reproduction (Levinson & Holland, 1996). School knowledge is internalized through "habitus" (a set of dispositions), and what appears to be natural and neutral are oppressive practices that are political and historical in nature (Bourdieu, 1977, p. 19). Gender, culture, and social class are aspects of the hierarchy that influence the social context; the sense that individuals make of a situation depends on their relative position in that social structure (Lemke, 1989). Mainstream dominant discourses such as those practiced by middle-class whites privilege those who have mastered particular ways of speaking and exclude those who have not (Gee, 1990). However, because humans are agents, they can respond to dominant discourses by adapting speech patterns to the dominant class (Foley, 1990), or by resisting, yet also reproducing, existing structures (Willis, 1977), or by reconstructing themselves within particular spaces (Dressman, 1997).

Power and Language in the Classroom

Power is the means through which social structures sort people, "the determining force that causes some people to get less and some more of whatever is considered desirable in a social world" (Lemert, 1997, p. 127). Ideological power, projecting one's practices as universal and common sense, is exercised through discourse; those who have power can use coercion or consent to exercise and maintain power. Individuals make sense of their reality and social positions as the domains of the interactional, ideological, and local intersect through language and text. Although individuals occupy subject positions and are thus constrained by particular discoursal rights and obligations, as social agents they are also active and creative, combining discourse types to meet ever-changing situations. Therefore, "power is won, held, and lost in social struggles," and "discourse is the site of power struggles" (Fairclough, 1989, p. 74).

Power is constituted through language at both the macrolevel of the institutions and within local classrooms. Classrooms have normative patterns or scripts for defining appropriate behaviors, and as cultural spaces, classrooms are the sites of tension and conflicting beliefs (Gutierrez, Baquedano-Lopez, & Turner, 1997). Oppressive practices can occur when teachers assume that students share the same cultural practices they do and impose their scripts on students. However, students can "re-key" the teacher script by creating a counter-script that disrupts the teacher's (Gutierrez, Rymes, & Larson, 1995, p. 459). Although some re-keying is not successful because the teacher will not abandon the teacher script, other forms of disruption can result in the teacher and student meeting in a shared space: the "unscripted third space" (p. 459). This third space emerging from the conflict allows student interests to merge with instructional goals: "It is within this third space that students and teachers can bridge the various social spaces within classrooms" (p. 467). In classrooms where learning and language use is constructed narrowly, students may be limited in opportunities for becoming strategic learners. In contrast, in classrooms that reflect a "third space," the curriculum

15

utilizes the potential of students' own language and knowledge, and learning is facilitated by guided participation rather than through authoritarian means (Gutierrez et al., 1997).

Classroom Literacy Practices

Recent studies have highlighted the relationship among cultural practices, literacy learning, and identity construction. My (McCarthey, 1998) examination of third and fourth graders revealed that students reconstructed their subjectivities based on the demands of the social setting. Students' classroom participation was influenced not only by race, class, and gender but also by the classroom tasks presented to them. Dillon and Moje (1998) found that adolescents assumed a variety of subject positions in different classrooms, sometimes complacent and sometimes resistant, in relation to the teacher, student teacher, and peers. In her study of seven sixth-grade girls from affluent families in Canada, Cherland (1994) explored the connections between discourse and subjectivity and found that the students clearly enacted gendered literacy practices. The girls read fiction quite avidly (8 to 10 novels a month) to emulate their own mothers who were avid novel readers, to sustain their friendship with other girls in the group, and as a way to express their emotions. Through the reading of fiction, the girls were able to explore various models of agency and express their own senses of agency by renegotiating the cultural messages of the texts. Finders (1997) found that literacy played an important role in the ways that girls made allegiances and constructed boundaries in their friendship circles. While one group of girls who engaged in note passing, writing graffiti, and reading teen magazines constructed literacy as a social event to mark allegiance and sustain social roles, another group distinguished between school assignments and texts written for private purposes. Egan-Robertson's (1998) study of a small group of eighth-grade girls in a writing club found that students seized opportunities to reshape discourses about themselves when provided an appropriate forum. Girls experienced shifts in their perceptions of themselves from that of low-achieving students to writers who could talk about racial and ethnic identity and issues of culture and power. Blake's (1997) study of 11 poor Latina and African American girls in a fifth-grade urban classroom explored their struggle to transform their violent worlds into more peaceful ones through activist writing stances. Through writing, the girls began to struggle with issues of power, identity, sexuality, race, and gender.

Many of these studies took place in sites outside the traditional setting or in classrooms that were attempting to enact more "invisible pedagogies" (Bernstein, 1973, p. 24), that is, curricular practices in which subjects tended to be more integrated and students had more choices than in traditional settings. Progressive settings seem to provide students with more opportunities to consider who they are and how they use literacy in their everyday lives, because they support using literacy beyond the classroom. Further analyses of how students enact theories of student identity within classroom contexts can help us to identify supportive settings for student learning. For example, Au (1993, 1998) identifies reading and writing workshops as avenues for promoting literacy for students from diverse backgrounds and suggests that practices should focus on making literacy personally meaningful for students by drawing from their interests and experiences, by teaching skills within context, and by including multicultural literature in the curriculum.

Writing Workshops and Literature-Based Instruction

The writing workshop allows teachers and students to interact around students' writing. The teacher provides time and opportunities for students to engage in writing, to talk with the teacher, and to share their writing with peers. Calkins (1986) suggests that time be set aside each school day for the workshop, consisting of (1) a minilesson in which the teacher conveys information about topics, processes, or procedures related to writing; (2) writing time in which students draft or revise their work; (3) conferences in which the teacher reads and responds to students' texts individually or in small groups; and (4) share sessions in which students respond to one another's work. Topic choice, strategies for writing, and revision are aspects of the workshop that are stressed. The teacher's role is to provide time, materials, and a structure for writing and talking about writing. The teacher also models good writing by sharing examples from his or her own writing, literature, or other students' writing; by encouraging students to write by helping with topic choice; and by supporting students to become better writers through dialogue about writing.

The teacher's role in literature-based instruction is somewhat similar to writing workshop. The teacher is expected to share literature with students and to act as an observer, encourager, and responder (Routman, 1991). Students have opportunities for shared reading, being read to aloud, guided reading, and independent reading. In each of these settings, students read poems or books from different genres that represent the spectrum of children's literature. Skills such as sight words, phonics, spelling, and vocabulary are taught within the context of reading and writing. The focus is on students' application of strategies for authentic purposes. The teacher provides students with multiple opportunities to respond to texts orally and in writing. Theme units are often part of literature-based instruction as students engage in tasks to research and to apply information in many content areas throughout the school day. Including books that highlight the experiences of diverse cultural groups has also become a part of many literature-based classrooms (Au, 1993; Harris, 1992).

The literacy practices associated with writing workshops and literature-based instruction have aimed to motivate students to become engaged in reading and writing. Yet several studies have pointed out the limitations of reading and writing workshops, especially for nonmainstream students. Delpit (1995), for example, believes that workshops fail to provide children of color with needed skills and access to codes of power. Dressman (1993) points out that the individualistic orientation of reading workshops privileges white middle-class students over nonmainstream students who may be more accustomed to communal practices. Students from diverse backgrounds may not feel comfortable selecting topics that reflect their own cultural backgrounds and sharing their writing with teachers and peers who value only mainstream topics and genres (Willis, 1995). Lensmire (1993, 2000) found that third-grade students used texts to harm each other and to isolate certain students along social-class lines. He critiqued workshop advocates for characterizing writing as personal and individual, for ignoring conflict, and for not engaging students in needed deliberation of texts.

Previous research has shown that students' views of themselves as readers and writers and their views of literacy tasks may have lasting effects on students' achievement as well as their motivation to engage in literate activities. Students who feel good about themselves as readers spend more time reading independently and have confidence in their ability to read successfully in the future (Guthrie &

Anderson, 1999). In a U.S. national survey, McKenna, Kear, and Ellsworth (1995) found that attitudes toward recreational and academic reading became more negative over the elementary school years and were the most negative for the least able readers. Good readers reported understanding what they read, talking more, and reading more frequently at home for enjoyment than did poor readers (Canaday & Krantz, 1996). To promote competent readers who are confident in their abilities, we need to understand what motivates students and how to engage them in the reading and writing processes.

Students' Views of Reading and Writing

Several researchers have suggested that individual views of reading and writing are closely connected to cultural views of literacy (Faigley, Cherry, Jolliffe, & Skinner, 1985). Holdaway (1986) and Templeton (1986) argue for specific effects of literacy on the individual, suggesting that literacy can affect our sense of ourselves. Ferdman (1990) suggests that literacy and culture have a reciprocal relationship at the level of the individual and that a person's identification with a particular ethnic or cultural group is connected to her or his perception of literacy. Although cultural identity mediates the learning and use of literacy, literacy will subsequently alter an individual's view of him- or herself. Mahiri and Godley (1998) found evidence that the strong connection between societal literacy practices and individual views of literacy affected a person's identity. Viviana, the subject of their study, had used her literacy skills to empower her parents as well as herself. When she could no longer physically write because of Carpal Tunnel Syndrome, she began to feel that she was less intelligent and unable to aid her parents with negotiating in written English. Her view of herself as a highly educated, good daughter who could mediate between her Latino culture and mainstream America was revised.

Classroom practices such as ability grouping and rewarding students can negatively affect students' views of their own reading and writing capabilities. For example, Borko and Eisenhart (1986) found that students in higher ability groups were more motivated to read and had more positive views of themselves than did students in lower groups. Evans's (1993) study showed that when students saw reading and writing as demonstrations of what they knew for the purpose of pleasing the teacher and getting high grades, they began to see themselves as incompetent, no longer enjoyed literacy activities, and avoided reading and writing altogether.

Studies of avid writers point to some features of classrooms and homes that hold promise for encouraging students to view writing as purposeful and enjoyable. Hudson (1986) found that self-sponsored writing at home featured a wider range of audiences, purposes for writing, and genres than assigned and self-sponsored writing at school. Abbott (1996) suggests that children's sense of choice and control are central to their willingness to engage in self-sponsored writing. In Abbott's study, students who engaged in self-sponsored writing came from families who valued literacy, developed supportive relationships with family members, had choices over aspects of daily life, and had supportive relationships with teachers and peers at school.

Together, the studies about literacy practices reviewed here suggest that students are motivated to read and write in contexts that provide them with choice, support, and control rather than extrinsic rewards or pleasing others. These contexts provide opportunities for students to explore their identities while reading and writing for authentic purposes. It is within this frame that I investigated the following research question: How do students construct their identities as readers and writers within home and school contexts? Related to the major issue are the following subquestions:

- How do students see themselves as readers and writers?
- What do students see as the purposes of reading and writing?
- How do students respond to classroom contexts?

To investigate students as readers and writers, I collected data at three sites in the United States. The following description of methods used provides an overview of the settings, teachers, and students who participated in three different studies conducted during the 1990s.

Methods

For each of the three studies, I was interested in how students participated in literacy practices within settings that allowed them opportunities to have choices about what they could read and write and to engage in dialogue about their literacy learning. Who they were as readers and writers was central to each study. Initially, I did not select the sites in order to do a comparative analysis. I selected each site for the understandings I could gain about individual students in particular settings and, later, found that some themes cut across sites and were worth explicating.

I chose the site in New York City because I had been working on a national project investigating 11 teacher-education programs in the United States, including the Columbia University Teachers College Writing Project (National Center for Research on Teacher Education, 1988). The particular classroom that supported the general principles of the writing project provided an opportunity to study student-teacher interactions in detail through the writing workshop. As developing writers, the students provided much data about the purposes of writing, audience, context, and their views of themselves as writers.

When I moved to Texas, a state known for its emphasis on testing and standards, I looked for sites in which teachers were attempting to teach outside the traditional teaching for the test. A graduate student informed me of a school in which there was a shifting from the norms of individual classrooms to team teaching and to designing multiage groupings. The principal of the school suggested that I meet with a team of third- and fourth-grade teachers whose curricular focus was on literature-based instruction, writing workshop, and thematic units. Their classroom provided an exemplary site in which teachers and students were experimenting with a wide variety of literacy practices, thus providing me with an opportunity to see how students saw themselves as literacy learners.

I learned about the third site, again located in Texas, from colleagues who had used a particular teacher's classroom to place student teachers. Having taught this teacher 7 years before as an undergraduate student, I was excited to learn that she was using many of the literature-based practices we had emphasized in the teacher-education program. It seemed an ideal site in which to find out how students were constructing their literate identities.

In all three studies, I used ethnographic case-study methods as described by Merriam (1998) to examine individual students within literacy contexts. Case studies are particularistic; they focus on individuals, situations, or events. They are intended to be descriptive by providing in-depth documentation of events and perspectives of those involved. Cases also are inductive and rely on building conceptual categories from the data rather than beginning with categories. To collect data for the case studies, I interviewed students on three or more occasions and interviewed the teacher at least twice at each site. Additionally, I conducted classroom observations and collected samples of students' writing. At two sites, I also interviewed parents.

Within each site, I used purposeful sampling, that is, "a sample from which one can learn the most, which fits a set of criteria" (Merriam, 1998, p. 48). Criteria for selection may include cases that are extreme or typical, have maximum variation, are politically important or sensitive, or are convenient (Patton, 1980). I identified the following criteria to maximize the potential for learning about students: (1) parents and child agreed to the child's participation in the study, (2) students represented a spectrum of low to high achievers as designated by the teacher, and (3) students were representative of the cultural diversity within the classroom. Variations in data collection procedures occurred in order to be sensitive to the particular contexts and are described here.

New York City Site

The setting for the first study was a fifth/sixth-grade classroom in a public school in the heart of Manhattan. The school was located in a middle-class neighborhood but drew students from all parts of the city. The student population consisted of 53% European American, 16% African American, 17% Latino, and 14% Asian American, with about 30% of the school population receiving free or reduced lunch. I collected data over a 5-week period in the fall of 1990 as students participated in a writing workshop.

Teacher Selection and Data Collection

The teacher had 18 years of experience, had attended the Summer Institute at Columbia University Teachers College, and had been implementing the writing workshop for 4 years. I interviewed the teacher on two occasions about her goals for a range of writing activities and her perceptions of students. Questions focused on her goals for the case-study students during the writing time, her perceptions of the students as writers, and her perceptions of the texts that students had produced.

Classroom Observations

I observed writing workshop daily for 5 weeks. Classroom observations of activities during writing time included (1) teacher-directed lessons in which the teacher and students discussed issues related to writing (minilessons), (2) writing time in which students worked on their individual texts, (3) teacher-student writing conferences in which the teacher discussed the students' texts with them, and (4) share sessions in which a student shared a text and the whole class responded.

Student Selection and Data Collection

I collected data on five students: three African Americans and two Latinos. Two were high-achieving students, two were average, and one was considered low achieving. Formal and informal interviews were conducted with each student. Formal interviews took place at the beginning (entry interviews) and at the end of data collection (exit interviews), occurred outside the classroom context, and used a set of predetermined questions for all students. Questions in the entry interview focused on students' backgrounds, their beliefs and attitudes about writing, and the texts from their notebooks. Questions in the exit interview focused on their completed drafts and events that had occurred within the classroom.

Informal interviews were conducted within the classroom context on a frequent basis. For instance, after a writing conference with the teacher, I asked students questions about the interaction. In addition, I talked to students at least twice a week about their texts and the changes they had made.

Student Work

I collected and photocopied all notebook entries students had written since the beginning of the year and all drafts of projects. Some students, like Ella, shared with me additional work that they had written outside the classroom context.

Texas Site: Hillside School

The setting for the second study was located in a central Texas city, with the school population consisting of 57% Latino, 39% European American, and 4% African American, with 64% of the students on a free- or reduced-lunch program. The neighborhoods where students lived consisted of both middle-class and working-class families; the wealthier, professional families tended to live in older homes near the school, while the working-class families lived in modest homes or apartments further from the school.

Teacher Selection and Data Collection

Initially, I worked in two classrooms with two teams of teachers who had been recommended to me by a graduate student familiar with innovative schools and literature-based practices. In this book, I focus on three of the five teachers and their students. The three European American teachers were part of an instructional "block" responsible for about 49 students (in two large, joined classrooms). Ms. Allen had been teaching at Hillside School for 7 years and had been team teaching with Ms. Martin for the last 3 years. Joined by their interests in working on something "other than just what the textbook offered," both teachers found teaming a rewarding experience. At the beginning of the year, they were joined by a third teacher, Ms. Burton, whose primary responsibility was for all the bilingual children (native Spanish speakers who were learning English as a second language) in the block, and she also taught Spanish twice a week to all students.

I first interviewed the three teachers individually at the end of September about their own backgrounds, goals for literacy instruction, and views about instructional practice. I then interviewed them as a team at the beginning of November and again in March about particular students and their curricular plans.

Classroom Observations

I conducted 1- to 3-hour classroom observations approximately three times weekly during the 1994–1995 school year. During the observations, I focused on literacy instruction occurring in a variety of contexts: writing workshop, book response, and research projects related to topics in the books; however, more time was spent observing book response because of its centrality to the curriculum.

Student Selection and Data Collection

The original sample of students included 15 students from two classrooms. I then narrowed the sample to 9 students (4 European American, 4 Latino, and 1 African American: 3 high achieving, 5 average, and 1 struggling reader) whom I followed over the course of the year. I conducted four rounds of 30-minute interviews throughout the year with each student, focusing on his or her perceptions of home and school literacy activities, and talking to students informally during or after literacy events. All interviews were transcribed verbatim.

Student Work

I collected and photocopied all students' journals, response logs, and writing workshop folders. Students' journals included work from August through April. The teachers had created a response log for each book read aloud from September through May; the response logs contained blank, lined pages surrounded by interesting symbols related to each topic, for example, Egyptian pharaohs. Writing workshop pieces were kept in a separate folder. In addition, I photocopied and placed in another folder any other work the students shared with me, and I made copies of their portfolios in which they had selected their best pieces and written comments about what they learned from the projects.

Parent Interviews

I conducted home visits consisting of a 1-hour interview with one or more family members of eight of the nine students. Questions focused on parents' occupations, educational backgrounds, and literacy habits at home; their perceptions of their children's literacy habits at home and in school; their descriptions of students' classrooms; and their descriptions of opportunities to attend school functions and meet with the teachers. In homes where Spanish was the dominant language spoken, a translator accompanied me.

Texas Site: Valley School

The setting of the third study was located in an area that served inner-city, suburban, and rural children: 80% were Latino, 15% were European American, and 5% were African American. More than 90% of the students came from low socioeconomic status (SES) homes, qualifying the school as Title I. The Valley School was large (735 students), serving third through sixth graders, many of whom were housed in portable classrooms. Valley was designated a "national blue-ribbon school" by a national panel, and the school focused on the statewide Texas Assessment of Academic Skills (TAAS) test. Many of the teachers aligned their curriculum to the tests and spent a great deal of time practicing TAAS worksheets. However, at least two teachers in the school provided an alternative language arts curriculum using reading and writing workshops and literature-based approaches (Atwell, 1987; Calkins, 1986; Routman, 1991).

Teacher Selection and Data Collection

Ms. Le Blanc was one of two teachers who used reading and writing workshops and literature-based programs in her instruction. She taught two sections of language arts to her homeroom students and to students from another fifth-grade classroom. (In turn, the other teacher taught both sections of mathematics.) Ms. Le Blanc, a European American, had 7 years of experience teaching students from diverse backgrounds while using a literature-based program and a multicultural emphasis in her curriculum. She had three major components in her language arts program: reading workshop; writing workshop; and Reading Renaissance, a schoolwide computerized reading comprehension program.

I interviewed Ms. Le Blanc on two occasions in 1999 for a total of 4 hours. She provided a detailed explanation of her language arts program and a description of each of the 12 students. I developed the interview questions from observations made in her classroom and my interest in her perceptions of the students.

Classroom Observations

The interview data were supported by my classroom observations conducted twice a week over the course of one semester. These observations focused on teacher-student interaction during read-alouds, subsequent discussions, and follow-up activities. I also observed students during the initial periods of working on skill sheets or related activities.

Student Selection and Data Collection

Of the sample 12 students (20% of the total number of students from both classes), 6 were from each of the language arts classes, and all received free or reduced lunch. The sample reflected the ethnic and cultural diversity of the classroom (7 Latino/Latina students, 2 African American, 1 Asian American, 1 European American, and 1 of Latina and German background). Five students were high level readers, four were average, and three were struggling readers.

I interviewed each student for an average of 45 minutes three times during the semester. The first interview (about 1 hour) focused on students' family backgrounds, their interests in and out of school, their views of themselves as readers and writers, and their perceptions of reading and writing. The second interview (about 45 minutes) focused on students' descriptions of themselves and opinions of books read within the classroom context. I also asked students to describe their peers in general terms and to describe their peers' success with and interest in reading and writing. The third interview (about 30 minutes) focused on book-selection strategies and perceptions of the schoolwide reading program.

Student Work

I collected and photocopied writing samples from each student in the study. Samples consisted of students' journal entries in response to the books read aloud from January through April, letters written to peers, and any other materials including letters from the students who had elected to correspond with me from March through May.

Parent Interviews

I interviewed the students' parents who agreed to either a telephone or a face-to-face interview (7 of the 12 students' mothers agreed to the interview). These interviews focused on the parents' views of their children both in general terms and with regard to their interests and success with literacy. I also asked parents about their perceptions of the classroom context and their communication with the teacher and school. The interviews varied from 25 minutes to 60 minutes.

Researcher's Stance

I am a middle-class, European American woman who has often embraced principles underlying literature-based classrooms and writing workshops. Each of the three sites was recommended to me by educators who were familiar with the sites and believed that the teachers enacted practices consistent with process writing and literature-based ideals. My own role as a researcher in classrooms shifted over the three studies, and I am continually in the process of evaluating it.

In the New York City (NYC) site, I was a beginning researcher who was trying to understand the role of students as writers and the ways in which they appropriated the dialogue from the classroom to use in their own texts and talk. Although I regarded myself as an ethnographer who tried to understand both the students' and the teacher's points of view, I found that the students were treating me as a confidant and that I was becoming somewhat critical of some of the teacher's practices. I, thus, saw myself as more of an advocate for the students, and may have lost some of the teacher's perspective.

My original intention with regard to becoming a researcher at Hillside School in Texas was to work with the team of teachers to increase my understanding of their practices while, at the same time, helping them to engage in inquiry about their own teaching. The yearlong relationship with the team of teachers shifted to a more traditional participant-observer role as I became more interested in how students and their families were making sense of the classroom practices.

At the third site, Valley School in Texas, I took on the role of participant-observer in the classroom. However, I relied less on observations and more on data from my one-on-one interactions with students, their parents, and the teacher for understanding the perceptions of students as literacy learners. Having students write letters to me was the teacher's idea that subsequently enhanced my relationships with the students who chose to correspond with me. The focus in this study was clearly on the students, with the teachers and parents providing background information about literacy practices.

Throughout the course of the three studies, I became increasingly cognizant of my role as a researcher studying the literacy practices of students and families who have different ethnic and social backgrounds from mine. Relying on the students' and teacher's points of view in the NYC study pointed out to me the need to get to know students in different contexts and to learn more of their family backgrounds. Thus, I sought the parents' views in the second study, and parents' descriptions of their home literacy practices helped me to challenge the widely held but inaccurate notion that many working-class and poor families have little literacy in their homes. Yet, I was aware of being "the other" in my interactions with some of the Latino and African American parents, especially with regard to my status as an outsider to the Spanish language. Bringing Spanish speakers into the interview process enhanced my understanding of literacy practices and made me more cognizant of the need for increased understanding of students' backgrounds. I attempted to develop my own understandings by reading more about cultures other than my own and by examining my position as an outsider investigating others' lives.

Analysis and Selection of Cases

Because these data came from three different sites and three different time periods, I needed a framework to select and analyze students' identities as readers and writers across the sites. As I examined the data both within particular sites and across the three sites, it became clear that there were some students who were quite adept at understanding the teachers' expectations and adjusting to them, while other students were not successful in these classrooms. Students' attitudes toward literacy seemed to be shaped by the classroom contexts and also by their relationships with the teachers. Some students' views of reading and writing seemed to open them up to the possibilities of literacy, while other attitudes limited their own practices. I began to consider frames that might aid in conceptualizing students' identities as readers and writers at the same time the theories provided an explanation for students' interactions within the classroom settings.

Harré's (1984) theory of internalization provided one suitable frame for situating students' responses to classroom settings. In his model of internalization, Harré suggests that learners move through a cycle from appropriation of the social dialogue to transformation of that dialogue for their own purposes. Bakhtin's (1981) description of the two ways of assimilating social discourse by the individual (1) "reciting by heart," or using another's words in the form of models, rules, and directions, and (2) "retelling in one's own words" (p. 341), allowing flexibility and creativity, also aided in analysis of students' understanding of classroom expectations. I have borrowed the term *resistance* from researchers such as Willis (1977), Foley (1990), and Dressman (1997) to characterize attempts by students to avoid or challenge the teacher's authority.

From these theories, I developed the categories of *appropriation*, *resistance*, and *transformation* to characterize students' primary means of interacting with the norms and expectations established by the teachers in each of the three sites. I found that some of the students in the three sites *appropriated* the teacher's expectations and norms of classroom interaction. The students understood the purposes of the literacy tasks and were able to fulfill assignments and conform to the rules and roles designed by the teacher and peers. These students tended to see reading and writing as classroom activities that had limited use outside of the classroom. They accepted the "teacher's script" (Gutierrez et al., 1995, p. 454) and their responses to the classroom were aligned with what Dressman (1997) describes as "congruence" (p. 83) between students' social backgrounds and school values.

In each school setting, there were students who were not successful and either actively or passively *resisted* the curriculum as a whole, the teacher's specific assignments, or the teachers' implicit expectations about reading and writing. These students often had conflicts with the teacher or the curricular context and found ways around classroom assignments through avoidance or distraction. These students developed "counterscripts" to the classroom (Gutierrez et al., 1995), yet like the students in Willis's (1977) study and in Dressman's (1997) studies, their resistance did not enable them to beat the system. Instead, their reading and writing activities in school were limited both by the classroom conditions and their own resistance.

There were also students in each setting who went beyond understanding and fulfilling the tasks and were able to *transform* the assignments and goals in ways that allowed them to see reading and writing as practices that they could apply to other settings. Their texts tended to reflect Bakhtin's (1981) notion of "internally persuasive discourse" (p. 342) because they appropriated voices they encountered but changed them to fit within their own purposes. By establishing a "third space" with the teacher (Gutierrez et al., 1995, p. 454), these students were successful in altering the classroom norms enough to create spaces in which they could be successful inside and outside the classroom. Having experienced some form of conflict with the classroom norms, the students were able to reconstruct their identities (Dressman, 1997) as readers and writers to both fit in and alter the classroom space.

In selecting the three cases to present in each chapter, I have chosen to align them within the framework of appropriation, resistance, and transformation in relation to classroom expectations. This frame has the advantage of showing the variations among students at each site, while also demonstrating similarities across different contexts. In using these categories, I do not intend to suggest a fixed conception of identity, but rather I intend to capture a dynamic at a point in time. Chapter 2 demonstrates this variation within the New York City site.

CHAPTER 2

Appropriation, Resistance, and Transformation in a Writing Workshop

My study at the New York City (NYC) site occurred during the early 1990s when process approaches to writing were flourishing. The Teachers College Writing Project at Columbia University, New York, had successfully negotiated with several NYC public schools to allow trainers from the project to work with several schools in the boroughs of Manhattan and Queens. Under the direction of Lucy Calkins, the project featured summer institutes for teachers and hands-on training in which members of the project modeled approaches to writing with students in NYC classrooms. Teachers had opportunities to implement practices, be observed by project trainers, and discuss their practices with the trainers and other teachers. The school in which I conducted my study had the full support of the principal, and several teachers were implementing the project.

The study included 28 students (14 European Americans, 7 African Americans, 4 Latino Americans, and 3 Asian Americans) from both working-class and middle-class backgrounds in the combination fifth/sixth-grade classroom. Ms. Meyer, a middle-class white teacher, had been implementing for more than 4 years a writing workshop similar to the one described by Calkins (1986). Her views that writing could empower students, students ought to have a choice of topics, conventions should be taught within the context of students' own writing, and the teacher's role is to support the student were consistent with the goals of the Teachers College Writing Project.

Students kept notebooks about their personal experiences and then selected a topic, issue, or theme to pursue in more depth, in the form of a project, and for a particular audience (Calkins, 1991).

The physical classroom reflected many of the elements often found in process-writing classrooms. The room was divided into the rug area and the table area; bookshelves contained many picture books and novels that were easily accessible to the students; and there was time set aside each day for writing workshop activities. Ms. Meyer adapted and modified ideas from Calkins's *The Art of Teaching Writing* (1986) and *Living Between the Lines* (1991). The structure of the workshop consisted of lively, teacher-directed minilessons in which the teacher (or sometimes the trainer from Teachers College) read pieces of literature to students and discussed the qualities of good writing. The minilessons were fast paced and the teacher often joked with students. She dominated the discourse by asking them questions, but also frequently offered her own opinions. During writing time, which lasted 20 to 25 minutes, students wrote at individual desks and were to remain quiet in order to eliminate distractions. While students were writing, the teacher conducted individual conferences with six to eight students. Conferences occurred in a variety of places: at the student's desk, on the rug, or at a table designated for conferences. Ms. Meyer usually opened with "How's it going?" then proceeded to ask questions, summarize what the student had said, and provide recommendations for revisions. The workshop culminated with sharing time on the rug where students volunteered to read aloud their work and teachers and peers made comments.

During the workshop, Ms. Meyer focused on the qualities of good writing. She emphasized writing from personal experience, writing for a particular audience, and using imagery and figurative language. Her emphasis on personal experience came through in her rationale for having students keep notebooks:

> I think what I want from them is to be able to just get them to become chroniclers of life—of their lives. I think for me the most important thing is that I give them this gift of being able to observe their lives, and to look at themselves and what they're doing and their place in the world, and be able to keep track of that.

Ms. Meyer communicated her emphasis on writing from personal experience through modeling—reading from her own notebook—through examples from children's literature in which the central characters wrote about their own experience, through the assignments she gave such as having students record important events in their lives, and through her conferences in which she suggested that students write about a relative or a memory. She encouraged students to write for a particular audience by asking, "Who is this going to be for?" in whole-group sessions and individual conferences. Her emphasis on imagery and figurative language came through in her text selections from children's literature and her language cues such as the need for using description or including details.

Ms. Meyer cited the institutes at Teachers College as the main sources of her inspiration for her emphasis on qualities of good writing and the importance of communicating one's own experience to an audience. She believed that modeling was essential for students to become good writers, and she evaluated her own teaching in terms of how successful students were in producing high-quality notebook pieces. Conferences with students, demonstrations, and bringing in outsiders were strategies she used for shaping students' writing.

Although all students were in the same classroom and had opportunities to participate in the writing workshop, the students held quite different views of the purposes of writing and responded to the classroom norms in a variety of ways. For example, Miguel conformed to the classroom norms and saw writing as an important tool for learning and for fulfilling classroom assignments. In contrast, Anita resisted the classroom norms and viewed writing as a dialogue with herself to be done outside of school. Ella experienced writing as a creative process for an audience and was able to transform the classroom norms to maintain her identity as a fiction writer.

Miguel: Appropriating the Norms of the Workshop

Miguel was an 11-year-old sixth grader who came to the United States from Guatemala as a third grader speaking only Spanish. He was from a working class background and lived with his mother and brother in an apartment shared by several families. Miguel's mother worked as a babysitter at the homes of other families. There were no Spanish-speaking teachers in the school, so he learned English quickly because, "I was in the school and had to." Miguel reported that he was proficient enough to correct his mother's English. In fact, his facility with English was notable—he was fluent, articulate, used extensive vocabulary, and was a delightful conversationalist, often interspersing his comments with figurative language. He also felt connected to his Latino background as evidenced by his writing in his notebook about the difference between New Year's celebrations in the United States, which were quite boring, and in Guatemala where children were allowed to set off firecrackers.

Miguel was achievement-oriented, artistic, and articulate in conversations. He read extensively both fiction and nonfiction books. He had learned to read in Guatemala and remembered having experiences in which his uncle "used the belt" if he did not successfully pronounce the words. He wrote the following in his notebook:

> I didn't know how to read, but with a belt on my uncles hand, I soon dashed through the words. They seemed pretty hard, but I tried hard, so I wouldn't get belted by my uncle. He was serious about it to, when I got a paragraph right, he would give me a piece of gum, but when I got it wrong, well I can tell you it was terrible.

Miguel incorporated some of his early memories into his writing and had developed positive attitudes about literacy. Having been in writing process classrooms previously, Miguel was familiar with planning, drafting, and revising his writing. His notebook contained a range of entries from pieces about himself and his family to space and how things worked. He was concerned about environmental issues, especially whales, and his final project for a larger audience consisted of comparing himself to a killer whale.

Ms. Meyer held positive views about Miguel, describing him as "the greatest kid, the greatest kid, he really is," which were reflected in her notes to him about his notebook:

> Dear Miguel,
>
> It's amazing to read a notebook as honest as yours. For a boy your age to be so up-front is so special. You have a real knack for seeing yourself clearly and writing it down. Your entries are all so different and so interesting. I love your notebook and am honored to be your teacher.
>
> Fondly,
>
> Ms. Meyer

Literacy Practices

Miguel viewed writing as a combination of epiphany and effort. He described his idea-gathering process in the following way: "I sit down there and think or I may look everywhere in the room or outside the window. But I don't get ideas when people talk about their writing." He believed that ideas would come to him if he were quiet and observant. However, when he actually started writing, he found that it took a great deal of effort. He placed pressure on himself to perform well as a writer and saw being a good writer as going hand-in-hand with being a good student. When asked about the process he went through to compose a piece, he said, "I say, 'you better write something or you'll get an F.'" His teacher also recognized that he conformed to her expectations. When talking about his project, she said, "I think he's forcing his project because he had to do it, but I'm not sure it is something that he's really that interested in."

Miguel was influenced by the classroom expectations set by the teacher. He drew heavily from the classroom dialogue and talked about features of good writing such as good description, comparisons, and imagination. For example, when discussing what he liked about his work "Man's Best Friend," he said, "I like the way I described it and described the car and I compared it to a dog." He was also sensitive to audience interest and suggested that "it depended on the reader," and that he was able "to keep them, [the audience] on their toes and I surprised them." He was able to transfer his understanding of good writing to seeing description in books; about *Lord of the Rings* (1974), he noted, "Tolkien uses lots of imagination, and he uses a lot of language, and he describes like the elves and everything, and he uses a lot of imagination at the same time." He attributed his success with writing to the teacher. For example, he said, "Without a teacher like Ms. Meyer, I wouldn't get the idea from getting description from the book...this year Ms. Meyer got me into description, so that every time I saw description in the book, I put a [sticky note] on that and wrote something like 'having a great sense of humor.'" He also appreciated the teacher writing notes to him on a separate piece of paper in response to his work: "Ms. Meyer is really good because she doesn't write in your notebook and she uses a lot of imagination, and she puts an envelope in mine which is back here and she puts a note in it."

Miguel's strong relationship with the teacher was evident in the writing conferences he had with her. Within a 5-week period, the teacher had several brief conversations with Miguel about his writing, as well as one lengthy conversation. She sat close to him during conferences and often nodded in appreciation of his language choice. In the conference in which Miguel was trying to identify a topic from his notebook to expand on, the teacher and Miguel seemed to develop synchrony as witnessed by their body language and uptake of each other's words.

After Miguel had read parts of his two entries and Ms. Meyer asked questions, she suggested that he may not be ready to do a project. However, in this portion of the conference, we can see how each speaker incorporated words of the other in his or her turn, which led to Miguel finding a topic:

Ms. Meyer: Hmm. So what do you think you want to do, Miguel? You think you may not be ready to do a project yet? Nothing really stands out as being important to you in here? You can't kind of put your finger on what's important to you?

Miguel: Well...

Ms. Meyer: OK, so...

Miguel: Mostly the killer whale.

Ms. Meyer: Uh, huh.

Miguel: It's my favorite whale and I like the way it stands out.

Ms. Meyer: Mhmmm.

Miguel: It's the colors it has.

Here the teacher had introduced the idea of "standing out," which Miguel seemed to pick up on in such a way that he associated the meaning with a killer whale standing out among other whales, perhaps because of its colors. Miguel picked up the idea of choosing a topic that was important, while making use of the term *stand out*. The teacher and Miguel seemed to arrive at a shared understanding of what the topic of the project would be; it was the pivotal point for subsequent discussions about the project. When Miguel explained that the killer whale could be mean or friendly, Ms. Meyer asked him if he thought that he was at all like a killer whale. When he responded affirmatively, she suggested that he write a comparison of himself and the killer whale. Miguel readily agreed with the idea and suggested that he knew a lot of information about the whale that he could include. In an interview, Miguel described how he saw his teacher helping him:

> I was telling her [Ms. Meyer] about my project. So I was only writing the killer whales and then she said that I have a lot of entries about myself. So I just said, "yea, I do" and then when I said I had a killer whale in me, so then she said you can compare both of them, so then I did.

Ms. Meyer continued to support his efforts in subsequent conferences by providing him with books about killer whales and by having him think about the audience for his piece. In their third conference, Miguel explained to her how he was comparing the killer whale to himself. When she looked at his paper, she pointed to aspects that she found particularly interesting and encouraged him to find more connections. Miguel initiated the exchange, and their conference continued:

Ms. Meyer: How is it coming?

Miguel: I am taking the pieces, and on, like on this piece, I write, "Killer whales can live up to 60 years…"

Ms. Meyer: Uh, huh.

Miguel: …60 to 70 years. Then I took something from myself and I said, "But guess what? So can I!" [enthusiastic]

Ms. Meyer: OK, but why can you? See this is where the part that could become really really interesting because you are going to take really good care of yourself, you are going to see yourself like all that part about seeing yourself in the future, and you are going to exercise and stuff like that. And maybe you do a lot of swimming like the killer whale. You know what I mean? [pace increases as she becomes more involved]

Miguel: Yeah.

Ms. Meyer: You can kind of get it all into that; it is really neat. [emphatic]

Miguel had the opportunity to explain aspects he had added to his piece, while the teacher focused on aspects she liked. She then suggested another comparison he could add—that of swimming like the killer whale. Synchrony between teacher and student was particularly apparent in this interaction as teacher and student sat close together; Ms. Meyer was quite enthusiastic in her tone of voice, and Miguel nodded and smiled during their brief conference. He also became excited when he told her about the connection he had made between the killer whale being able to live 60 to 70 years and his own life span. In another interview he reiterated how much the teacher had helped him by saying,

> One day, she really got me into it because she said, because I was writing it. I was writing that the killer whale can…can live up to 70 years, 60 through 70 years, and I was just going to leave it like that and I was going to say, "but so can I." And now, I was just going to leave it like that, but she said you can write *how* you can live up to 70 years, and I wrote like a paragraph about it.

The writing conferences, interviews, and Miguel's texts all demonstrated that the teacher and student developed a shared understanding of writing tasks. Their body language and their emphasis on particular words provided evidence of their being in synchrony with each other during conferences. The interviews showed that each valued the other and that Miguel sought teacher approval. His texts reflected the teacher's voice: He compared the killer whale to himself at her suggestion, he used description and imagery in a way that was consistent with the classroom norms, and he included some of the teacher's specific ideas (see Figure 1).

Figure 1
Miguel's Writing Sample

Killer Whale

> I am a human being
> But can't be seen
> I express myself as a killer whale
> But I am not a killer
> I am friendly as a trained dog
> But I can be fierce as a killer whale hunting
> I can be your friend
> But I can ignore

You know, when I go swimming I just get the feeling of being a killer whale in the deep blue ocean. Then again I feel like I am being followed by a shark, so then I get scared and I get out of the water. But thinking of being a killer whale, I then dash to the water without being scared of he shark. But imagining the shark, how fierce it would be, hurdling through the water, mouth open, wantin to crunch on my bones and rip my flesh off my bones. Boy that would be scary!

But wait, I'm a killer whale so then I would be able to tear the shark's flesh and crunch on it's bones.

With my 30 ft. body and the shark being only 15 ft., boy would I crunch him for lunch I would slap the shark on it's head with my great and powerful fluke, and let it swim away.

Killer whales can live up to 60-70 years, but guess what?

So can I! I know, because I am going to exercise, swim [but of course not as fast as the killer whale], eat properly and I am going to be as strong as the killer whale, and as brave as the killer whale.

The dorsal fin of a killer whale is 6 ft. The killer whale is like a submarine. It's great 8 ton body hurdling through the water.

It's great powerful fluke can knock off a human being's head with just one swing, as if it was playing baseball. New borns are 8 ft. long. Killer whales live in family groups of several hundred—remaining in them for life—in all oceans, mostly in cooler coastal waters. This expremely powerful whale is tame and gentle and survives well in captivity.

Summary

Miguel's home and school literacy practices blended together. He was able to incorporate his identity as a Spanish speaker from Guatemala by writing about his experiences in his notebook. Although he lived his early years in a context quite different from his current one, he did not seem to experience a clash between home and school norms. His early valuing of literacy, even though developed through "the belt," appeared to aid him in fitting with the classroom norms. Miguel was successful in understanding the classroom norms and composing a piece that met the demands of that community, that of composing a personal piece that included imagery and description. The teacher helped him to understand those expectations through the classroom demonstrations and through her conferences with him. Miguel seemed to have internalized the social-cognitive norms of the classroom, which provides an example of smooth interactions between teacher and student.

Miguel's identity as a writer was defined mostly in terms of the classroom norms such as using descriptive language, including metaphor and writing an interesting piece for an audience. He is an example of a student who appropriated and used classroom norms—from a Bakhtinian (1981) framework his writing was filled with the teachers' words, but he also used writing for his own purposes. Miguel's identity as a writer fit well within the cultural model of the classroom. As enacted in this classroom, there seemed to be no conflict with the primary discourses he had learned at home (although he was a second-language learner) and the secondary discourses learned at school (Gee, 1990). He seemed to accept the somewhat taken-for-granted cultural model of the classroom that embraced writing about an important person and using descriptive language. In contrast, Anita's identity as a writer was in opposition to the classroom. She resisted classroom expectations by not participating in share sessions and by choosing a topic that was not sanctioned by the teacher.

Anita: Resisting Teacher Expectations

Anita was an 11-year-old sixth grader who had come from Jamaica and now lived in the Bronx Borough of NYC with her brother and her mother, who worked as a housekeeper. Anita took the train to school each morning by herself and reported that she entertained passengers on the train. She liked singing and dancing and entertaining people in nonschool settings, but was very withdrawn in whole-group class discussions. In fact, Anita never contributed to any of the classroom discussions, nor did she share her writing with the whole class. Anita seemed to have two quite distinct identities—her active, social self who was comfortable with adults outside of school and her withdrawn school self.

Ms. Meyer viewed Anita as a failing student who did not achieve in any subject and scored in less than the 10th percentile on standardized tests. The teacher admitted she had difficulty with her: "I haven't met her mother, her mother refuses to come to school, which is a real indication of you know, I just can't get a fix on her. I just don't like her…I think she's very, very slow." In terms of Anita's writing project, the teacher felt that she could not help her very much because "I can't make a connection with her…because I have so much trouble with her the rest of the day."

In the classroom sessions observed, Anita never made a single contribution. She had conflicting feelings about sharing her writing with the teacher, and said, "I don't want her to talk to me at all…she never does, so why should I want her to?"

Literacy Practices

Anita had had few opportunities to participate in writing process classrooms previously; she reported having done little writing before, and this was her first year at this school. Thus, she was at a disadvantage in this school where many of the students had been socialized to writing process previously. However, Anita valued her notebook as a place where she could write down her experiences and explained that her notebook is "something you write stuff in that makes you feel sad, happy, and stuff like that—if you think someone is trying to hurt you, you just write it in your notebook."

Writing appeared to Anita to be a personal and private journey to communicate with her inner self. Writing seemed to be a kind of therapy where she recorded unpleasant experiences and memories. She offered, "I hate writing reading entries because there is hardly anything in the book to write about that happens in your life. My life is harder because my father is really out of shape." She had several entries about experiences from her life and several references to her father, implying, but not specifically stating, some abuse.

Anita used writing as dialogue with herself rather than as communication with an audience. She feared rejection from the teacher and did not seek help from her: "If I did not go to her, she might not talk to me," and later, "she doesn't talk to me about anything." Although she recognized that Ms. Meyer was interested in teaching them about description, Anita did not consciously integrate what she learned in class into her writing. She was more concerned with recording her memorable experiences rather than learning the teacher's agenda. Anita seemed to connect the topic of writing with writing itself, not distancing herself from the process. For example, when asked which texts she liked and why, she chose the pieces that reflected her experiences and the people and things she valued. For example, she liked a notebook entry about her grandfather because, "I like the way he loves people, was nice to them, the way he cared about them" and thought a piece about her dog was her best because, "I really love my dog a lot." Although Anita used a skill she had learned in school—writing in a notebook—and incorporated it in her home life through her notebook entries, her writing was not valued by the teacher.

During their extended conference of more than 7 minutes, Ms. Meyer and Anita had difficulty developing a shared understanding about the topic for the project. In the first part of the conference, the teacher asked Anita what piece she was thinking of developing for her project. When Anita pointed to her piece titled "Lenox Hill Camp" that she had been working on daily for over 2 weeks, the teacher tried to dissuade Anita from writing about this topic. Despite Anita's introduction of several topics related to her experiences at Lenox Hill, the teacher rarely pursued those topics. Instead, Ms. Meyer introduced the topic of Anita's father on several occasions, suggesting that writing about the good and bad experiences with her father might be more "important." Anita resisted pursuing the teacher's leads related to her father, though she answered the teacher's direct questions. The lack of synchrony between teacher and student is apparent:

Ms. Meyer: It is so interesting, Anita, that you talk about writing that because there are so many entries when I look through this. I would have thought that the thing that would have stood out to you most would have been about your father. You have so many entries about your father in here. [pace slows down; she reads from text slowly with feeling.] "When I was living in Jamaica I had a farm. We had chickens and my father has something like an idea to let the chickens..."

Anita: Lay eggs...

Ms. Meyer: "Lay eggs and sell them." I mean I could just see this becoming all the like, you know, either the good times [pace slows down].... You had a lot of good times and a lot of bad times with your father, right? [pace quickens]

Anita:	Yeah. [agreeing unenthusiastically, falling tone]
Ms. Meyer:	You know, it seems to me that you have all these entries about the good and the bad times about your father, and maybe you should just pick one. You know, I'm not trying to tell you what to do, you know, but, it seems to me that you have more important stuff in here than Lenox Hill camp. You know what I mean? Unless you don't really want to write about it. Do you have other good entries about your father here besides this one?
Anita:	Not really. [drawn out syllables]

They look through the notebook together. Anita puts her hands on the notebook and tries to flip pages.

Anita:	That is the first day of school when Nick was bothering me.
Ms. Meyer:	Mhmmm [long pause]. So many of your entries have to do with your father...
Anita:	This is about...
Ms. Meyer:	Mhmmm...

Each time Anita introduced a possible topic, Ms. Meyer ignored it. Likewise, when the teacher brought up her father, Anita focused on a different topic. In their inflections, they emphasized different words. Essentially, no overlap of ideas existed in the conference between Ms. Meyer and Anita. This lack of overlap continued throughout the conference because the teacher did not build on Anita's ideas, but focused on what she considered important.

| Ms. Meyer: | Mhmmm. I don't know [sighs, long pause]. I think you need to think, I think you really need to go through this book, right? Really go through this book really carefully and read it very carefully. And take another color pen, OK, and underline all the sentences in your book, all of the places in your book where you think you wrote something so beautifully and that it was so important for you, OK? Because I think, Anita, that you have really, really deep and important things to say about |

relationships and about your mother and your father, and I just don't think that Lenox Hill is the
most important thing for you in here. If you decide
that that is what you want to do, OK. If it turns [out]
that after this you can't find some big important
idea that comes out of this for you that you would
like to write about…[pace slows down, says delib-
erately] Maybe it's going to be wishing, you know,
that your father were different, that you could have
more good times like the time in Jamaica [pace
speeds up]. Maybe you could really really write up
that time in Jamaica because that was a really good
time, wasn't it?

The teacher suggested to Anita that she describe what Jamaica
looked like and that she write a letter to her father. She ended the
conference by correcting Anita about the length of time the camp
lasted and recommending that if Anita wrote about Lenox Hill Camp,
she needed to think about what was important to her about camp.

The nonverbal actions during the conference were informative as
well. When Anita talked about Lenox Hill Camp, the teacher engaged
in a series of nervous gestures such as brushing her hand, scratching
her face, and picking lint off her sweater. When Ms. Meyer asked
questions about what was important, Anita looked at the rug, but never directly at the teacher. As soon as the teacher mentioned Anita's
entries about her father, Anita's shoulders stiffened and she looked at
the ground. After this, the teacher and student never made eye contact.
Throughout this conference, the teacher and student did not establish
a shared understanding of topic or audience.

Both participants had strong feelings about their interactions during the conferences and about the texts discussed. Anita indicated
that her experience at the camp was one of the best times in her life,
thus, she wanted to write about it. Ms. Meyer believed that there was
more compelling material in the notebook that Anita could develop
other than the Lenox Hill Camp story. Ms. Meyer said in an interview,

I wanted her to try to see what was at the bottom of all this, you know
what I mean, all these horrible pieces that she has, all these bad luck
things…I was hoping that she would, you know, she's got all of these

44

horrible stories…. And I didn't want to let her do that [write about Lenox Hill Camp] because that would have been just one of those, you know, "I went to Great Adventure" kind of things, "I had a lot of fun, I hid in the woods."

Ms. Meyer had suggested that Anita's story lacked getting to the bottom of something, meaning for the author to explain why something had occurred or what difference an event had made in one's life. Getting to the bottom of something seemed to entail being reflective about an event or person and describing its emotional impact. In contrast, the teacher viewed writing about Lenox Hill Camp as the "Great Adventure" genre that lacked emotional impact and focus.

The overall classroom norms, as well as the teacher-student interactions, seemed to be oppressive to Anita, and she sought ways to resist them. In terms of language and style, Anita had used very little imagery or figurative language that were introduced during the whole-group sessions. Her Lenox Hill Camp piece was long, but contained relatively few adjectives that might "give the reader a picture in his mind" (a phrase that was emphasized in whole-group minilessons), and she did not use metaphors or comparisons (see Figure 2).

Figure 2
Anita's Writing Sample

Lenox Hill Camp

My teacher was saying something and I remember the time when my old class went to Lenox Hill camp we had a lot of fun My bus was the first bus to leave a couple of us was in the bus I'll name the people. Ophelia, Cindy, Jasmin, bosise, Micle, Antony, marcus, patric, Joey, and me our bus was the first to leave After that the other bus came The teacher disided to pick out the rooms for girls and boys We were in scode [squad] one and the other class was in scoude [squad] two well [while] the girls were less. what I mean was that there were less girls. The scond [second] day that we were there the boys were Trying to come in our room. and then we plade [played] a game, spin the botle. it was a realy bad game. I'll tell you how it gose you take a botle and spin it and if it lands on a girl, then they have to wate [wait] and then you spin it agian and if it points at a boy, the girl and the boy have to go in the colset and do something and if you don't

45

you get a slap so when I went in the closet with the boy we acted like we were doing something But we were not and I put spit all over my mouth and came out of there and they said Had fun I was like yes I had a lot of fun. and then our class introctor [instructor] came and brought us outside and we went on the seld [sled] and hade a lot of fun we went down a little hill and went on the seld and then my friend Ophlea and I were talking [taking] some ice out of the water. it was winter. It was realy cool and it was the Bigest piece of ice you ever seen. I Loved Lonx hill camp. it was like we went hikeing and I wore my water baiters [boots] and it had a hole in it and my feet were frezing so much you could do me thing [something] with it. Well then that night my teacher read us a horrour story and I got real Scared and then I could hardly sleep and one Time we aske the teacher to get a drink of water. She looked kind of wear [weird]. When she said yes, I saw some smoke come out of her mouth. I was really sick. I was so scared that the, that she might be smoking crack because she was like acting like strange all the time. Every morning and every day every morning and everybody is like was she really smoking at my table the ones that were in my group and maybe a litle and the next day maybe a litle The next day we had to go hiking so we went we learned about foot tracks, animals I don't remember how the squirel looked and anyway we went on the bridge blindfold and my friend Jasmin was Ok when I did her and when she did me I almost fell off she was so dumb. we went back to the camp it was fun Fun. we went on the hike but I got really scared because she put me at the edge of the bridge I was like get this thing off of me and I almost throw up on her. So I took off the blindfold and I was at the edge of the bridge. She was very careless. She put me at the edge of the bridge.

Anita did write from personal experience, but her story did not focus on one or two aspects of a person or an event or contain thick description. Thus, her text did not match the teacher's image of a good text. Yet, her text contained many interesting features including several dramatic points within a structure, but these remained unacknowledged by the teacher. Her Lenox Hill piece also reflected more of a topic-association style of writing (Michaels, 1987) in which Anita introduced an idea connected to her experience at camp and then provided a number of details about that idea. Her text is similar to stories characteristic of many African American children who "plot numerous sequences of events within the context of the individual experiences combined" (McCabe, 1997, p. 460, citing Rodino et al., 1991). Her story also appears to be an oral text—she used many *ands* and *thens* to connect events, she explained some of the features of her text, and wrote as if she were telling an audience, "By the way you might be wondering how the squirrel looked, but I don't remember." She did seem to internalize some of the classroom expectations about using description, but she also expressed fear about the adult possibly using crack cocaine. As a reader, I could imagine many topics the teacher might have pursued with Anita that might have clarified her texts. Yet, the many tensions and story lines remained unexplored in the conference.

Initially, Anita planned to resist the teacher's authority, because when asked whether she was going to stick with the Lenox Hill Camp topic for her final project, she said, "Yes, because I feel like it." However, she eventually changed her mind, enlisted another student's help rather than the teacher's, and wrote a poem about her grandfather, abandoning the Lenox Hill Camp piece.

Anita's relationship with the teacher seems to have contributed to her resistance to the classroom norms and her attempts to fashion an identity as a writer outside the classroom. Anita was conflicted about her relationship with the teacher because she had to function in the classroom knowing that her work was not valued. As evidenced by the conference with the teacher, Anita's concept of text and her topic choice did not match the teacher's image of a good text for this assignment. During the course of the writing conference, Ms. Meyer never looked at Anita's story on Lenox Hill Camp. The conversation was really never about Anita's text or topic; instead, the conference revolved around finding an alternative topic. The implicit messages to Anita were most likely that the text she wrote was not valued and that it was better to write about something "important" such as her father, even if that meant writing about a painful relationship. Yet, the teacher did little to help Anita understand how to select what she considered an appropriate topic for a project. The fact that Anita was Jamaican and may not have a shared the teacher's value on traditional European American literary language seemed to have influenced the teacher's interactions with her.

Anita's story demonstrates what can go awry when teacher and student do not develop a shared understanding of topic or the criteria for writing a text. It also points out that although the teacher may have enormous impact on the student, some students can be resilient and find ways to resist overtly or covertly. Anita was not defeated as a writer by her interactions with the teacher; instead, she continued to write in her notebook but for a different audience than the classroom—herself—and for a different purpose—therapy. She also continued to value her own work and found that she liked many of the phrases and ideas she had included in her notebook.

Summary

Anita's resistance to the classroom norms was quite admirable in many ways. Although the teacher derailed Anita's initial project and very easily could have left her feeling defeated and lacking any confidence as a writer, Anita persisted with her writing. She chose another project, she continued to use her notebook for therapy, and she shared aspects of herself with others outside the school community such as the people on the train. In these ways she demonstrated that she was quite literate—she used language in a variety of formats (notebooks, singing, dancing) to "think about and act on the world" (Gee, 2001, p. 714). However, her identity as a writer at school was limited because she felt that she needed to keep her writing private. The notebooks may have been therapeutic for her, allowing her to survive some difficult times, and connected her to an audience on the train; however, her writing did not give her entrée into the larger community at school.

The conflicts she encountered suggest that larger institutional forces were at work. Conflicts existed between her working-class, Jamaican background and the middle-class values and ways of speaking of the white teacher (Gee, 1990). She did not accept the cultural model of the classroom (which may have been invisible to her) with its emphasis on descriptive language and personal experience of a particular type (Gee, 2001). She tried to find alternative ways to enact her identity as a literate individual but may have been limited because of her challenges at school.

Anita's background and classroom experiences differed remarkably from Ella who found ways to meet the demands of the classroom while maintaining her identity as a fiction writer and transforming her classroom experiences into texts.

Ella: Transforming Classroom Norms Through a Fictional Voice

Ella was a tall, African American, fifth-grade girl. She lived with her mother in an apartment in the Spanish Harlem section of NYC and was from a middle-class background. Her mother worked as a proof-reader in a publishing company; her father was a university professor who worked with computers. She had been at the school since kindergarten and had many opportunities to participate in process writing classrooms. Ella enjoyed engaging adults in conversations in which she would tell humorous anecdotes, interweaving books she had read, games she had played, and stories she had written. Ella read extensively, mostly fiction and detective novels, and enjoyed writing fiction as well as more personal narratives. She believed that the one thing she had gained from Ms. Meyer's class was the importance of literature in supplying ideas for writing: "I learned that you can use your best writing off of books. Books can give you some good ideas."

Ella believed having a career as a writer would afford her the opportunity to write about whatever she wanted. She wrote at home as well as in the school context, sometimes writing with a friend during recess. Ella kept two notebooks—a small one for her classroom writings, or as she said, "one that you use for things that have happened in your life" and a larger one for her fiction writing or the writing of "humorous stories." She kept the larger notebook secret because the writing of fiction was not sanctioned in the classroom. Her secret notebook contained several fictional pieces, some with several chapters, including a book titled *Morris and Marsha, P. I.* (the "I" is cleverly drawn in the form of an eye). Inside were three stories: "The Case of the Dog de Menson," "The Case of the Foggie Building," and "The Vanishing Castle." Each story had several chapters, with the book totaling 32 pages. This notebook also contained the story that she and her friend, Serena, had written together, much of it on the telephone.

Writing served multiple purposes for Ella, and she was forthcoming about her enjoyment of the process: "I like writing. I don't know why I like writing detective stories so much but I just do." She was aware that writing could be context specific and when asked if she considered herself a good writer, Ella responded, "It depends on what kind of a story it is" then added that she was best at writing fiction. Although she found that writing could be a tool for self-reflection, she was most interested in writing collaboratively with her friend and for an audience. She had examined earlier pieces and wanted to revise them, "because as you go along, you get new ideas…you cross out things, put in new things." She was most interested in writing when she could choose her own topics and was not forced to write. Ella was able to keep her identity as a fiction writer at the same time she fulfilled classroom assignments. Additionally, she succeeded in transforming classroom norms to suit her own purposes; for example, she inserted her "fictional voice" into the classroom notebook pieces.

Ms. Meyer felt positively toward Ella, but she did not encourage her to write fiction. She described her as an excellent student who scored in the 99th percentile on standardized achievement tests. She found that Ella had good ideas and seemed in control of school and of her writing:

> As far as her work is concerned, she really does fine. She pays attention in class, she's really a really neat kid, I really like her. I think her notebook is lovely. I mean I think it's honest, and it's really lovely, and you know there's a lot of really great things happening there. I think perhaps her project will really be very nice, you know she'll pull out those really nice pieces about her aunt and do some really nice writing about them.

Although Ms. Meyer clearly approved of Ella's notebook pieces, she was less enthusiastic about Ella or other students' fiction writing. Her dislike of children writing fiction at this point in the year rested on her assumptions that the students were too unsophisticated to see that fiction writing was based on truth—the personal experience of authors. She believed that writers used notebooks to generate ideas for fiction, but that notebooks recorded events of writers' lives that could be used for development into stories:

> [Students] don't have an idea that it really is the same and that fiction writing should really be based on truth from their notebooks. In other words, nobody goes out, Katherine Paterson [an author of children's books], nobody goes out and writes a piece of fiction that isn't based on truth somehow or somewhere. You know what I mean, and if they did do

fiction, it should really have come, should come from their notebooks at some point.

Ms. Meyer felt strongly that students should base their writing on research or the reality that they observe around them. She expressed that students have to write from their own experience because

> that's the way it has to be for young kids. Otherwise you get these stories about Ninja Turtles, and that G.I. Joe is coming alive, and about people living on the moon. It's not based in any kind of fact or any kind of research or any kind of reality. Whatever their story is about, they're not doing any research into the reality of the fiction, you know?

Literacy Practices

The previous examples from the teacher's interview provide background for understanding Ella's interactions with Ms. Meyer during writing conferences. The first conference focused on finding an appropriate theme or topic from the notebook to develop into a project. When Ella and the teacher began their first conference, they did not have a shared understanding about the project or what the word *important* implied. The teacher believed *important* should be something deeply personal, while Ella believed important had to do with items that were newsworthy. Ella had expressed her ideas about what constituted important issues about which to write in an interview prior to the conference:

> I don't know what I'm going to do…because, because there's no really big, important issues in here [indicating her notebook]. Except for this, I wrote about the news. I was mad though because this guy was missing since Sunday, and they found him in the lake drowned, and they didn't put it on the news or anything.

Their lack of a shared understanding is reflected near the opening of their conference:

Ms. Meyer:	Mhmm. And nothing seems to stand out for you as being important?
Ella:	Not really.
Ms. Meyer:	Mhmm. Is there something you seem to write about more often than not?

51

Ella:	Yeah.
Ms. Meyer:	What do you think that is?
Ella:	Um, well, about um, usually about me and when I was little.

Although the teacher and student did not use each other's words in the subsequent sentences, they were responding to one another in such a way that communication seemed to have been clear. Ella came to understand that the topic of the project should be something she wrote about frequently in her notebook. As the conference continued, Ella said she had written some pieces about her aunt, and Ms. Meyer revisited the issue of finding out what was important about her relationship with her aunt.

Ms. Meyer:	OK, so you, so you are missing her, is that what you're saying?
Ella:	Yeah.
Ms. Meyer:	Ahhh. So you're saying that the bottom of all this is that you're missing your Aunt Delores now and you're remembering all the wonderful times?
Ella:	[Nods] And I'm mad at my grandparents because they're going to see her and they're not taking me.
Ms. Meyer:	So, don't you think, what does that sound like to you…that maybe this would be that, that you have all those stories about when you used to do things with her? Well, what about if you turned them into a kind of a letter to her? That would be a really neat project, a real neat letter to her where you went on and on and talked to her about all the wonderful times, as a way to say to her I miss you so much. Maybe in a way to plan a time where you could get together? Yeah? Does that sound like something you might want to do?

Ella had become engaged in the conversation about her aunt and seemed to have found this a satisfactory topic about which to write her project. The teacher suggested that she write a letter, and this seemed to strike Ella as a good idea, evidenced by the nodding of her head at several different points. The teacher emphasized several words such as *stories*, *letter*, and *miss*, indicating these were the important ideas. In her recommendations to Ella, she also placed her inflection on *neat*, giving the implicit message that writing a letter was a good idea. However, conflict arose when Ella indicated that she had also been doing a fiction project with a classmate, Serena. Ms. Meyer did not encourage this topic and became more explicit about the procedures that Ella should go through to complete the letter to her aunt. She went on to tell Ella how to select the entries about her aunt and to turn those into a project, focusing on why those were important. In the process, she discouraged Ella from writing any fiction. The conference ended with Ella getting up from the floor and going back to her seat where she began to select existing pieces from her notebook for her project, complying with the teacher's requests.

Ella responded positively, if not enthusiastically, to her conference with the teacher. In an informal interview after the conference, Ella explained that she now felt that she understood what a project was because the teacher had explained it to her. Ella summarized her interaction with the teacher by saying that she had told the teacher she had a lot of entries about her Aunt Delores and that the teacher then recommended turning those entries into a letter to her aunt. When I asked Ella if the teacher's idea was a good one, she said, "I'm going to go ahead with it." In response to whether that was something she wanted to do, Ella responded, "Yeah. And she's [Aunt Delores] been begging me to write her a letter so it won't run up my grandparents' phone bill."

Looking back at the writing conference, it seems that initially Ella suggested that she had written several entries about her Aunt Delores. Ms. Meyer picked up on this and encouraged Ella to write about this topic for her project. Ms. Meyer also suggested Ella turn these entries into a letter that seemed satisfactory to her, because she could meet the teacher's criterion of an appropriate topic, while meeting her own interest in contacting her aunt without creating an expensive telephone bill. The teacher and student had come to a shared understanding of the project. Altlhough Ella temporarily had gotten excited about writing a fiction project, her interest waned when the teacher did not encourage her to write fiction for this project. Ella may have compromised her own interests to satisfy the teacher, but she did so in a way that allowed her to find a topic that she was interested in pursuing.

Ella's interest in the letter to her aunt developed over the next several days. She worked on her project, selecting work from her notebook and expanding upon those entries. Ms. Meyer initiated a second writing conference by calling Ella to the back table. Ella handed her paper to Ms. Meyer, who then looked through Ella's sheets of paper and started the conference by asking where the beginning was and if she had placed the entries in the form of a letter. In the next sequence, the teacher pointed out how Ella needed an introduction that would be more fitting to a letter, after establishing that there was a conflict between writing a letter (which required second person) and a story (which required the use of either first person or third person).

Ms. Meyer:	Oh OK. So first you are copying all the entries, then you are going to go through this, and you are going to find how to make this because it can't be [speeds up pace] "Dear Aunt Delores, Me and my Aunt Delores have always been close." See what I am saying? [pause] So how are you going to do that? That, that's your challenge.
Ella:	I have to have a new start [inaudible] something like [inaudible] I changed…
Ms. Meyer:	But you need to have the whole tone change. In other words, you have to be speaking to her as if it is in a letter. See what I am saying? So if you were writing all this to her, you wouldn't be saying it like "summers were no different, something always happened like when" [reads a part from Ella's text very quickly]. You might want to say, "Remember, Aunt Delores, when" [says this slowly] or you know, remember when, or "Boy, I laugh when I think about us." It's kind of like you kind of need to be talking to her as if you would in a letter.
Ella:	I started doing that, it was like I was telling it to Serena [laughs].
Ms. Meyer:	Ahh, yeah, it's a good idea.

At the point where Ms. Meyer gave specific suggestions about how Ella could start her piece, teacher and student seemed to connect. Ms. Meyer leaned toward Ella who sat down, closing the physical gap between them to a distance of about one foot. Ella began to tell the teacher about how she had started to do that and had even tried it out on her friend, Serena. The two resumed their conference when Ella showed the teacher the last entry.

Ella:	I'm on the last entry.
Ms. Meyer:	OK, so that's when you need to kind of take all this stuff and decide how you can turn this in.
Ella:	My mother said, my mother said, she um, like she got her friend to like we are making a tape.
Ms. Meyer:	You are going to tape it and send it to her also?
Ella:	Yeah.
Ms. Meyer:	That's wonderful. [draws out word]

The teacher responded positively to Ella's suggestion that she send a tape along with her letter as evidenced by the teacher's enthusiasm in her voice. In this segment there is a much more cooperative element to their interactions. Ella initiated this part of the exchange by offering to show Ms. Meyer the last entry. Additionally, each speaker said about the same amount within a turn, and both speakers incorporated the ideas of the previous speaker. For instance, Ella stressed the word *tape*, which Ms. Meyer then picked up on, emphasizing the same word. Although the teacher provided suggestions, the dialogue was negotiated between them. Their body language also demonstrated a kind of synchrony: Both looked at the papers at the same time, looked back at one another simultaneously, looked at the papers again, and then made eye contact. Synchrony between teacher and student continued as they both laughed at some phrases and agreed on a way to begin the letter (see Figure 3). Ella agreed that she would write a letter to her aunt and began to select entries from her notebook to use for the project.

Figure 3
Ella's Writing Sample

Dear, Aunt Delores,

I finally decided to listen to you. Instead of running up your or Grandma's phone bill I'm writing you a letter. Remember those stories you used to tell me about when I was little. "I know" "I know." Of course you remember them. Well you're going to hear them again. My way! Here's one you've told me only once, you'll remember it once you hear it. Here it goes: It was snowing, ice covered the ground. We were on are way to the grocery store for Grandma. I had to skip to keep up with you. Snow drifted down onto my nose We giggled as we walked even though I had something else on my mind—"mischief"! I waited for the perfect moment then wriggled out of your grasp. I ran with the wind and slipped and fell and sat there for a few seconds then burst out laughing. Meanwhile you had run after me and slipped and fell, almost landing on top of me. "Yikes" I said as I scrambled to the side. Your face turned red as a beet but then you started laughing. We tried to get up but we could'nt. Finally sombody got us up. You carried me there and back.

Sound familiar? There's your all-time favorite. Oh by the way could you and a few other family members come to my recital in June? I would really like you to be there and hopefully you'll meet my sister! Well here comes the story. It was a sunny summer day. I was staying at your apartment and we were eating breakfast. I glanced over to your plate and noticed that you had more sausage than I did. "I want some orange juice please" I said. I watched you get the juice. Before I quickly swiped one of your sausages onto my plate, you came back with the juice. "Hey," you said "how come I only have 3 sausages and you have 4?" "I don't know," I answered You didn't say anything else after that. I wondered why.

I love you and I miss you and I hope I'll see you soon.
though times were hard
and we were spread apart
I've always had faith in
you cause you were in my heart.

P.S. Please write back.
Love
Ella
P.P.S I know you told me to stop growing, but I couldn't help being 5'2 ½".

Ella's texts showed that she not only used the teacher's suggestions, but she was able to keep her own voice. For example, in each revision of the drafts of the letter to her aunt, Ella changed the end of the story. She was able to include fictional elements that she so highly valued by writing a story in the first person (meeting the teacher's expectations), yet adding a variety of endings (her own fictional voice). In Ella's final project (Figure 3), she made use of the dialogue from the classroom, her writing conferences with the teacher, and previous experiences with literature and fiction writing. Her letter shows the direct influence of the teacher in using a letter format and in the opening line, "Dear, Aunt Delores. I finally decided to listen to you." The description she used such as "wriggled," "snow drifting," and "swiped" reflects the teacher's value on using detail and colorful language. Ella also made use of a fictional voice by setting the winter scene and adding dialogue to tell the stories within the letter. The final project combines elements—letter, narrative, and invitation to her performance. Yet, we get the sense that Ella indeed will send this to her aunt, thus developing her classroom writing assignment into a piece for an audience. Ella, then, was able to transform the classroom dialogue to fit with her previous experiences and emergent style to share with an audience beyond the classroom.

Summary

Ella's case demonstrates how a student can comply with classroom norms yet transform them to meet her own criteria. Although disagreeing with the teacher about several aspects of writing such as writing collaboratively versus writing alone (which the teacher valued) and writing fiction as opposed to writing from personal experience, Ella had quality interactions with her teacher during the two writing conferences. These conferences were pivotal in Ella's subsequent texts, because she was clearly influenced by these conversations and included the teacher's ideas in her project. However, by including a fictional voice in her project, she used the ideas in a unique way and did not just submit to the teacher's authority. She showed that she understood the classroom norms and the teacher's expectations, but she was able to combine those features she thought the teacher valued, such as writing about the personal and using description, while developing her own style. Ella was particularly adept at finding ways to serve her own purposes within the context of the classroom. She exemplified Bahktin's (1981) "internally persuasive discourse" (p. 342) because she was flexible and able to apply her knowledge into a new setting.

Ella's background allowed her entrée into the cultural models of the classroom. Because she had a middle-class background and professional parents who supported her out-of-school writing, Ella had many opportunities to write in a variety of genres. Although some of these genres were not valued in this particular classroom, she had positive experiences in other writing process classrooms that gave her confidence in her work. Her articulate narrative style, learned at home, also provided her with opportunities to link her primary home discourse with school discourse (Gee, 1990).

What These Cases Might Mean for Developing Students' Identities as Writers

The cases of Miguel, Anita, and Ella highlight the differences in how students viewed the purposes of writing and their views of themselves as writers. Miguel saw good writing as a part of being a good student, the result of effort and epiphany. His vision of writing aligned well with classroom expectations and allowed him to be quite successful within the classroom. His values on writing were congruent with the teacher's, and he followed the teacher script (Gutierrez, Rymes, & Larson, 1995). Anita, by contrast, was not seen as a successful writer in this classroom and resisted the teacher's attempts to write about her father or to use the type of figurative language the teacher wanted. However, she continued to value her own work and to write for herself—quite a feat given her relationship with the teacher. Yet writing only for therapeutic purposes limited her to a one-person community, and at the same time her resistance (albeit understandable) to share her work in the larger setting prevented her from joining the larger school community. Anita was caught between pleasing the teacher and writing about something meaningful to her. In effect, her primary discourse learned at home, influenced by her status as a working-class, Jamaican immigrant, conflicted with the middle-class norms of the classroom teacher who enacted a particular cultural model of writing (Gee, 2001).

Ella, who was able to develop a "third space" (Gutierrez et al., 1995) with the teacher, became aware of the teacher's values relating to a particular kind of writing. Once she understood the teacher's implicit assumptions about writing, she transformed her pieces to include fictional ideas, as well as other elements to satisfy the teacher. In this way, she was utilizing Bakhtin's (1981) internally persuasive discourse, combining her own past work as a fiction writer with the teacher's voice of narrative through letter writing. Ella found a "liminal space" (Dressman, 1997, p. 42) or alternative space where she could create a "hybrid text" (Fecho, 2001, p. 7).

Through a comparison of the three cases, we can see how these students were both empowered and deterred as writers. While Miguel seemed to flourish in the classroom, Anita had many challenges, but she was able to find a purpose for writing in spite of the teacher. Ella was enabled by the classroom to write to her aunt, yet she also found her voice through some resistance to the classroom expectations. All three students demonstrated many literate practices: Miguel read the literal word, but also the world, for his mother, by interpreting U.S. culture and supporting her in learning English; Anita enacted quite different literate selves on the train versus in the classroom; and Ella found ways to write individually and collaboratively in different genres. Some of the students' literate practices were valued in this classroom, while some were not.

The writing workshop in this New York City classroom demonstrated the tremendous influence that the teacher-student relationship may have on students' writing and beliefs about themselves as writers. The teacher had a strong relationship with some students, and they developed a shared understanding about topics to write about and how to revise their texts into projects for an audience; at the same time, she ignored and did not value other students' texts and, by extension, their literate identities.

The conferences provide a close-up look at the relationships between teacher and students. When synchrony developed between the teacher and student, the student appropriated information and applied it to her or his writing. The conferences also allow us to see how the teacher imposed her view of good writing on the students. She drew from literature and students' writing in her demonstrations, but her interactions with students showed that she was actually quite prescriptive. By being enthusiastic about some students' topics and not others and by providing suggestions about what genres to use, the teacher communicated her own values. She held a particular cultural model (Gee, 2001) about what constituted good writing, which included selecting important personal experiences as topics, using description and imagery as features of good writing, and sharing with an audience rather than writing for oneself as the primary purpose of writing. These values were the ones that counted as valid and normal in her classroom. When a student such as Anita held a different model or was unable to read exactly what Ms. Meyer wanted, the result was unsatisfactory at best or disastrous at worst.

The conferences provide a microcosm of larger institutional forces at work. They are an example of Fairclough's (1992) suggestion that classrooms are cultural sites where local and institutional forces play out. Although the three students expressed agency within their writing, their responses were shaped by home values and discourses, by the teacher's models of writing, and by the larger institution of schooling that gives power to teachers. Likewise, Ms. Meyer's identity as a teacher had been formed by being middle-class, white, and Jewish with a long history of living and teaching in New York City. Her own views of writing were influenced by the Teachers College Writing Project that valued personal writing from a specific genre. She was enacting the discourses of the Writing Project, focusing on students as individuals who needed to express themselves, just as she was enacting larger norms connected to the institution—that is, students should be able to comprehend and conform to classroom expectations (Gee, 2001).

The teacher-student interactions within the writing workshop have much to teach us about how students' identities are formed and reshaped within the workshop. Although the intentions of the writing workshop are to promote student choice and motivation to become lifelong writers, the curriculum in this classroom was rather prescriptive. Students like Miguel can be quite successful in understanding the classroom norms and thriving within them. Students like Ella may be able to satisfy both the teacher and themselves by retaining their own identities as writers within the classroom context. However, students like Anita, whose home discourse may differ from that valued in the classroom and who have a difficult relationship with the teacher, may find their identities as writers unsupported. This lack of support can lead to increased resistance, resulting in fewer opportunities to share writing and thus, to enact their literate selves.

From these cases, it seems important to realize that students have rich, literate backgrounds and potentially competing identities. Who Anita was as a writer in the classroom differed substantially from who she was on the train, entertaining adults. Ella, too, had a more collaborative side to her, but she blended her fictional writing into her personal experiences. The cases demonstrate what Sarup (1996) describes as a blending (Ella) or clashing (Anita) of identities. Understanding students' backgrounds and allowing them to use their experiences and values in school literacy activities may encourage them to develop many literacies and identities rather than feeling the need to submerge aspects of themselves.

The cases also suggest that the teacher-student relationship is important to developing writers who take pride in their achievements. Writing conferences can serve as a powerful means to develop the teacher-student relationship; however, this close-up, face-to-face interaction also poses some risks (McCarthey, 1994). The lesson may be that we all need to become more cognizant of the powerful effects of our talk about writing with students. Teachers may wish to examine their implicit assumptions about what constitutes effective writing pieces, as well as consider how we can help students improve their writing without imposing our view on students or denying what they consider important enough to render into writing. We may need to create spaces in classrooms where students can learn about many definitions of good writing, but where they can have opportunities to try out a variety of genres.

Appropriating, Resisting, and Transforming Norms in a Literature-Based, Multiage Classroom

Hillside School, located in a neighborhood with middle-class professional families and working-class and working-poor families in a city
in south central Texas, had engaged in a number of schoolwide innovations in the 1990s. With the support of a dynamic principal, the
school had begun a multiage grouping program in which teachers
team-taught students from two grade levels for 2 years. Several teachers had begun experimenting with team teaching and multiage grouping in the early 1990s, and the rest of the school adopted the plan in
the mid-1990s. Construction of additional classroom space reflected
the philosophy that students should be grouped in diverse ways; thus,
new designs joined classrooms with folding doors to encourage
different grouping patterns. The teachers believed that multiage classrooms provided continuity of students' curricular experiences, allowed for opening and integrating curriculum, and provided the
impetus for team teaching. Team teaching allowed the teachers to pool
their strengths at the same time they specialized in areas within the
curriculum and modeled for students problem-solving strategies and
conflict management.

Along with the multiage grouping, teachers implemented a
literature-based reading program and used portfolio assessment

instead of traditional grading. The school had several bilingual teachers and made efforts to link to the larger Latino community they served. Students were required to take the Texas Assessment of Academic Skills (TAAS), but most teachers felt that they could prepare students for the test without sacrificing their literature-based programs. This attitude shifted shortly after the principal retired, and the school and district encountered problems with the state over testing. The study discussed in this chapter took place at the height of the principal and school's innovations when the district supported the school's curriculum; many visitors came to the school to observe the programs and several of the teachers were asked to make presentations throughout the state.

The three teachers I studied formed an instructional team responsible for 49 third and fourth graders. They planned all curricular activities together and emphasized innovative reading and writing practices that they had learned from whole language workshops led by educators in New Zealand. The teachers integrated curriculum across the subject areas, provided many opportunities for students to read and write, and allowed students to pursue interests through research projects. The classroom was considered a bilingual classroom because one of the teachers spoke fluent Spanish, conducted ESL instruction for Spanish-speaking students, and taught Spanish as a class to all of the third and fourth graders. The teachers were committed to all aspects of the program: the multiage component, the literature-based and writing workshop aspects, and the thematic units. They believed that they were allowed considerable freedom in designing their curriculum and meeting the needs of their students as long as the students continued to perform well on TAAS.

Classroom Literacy Activities

The school day generally began with students writing in their personal journals; students were allowed to write about anything they wanted and the teachers read their entries and initialed them, but did not comment on them. Interspersed throughout the day were literacy activities such as research, writing workshop, and writing articles for the weekly class newspaper. Research occurred in conjunction with the units of study, while writing workshop occurred only about once a week.

Book response was a central feature of the literacy activities around which many of the others revolved. The teachers selected a children's book, which became the focus of a unit of study (from 2 to 12 weeks) and connected social studies and science concepts to the novels. For example, during the unit on *Pedro's Journal* (Conrad, 1991), a first-person narrative about Columbus's landing in America, students learned about sailing and did research projects on events connected to that time in history, for example, the bubonic plague or Florence, Italy, as a center of culture. Daily book response consisted of all students gathering together on the rug to listen to a chapter or two read aloud from the novel. While one teacher read aloud, the other teacher wrote a summary of the events on a chart (the bilingual teacher wrote an additional summary in Spanish). At the end of the read-aloud, students wrote in their response logs (open-ended response journals) for 5 minutes. The emphasis was on students writing their ideas without concern for spelling or punctuation.

Because the teachers believed it was important for students to hear one another's ideas, they encouraged students to share their response logs with the entire group. The teaming situation allowed all teachers to respond to students, freely chiming in when they felt it necessary without assigning teacher roles. One of the teachers wrote several words (what they referred to as "colorful language") used by the students on a chart for the purpose of building vocabulary. Ms. Martin said, "I can't think of a better way for these children to start using some of these [vocabulary from the novels] than posting it in the room so they actually see it all day long, so not only are they using it in their response logs but also in their other writing." Although the teachers did not discourage students from summarizing the story, they hoped that students would go beyond summaries to adopt the characters' perspectives and to include interesting vocabulary.

Books and Related Tasks

The first book read aloud during book response, *Pedro's Journal*, tells the story of Columbus's landing in America through the eyes of a young cabin boy. The book attempts to present a balanced view of the relationship between Columbus and the natives by evoking sympathy for the plight of both: Columbus and his men were thousands of miles from home with dwindling supplies, and the natives, some of whom were friendly, could be hostile. Although the teachers suggested that students should "put yourself in the place of Pedro," they allowed students to write open-ended responses. The classroom followed a similar format after reading *James and the Giant Peach* (Dahl, 1961). The teachers read aloud one or more chapters, students wrote in their journals from the perspective of James, and teachers called on individual students to read their responses. Teachers recorded students' responses on a chart. After hearing some students' responses, the teachers noted that students "were just retelling the story" and responded to two girls who had complained about having to take on the perspective of another male character by altering the assignment to "You're observing the story as it's unfolding."

The format was altered for a 2-week period in late November; students met in small groups and completed worksheets together that included specific comprehension questions. *Eating the Plates* (Penner, 1991), an expository text filled with details about the Pilgrims' lives—the kinds of houses they built, the food they ate, and their habits and manners—served as the text. The final books in December were a series of picture books about different early U.S. traditions of celebrating Christmas. Some books dealt with the lives of 19th-century immigrants (of European descent), while others explored their legends or traditions, such as *The Baker's Dozen* (Shepard, 1995), but all assumed a Christian audience. Teachers used a large chart to display the names, authors, and students' responses to the books.

In the second semester, the teachers and students spent about 2 months on a unit about ancient Egypt by beginning with the mystery book *The Egypt Game* (Snyder, 1986). In the book, two young girls turn a deserted storage yard behind an antique store into a game in which they pretend they are in ancient Egypt by wearing costumes and assuming roles; other children join the game and help them solve a murder. A typical reading-response session went as follows:

One teacher, Ms. Allen, asks students to close their eyes, and she begins the imaging:

Think back to California, on Orchard Street, the old professor's store. Look inside the windows. You see two girls, one rather tall wearing a ratty old stole and false eyelashes, the other has dark skin. There is a little boy running around; his name is Marshall. Listen to what they are talking about. What will happen now that there are three people in *The Egypt Game*?

Greg interrupts to say there are now four people in the game. The teachers ignore his comments. Mandy raises her hand and asks if it is OK when they are writing to be one of the girls. Ms. Allen responds that it is up to them to be one of the bystanders, one of the girls, or Marshall. The other teacher, Ms. Martin, writes a summary of events on the chart. Then students begin their responses and share them:

Emily [reads]:	"Look April asked…she looks like Nefertiti with her magical smile."
Ms. Martin:	I loved the choice of words, *magical* [gasping].
Geoffrey [reads]:	"I think they will let her in [the game]. That is why the chapter is called 'Neferbeth,' because it is Nefertiti and Elizabeth."
Ms. Allen:	So they have combined two names—Nefertiti and Elizabeth.
Greg [calls out]:	It is like my god. I combined it with ferret and Nefertiti and got Feretini.
Ms. Allen:	What was your god? Well, maybe we will talk about that later.
Greg:	It is named after my ferret.
Trina [reads]:	"I think if they let her it would not hurt their imaginary game, the Egypt game. I think it would be fascinating if they let the new girl in because her neck is shaped like the figure of Nefertiti so I think it would be wonderful."
Ms. Allen:	These are great, guys.
Mandy [reads]:	"Another girl and she is 9. I wonder how her imagination works? How does Melanie like this? Can I trust her to keep a secret? Maybe she'll teach the whole world about Melanie and I and the Egypt game. Then we'd be in trouble."
Ms. Martin:	I like that you have chosen to take the role of April. I like that.

The response session demonstrates how the teachers set the stage for listening to the novel and for students to assume a perspective of one of the characters. The teachers' responses indicate their emphasis on including descriptive language in their pieces. The teachers did not consider this a time to discuss the chapter per se, but rather hoped that students would use their responses as an opportunity to write insights about the book and to improve their writing.

During the Egypt unit, the teachers used picture books about discoveries of mummies and artifacts to supplement the study of Egypt. Students engaged in a variety of literacy, science, and social studies activities related to the topic; for example, students mummified a chicken, made their own mummies from papier maché, put together a news show, and made tools like those used in ancient Egypt. As part of each unit, students also completed a packet of worksheets and activities that included vocabulary and skills; for example, with the Egypt unit, students learned vocabulary related to Egypt, completed maps of the country and the surrounding area, completed sheets on gods and goddesses, and deciphered hieroglyphics.

The following three cases show the way in which students responded differently to the opportunities afforded in the classrooms. While Rita applied herself to learn the set of expectations and to become a successful writer in two languages, Greg struggled to gain acceptance from his teacher and peers. Mandy, equipped to write from a variety of perspectives, was able to alter the norms ever so slightly to achieve her goals of gender equity.

Rita: Appropriating Classroom Norms in Spanish and English

Rita was a fourth grader who was older than most of the students because she completed third grade twice due to an initial misunderstanding about her placement in a bilingual classroom. She arrived from Mexico as a kindergartner and spoke primarily Spanish at home with her mother, but spoke some English with her sisters who were high school-age. She came from a large family—a mother, a brother, and several sisters; her mother and three of Rita's sisters lived in central Texas. Different family members lived in different apartments in the city, and Rita lived with an older sister, but there was a great deal of fluidity among the households. Rita's mother and eldest sister were teachers in Mexico, but had to settle for lower status jobs in Texas; her mother could not work at all due to her diabetes.

The teachers had little contact with Rita's family, but my interviews with her family revealed that they felt frustrated with the education she was receiving. They believed that the school was trying to meet individual needs and not pressure students, but that the emphasis was not on academics. In contrast to the traditional education experiences they had in Mexico, they felt that the classrooms were too chaotic, allowed too much choice, and lacked structure. They felt the need to supplement what Rita was receiving at school by providing textbooks from Mexico at home, so she would be more challenged. They also expressed dissatisfaction with the language teaching at the school, suggesting that there were actually two groups, one for native English speakers and one for ESL students who were not receiving adequate instruction in either language. For example, the sisters believed that students should not be allowed to choose which language to use to complete worksheets, that English language acquisition should be emphasized before anything else, and that the Spanish in the school was "street Spanish" filled with slang rather than the Spanish of educated people. The family members indicated that these differences in values created conflicts for Rita in the classroom.

Rita, however, took all this in stride. She seemed to move quite easily from home to school, from Spanish to English. She reported that she read the Mexican textbooks at home required by her mother, and she helped her mother with English reading and pronunciation; she also conversed in Spanish and English with cousins and friends, wrote in both Spanish and English, and watched television in both languages. Rita made great efforts to learn English and retain Spanish while she negotiated the classroom expectations. Her after-school activities included ballet and swimming classes and watching television and movies at home.

Literacy Practices

Although she did not particularly enjoy reading or writing, Rita wanted to be successful in the classroom. She did not want to read over the summer, but would do so if her mother required it of her. Although she had books at home, she preferred to watch movies. Yet, she loved the read-alouds at school and sought to visualize the stories. She also enjoyed listening to peers share their writing, but did not want to read her own work to the large group: "I could hear how people say things they heard in the books, so I could another time remember the things they said. But I usually don't want to share." Rita knew that the teachers wanted students to share their work: "When the teacher says it's sharing time, they could raise their hands and then they could read what they had written." She also understood that the teachers valued some writing over others: "If they like what they [students] wrote, they'll say, 'that was very nice,' and if they don't, they just say, 'Thank you for sharing.'"

Rita not only understood some of the teacher's implicit messages, but she demonstrated competence in both Spanish and English in her own writing. Her journal writing in which she began each entry with "Querido Diario" [Dear Diary] had at least a half page—usually an entire page—for each day of school. Her topics reflected her everyday interests and concerns with life in and out of school. For example, she wrote about the first day of school, her teachers, ballet class, going to the park, birthdays, and friends. These entries were almost always written in Spanish, although she wrote in English on several occasions. Rita believed that the thoughts she was trying to convey determined her choice of language; she said, "I just start writing, and I don't know what language I'm doing, and I look and it's either Spanish or English, and then I continue to write in that language."

The importance of her identity as Latina and her connections to family in Mexico were evident in her writing. For example, she wrote about her family members who were still in Mexico and ended the entry with a tribute to her mother: "A todos los quiero mucho especialmente a mi mamá" (I love all of them very much, especially my mama). She was proud of her heritage, and in the fall chose to investigate the Mayan culture for a research project. She used the encyclopedia to find information and wrote the following brief description of the Mayans in both English and Spanish:

The Mayans
They lived 1,100 years ago they lived in Belize, Guatemala, Honduras, El Salvador and Mexico. They were farmers. The kids played music. The father chose who they were going to marry.

As part of her portfolio evaluation she wrote, "I realy enjoy doing this project because my mother and the rest of my sisters are part of Mayans, but I am not." She also wrote that she had chosen to do research on the Mayans "because my family have somethig of Mayans," but gave no further explanation in writing or orally of her background.

Rita's response log contained entries after each chapter read aloud. Her responses to *James and the Giant Peach*, taught in the fall, were careful summaries of each chapter written in Spanish. At the beginning of the Egypt unit, the teachers had provided questions for students to respond to, and then later they went back to the format of having students write free responses to the book chapter. Rita's responses were in English from January to March 19, in Spanish from March 20 to April 6, and then again in English during the remaining sessions in April. Her responses met the classroom expectations of writing summaries of events, making predictions about what might happen, and providing her own opinions. Although she did not volunteer to share her writing, the teachers were aware that she completed the assignments and were pleased with her work.

Rita's peers respected her, especially those who were learning English. She was willing to help them, and was often seen translating directions from English into Spanish for them. Rita achieved her greatest success when she led her group to create a bilingual fashion show for the class news broadcast about Egypt. Her team elected her to be captain and, initially, she experienced some emotional discomfort in her role as leader, as evidenced in her journal in which she wrote in Spanish about how the group was not yet prepared and expressed her hope that the project would be a success. Not only did Rita contribute much to the dialogues in both languages, but she also arbitrated the disputes among students about their various roles and contributions to the show. Later, she reported, "I learned how to work with other people and how to solve their problems." She also described the success of her group in writing when students were asked to reflect on the Egypt unit: "I think my group did an excellent job because we were the first group that did the talking in Spanish and English. I think my group did a very good job. I learned to help people if they didn't remember."

Continually trying to fit in and be accepted, Rita was successful by most standards. She wrote in both Spanish and English and found acceptance by teachers and peers for both; she completed her assigned work and was able to negotiate quite successfully the complex, sometimes conflicting, set of school and home values. The only area in which she never felt comfortable was sharing her writing with the larger group, always preferring small groups. She expressed in an interview that she would have liked to share her writing with only the ESL group, but was never afforded the opportunity: "I would want to change like when some people could share on the carpet. Like if we didn't share on the carpet, we could share after—when it was ESL time—because you [will not be] embarrassed."

Summary

For Rita, literacy was a means to gain social acceptance into the classroom. She saw making friends and completing her work as the tools for being successful. Rita wanted to fit into the classroom and identified the smart students as those who followed the rules: "You have to follow their rules. Listen to the teacher and do what the teacher says." She did not necessarily see writing as a means to be creative, believing that the most important aspects of writing were to "use vocabulary words" introduced by the teachers. However, she used literacy to establish her identity as a Latina and to connect with others—teachers, family, and friends. Literacy was a means to achieve success in the United States, and she believed that, like her sister, she could be recognized. She stated, "My sister, she got a ribbon, and she was bilingual and a good student, and she had a $500 award for a university. She gets lots of cards and stuff. I want to be like her."

Rita successfully negotiated her literate identities in her various worlds. Although there were some boundaries between her home language of more upper-class Spanish and the school-street Spanish disapproved of by her sisters, as well as the discourses of school versus home (Gee, 1990), Rita managed to please her family and her teachers. Rather than experiencing a clashing of identities, she was able to either keep her literate identities somewhat separate (reading Mexican textbooks at home and literature at school) or blend her identities in Spanish and English in school projects (Sarup, 1996). She seemed to understand the cultural model of the need to be successful in school and speak a particular style of Spanish from her Mexican immigrant home, as well as the teachers' cultural model of writing in certain forms in the classroom (Gee, 2001).

Although Rita was an example of a student who embraced the classroom expectations about writing and behavior, Greg was at odds with the teachers and his peers on many occasions. He tended to resist the teachers' expectations through off-task behavior and by not writing at all.

Greg: Resisting Classroom Norms Through Behavior

Greg, a European American third grader, was bright, articulate, and well-read, and was the only child of middle-class, well-educated parents. His mother was a family practice doctor, and his father was an attorney for a liberal group helping farm workers. His home was filled with books of all kinds and both parents read about diverse topics ranging from medicine to anthropology. Greg's own shelves contained a large collection of children's and adult books about war and other topics. He reported that he played soccer, took walks with his mother, and watched television, but his favorite things to do were to play computer games and read books. His mother read to him nightly such books as *The Forgotten Door* (Key, 1989) and The Redwall series (Jacques, 1986), and he read a large number of books on his own.

Games and books about war, especially World War II and the Civil War, fascinated Greg. He described his favorite computer game as "'Aces Over the Pacific,' which is this World War II game where you can fly different planes," and he was reading nonfiction books about jets and planes. His knowledge was extensive and he could name many of the types of planes and provide relevant information about them such as, "The war ended before they could be used. Like the Shooting star, the Bear cat, the Tiger Cat, the FU-4 G force air which is an E model of the force air, which is a model of the Corsair." His parents provided opportunities for him to build on his knowledge by taking him on field trips. For example, Greg and his father spent 6 weeks together driving and visiting battlegrounds in the southern United States and discussing artifacts, and he received a "huge, [in] virtually perfect condition, 12-pound Napoleon cannon ball" for Christmas. His interest in wars and battles provided him with numerous topics to write about, and his enthusiasm bubbled over into school. However, Greg's attempts to bring his world of war into the classroom were not greeted with enthusiasm by the teachers. For show and tell, Greg had at different times brought a Civil War bullet and a grenade, one in which "they drilled out the explosives." Greg was aware that it might not have been a good idea because, "lesson number one, it's still dangerous and you can do a fair amount of damage if you poke someone in the head with it. It's basically a weapon, a 10-pound weapon."

Greg's mother was quite aware of Greg's interest in the Civil War and World War II, and described how he was particularly interested in artifacts. She found that, "He is really into computers, very computer literate for his age. He can search files and find things. He can access games; he is into story games where they go into a particular area and explore things." One of Greg's qualities she most valued was his quirky sense of humor, "kind of Monty Python—he gets rained on by cans of Spam, [he likes the] wild antics of this character. He likes parody, quirky British humor."

She described him as a voracious reader who tackled adult books about World War II and the Civil War, and learned a lot of geography about Europe and the southern United States as a result of his interests. She felt that his 6-week field trip with his father to battlegrounds contributed substantially to his education, but because of this intimate, one-on-one involvement with his father, he may have felt frustration in the classroom where there were many children competing for attention.

Greg's mother was pleased with the learning environment in the multiage classroom, especially the fact that they studied topics in depth. Greg reported to her some of the facts that he had learned about Egypt, but he was interested in telling her what was going on with other students, especially that he wanted to work with certain students or by himself. She sensed that he did not participate in the book response time the way the teachers felt he should. Greg's mother identified his writing as creative and found that he wrote more freely on computer than by hand.

Greg demonstrated enthusiasm in interviews about many of the projects done at school such as the Egypt unit and mummifying chickens, but it was clear that he struggled for teacher and peer acceptance. Because there was much collaborative work in the classroom, Greg had opportunities to work with others. He wanted to work on projects with some of the "popular, smart boys," but felt that he was rejected and had to work with Jack, an unpopular, off-task student who rarely completed his work. He explained, "Jack was the only person left, unfortunately. It's like the only reason why he's the only one left, everyone knows never be Jack's partner." Greg subsequently blamed Jack when the project was not completed, "We made an agreement. I would do the map. He would do the dialogue—I do the map in one night. We wait 3 weeks. I ask Jack finally at the end of 3 weeks, 'How close are you to finishing the dialogue?' And he says, 'I was supposed to do that?'"

Instead of working with a partner and for fear he might get stuck with Jack, Greg often chose to work alone. He was not happy about his role in the classroom and expressed it in his journal:

> My life is a living nightmare. Nowhon likes me. Well maby Michael and Huoston, but they live 500 miles away. I want to move back to Harlingen. I wish at least one person would like me. I loose my pencils nobody will help me find them. Every won thinks I'm a troublemaker and I want to get in trouble. I really don't. I'm sorry I will write in cursive.

The teachers were aware of Greg's isolation and unhappiness. They reported that by November they had met with the parents on three occasions and had numerous phone calls about Greg's disruptive behavior. At first, they thought that Greg's adjustment to the new school and stimulating environment of their multiage classroom might have been the source of the problem, but the parents began to share with them that he had experienced problems in his previous school. When the teachers examined his transcripts, they found that he had high test scores, but "N minus" in social skills. Ms. Allen described him as having read many books, and "he knows something about everything." However, both teachers found his social skills to be "lacking for his age." They found that he was unwilling to stay on task, "not getting his work done, the class waiting on him." He had antagonized the class such that the teachers felt, "he needs to have friends, but now he has a reputation in the classroom, and I don't know how he's going to make friends." The teachers viewed him as an underachiever who had much potential because of his depth of knowledge, but they felt that his lack of social skills and unwillingness to follow classroom rules impeded his learning. For example, they found him reading books by himself in the library center instead of being involved in the lesson with the rest of the class.

Literacy Practices

Greg was aware of how to be successful in this classroom, such as writing in cursive and responding to the read-alouds. He noted that to be successful during book response time, "you have to be able to write the summary of the story" and to use colorful language:

> "As the seagull wailed around in the sky. A foremost island where the dark people lurked in the shadows." That's what you have to do. You can't just say "There was a bunch of water and there were bunch of little fishies in there."

Greg also knew how to be successful in writer's workshop, "you have to know how to create stories," but his stories were not always acceptable because they were gory or violent. He used examples of "Bloody Mary" in which he talked about seeing "a heap of bones and blood, also a stomach" or "as he hydro-slammed his head into a door and we ran out" to illustrate his point. Although he knew the teachers did not accept these pieces, he continued to write them for his own entertainment. Although he knew his teachers wanted him to write in cursive, he reverted back to printing after his trial runs at cursive writing in his journal.

Greg also knew that he was expected to be quiet during book response time and then write a response, yet he often displayed a lack of interest in the chapters read or in responding to them. His responses to the books were quite inconsistent; sometimes he wrote one line and sometimes he wrote about one page (20 lines). His writing seemed to directly reflect his interest in the particular chapter or topic. For example, one day he wrote, "James has some magic" for his entire entry, a week later he wrote only the date, and the following week he wrote a page-length summary of the chapter complete with descriptive words and dialogue to *James and the Giant Peach*. His journal entries about his everyday life were brief and mundane (except for the entry about how miserable he was at school), but his entries in which he wrote facts about wars were lengthy, detailed, and supplemented with drawings of battles and guns. For example, on December 12, he wrote,

The Civil War was the bloodest war in Amercan History. About 5,000,0 people were killd

The south had very little factories to begin with but as its factories fell the couldn't produce the weeapons it's armys so valubly needed. But the south had one thing the north didn't cotton you might think cotton isn't very importit It real is you make rope uniforms and gun pouter sacks. [He has drawn a picture to show someone shooting and a 100 pound cannon.]

The civil war was a war with many casuletys and many battles with no way of knowing were one part of a army is. One of the most famos battles like the was the wilderness were many troops were deep in enemy lines and still thought they were in friendly tertory.

This journal entry and many related to war read like a textbook, and his talk often reflected adult inflections and book language. However, his contributions in class, which contained the same adult-like phrasing and factual accounting put off some of his peers. During small-group work, he shared a drawing with his group and they ignored him. He commented as an aside, "I guess they don't like it."

During class discussion, he often raised his hand or called out to answer questions asked by the teachers. Often he was reprimanded for calling out or not sitting up, occasionally he was dismissed from the group for being off-task, but often he was called on to define vocabulary words. The teachers often called on him to provide an answer when nobody else could, but they also demonstrated some conflict and felt the need to call on others. During a response session to the Thanksgiving book, Greg provided so many responses (some elicited, some not) that one of the teachers asked, "Have you read this book before, Greg?" to which he responded, "No, I just knew that from history." In the same session she said, "What do you think a treaty is, and I don't want to hear from Greg. Let's give somebody else a chance to show me what they know." Later on, though, when David had difficulty defining an ember she asked, "Can somebody help David?" When no one else responded, she called on Greg who said, "A little piece of wood burns off, it is glowing hot. It is like an ash, a cinder, it is hot." The teacher then commented it was right, and told David, "I know you were thinking of that."

Although he was often called on to contribute his factual knowledge to book response time, he was rarely called on to share his writing from his response log. He felt that it was a "hopeless cause" to share and described what happened: "I finish writing and then I raise my hand, then they pick Emily, then they pick David, then they pick Jamie, then Angie, then they pick everyone, then they say, 'Greg, you can do it tomorrow.'" It was difficult to understand why the teachers did not allow him to share. Some possibilities include feeling that he had already contributed during the reading of the chapter, ignoring him because he did not sit up and listen and often appeared to be disengaged, or just overlooking him because of the large number of students who could share. Although he seemed to thrive on response and attention, Greg did not receive much response to his writing; he did not share his response logs with the whole class, and his journal entries were read but not responded to by the teachers.

Summary

Greg and the adults in his life seemed to share a view of Greg as a voracious reader who was very knowledgeable about a range of topics. However, he experienced conflicts in the classroom with the teachers because he did not obey the rules or conform to some of the classroom expectations. He felt rejected by peers and experienced loneliness and distress that often resulted in arguments with or rejection by other children. His identity as a reader and writer seemed to be shaped more by opportunities at home where he could talk at length about wars with his father, read with his mother, and play computer games by himself. Although he was successful in his home literacy environment, he did not feel supported or valued at school. His response was to try and fit in by sharing his knowledge, but also by resisting; that is, he often chose not to write during novel time, wrote about topics other than personal experience in his journal, used violent language, and argued with his peers. Greg exemplified many of the classic characteristics of a bright child who was rejected by his peers and resisted completing assignments he found unimportant.

Greg experienced the school environment as oppressive, a place that did not encourage him to express his home discourse—that of professionals who read a great deal of nonfiction and talked about history and current affairs. Although his home discourse might have appeared to be more aligned with the teachers' than was Rita's because he was a native English speaker with educated parents, Greg's discourse actually conflicted with the traditional school patterns that allow little time for individual speakers to express their ideas (Cazden, 1988). His identity as a middle-class, white male from an educated family, which privileges him in society in general, did not necessarily privilege him in this classroom setting. Greg had many literate identities developed from his experiences at home and school that tended to clash (Sarup, 1996). He was not able to successfully negotiate his various literacies within this classroom; and in this way, he differed from Rita who appropriated classroom norms but did not go beyond them, and Mandy who found ways to slightly alter the expectations, especially for writing.

Mandy: Transformation Through Social Justice

Mandy, a European American third grader, was the daughter of a teacher in the school and a cabinetmaker. She lived in a house with her parents and an older sister who had attended the school in recent years. Mandy reported that her father read to her, and her sister often joined in. Mandy said that both her parents read frequently: novels, picture books, children's magazines, her mother's school books, and books on tape. Her mother added to this information in the interview, remarking, "I love to read...for pure enjoyment.... I was an English lit major." She and her husband were reading the same book about a man who kept a diary during the Civil War. Mandy's mother also wrote articles about teaching and had submitted them for publication.

Mandy's mother indicated that besides engaging in literacy activities, her daughter also played basketball and took jazz dance lessons. Her description of her daughter included the following, "I think she's very bright, and she amazes me at the things she thinks about and how deeply she feels about them. And I really think she has a very big heart; I'm proud of her for that."

Mandy's teachers suggested that they knew her family well because they had taught her older sister, and her mother had taught at the school for a number of years. They described Mandy as "independent, very capable academically" with "lots of opportunities for experiences" such as a trip to Australia. They found that she cared about others' opinions of her. This was supported by Mandy herself who said when asked about teachers' responses to her writing, "Well it made me feel good that I really did a good job and not just I thought so, that other people thought it was good too." However, she did not depend on others' views of her entirely and believed that she would persevere to get what she wanted like the character April in *The Egypt Game* (Snyder, 1986): "She kind of acted like me because if she really wanted something she had her own way of getting it."

Literacy Practices

Mandy was an avid reader and writer, was articulate in interviews, and was a very active participant in class discussions. She read a range of books including a biography of Helen Keller, Baby-Sitters Club books, comic books, mystery books, and information books about dogs. She used her extensive reading about breeds of dogs to persuade her parents to get her a dog and convinced them that she could care for it because of her deep knowledge. She wrote in a diary and created stories to read to audiences that included her mother and grandfather: "I write them and send them to him when I'm not there."

Mandy's interest in reading and writing at home helped her to fit with the classroom norms and expectations. The teachers wanted students to focus on ideas in their response logs without concern for spelling or punctuation. Mandy internalized this concept well:

> Well, it makes you feel really good about what you're writing. Not that just if you write nobody can edit it, they're not really looking at your work, they're looking at what you say if you were really listening and how they feel about your work. Not about your writing and how perfect it is. Cause I mean I don't always use like commas and exclamation marks and stuff. I just write it cause I really write really fast sometimes, it gets messy. But I like to fit everything in my mind on the piece of paper.

Mandy had a strong sense of audience and idea development, and had little concern for grammar or punctuation. She also felt comfortable with the expectations of the writing workshop. She described topics for the workshop as, "it can be about your life or something you have or your favorite sport, or it can be just a story that you made up." Mandy wrote about her own life, often drawing from experiences out of school (e.g., visiting her father's birthplace, breaking her leg, playing basketball, and attending sporting events). She was quite comfortable with the personal expressive mode and then later moving into the fiction genre:

Well right now I'm just working about stuff that happens to me and I think after I finish all of the stories that I really want to do then I'll start making up stories for myself because that's what I like to do. But I want to write a lot of things about my life.

Mandy volunteered and was often called on to share her writing with the class, and her colorful language was often reflected on the class charts. She acknowledged that she "shared her writing often" and that she enjoyed it because, "Well it's like you really get to express how you feel about this story, not just about how Pedro feels. I mean you're pretending you're Pedro, but it's talking in your own words."

For Mandy, responding in the logs went beyond merely summarizing but allowed her to express her own ideas. She used descriptive language and similes in her writing, and these endeared her to the teacher. For example, in response to *Into the Mummy's Tomb's* (Reeves, 1993), she wrote,

The dust flickered behind me as I drove away from Highclear Castle. The grains looked like pieces of Carter's sole [soul] melting away like an ice cube on a peach. Suddenly I felt [indecipherable]. Carter died in pain and agony. I don't know about anyone else but I would long for him.

Although Mandy was very successful at understanding and fitting into the classroom norms, she also found ways to transform them through her flexibility and her commitment to social justice. For example, she could write well in several genres, easily moving from personal expressive to fantasy stories modeled on books she had read. Her flexibility was most noted in her ability to take on the perspectives of the various characters in books read aloud. She easily inserted herself into *Pedro's Journal* by taking the perspective of Pedro:

How will I ever tell my mother? I am ashamed. I can't believe I sunk the Santa Maria. How could I ever do such a thing? And the Nina drifted away as if it were in outer space.

And in a later entry she found a way to express the disgust that she related to in the crew's treatment of the natives:

I feel ashamed of taking those natives with us. My mother would feel the same. They are being torn apart from their family. But I know how they feel. Late at night the natives mothers and fathers came and asked to come to. I felt like they were sacrificing themselves for no reason.

In subsequent novels and picture books, especially about Egypt, Mandy also inserted herself in the text. Whether it was April in *The Egypt Game*, Aida in the book *Aida* (Price, 1990), or the jaguar in a book about rain forests, Mandy assumed the role of one of the characters, not always the protagonist, in a clear and creative fashion.

Mandy had helped create the conditions for her and her classmates to take alternative viewpoints. For responses to the first two books, students were assigned to pretend they were the protagonist and write from that perspective. Mandy complained to me and the teachers about the difficulty of always taking a boy's perspective, "Because it's like you don't really know much about the boys, you just know a lot about the girls." Partway through the second book, *James and the Giant Peach*, Mandy said, "You know, we're always having to be boys. We had to be Pedro, now we have to be James." The teachers responded positively to her resistance to identification with the male characters and altered the writing task for the response logs. They suggested that students could be "observing the story as it is unfolding" or to take any character's perspective. Mandy was pleased to report that the teachers had changed the assignment:

> See what they said is that, they said that you could be anything that you wanted, you could be James, you could be an insect, or you could just be like writing a story, or you could be just like watching them and saying like, "I can see James right now," or you just be writing the story. I really just pretended I'm writing the story...but it's in a different version.

When she saw something that she perceived as unjust, she went to the teachers and pointed it out or found a way of addressing her concerns. One concern seemed to be with gender and racial equity, and she raised questions about both at different times. For example, her mother reported that Mandy had "a real strong sense of social justice" and "thinks about the way women are treated." Mandy had asked why all the wait staff at a restaurant were black or Hispanic and the customers white and went on to suggest that it was quite unfair for the minorities to have those low-status jobs. Mandy reported, "I think about people being racist and sexist...because I think that everybody in the world should be treated evenly, and even those are not being, I really don't think that's fair."

Mandy attempted to transform her concern with racial equity into a story she had just begun writing that included characters from diverse backgrounds. She had just begun thinking about the characters and their relationships with one another: "There's one girl named Melanie, and she's Hispanic, and then Hosea's Hispanic, and Sandra is black, and Allen is white." Although the end of data collection precluded my seeing whether the story expressed themes of social justice, Mandy demonstrated that she was aware of racial differences and sought to include characters from diverse backgrounds.

In some ways Mandy was aware of her middle-class background as being privileged, "because a bunch of my friends aren't really as privileged as me," but she also attributed her success to her mother, who always worked with her. Mandy had a mature view of the strengths of other students. She suggested that "a lot of the different kids are smarter in every kind of way…some kids can't read very well but they're really good at thinking. And some kids can't really do math, but they can read the problems so that helps them."

Summary

Mandy engaged in many literate practices at home including being read to, reading aloud to her parents, and reading independently. She also wrote diary entries, letters, and stories and shared them with her family members. She was very successful in school literacy activities, but she also found ways to insert herself and her own views of what seemed unjust into the school setting. Through her motivated and extensive literacy practices, Mandy was able to transform some classroom practices to provide more opportunities for herself and other students to write from different perspectives and to begin to consider equity issues. Her status as a successful student who was white and middle class, as well as a daughter of a teacher in the school, provided her with a kind of privilege that, no doubt, made her views acceptable to the teachers. Because her discourses from home and her cultural models fit well with school expectations (Gee, 2001), Mandy had many advantages that helped her to get the teachers to adjust the norms. No doubt, her mother helped inculcate the values of reading and writing in school-like fashion, but also encouraged her to question racial and gender inequities. Would the teachers have been so willing to look at their practices if a working-class Latina who used a different discourse style than they had raised the issues?

What Do These Cases Mean for Students' Identities as Writers?

The ways in which students appropriated, resisted, or transformed the classroom expectations in the Hillside classrooms highlight the public and private forums for students' development of their literate identities. Although Rita did not share her work publicly, the bilingual teacher did read and correct her grammar in her journals. Much of herself as a writer was buried in her journals and her response logs, but she continued to comply with expectations and have her work valued in the classroom. The achievement of which she was most proud became public when she and her group performed their Egyptian fashion show.

In the meantime, Greg had few opportunities to share his writing publicly because he wrote journal entries that were not responded to, and he was not called on to share his writing. He did, however, have the public forum of calling out answers to questions posed by the teachers, yet his peers did not necessarily value his responses. His resistance to doing his work was more public because the teachers reprimanded him for not listening or not writing in his response log. In contrast, Mandy wrote in a variety of genres, seized any opportunity afforded in the classroom to share her work, and made public her concerns about gender roles. She drew from home and school support to develop a persuasive discourse in which she could tweak the classroom norms a bit. Like students in Phelps and Weaver's (1999) study, Greg and Mandy were better at negotiating the public space to insert their more private voices, while others like Rita were stifled by the public domain of the share sessions.

The students' texts reflect a spectrum from more authoritative reciting by heart to a more hybrid form of discourse (Bakhtin, 1981). Rita's writing tended to consist of recounting her day in her journal or summarizing the chapters in her response log. Because she was learning to read and write in two languages, the fact that her writing reflects more of an authoritative discourse is not surprising. Greg's journal entries varied from a kind of "authoritative discourse" drawn straight from academic discourse to his more personal entries such as his expression of unhappiness. Some of his log responses had the potential to be creative but remained undeveloped. At the other end, we see how Mandy developed a kind of hybrid text (Fecho, 2001) in which she brought in multiple perspectives and inserted her own more feminist views in the text.

All three students demonstrated an enormous capacity to engage in a range of literate activities and to negotiate different literacies. Rita, for example, "read" the world of her Mexican immigrant family, understanding their values while learning the language and values of school in an attempt to reduce conflict and "blend" her various selves (Sarup, 1996). Greg, while experiencing conflicts between opportunities at home and accepted school behaviors and discourse styles, also demonstrated a range of literate behaviors in his talk and writing. Mandy, whose home and school discourse styles were strongly connected and whose identities overlapped to a large degree, also had various literate identities enacted through her skills in a variety of genres. These cases demonstrate a range of literacies and identities that students assumed and enacted and suggest that as educators we need to look for and develop the range of literacies that students bring with them (Holdaway, 1986).

In this classroom, we can see how the expectation about including colorful language and vocabulary in one's writing, avoiding summarizing, and taking a (male) character's perspective were enacted. Teachers tended to praise students who used description or metaphor, therefore those aspects were counted as "normal and natural" (Gee, 2001, p. 720), and other writing was regarded as deviant. Although the teachers provided students with choices about projects to explore and emphasized students' development of voice, the teachers undermined some of their own values by emphasizing a particular kind of writing during book response to the exclusion of others. Because they only initialed students' journal writing without responding to it and did not encourage students to read their work aloud, the teachers did not value highly students' efforts to communicate their home and school experiences. Students who wrote a particular kind of piece were more likely to be valued than those who summarized or wrote factual World

War II pieces. Although not as overt in their talk with students about the qualities of good writing as Ms. Meyer in New York City, these teachers did hold certain values and communicated them through the ways they responded (or did not) to students' writing. The teachers' authority and instruction, then, tended to provide differential instruction for students and undermined their otherwise important contributions to providing an inclusive curriculum.

The three cases raise questions about the expectations we have for students and how we communicate our values. Is descriptive language the only way to write creatively? Must one always be another character? Must that character be male? The data might also suggest the importance of responding to students, not necessarily always in a public forum, in a supportive manner. Although responding daily to 49 journals would be an enormously time-consuming task for teachers, opening a dialogue with students about what they write could provide students with a reason for journal writing other than completing an assignment. Valuing a variety of genres (even recounting facts from a Civil War book) and allowing students to bring in their outside knowledge might enhance other students' learning.

Although considering the suggestions about how teachers might validate students' home experiences, we also need to keep in mind the larger context in which these teachers were working. Despite the support they received from their principal and colleagues, they were still undertaking an enormous task—changing from a traditional basal curriculum to one that is literature-based, changing from a traditional grading system to portfolios, and challenging the norms of how students are arranged in classrooms. And, they were doing this at the same time as they were preparing their students to pass a high-stakes test. As many authors (e.g., Cohen, 1988; Cuban & Tyack, 1993) have pointed out, changing the traditional structure of schooling is an enormous task, and the fact that the teachers' interactions with students reproduced traditional patterns is not surprising (Aronowitz & Giroux, 1991).

Appropriation, Resistance, and Transformation in Reading Workshop and Reading Renaissance

The Valley School in Texas had adopted Reading Renaissance, an offshoot of the computerized program Accelerated Reader, as the reading program throughout the school. All the books in the library were color-coded, and students were required to choose books by color, which was determined by computerized comprehension tests. Students received points for reading books and passing tests, and classrooms were rewarded with pizza parties when all students reached particular goals. The testing and standardized reading program were institutional factors that clearly affected the teachers' day-to-day practices. However, two teachers in the school who had attended universities that supported more literature-based programs added these features to their language arts programs.

One of these teachers, Ms. Le Blanc, had been a student of mine 8 years before at The University of Texas, Austin, in a course on literacy acquisition. She had taught in a variety of inner-city settings in Texas and brought a practical, down-to-earth perspective to her classroom. Although she embraced many of the ideals of literature-based curriculum and wanted students to engage in meaningful tasks while reading and writing, she understood the reality of preparing students for the state tests. She compromised by combining the TAAS skills with her reading workshop:

> I'm able to work in the TAAS skills in the reading workshop freely.... I usually teach them through novel units, since I teach fifth grade. Every now and then I'll pull in a picture book unit with a theme just for variation and fun. But normally we do novel units. And I usually get through about 9 to 10 novels in a school year.

Ms. Le Blanc had many objections to the Reading Renaissance program but believed she had to go along with the principal and her colleagues in using it:

> The program is very structured. Last year, we turned in reports weekly, which was extremely time consuming and controlling of the children's reading. I feel like a Nazi doing those reports, taking off who is at risk. Last year I was a new teacher at the school, and I knew the Reading Renaissance program was very important to the principal. We had model classrooms with Reading Renaissance. We were a Reading Renaissance Model School. So there was pressure to make sure At-Risk Reports looked really good. Oh my god! It will wear you out. Wear the kids out.

She did not believe in rewarding students for reading and, unlike many of her colleagues, did not think that Reading Renaissance was a sufficient language arts program. She compromised by going along with the school guidelines but adding other features to her language arts program.

Ms. Le Blanc's fifth-grade language arts program consisted of three components: reading workshop, writing workshop, and Reading Renaissance. Her reading workshop differed from other educators' such as Atwell's (1987) definition, because it involved the teacher selecting novels to read aloud and discuss with students rather than students selecting their own books to read and write about. After reading aloud one or more chapters of the book, Ms. Le Blanc asked students to discuss or respond in their journals to particular aspects of the novels. The two novels used in the reading-workshop portion of the curriculum in January through March were both Newbery Award winners, *Maniac Magee* (Spinelli, 1990) and *Roll of Thunder, Hear My Cry* (Taylor, 1976). Written by a European American man, *Maniac Magee* is the story of a homeless 12-year-old boy who can hit a ball farther and run faster than other children. He crosses the boundary between the white west end and the black east end of town and tries to soothe rival factions from the two sides. Written by an African American woman, *Roll of Thunder, Hear My Cry* focuses on the struggle of a black family trying to hold onto their land in the southern United States during the Depression. The book portrays the family's defiance of racism amid the nightriders and burnings.

The teacher selected the novels for units with specific goals in mind. She drew from students' interests, her knowledge of their cultural and social backgrounds, and her own emphasis on books that deal with race, economics, or gender issues. Although most of her students were Latino and she believed it was important to select books that connected to students' lives, she tended to select books about issues or themes rather than books with Latino characters or authors. She selected *Maniac Magee* because it deals with

> a boy who has many challenges in his life and has to come up with ways to overcome those challenges. I felt like our students needed to know that it's OK to have challenges in your life, that our lives are not perfect. And that especially as a kid, it's OK to have problems, but you need to know how to deal with those problems in a positive way. And the second reason is because it dealt directly with race issues.

Ms. Le Blanc chose *Roll of Thunder, Hear My Cry* because it not only addresses discrimination, but it also shows "generations of strong women." She wanted to focus on strong women for not only her African American girls but also for her Hispanic girls who "tend to be from very traditional families.... I feel like I just need to bring out different qualities in what girls and women can do." Additionally, she had noticed that in the classroom students of African American, Anglo, and Hispanic backgrounds (her designations) mingled, but at recess they chose to play with children from their own ethnic groups, and she found this troubling. There were also specific racial tensions that occurred at school, and she was aware that there were racial tensions in some of the apartment complexes where students lived as well. She wanted students to become more aware of social issues and to become more tolerant of one another. She also had an agenda of teaching students to problem solve in nonviolent ways. She stated that her goals were to have the students develop

> a sense of fairness in the world and seeing people more for who they are than for where they come from or the color of their skin. In both

stories, the characters have problems in their lives. They generally tend to solve them positively through actions—actions that would make some changes through law or changing people's ideas of how they think. More nonviolent protest. I just want them to get a sense of fairness so they'll think [about] how they treat people and act.

The teacher then designed activities or questions for journals that asked for students to engage in a range of tasks, from asking students to define words to predicting what will happen next in the book, to connecting issues to their own lives. For example, the journal questions for *Maniac Magee* included "Find *legend* in the dictionary. Do you think Maniac will leave the Beals family? What would you do?" and "Tell me about a challenge in your own life and how you overcame it." Students also completed charts that listed columns for "main ideas, facts, opinions, and future outcomes" together as a class—many of these incorporated the TAAS objectives.

A less emphasized but valued aspect of the classroom curriculum was writing workshop. The teacher could devote less time to this because the school required teachers to teach the four TAAS test genres of writing: persuasive, how-to, compare and contrast, and narrative. It took at least 2 weeks to teach each of those, so "we don't get as much of the writing workshop as I would like." However, Ms. Le Blanc added a letter-writing component that encouraged students to write letters to another member of the class during the second semester of the school year.

The third component of the language arts curriculum was the schoolwide reading program, Reading Renaissance. Students took a test the first week of school to determine their reading levels and were placed according to a corresponding color. Students could select one or two books to check out that were their color and an additional non–Accelerated Reader book. After reading the book, students took computerized tests that checked their comprehension and determined their pass rate. When all children passed, the class received rewards such as pizza parties. Students were required to read their Reading Renaissance books for 1 hour each day in school and for 20 to 30 minutes at home.

Ms. Le Blanc had mixed feelings about the program but felt that it had more negative points than positive. Although she saw value in students' having goals and something to work toward and felt that the immediate feedback they received was important, she was concerned about the trivial comprehension questions:

> Like in *The Skirt* by Gary Soto [1992], one of the questions was, "The girl climbed *over* the fence, *through* the fence, or *under* the fence?" I mean. I couldn't remember how the girl got into it. Who cares if she climbed through the fence or over the fence? It doesn't matter. For the really high achievers, that kills them to get those questions because we don't talk about details like that in our discussions because they have no meaning.

Ms. Le Blanc believed that the program hurt both the high achievers and the low achievers:

> It certainly has many drawbacks. For a kid like Daniel, who reads at an eighth-grade level, he had the pressure to get through a novel in 2 weeks because that's when the At-Risk Report comes. Otherwise, the At-Risk Report that's turned in to the principal shows he hasn't taken a test in 2 weeks so it looks like he is not reading. For a kid like Daniel who is going to take 3 or 4 weeks [because he is reading lengthy books] and who loves to read, bad reports come out. He has an A on the At-Risk. "A" means you haven't taken the tests. He is bummed. I mean he will go to tears. And then kids like Natalie and Tanya, who have been reading a first-grade book for the entire month and still haven't taken a test, they just dread [the reports]. When you have reward parties, Tanya and Natalie are never going to be off that list [the At-Risk list]. Then those kids—and this is the real kicker—those kids are supposed to read in another room. So that's why reading is a punishment.

The multifaceted curriculum with somewhat competing goals had different effects on students. Jennifer, a successful student who was concerned with pleasing authority, fit in well with the classroom expectations across the curricular areas. In contrast, Lucas, a struggling ESL student, resisted reading his Reading Renaissance books and chose not to respond to the books. Daniel created interesting texts that represented his strong views about diversity that decried violence and shared them with the class.

Jennifer: Appropriating Classroom Norms

Jennifer was Latina from a working-class background. Her mother worked as a hairdresser to support Jennifer, her two sisters, and two brothers. Her parents were divorced, but Jennifer spent some week-ends with her father, who also brought lunch to her occasionally at school. Her father worked for a moving company. The primary language spoken at home was English. Her mother spoke some Spanish with relatives and wanted to teach her children some Spanish.

Jennifer's mother felt that she had been a person who "slipped through the cracks," and she wanted to ensure that her children were successful in school. She felt that she could have been helped more, and was identified as a slow reader early in life and could not excel: "With reading, once they find you as slow, they put you down a lower grade instead of finding what your difficulties are." Jennifer's mother was pleased that she was able to go to business college and get a degree in word processing. Jennifer's mother did not find much opportunity to engage in literacy at home, but she did fill out paperwork for her job and read some romance novels at home.

Almost everyone close to Jennifer agreed that she was a nice girl who was quiet, yet friendly. She described herself as "nice" and her peers agreed. For her peers this meant that she was friendly to everyone, she helped other people, and that she did "everything the teacher says." Her friend, Paula, wrote to her in a letter, "You are relly, relly, relly [sic] smart. You are also relly, relly, relly [sic] nice." Her mother also found her to be "quiet—she's more to herself. She likes doing things by herself." Her teacher was very enthusiastic about Jennifer's contributions as the "errand girl." Ms. Le Blanc said, "she's the one kid I can trust to do anything and everything. She is a strong enough student both academically and [with regard to] her spirit to go to someone and ask what she missed." Jennifer enjoyed this role of errand girl and found that her teacher would describe her as "A big help. Usually in the morning when she has to do a lot of stuff, I will help her do errands."

The teacher, Jennifer, and her mother all shared similar perceptions of Jennifer's future career. The teacher explained that, "I always say, 'She's gonna be a teacher.' She's very helpful and caring. She's such a good tutor in the classroom." Her mother concurred, adding that she wanted her to be either a teacher or a pediatric doctor because she "likes to play with children, but in her own time when she wants to." Jennifer, too, stated that she wanted to be a teacher or a doctor. The shared perception by her teacher, mother, peers, and Jennifer that she was smart and nice was reflected in Jennifer's literacy practices.

Literacy Practices

Jennifer's success with reading apparently began at an early age, because her mother reported that "As a young child, I never had to help her with reading. She caught on real quick." Jennifer reported enjoying both reading and writing: "I like to read and write. When I was in the fourth grade, I would read books and then I would write different kinds of stories that were six pages long." Her interest continued into the fifth grade where she explained that she read everything from joke books to "plain books [books that talk about everything]" to grown-up books [books with small print]."

Everyone close to Jennifer agreed that she was an excellent reader. Her peers knew that she was on one of the highest levels in the Reading Renaissance program and nominated her consistently as one of the two best readers in the class. Jennifer gauged her own reading ability in terms of the color she was on and her grades, commenting, "I am smart because I get As and Bs on my report card." She believed the program was a good one because "kids know how to read when they grow up." She found that the levels helped her "because you could see if you need to read more and get more 100s and 90s and 80s to get on the grade level you're on." She even felt positively toward the tests because "they kind of challenge you." Jennifer was quite strategic in her choices for Reading Renaissance, describing how she chooses a book:

> First I look at my color. Then sometimes I look at how many pages is one chapter, and how much points it's worth. Then I look up how many chapters there are. Like if the pages are like four pages [in] one chapter, and there's 12 chapters, and it's worth six points, I'll get it. If the pages are five pages, and there's 21 chapters, and the book is worth three points, I won't get it.

Jennifer's responses to school tasks were to meet expectations and to do her work competently and thoroughly. Organized neatly and sequentially, Jennifer's journal reflected her orientation to do well, but did not necessarily show deep insights or challenge any of the themes related to the book. Her responses to the teacher-generated questions, for example, were one or two sentences, and were school-oriented. For instance, when asked to describe her greatest challenge, she wrote "a spelling bee I took in second grade. I overcame it by studying every day and I came in second place." In response to a question about challenges she faced in the fifth grade, she answered, "One was in math class, rotation, reflection, translation. I overcame it by studying charts." Jennifer clearly valued school tasks and sought to achieve through studying and applying herself. Her writing seemed to reflect the values she had gained from her parents as shown in her response to the question about *Roll of Thunder, Hear My Cry,* which asked, "Stacey gets a lecture from Hammer. Tell me about a lecture you've received." Jennifer wrote,

> My best friend told me that I am kind and nice to others. Also that she's proud to be my friend because I understand what she's telling me. Sometimes we disagree but whenever I'm wrong she'll explain it to me. I also get lectures from my dad like "you better do better on tests or you don't get any money on [for] your report card."

Jennifer stated that she liked writing in her free time at home and shared her work with family and friends. However, she did not elaborate or provide examples of pieces that she had written. She seemed to enjoy the classroom assignment of writing letters to a peer the most; in these letters she wrote brief summaries of what she did at home, including watching television and doing homework. She and I corresponded several times via letter in which she wrote about her baby brother and asked me questions about my son, who was then about 18 months old. Having a real audience with whom to correspond was an important factor in her motivation to write.

Jennifer's mother noted that her interest in writing tended to depend on the teacher she had, and Ms. Le Blanc found that writing was more difficult for Jennifer than reading. Jennifer believed that there were several good writers in the class, but she was good, too, because "sometimes their [classmates] faces get lit up." Jennifer believed that good writing involved "putting emotion into it" and communication with an audience, yet her topics and audiences, at least in the fifth grade, were limited to school assignments.

Summary

Jennifer seemed to experience much success in school and support at home for conforming to classroom expectations. She cheerfully did errands for the teacher, she participated in all school reading and writing tasks, and she was perceived positively by her teacher and peers. Jennifer enjoyed school, and her teacher and mother had a strong relationship with each other. The teacher said she saw her parents at school quite frequently, and Jennifer's mother felt comfortable with the teacher and would respond to notes or call if she experienced any concerns. Jennifer's writing about her father suggests that he, too, reinforced the importance of doing well at school. School and home norms were well aligned as evidenced by the school curricula that provided rewards for reading books in a similar way to Jennifer's father's reinforcing good grades with monetary rewards. There was a shared cultural model in which home and school had similar values about the role of literacy and the role of authority (Gee, 2001).

Although Jennifer was successful in school by the standards of almost everyone close to her, the purposes for reading and writing were mostly limited to fulfilling school assignments. She did not view herself, nor did others view her, as particularly creative or extraordinary, but she was clearly successful. The authoritative voice of Bakhtin (1981) resonates in the case of Jennifer because of the ways in which she assimilated voices from home and school. The purposes of literacy did not seem to extend beyond the classroom bounds, but literacy, especially in the case of letter writing, did serve as a means to connect home and school, because she could communicate her daily activities to me and to others.

Lucas: Resisting Classroom Norms Through Avoidance

Lucas was from a working-class home where Spanish was the primary language spoken; he was considered ESL and had received some help at school. Lucas lived with his mother, stepfather, 4-year-old sister, and baby brother. His mother stayed at home and his stepfather worked as a welder. Lucas enjoyed time that he spent with an aunt who took him shopping and allowed him to make choices while shopping.

Lucas described himself as "not a very good student" and believed the teachers would describe him as "not very smart." He believed his parents compared him to his cousins who made better grades than he did. Several of his peers noted that he was not a good student. His teacher agreed with this assessment, suggesting that he was not motivated, received straight Fs on his report card, and was in danger of failing fifth grade. His teacher seemed to think that his lack of success was rooted in a lack of motivation. She also found that he was socially immature, silly, and often got into trouble.

Lucas was somewhat aware of the effect he had on others. He described an incident in which he had pulled the emergency exit on the bus causing the bell to ring. He said, "then the little bell rang and I was in trouble," but he saw this as an example of being "curious." He also thought that one of his teachers would describe him as "a real active kid." He saw himself as a "wild" child because he liked to climb trees and he had often fallen down, and felt that his parents would describe him as "a crazy person." Indeed, his peers noticed his active nature. One student said, "He likes to play around" while another found him to "like action." Although some students found his activity level "funny," several girls were not amused by it, describing him as "annoying" and "irritating." His teacher suggested that his classroom behavior consisted of "wandering around and goofing off, playing slapstick funny in the room." Lucas felt that he could relate to the character of Little Man in *Roll of Thunder, Hear My Cry* because, "he's always acting silly, like me, and always acting crazy."

Literacy Practices

There was a great deal of consensus that Lucas was not a good reader or writer. He said he was "not a very good reader," and he knew this because "on my report cards and progress reports I don't get really good grades on them." He thought that his parents saw him as a slow reader who did not use a lot of expression: "I don't act like real readers do, like teachers and how they read and stuff." His peers noted that he was not a good reader and that he was usually talking during reading time. His teacher's only comment about his reading was, "He doesn't read." She also remarked that he did not write and that his handwriting was very difficult to read,

> [He] writes like a first grader except I can't read his handwriting. It's definitely not a language barrier. His pages will be kind of spotty, chicken scratches here and there on a page. He does it all at the end in an hour—whole months' worth in an hour.

Lucas agreed that his handwriting was difficult to read and remarked that it was "sloppy."

Although Lucas noted that he was not a good reader, he also said that he read more than his parents did at home. He said his parents read to him some when he was younger, but no one currently read to him: Because he had to read 30 minutes a night for homework, he chose material about NASA (National Aeronautics and Space Administration) and outer space to read before he went to sleep. Lucas said that when he was younger, he copied poems and other things from books using a typewriter, but the typewriter had broken and it was not enjoyable to copy them by hand. Although not much reading went on at home according to Lucas, family members occasionally wrote to his grandmother in El Paso, Texas. Lucas liked the class activity in which students wrote letters to each other because "it's fun; it's better than reading journal." He read aloud the following letter, which he wrote to another student:

> Dear Emerald, As soon as I got home from school, I went to my cousin's house, Omar. Then we went to Sonic on our bike…by our house on the bikes. When we got there, Omar ordered a frito pie. Then I ordered a chicken strip dinner. It was good. Then I went home on my bike. It was real fun.

Another letter he read aloud followed a similar format of reporting his activities of the day:

> Dear Valen, I will tell you what I did yesterday. First of all, I went to the playground at 2:55 and got a snack from Mr. Tamez. It was good. Then I went to my two classes, and my dad picked me up at 5:15. Then we went home, ate Ms. Le Blanc's yummy recipe, and took a shower, and got ready for bed, and went to bed.

Although Lucas resisted classroom expectations by refusing to read the Reading Renaissance books, by playing around during reading time, and by failing, he also developed some interesting adaptive strategies. For example, he stated that when selecting a book to read, he always read page 13; if it was interesting, he checked out the book. However, Lucas did not see a purpose in his life for reading—it did not seem to help him attain the things he wanted. His orientation toward reading was for points rather than for enjoyment or learning information. He said, "I am trying to keep up on my reading because I am failing. Trying to read more every night and more in the classroom. Trying to check out books that have higher points." He went on to explain his rationale for choosing a book titled *Adventure in Legoland* (Matas, 1992): "It is worth more points and it is shorter. [Teacher: Do you think about length?] It does not matter as long as it has the points. I always go to the [chart] and see the points." Lucas's comments suggest that he had not given up on school and that he sought to improve his reading; however, his reasons for reading were limited to the notion of obtaining points.

Summary

Lucas was limited by his own perceptions and those of others that he was a poor reader, by lack of resources at home for school literacy practices (e.g., the typewriter had broken and the teachers had difficulty establishing contact with the parents), and by a narrowed view of the purposes of reading (reinforced by the school reading program) as an activity only for obtaining points. The classroom curriculum clearly influenced him, constraining his potential to become a reader who sees wider purposes for reading, and possibly, preventing him from becoming a competent reader because he received little help within the classroom to work on strategies. Like many of the second language students Reyes (1991) describes in process-writing classrooms, Lucas may have been limited by not receiving enough explicit skills instruction in either reading or writing. Here we see the local, institutional, and societal forces all contributing to Lucas's struggles (Fairclough, 1989). At the classroom level, he received little help to learn the skills necessary to read and write in English. At the institutional level of the school, he was limited by the Reading Renaissance program that allowed access to a narrow range of books and evaluated a narrow range of specific comprehension abilities. Because Lucas was a newly arrived ESL student whose family had few economic resources, he was limited at the societal level. The combined forces made it difficult for Lucas to succeed as a reader and writer. As a student in a less powerful position, his contributions were continually constrained at every level (Fairclough, 1989).

Despite Lucas's struggle with reading and writing, he was aware of the difficulties, and he felt "pretty proud to come to school because a lot of people don't have chances to come to school." He saw that his resistance was not paying off, he was motivated to do better, and he seized opportunities to express his ideas when provided a more authentic venue in the classroom, such as writing letters to classmates. Yet Lucas faced many obstacles in becoming a competent reader and writer, and seemed to be on the losing end of the social struggle for power or even some recognition in the classroom.

Whereas Lucas did not seem to have access to what was considered normal and natural in this classroom (Gee, 2001), and he resisted many of the classroom literacy practices, another student, Daniel, embraced them. Like Lucas, Daniel was Latino from a working-class background; however, Daniel was a fluent English speaker who was born in the United States. Yet Daniel experienced his own set of conflicts in developing a voice that would allow him to insert his ideas about social justice into classroom assignments and to go beyond the teacher's expectations.

Daniel: Transforming Classroom Norms Through Writing

Daniel was the older of two children from a single-parent family. His mother was Latina and his younger sister was biracial—African American and Latina. English was the primary language spoken in the home, although everyone understood Spanish. Daniel's mother had worked in a law office and wanted Daniel to become a lawyer, because she met "a lot of nice lawyers that did civil rights." She hoped that he would graduate from college "because in our family no one has graduated high school. I went to community college, and I was the first in my family. I want Daniel to see that it's not impossible because we don't have money." His mother had to quit the law office to spend more time with her children, and she was now making ends meet by working at a department store and substitute teaching.

Daniel's mother placed a high value on education, in part because she dropped out of high school when she became pregnant with Daniel, but went back to community college. She said,

> I try to stress with Daniel and [his sister] how important education is. It makes the difference between success and failure. We're not living in a great place, but we make it. We don't get help from welfare, and I think it has to do with the fact that I did get it [education], even though it is just a 2-year degree.

Daniel felt quite close to his family, saying, "My family always sticks together; we try to help my grandpa. I'm close to my cousins in Houston. We celebrate Christmas. We help each other with problems." One of the important events in his life had been his sister's birth because "finally [there was] somebody to share everything with and to have fun with." His mother found opportunities to go to school and have lunch with Daniel. She reported that Daniel said, "Mom, when are you gonna come back?" after sharing lunch in the cafeteria.

Daniel's mother described him as both cautious and curious. She explained that when "he was taking his first steps, he wouldn't walk until he was sure he could walk. He's very cautious." On the other hand, she found him to be

> unique, he's not your typical kid. He's a thinker and writer. He probably challenges her [his teacher] with different questions. He's always been very, very curious. That's his nature. He wants to know everything and sometimes it gets frustrating because it's like question after question.

The teacher did find Daniel to be "an interesting young man." However, she found him to be "too serious…he's very hard on himself. He sets high expectations for himself. He's in tears almost every day about grades, about school." She also noted that adult approval was important to Daniel, especially pleasing his mother. The teacher shared that Daniel had been very depressed and had not been able to get out of bed because he was so hard on himself. His mother did not mention Daniel's depression, but did note that he had a horrible time in a previous school. The previous teacher had suggested Ritalin for hyperactivity and explained to Daniel's mother that most of the boys in the class were on it—not to worry. The doctor had prescribed Ritalin based on the teacher's recommendation. However, Daniel's mother went to the library and read up on Attention Deficit Disorder (ADD):

> I had never heard of ADD; I went to the library and I checked out 10 books, and I went through them. I went through the symptoms, and I was like, this is not my child. That is not the imaginative, creative son I know. I didn't put him on the medication, and the next year we went to [this school], and he excelled.

Apparently Daniel was not depressed around his peers. They described him as "funny" because he told jokes, "nice" because he shared things, and "friendly." Daniel was quite serious in his conversations with me and compared himself to a "ram because I'm real stubborn, and I have a lot of courage and faith and hope when I need it." He went on to explain that when his grandmother died, "I really needed to use it [courage] to help my family and me." He also described himself as "energetic" because he liked to run, "talkative," and "happy." It is interesting to note that Daniel said, "I barely get sad or down." He also seemed to have a strong sense of self-esteem, something his mother stressed and felt that she had not had enough of as a child. In a letter to me, Daniel wrote a poem that read,

> I wish I was an astronaut
> I wish I was a bird
> I wish I was a pirate
> with a big and shiny sword,
> but what ever I wish for
> I am happy being me.

Literacy Practices

Literacy was highly valued by Daniel and his mother. His mother talked about reading daily, mentioning that she often skipped "from book to book." Daniel was aware of his mother's interest in literacy and said she read

> everything—books and magazines and the newspaper. She writes to people that are in other cities or states. She likes to write things, poems and little stories, and she takes them to everybody else in our family and they read it.

Daniel shared this love of literacy. He stated, "I like to read a lot. I've always liked reading [since] the first time I picked up a book." He went on to explain that he read in class and at home as well as on trips: "I go to Houston to visit aunts and uncles, and I read in the car going there. Whenever I want to, I read." He was aware that he was a good reader, saying "A lot of people say I'm good too." He knew that his mother and his teacher shared the view that he was an excellent reader. Each of his peers responded that Daniel was either the best reader in the class or one of two best readers. His mother explained that he had shown an interest in reading at a young age.

It was Daniel's writing that set him apart from his peers. Each of his peers stated that Daniel was a very good writer and mentioned that the teacher often had him read his work aloud. His peers found his stories to be very interesting, especially the ones that had scary parts. The teacher described him as "a writer." She said,

> I think he sees himself as a strong leader and writer. I hope he does anyway. He really shined (sic) when we did our black history packets…the kids wanted him to read the packet front to back and they were asking for his autograph because they said, "One day he's gonna be a famous author."

Not only did Daniel write at school, he also wrote at home because he had more time. He said, "that's where [home] I write most of my stories and poems. And I read to other people in my family." His mother noted his interest in writing as well: "He likes to write poems. He shares that with me, and he likes to write short stories, mostly like sci-fi. It's like inherent in him. He just started doing it without me showing him." He also enjoyed writing fictional stories, as evidenced by his lengthy story about his cousin's frightening encounter with a wolf.

Daniel used his reading and writing skills to express his views of current events and, in this way, went beyond school expectations. The teacher had provided students with the opportunity to write about the tragic school shootings in Littleton, Colorado, and he wrote the following:

Trenchcoat Man Massacre

In Colorado there was gunfire. 25 people died in this horrible massacre. It took place in a school there were two people shooting with semi-automatic guns. After the shooting they killed themselves. It lasted 4 hours.

I feel like most people cannot be trusted. How can people be so deadly. The thought that it happened in a school frightens me. What if this happens in our school? What would make two people want to run loose in a school and kill people. The other thing is a lot of these people still had a long life ahead of them and the parents must feel bad too.

This piece shows some of Daniel's deep thinking about current issues and the fears that such violence evoked in him. Writing seemed to be an outlet for his emotions that he did not often share in interviews or conversations with others. Although he did participate in classroom discussions, he felt most comfortable writing his responses in the journals and then reading them aloud to classmates. Daniel was clearly affected by the classroom talk about race, and he shared this piece from his journal with me:

If there were only one race in the entire world, the world would be a boring place. Everybody would be the same race, which means you would wake up every morning and go outside to see the same color of people each and every day. The world would be no fun anymore. Nobody would know the true meaning of color. It would be demolished. The only different life forms would be animals. The everlasting rainbow on earth would be nothing to people. Color matters so much, but not in the way of hate, but life on earth. People should be glad there is a rainbow. Blacks, whites, yellow, copper, red and many other colors are the colors that keep life moving. Without them, the world is hopeless. But with them, the world is truly beautiful. That is why one race would be so dull.

This piece was not written as part of a classroom assignment, but the teacher allowed him to read it to the entire class. He took the opportunity to make his private ruminations more public.

Summary

Daniel's identity was closely tied to being a successful and avid reader and writer. Both home and school contexts provided him with an audience, as well as many opportunities to create stories and to write about issues of concern to him. Rather than just doing school assignments, Daniel seized opportunities to write about issues that were important to him, such as the above piece. His writing reflects Bakhtin's (1981) notion of "internally persuasive discourse" (p. 345), because he drew from other sources to create something new. Although his reading and writing activities were public, he kept to himself and seemed to be more private about his home life and past struggles. He seemed to act differently with his peers than with adults, who saw a deep, reflective side to him. These conflicts may have provided an impetus to transform his experiences though writing. Daniel's struggles to establish a variety of literacy practices in different contexts links to Sarup's (1996) belief that aspects of individuals' identities may clash in particular spaces. For Daniel, the classroom was a place where his literate and other identities both blended and clashed, but allowed him opportunities to transform his identities.

What Might These Cases Mean for Understanding Students' Identities as Readers and Writers?

Students in this classroom, which featured reading and writing workshops as well as the Reading Renaissance program, responded to the curriculum in different ways. Jennifer did not question the classroom norms and sought to be successful within them; Lucas wanted to be successful in school but was limited by classroom, institutional, and societal constraints and undermined his own attempts by playing around or not reading; and Daniel complied, but also found opportunities to write about issues of interest to him such as racial prejudice. Jennifer completed assignments and was very successful in school, and found no reason to question or challenge school expectations. When connecting novel themes to her own life, she did so at a literal level that successfully addressed the questions but did not go beyond them. Lucas, by contrast, was a student who struggled to read and write, and resisted the process as well. Although he found an audience—a friend to correspond with in the school-sponsored activity of writing letters—he did not seem to have a larger audience of friends, the teacher, or family with whom to use literacy in meaningful contexts. Purposes of reading and writing seemed to be limited to school tasks, and he was not successful at performing them. Institutional forces, including his lack of access to the language of power, seemed to play a large role in preventing him from succeeding, while his own resistance seemed to contribute to his lack of success in school. Daniel, who was perceived as a good reader and writer and a complex person by teacher and peers, was able to transform the classroom norms to suit his own purposes. He found audiences both in school and out of school and used writing not only to communicate, but to reflect on his own views of violence and race relations. Rather than simply fulfilling classroom assignments, Daniel sought opportunities to write about his feelings and share them with others. The support he received from his teacher and his mother seemed to play a clear role in promoting his literate identity and encouraging him to communicate and transform his own experiences.

The cases demonstrate how students negotiated their identities in different contexts (Gee, 2001). All three had a set of literate practices that influenced how they related to different people. For Jennifer, home and school expectations were quite aligned, and she was able to demonstrate her literacies in both contexts. Although Daniel kept many aspects of himself more private, the complexity of his literate practices is noteworthy. He was supported at home as well as at school in pursuing his interests in reading and writing. Although Lucas did not seem successful in this classroom, he had clearly obtained some strategies for book selection and for communicating with peers. Given the challenges that he had in the classroom, Lucas, too, had developed literate practices that defined who he was. In all three examples we can see the relationships between literacy and identity and the complex ways in which they informed one another (Holdaway, 1986).

The three cases of the students at Valley School demonstrate the powerful effect of institutionalized curriculum on students' identities The language arts curriculum in this fifth-grade classroom was multifaceted, both in terms of the explicit programs and the implicit messages derived from the competing norms. Although some aspects of the curriculum were quite prescribed, such as Reading Renaissance with its color coding, tests, and reward systems, other aspects such as literature response and writing workshop allowed students opportunities to see reading and writing as more than a set of classroom exercises. The influence of Reading Renaissance is clear from seeing that the students evaluated their reading abilities and interests in terms of what color they were on in the schoolwide program. They rated themselves against others and developed strategies for taking tests and thus gaining points. In contrast, the reading workshop provided opportunities for students to become engaged in texts through listening, discussing, and writing responses. The teacher had sought to address issues of racial discrimination and tension through literature, and students were able to discuss their understandings of the themes of the book both in classroom discussions and in interviews. Yet, the response to the novel tasks were somewhat prescribed; although the questions asked students to connect the books to their lives, they did so in particular ways such as describing a challenge or a time they felt jealous. These tasks corresponded in some ways to the TAAS skills and provide evidence of the ways in which the teacher felt pressured to prepare her students for the tests. Here, we see the discourse of the teacher was as constrained as the students' by the institutional effects of a particular program and the focus on testing (Fairclough, 1989).

Students such as Jennifer and Daniel were able to successfully negotiate the different tasks and expectations within the classroom. However, quite different expectations for each of the curricular areas may have posed particular challenges for students such as Lucas. Although there were choices about books to read within the prescribed curriculum and some opportunities for open-ended responses, Lucas seemed to need much more instruction in decoding and comprehension strategies than was being provided. Having him read in isolation and testing him on a narrow range of comprehension questions only seemed to compound his problems and did not seem to provide him access to full classroom participation. As a result, he seemed to have a narrowed view of the purposes of reading and writing, and in the end, he had few choices.

The findings that the classroom curriculum had a powerful effect on the students have some implications for practice. First, students who identify themselves as readers primarily in terms of a color scheme could develop a limited view of reading—seeing reading as a means to gain points or win prizes rather than a process to aid them in acquiring information (see Sailors, Worthy, Assaf, & Mast, 2000). Second, there is also the danger of reducing complex literacy skills and strategies to a single dimension and suggesting to students that literacy is equal to a color on a chart. These consequences suggest that schools need to be careful about the imposition of particular programs on all teachers and students (Biggers, 2001). The risks of a standardized program seem to outweigh the rewards.

Not only were the students affected by the curriculum, but it is clear that the teacher was pressured into teaching in ways that she found offensive. In the teacher's view the institutional norm of using the program, posting students' scores, and having reward parties affected how they saw themselves as literacy learners and had harmful effects on both high and low achievers. Being a "Model School for Reading Renaissance," as well as preparing students for the TAAS tests, affected how the teacher conducted her classroom and her views of curriculum. Here we see in a rather specific way how a teacher operated within social and institutional boundaries as well as her own cultural milieu (Aronowitz & Giroux, 1991). Given the intense pressures the teacher experienced, it seems remarkable that she was able to negotiate the curricular terrain and provide opportunities for students to explore their literate identities in a number of contexts.

CHAPTER 5

Understanding Students Within Their Social Contexts

Although these nine cases of students are specific to their sites, the cases also represent a larger picture of teaching and learning in U.S. classrooms. What emerges from the analyses is an image of complex interactions between teachers and students in which students are continually negotiating who they are within culturally inscribed spaces. Although each child responded to the classroom setting in a different way, themes emerged across the three sites: the influence of power and authority as communicated through the teacher's role and classroom curriculum, issues of purposes and audiences for writing, and the need for creating spaces within existing classrooms. In this concluding chapter, I compare students' constructions of literate identities, analyze the classroom contexts that influenced students, and suggest some implications for practice.

Comparing Students' Constructions of Literate Identities

Although students interacted in specific ways with their teachers and peers, there were also some commonalties among students who appropriated, resisted, or transformed their classroom contexts. The following comparison across sites provides some insight into how students engaged in complex negotiations with regard to their literacy learning and identity construction.

Appropriation of Classroom Norms

Miguel, Rita, and Jennifer were all successful in appropriating the classroom norms and expectations. They conformed to the teacher's rules, whether it was writing from personal experience, writing summaries of novels, or reading within the accepted range of Accelerated Reading books. Miguel generally conformed to the teacher's instructions; for example, he used sticky notes to mark his writing as he had been taught by the teacher, he used index cards to mark vocabulary he wanted to learn, and he wrote journal entries in accordance with the teacher's expectations. Miguel internalized what he had learned from the teacher and the classroom and had applied the information about writing for an audience, writing from personal experience, and using description in his own writing. Rita, too, was very conscious of pleasing the teacher. She wrote journal entries about her life, summarized the books read aloud, and attempted to include descriptive language in her work. Jennifer excelled in the reading program and fulfilled all her assignments. She was strategic about moving ahead through the reading levels, and she sought her teacher's approval.

Each student had developed a strong relationship with the teacher and found his or her work valued and supported in the classroom context. Ms. Meyer respected Miguel's work and appreciated his contributions. She felt very positive toward him, describing him as "the greatest kid," and her interactions, particularly in writing conferences, continually encouraged him. Likewise, Rita's teachers encouraged her to fit into the classroom and to develop her writing in Spanish and English. Although she never felt comfortable enough to share her writing with the large class, she did have opportunities to demonstrate her language and literacy competence in both languages. Jennifer, highly regarded by Ms. Le Blanc, became the teacher's errand girl and the person she could count on at all times.

Authority figured largely in students' relationships with teachers and with literacy practices. Miguel viewed his teacher as the primary influence on his writing and valued her input. When he struggled to find a topic for his project, he felt that she saved him and helped him see that he wanted to compare himself to a killer whale. He reported that she had opened new horizons for him and helped him by meeting with him in conferences and modeling descriptive writing in the classroom. Rita also wanted to please the teacher and had internalized the idea that if she followed the teacher's rules, she would get ahead like her sister. Her attitudes toward authority were consistent with those at home. Although her family members, who had emigrated from Mexico, were not happy with some of the school literacy practices, they expected Rita to follow the school rules. Jennifer, too, had a fairly straightforward relationship with authority—attending to her work allowed her to be free to do errands for the teacher and to gain acceptance. Her father reinforced the value of doing well in school by rewarding her for good grades.

From a perspective that values students' understanding and applying school norms, these students were very successful. They had figured out how to play the game of school and had used available resources to fit into U.S. classrooms. From a cultural reproductive stance (Bourdieu, 1977), these students were acquiring the cultural capital to help them succeed in monetary ways in the future. The three students, all Latino from working-class backgrounds, occupied particular subject positions in their classrooms—they were in less powerful positions than the teacher because they were students from economic and social circumstances that did not privilege them. Yet, they participated in classroom norms and, in a sense, reproduced those norms by consenting to the teachers' authority and fulfilling their expected social roles (Fairclough, 1989).

From a more critical perspective in which schools ought to do more than simply reinforce existing values, these students were missing out (Giroux, 1988). They viewed reading and writing as tools for fulfilling classroom assignments rather than as opportunities to extend beyond school or to transform their worlds in some way. Miguel was satisfied with his killer whale project because he was able to combine his knowledge of whales with the expectation to write a personal narrative. Rita was able to combine her facilities with both Spanish and English to contribute to a group fashion show on ancient Egypt. Jennifer completed her assignments to move up in the Accelerated Reading program. These students enacted the broader discourse patterns of schooling in which teachers have power and authority, and the students submit to it without questioning those relationships (Giroux, 1988).

Audiences for literacy behaviors sometimes included students' families, but these students generally saw reading and writing as a means to improve themselves in school. Miguel wrote for peers at school because students were expected to share their work in writing workshop, but he cared deeply about the teacher's opinion. Miguel viewed good writing as going hand-in-hand with being a good student; Rita did not choose to read or write out of school, unless forced by her mother; and Jennifer, who had an early interest in reading and writing, had become more interested in other pre-teenage activities. Their views of reading and writing and their related identities as readers and writers will probably help them to continue to achieve in school. These students have overcome challenging economic and social circumstances—that is, being Latino and working class in a predominantly white and middle-class society—gaining access to the codes of power (Delpit, 1988). Their efforts, supported by parents and teachers, should be lauded. However, their success with schooling may inhibit them from changing a system that for the most part worked for them but may oppress others who were not as successful in the system (Bourdieu, 1977).

Resisting Classroom Expectations

The three students whom I have described as resisting classroom expectations challenged the dynamics of the classroom either through "acts of open opposition" or through subtler acts (Dressman, 1997, p. 38). Although Greg and Lucas refused to participate in certain classroom activities, Anita shifted the assignment in a more subtle act of opposition. They all seemed to find their classrooms oppressive, but for quite different reasons and with different consequences. In each case, a complex network of misunderstandings, personal factors, cultural mismatches, and larger institutional forces seemed to be operating. Anita and Ms. Meyer had a rocky relationship that affected the ways in which Anita interacted in the classroom. Although Anita did not share her writing in the large group or with peers, she did attempt to explain her topic and interest to the teacher in a conference. When Ms. Meyer did not support her topic choice or her narrative style, Anita initially resisted and was going to stick with her original topic. Even though she changed topics, her work was never really valued by the teacher because it did not reflect the teacher's value on description, metaphor, and exploration of an intimate personal relationship. Her working-class social status, her ethnicity—different from the teacher's—and her lack of academic success appeared to work against her; at the same time,

Ms. Meyer perpetuated the image of Anita as an unsuccessful writer and did little to help her find her voice. The discourse enacted in the writing conference displayed the difference in power between the teacher and Anita, as the teacher continually tried to control the conference. Besides the personal factors that influenced their relationship, we can see the institutional forces in which the "white middle-class gatekeeper," Ms. Meyer, constrained the discourse type (Fairclough, 1989, p. 47).

Greg's interactions with his teachers were complex. Although Ms. Martin and Ms. Allen valued his extensive knowledge of history and other fields, allowing him to respond to questions they asked during large-group read-alouds, they were uncomfortable with his refusal to participate in the expected way. They wanted Greg to participate in literacy activities during the scheduled times, to pay attention during novel time, to raise his hand and be called on before speaking, and to wait his turn to share. These expectations are fairly typical in U.S. classrooms, and Greg would have fit in better had he cooperated; however, Greg resisted through his behavior and, occasionally, through not writing at all during response time. The consequence was that he was often in conflict with his teachers and with his peers, who saw his resistance as disrupting their literacy opportunities. Greg, equipped with a great deal of cultural capital from home (Bourdieu, 1977), continued to write about war in his journals and took pride in including blood and gore in his stories. However, his form of resistance seemed to create a great deal of unresolved tension and discomfort, resulting in school as an oppressive force.

Lucas, who lacked the cultural capital and resources afforded to Greg, resisted working in his classroom setting as well. He did not have the facility in written English to participate fully, and he did not seem to be getting the help he needed. The curriculum of Reading Renaissance, in which students were expected to read and answer questions on their own, contributed to his failure. Because he had not acquired the basics of decoding and comprehension, simply having him take tests on materials he could not understand was not going to help him attain the necessary skills. Additionally, although listening to stories read aloud might have provided him with some opportunities to hear spoken English and to participate in discussions, the fact that Lucas was not receiving adequate instruction in texts he could read limited his access to literacy. For his part, Lucas essentially refused to read during the scheduled time, choosing to play and avoid work. His peers noted his lack of participation, and although many liked him, they attributed his difficulties to his own off-task behavior. The dynamic of institutional forces such as the Reading Renaissance program, the lack of support for his learning to read and write in English in the classroom, and his working-class new-immigrant status combined in ways that prevented his success in the classroom (Fairclough, 1989). For his part, Lucas's lack of participation prevented him from changing the dynamics in the classroom in any productive ways (Foley, 1990).

The interplay of the oppressive classroom settings and the students' resistance limited their literacy experiences within the classroom, but may not have limited their access to other forms of literacy in other settings. Anita did not share her work with a classroom audience, but she created opportunities to perform other literate identities through her journals and her singing and dancing on the train with a different audience. Greg wrote many interesting pieces in his journal, but the teachers did not respond to them or provide opportunities for him to share his written work in the classroom. As a result, Greg's extensive knowledge of World War II and the Civil War was largely unexplored by the teachers or his peers. However, Greg did have a receptive audience at home, and he continued to work on expressing his ideas in a variety of formats. At the same time as the Reading Renaissance curriculum and the read-alouds failed to address Lucas's specific needs, his reluctance to participate in the classroom activities limited his classroom literacy opportunities. Instead of attaining fluency in written and spoken English, he was falling behind. The writing that he had done at home was not supported continually at home and went unacknowledged in school. Reading and writing did not serve a purpose for him in his daily life, and at the same time, his lack of these tools was preventing him from being successful in school. Yet Lucas had developed literate strategies, such as book selection and writing to an audience of a friend, which provided him with some opportunities for attaining literacy.

In the three cases, students demonstrated resistance to classroom activities, but not to literacy per se. They found ways to enact their literate identities outside the classroom boundaries. Anita found an audience on the train, Greg continued his reading and writing at home, and Lucas found a friend with whom to correspond. They were able to find sources outside the classroom and other ways to represent themselves. Their identities were not totally constituted by the classroom settings, rather they took up different positions depending on the contexts (Dillon & Moje, 1998; Hagood, in press). Although they did not fit the cultural model established by the teachers and their behavior was considered deviant in some ways (Gee, 2001), these students all wanted to succeed in school. These were not students who had given up and withdrawn; instead, they continued to try to find ways to gain acceptance in their classroom settings. Anita switched topics, trying to please the teacher; Greg continued to give answers in large-group sessions; and Lucas sought to try harder to complete his homework. However, their current settings did not seem to provide hope for change: Anita's relationship with the teacher seemed doomed to failure, Greg did not see a reason to change his behavior, and Lucas needed more assistance in the basics of reading and writing. The students seemed to have little power to change their circumstances, and their own resistance only seemed to make matters worse. If these patterns of challenges are continued in school, these students may not succeed in attaining schooled literacy. However, their literate identities within other contexts may have provided them with resources to meet the demands in other settings. Although they were constrained by their social positions (in the cases of Anita and Lucas) and by institutional barriers, they were still social agents who were "active and creative," who could "meet the ever-changing demands and contradictions of social situations" in new ways (Fairclough, 1989, p. 39).

Transforming Expectations Through Text

The students who transformed their identities as readers and writers were able to resist certain classroom expectations and "get away with it." Their attempts as active, creative social agents to change their classroom settings in some way were more successful than those of their resistant counterparts. That is, they each changed some aspect of their literacy practices or their classroom environments that resulted in creating a third space (Gutierrez et al., 1995). This third space involved the teacher and student understanding one another and engaging in active problem solving. For example, Ella and Ms. Meyer worked specifically on Ella's project after developing a shared understanding in a writing conference of the exact nature of the project. However, the creation of a third space did not necessarily occur in a one-on-one, teacher-student interaction. Mandy raised her concerns to Ms. Martin and Ms. Allen in class discussion about the gendered nature of the writing assignment and continued to raise the issue in subsequent assignments. The teachers recognized Mandy's concern and allowed her views to become part of the legitimate curriculum. Daniel seized opportunities outside the actual assignments to share his work with others. He used the study of *Roll of Thunder, Hear My Cry* (Taylor, 1976) and slavery to issue his own proclamation about the value of diversity in society. Ms. Le Blanc contributed to the development of the third space by allowing Daniel to write the piece instead of another assignment and encouraging him to share it with the whole class.

The result of the creation of a third space was that students created a "hybrid voice" (Fecho, 2001, p. 10). For Ella, that meant literally to superimpose her fictional voice onto her personal narrative. Instead of just writing a letter to her aunt recounting past experiences, she drew from her resources to create a story that is "half truth-half fiction." She was able to include fictional elements that she so highly valued by writing a story in the first person (meeting the teacher's expectations), yet adding a variety of endings (her own fictional voice). Ella made use of the dialogue from the classroom and developed her classroom writing assignment into a piece for an audience, her aunt. She had the knowledge and experience with using different genres that allowed her to create this hybrid. Although she did not directly challenge the teacher's authority, she found a way to combine her own interests with the teacher's expectations.

Mandy's hybrid voice manifested itself through her writing voices that were "half hers and half others'" (Bakhtin, 1981). She inserted herself into the book characters and had them express some of her own concerns about treatment of people of color. She developed flexibility with genres that allowed her to adapt to different situations, while writing from a female perspective. She also attempted to write a story with characters from diverse backgrounds, thereby imbuing her work with a sense of social justice. Daniel also used his writing to express his views of diversity, inequity, and social justice. His hybrid voice reflected some of the discussions held in the classroom, but went beyond them to argue for valuing diversity.

The development of a hybrid voice occurred through some conflict between the classroom expectations and the students' interests. In Ella's case, the teacher did not want her to write fiction. Instead of simply complying with or ignoring the teacher's expectation, Ella adjusted the assignment to fit her own interests. Mandy raised her concern about having to write from a male perspective, and the teachers responded by altering the assignment. Mandy developed the flexibility to write from a variety of points of view. Further, she was struck by her observations of the inequities in the workplace and looked for ways to address her concerns. With Daniel, the conflict seemed distant in time and relationship. In some ways he was still struggling with previous teachers' perceptions of him as a student with ADD and a behavior problem. Yet his more immediate struggle seemed to be with finding ways to express his strong feelings about racial injustice and school violence. These students were able to capitalize on the conflicts with teachers to write for audiences and purposes beyond the classroom and to develop broader views of reading and writing.

The students who attempted to transform aspects of their identities or the classroom norms did so through their classroom literate practices. Ella, Mandy, and Daniel were very successful students by school standards; they achieved high grades, the teachers thought highly of them, and they all were motivated to do well in school. The students' work was well accepted by the teachers and their peers. All found opportunities to share their work in the classroom setting, and peers usually responded positively to their work. They had developed shared cultural models with the teachers about what literacy practices were expected (Gee, 2001).

Yet they also went beyond the classroom expectations. Ella, Mandy, and Daniel used literacy for broader purposes than the classroom. All three read voraciously and widely at home and all wrote stories at home as well as at school. Ella kept her fictional notebook for her own purposes; Mandy entered writing contests in her spare time; Daniel wrote pieces at home too. Students' home literacy experiences reinforced much of what was going on at school. Although Ella's teacher did not want her to write fiction for her assignment, she certainly applauded the idea of writing in and outside the classroom and sharing her work with real audiences. Mandy's mother, who served dual roles as parent and teacher, nurtured her daughter's home literacy habits and, at the same time, kept her teachers well informed about her experiences. Daniel shared much of his work with his mother, developing an audience beyond the classroom and creating continuity between home and school. Students who were able to transform their contexts were active in negotiating their identities within school and other contexts and drew from several discourses to create new texts (Fairclough, 1989). The students anticipated a form of critical literacy in which learners are able to see the relevance of reading and writing in their everyday lives, but also to interrogate texts, and to see themselves as active participants in the transformation of their own multiple identities (Luke, 2000).

Understanding Students' Backgrounds

The focus of this study was on students' construction of their literate identities. However, it is neither possible—nor desirable—to separate who these students were as readers and writers from the social contexts in which those identities were formed. The fact that Anita was African American and working class seemed to affect her teacher's perceptions of her, while at the same time, Anita's style of representing her experiences was unfamiliar to the teacher. Ella was also African American, but she was middle class, which may have given her access to literate practices in her home that were congruent with school expectations. Miguel and Rita, both Latino immigrants who were competent English speakers despite having been in the United States for only a few years, were remarkable in how much they had achieved in adapting to U.S. schools. Yet, Lucas, who was also a recent immigrant, did not have the same access to literacy and was struggling to read and write in English. Greg, armed with middle-class, European American cultural capital from experiences with his parents, was not able to successfully transform those experiences in the classroom setting, while Daniel, who was working-class and somewhat depressed, was able to make his experiences count in the classroom.

What has emerged is a complex picture of the role of race, culture, social class, and gender. These forces interacted in dynamic ways that belie a mere reproductive role of schooling in promoting success or failure (Bourdieu, 1977), and that suggest that teachers and students had agency that they exercised within the local setting. The study, then, becomes an example of the intersection of the various levels of society, institution, and the local classroom through language and text that interact in complex ways (Fairclough, 1992). In the next section, I discuss the local settings of the classrooms and analyze features that contributed to students' views of themselves as readers and writers.

Analyzing the Classroom Contexts

In this book, I have focused on how students constructed their literate identities within specific classroom contexts. In comparing students across sites, I have found that the teacher-student relationship and the classroom curriculum have played major roles in contributing to students' understandings of who they are as readers and writers. These classrooms were, in turn, part of larger institutions and social forces that influenced how the teachers enacted literate practices (Giroux, 1988).

Teacher-Student Relationships

The nine cases I have described highlight the importance of the teacher-student relationship in influencing literacy learning. Classroom talk, whether through writing conferences, large-group share sessions, or discussion, can serve as a powerful means to enact the teacher-student relationship (Cazden, 1988). In the NYC classroom, Ms. Meyer's views of the students influenced her interactions with them in the classroom and, in particular, affected her writing conferences with them. Her positive interaction with Miguel encouraged him to revise his whale piece by including description and comparing himself to a whale. Her negative feelings about Anita were reflected in the writing conference where teacher and student never reached a shared understanding of the topic. Although Ms. Meyer disapproved of students writing fiction, she had positive images of Ella and expressed interest in her topic of relating personal experiences and her letter to her aunt. While Miguel and the teacher experienced synchrony, Ms. Meyer and Anita experienced unresolved conflict. With Ella, teacher and student reached a shared understanding after experiencing some tension.

In the Hillside School site, Rita made every effort to please all her teachers and was successful despite the fact that she would have preferred other venues in which to share her work. In contrast, Greg continually negotiated his relationship with Ms. Martin and Ms. Allen, sometimes successfully, but often there was tension, and he felt rejected and rebellious. Mandy was well-liked by the teachers and, because she was a successful reader and writer, seemed to have resources to draw from that aided her in expressing her conflicts with the writing assignments. The sharing of response logs during the whole-class sessions was a window for seeing how teachers and students negotiated their relationships.

The natures of the relationships between teacher and students were reflected not only in the teacher's interviews, but also in the ways Ms. Le Blanc responded to the students during Reading Renaissance time and the large-group discussions at Valley School. The teacher had a positive view of Jennifer and provided her with opportunities to help around the classroom and school such as running errands. Jennifer was pleased by this role and accepted the responsibility with enthusiasm. On the other hand, the teacher reacted negatively to Lucas's lack of responsibility in completing his work and struggled with how to help him, seeking assistance from his parents to help him pass fifth grade. Daniel and the teacher had a complex interaction in which she felt that he was depressed and anxious about his work. She enlisted the help of his mother and provided opportunities for him to excel, while at the same time attempting to reduce his anxiety.

In all three settings, we see the continuum from strong, caring relationships in which the teacher and student developed an understanding of each other to situations in which the teacher and student struggled to find common ground. Because all human relationships are complex, it is not surprising that teacher and students experienced conflict as well as congruence. However, the teacher-student relationship affected the access to literacy and influenced how students felt about themselves as readers and writers.

Teachers enacted their relationships with students within the curriculum. At two of the school sites, the teachers were relatively free from district requirements and emphases on test scores, which allowed students blocks of time to read and write or to engage with integrated units. At the third site, Valley School, the teacher combined the school-mandated curriculum, Reading Renaissance, with her own version of reading workshop. The teachers' views about what constituted good writing and effective literacy instruction, developed from their own experiences within the school cultures, influenced their curricular practices.

Teachers' Enactments of Writing Workshop and Literature-Based Curriculum

The curricular goals at each of the three school sites were consistent with writing workshop and literature-based instruction. The classrooms were student-centered to the extent that teachers assumed nontraditional roles, attempting to facilitate students' reading and writing in contrast to directing all activities. The focus was on the process of writing rather than on conventions. Students had choices about what to read, about topics for writing, or about projects for integrated units, and they were also encouraged to share their work with the teacher and peers (Calkins, 1986; Routman, 1991). Despite the surface appearance of openness and student choice, however, the teachers had implicit assumptions about what constituted effective reading and writing, which had a major impact on how students described themselves as readers and writers. Frequently, the teachers' assumptions contradicted their goals and ideals, opening possibilities for some students while creating dilemmas for others.

The writing workshop in NYC that emphasized writing process rather than conventions, student choice about topics, and writing for real audiences seemed quite enabling for some students. However, the teacher's enactment of the workshop, which included an emphasis on the "qualities of good writing" and writing from personal experience—for instance writing about a "deep and important relationship" as a genre—was a deterrent for some students like Anita. The ways in which the teacher communicated her value of writing about a deep and important topic during writing conferences seemed to be effective for only the students who could "read" her assumptions. However, for other students, like Anita, who did not have experience with writing workshop and who interpreted Ms. Meyer's focus on personal experience as an opportunity to write about experiences at camp, the teacher's stated views (i.e., "Select a topic from your own experience") contradicted her real intentions (i.e., "Write about an important relationship"). These conflicts, which could become the material for deliberation and community-building (Lensmire, 2000), were ignored and left unchallenged.

Likewise at the Hillside School site, the teachers encouraged students to respond openly to books read aloud. However, students' choices here, too, were limited by the teachers' values on what constituted good writing. Writing summaries did not really count—using colorful language and writing from a particular perspective did. Again, some students understood this assumption, while others grappled with the contradiction of writing freely but also pleasing the teacher. Because the journals were read but not responded to, students did not have access to models of the kind of journal writing the teachers valued. Trying to understand the teachers' intentions without being provided specific models was a challenging task for many of the students from diverse backgrounds (Delpit, 1988).

At the Valley School site, the contradictions in expectations for the major curricular topics must have challenged students like Lucas. On one hand, students were encouraged to respond freely to the chapters read aloud, but on the other, they were expected to read books for points and take tests for rewards. Again, some students understood and negotiated the different expectations or altered them to fit their own goals, while students such as Lucas did not operate successfully in either situation. Whereas the contradictions in expectations provided opportunities for some students to find ways to play with or subvert the system, these contradictions may have confused other students (Dressman, 1997).

Although the writing workshops and literature-based instruction opened possibilities for many students, the curriculum also became a "one-size fits all" (Reyes, 1991) situation that did not work for all students. Although the literature has often characterized traditional classroom instruction filled with worksheets and initiate-respond-evaluate (IRE) discourse patterns as limiting (Cazden, 1988), in some ways these classrooms where teachers struggled to teach against the grain, language and learning were still narrowly constructed (Gutierrez et al., 1997). The essential ingredient that seemed to be missing from the classrooms was an underlying value of the knowledge that every student brought to the learning setting (Willis, 1995). In the writing workshop in NYC, the teacher imposed her own views of the value of imagery and description and writing about an important relationship. She did not attempt to build on Anita's knowledge and experience at camp. The teachers at Hillside School allowed Rita to write in English and Spanish, thereby valuing her bilingualism; yet, their choices for books to read aloud to the class did not reflect many of the Latino students' backgrounds. And although they valued Greg's knowledge of the world, the teachers did not build on that knowledge or create opportunities for him to share his knowledge of wars and history. Ms. Le Blanc at Valley School created opportunities for students to relate their own experiences to literature through the questions she asked about text and by explicitly selecting novels that addressed racial issues. However, her text selections did not necessarily reflect the backgrounds of the majority of her students who were Latino, and she had not found a way to develop Lucas's fragile understanding of text. Some students, then, did not have access to "communities as effective practice" (Gutierrez & Meyer, 1995, p. 41) or have opportunities to relate their background knowledge to the texts read (Au, 1991).

All the teachers in the study brought their own assumptions about literacy, learning, and teaching to the classroom settings. Although the teachers were from different states and taught different populations in settings from urban to urban-rural, they shared many of the same assumptions about literacy. They also had many similarities in their backgrounds. Like the majority of teachers in U.S. schools (Sleeter, 1995), these teachers were white, middle class, and spoke English as their native language. They seemed to have a shared cultural model that defined what counted as normal and natural literacy practices and what counted as deviant or inappropriate behaviors in particular settings (Gee, 2001). For example, the teachers seemed to share the assumptions that they were in a position of authority and needed to control the discourse between teacher and students, that the curriculum needed to prepare students for later life (and their positions in the social structure), and that writing was most effective if performed in a particular genre and it contained certain features. However, these were also teachers who wanted to "teach against the grain" (Cochran-Smith & Lytle, 1993, p. 279) and engage in adventurous teaching (Cohen, 1988); they did not want to perpetuate traditional practices of basal readers, worksheets, testing comprehension, and working individually. They set up environments that allowed students to read and write authentic texts, to engage in meaningful activities, and to share their ideas with one another (Routman, 1991).

Despite their shared models of teaching, these teachers were constrained by larger institutional forces and societal pressures. Students at Hillside and Valley Schools still had to pass the TAAS test; teachers still felt the pressure of providing quality instruction for all students; and teachers were accountable to various audiences including the principal, parents, and the larger communities. Teachers experienced the contradictions between their goals of providing open-ended learning opportunities for all students and the institutional constraints of teaching a large number of students from diverse backgrounds. Like the teachers in McNeil's (1986) study, the teachers responded by controlling students' behavior in classrooms, controlling the tasks, and controlling the discourse. Just as the students were in unequal power positions with them, the teachers also occupied particular social positions that constrained their abilities to transform the curriculum and develop more caring relationships with all the students (Fairclough, 1989; Noddings, 1992).

The analyses of cases demonstrate the complex interplay between students and their settings. The students' identities as literacy learners developed in relation to their social contexts including home and school (Gee, 2001). For some students there was more consistency across their home and school settings, whereas for others, they demonstrated different literate abilities depending on the social support, the nature of the tasks, and the ways in which they positioned themselves relative to the teacher and their peers (Dillon & Moje, 1998; Evans, 1996; McCarthey, 1998). These identities also were constructed in relation to others' perceptions (Tatum, 1997). Students' literate identities were constructed by teachers, parents, and peers in relation to sometimes congruent and sometimes competing expectations from within their racial, cultural, and language discourse communities (Anzaldúa, 1999; Gee, 2001). The conflicts among aspects of students' identities created opportunities for some students who were able to alter the classroom norms and create a third space (Gutierrez et al., 1997), while those conflicts seemed unmanageable for students who experienced particularly oppressive conditions within the classrooms.

Social and institutional forces seemed to create more responsive environments for some students, while those same classrooms were oppressive for others. Race, social class, and linguistic status intersected, creating opportunities for some but limiting other students

(Aronowitz & Giroux, 1991). The relationship between power and language was quite complex; there were no straightforward connections between students' linguistic or social status and their literate practices in the classroom. The connections were much more subtle examples of the interplay among discourses, practices, and social positions. The cases are examples of the ways in which individuals made sense of their reality and social positions as the domains of the interactional, ideological, and local intersected through language and text in the classroom. The individual cases demonstrated how the students occupied different subject positions and thus were constrained by particular discoursal rights and obligations, at the same time as they were active and creative, contributing to their relative success or lack of success within the classroom settings (Fairclough, 1989). Appropriation, resistance, and transformation were forms through which students engaged in a dynamic interaction with the classroom and represented their views of literacy. These forms represent the conflicts between authoritative discourse and internally persuasive discourse that Bakhtin (1981) described as arising from the mix of voices we experience in our primary and secondary discourses (Gee, 1990).

Likewise, teachers were situated in particular communities and subject to institutional constraints and social norms; they worked long hours, were generally isolated in their classrooms (except for the team-teaching setting), and had little time for planning (Giroux, 1988). Their white, middle-class status played a role in the ways they established classroom environments and curriculum for their students. They shared cultural models of what was expected in schools, and they shared some expectations about what constituted writing workshop and literature-based instruction (Gee, 2001). The teachers operated within particular contexts and felt compelled to interact in accordance with program or district guidelines, whether it was the expectations to enact Calkins's (1986) writing workshop in a certain way or to be a model for the Reading Renaissance program. Yet, within those institutional constraints, teachers also showed agency in how they adapted models of teaching to fit their own belief systems or combined seemingly contradictory practices for what they hoped would be the learning of their students.

Because classrooms are dynamic settings in which teachers and students are continually negotiating their identities, we need to identify practices that will be sensitive to that complexity and make room for all students. In the following section, I draw from the three sites to suggest some principles for rethinking and revising literacy practices.

Implications for Practice

Underlying the recommendations I offer is a conception of identity that is fluid, dynamic, and relational (Mishler, 1999), and a view of literacy as a set of cultural practices that can promote democratic and emancipatory change (Freire, 1970). If we are to move away from the old "dead structures" (Lemert, 1997, p. 147) to more transformative practices, we need to consider ways that classrooms might change. Because classrooms are imbedded in larger institutional structures and social settings, we need "to find ways in which the pedagogical can be made more political and the political more pedagogical" (Giroux, 1988, p. 152).

Four major implications follow from this framework and the cross-site analyses. First, I recommend that we (teachers, researchers, teacher educators) reflect on our own assumptions about teaching and learning and, in particular, consider our own images of good writing and assumptions about literacy learning. Second, I emphasize the importance of getting to know particular students within their social and cultural contexts. Third, I recommend that we provide students with choices in a variety of genres to engage in literacy practices for multiple purposes. Fourth, I suggest that we engage students in explicit talk about the changing nature of identity.

Examining Assumptions and Making Expectations Clear

In each of the settings, teachers had particular views of reading and writing that students were able to understand and apply, resist, or transform. Ms. Meyer believed in the importance of representing important relationships and using imagery and description; the teachers in the multiage, literature-based setting focused on thematic units and taking characters' perspectives in creative ways; and Ms. Le Blanc valued responding to prompts about books. Although all of these seem to be interesting topics for students to explore and the teachers provided rationale for the selection of these topics, the teachers did not question whether these might be of value to all students. Is writing about an important person in your life, especially if there is suggestion of abuse, the most valuable topic to explore? Is taking the character's perspective the most effective way to interact with the novel? Is responding to particular questions the best way to relate a book to your life? Ultimately, as teachers we all make decisions about the most valuable topics to explore and the best books to read to achieve our goals. However, it is important to consider *what* and *who* is left out of the curriculum when we make the decisions we do (Sleeter, 1995) and to make efforts to provide inclusive curriculum (Nieto, 2002).

As we consider our choices for books to introduce to students and for topics about which students can write in particular genres, we need to be more cognizant of the powerful effects of our own values on students' literacy development. By virtue of our experience and knowledge, we are always walking the fine line between assisting students to become better readers and writers and imposing our views on them. It seems reasonable, then, for teachers to consider their values and to consider how they might conflict with those from other cultures. Examining our own assumptions about students, curriculum, and power relations is a prerequisite to developing the kinds of curricular opportunities we want for students of diverse backgrounds (Cochran-Smith & Lytle, 1993). Once we have examined our own assumptions and selected goals, resources, and methods, we need to think carefully about communicating our expectations to students.

If we have specific expectations about what we want students to learn, such as using description, we ought to make those expectations clear to students rather than simply devaluing what they do produce. No doubt, some students will still resist, but at least they will know what is expected rather than having to "read" what the teacher really wants. Likewise, if we want to narrow the writing topics for students, we need to communicate what the appropriate topics are to them. For example, if we do not want students to include violent content, we need to let them know the range of topics that are appropriate. Communicating clearly our expectations can assist particularly those students, such as Anita and Lucas, who may not have access to the "codes of power" (Delpit, 1988, p. 125), but can also promote understanding between teachers and students from all backgrounds.

In our quest to develop understanding, we should not forget that for some students within each site, conflict served as a springboard for change. Embracing conflict by trying to understand its source, whether from a lack of shared background or a misunderstanding about a particular task, can help us understand ourselves in relation to our students. Conflict can serve as the basis for a newer, deeper, and shared understanding that allows students to transform their literate identities. Engaging in dialogue with students, especially those who tend to resist classroom expectations, can provide much information about why a student may be resisting and what conditions underlie his or her behaviors.

Conflict can be set within the larger conversation about the importance of agency and critique. Because we occupy different social positions, conflict and struggle will exist, but these struggles can become the material for interrogating the dominant culture and schooling practices that are representative of it (Giroux, 1988). We can recognize the ways in which we may conflict with a student because of differences in values, roles, or social status and allow these differences to become part of the larger conversation. We need to create spaces in our curriculum where those conversations can occur. One of those places might be in literacy classes where students can have opportunities to talk about language itself.

Fairclough (1989) suggests that increasing consciousness about the role of language in the domination of some groups over others is the first step toward emancipation. He suggests that we need to develop critical language awareness that engages students in purposeful discourse at the same time as they begin to stretch and break conventions. By having students draw from and reflect on their own experiences with others in a systematic way, students can then develop awareness and increasingly purposeful discourse.

Understanding Students and Relating Curriculum to Their Backgrounds

To avoid creating the one-size-fits-all (Reyes, 1991) curriculum and to make room for the third space (Gutierrez et al., 1997), we need to create literacy experiences that are connected to students' lives. Essential to the process of connecting curriculum and students is to develop an understanding of students' diverse backgrounds. In her study of teachers of African American students, Ladson-Billings (1994) found that the most successful teachers learned a great deal about individual students and about their cultures and then developed culturally relevant curriculum. Learning about students may involve teachers in reading books about cultures other than their own and making home visits to understand the particular students in relation to their families. Like the teachers Moll and Gonzalez (1994) describe in their "funds of knowledge" project, we can increase our knowledge of students' cultures by actively seeking information.

Second, we may use our own understanding of children's lives to provide students with opportunities to connect their experiences to the curriculum. Selecting books that reflect the diverse society and the students' own backgrounds can help students connect literacy to their lives (Harris, 1992). When there are students from several different cultural backgrounds, it seems essential to bring in books that allow students to see members of their own culture represented in positive ways (Au, 1993). Further, teachers can use literature as a springboard to discussing students' own backgrounds as well as to introduce talk about race, class, and gender issues (Athaneses, 1998).

Allowing but not requiring students to write about personal experiences can help them see literacy as a powerful tool to which they can connect their lives and understand the potential of literacy beyond the classroom. Yet, personal experience writing does not have to be the only source of information. Reading and responding to topics of interest to students such as Greg's journals that were filled with facts about World War II also can provide information to teachers and allow students to connect home and school interests. Having students write about issues that they encounter every day or reflecting on catastrophic events such as the Columbine shootings (as Ms. Le Blanc did) or the destruction of the World Trade Center can allow students to read their world as well as the word (Freire, 1970).

Encouraging students to use their home languages can maximize students' learning of concepts, as well as help them feel valued in school (Gutierrez et al., 1997). Allowing students to use their home language, even if the teacher does not understand the words, also can increase teachers' understanding of students' competence with language.

Through listening to students' voices, learning about their backgrounds, and legitimizing their experiences, teachers can help students connect their experiences from in and out of school. Additionally, students can write about what it means to speak another language, affirming their identities as second-language learners (Nieto, 2002).

Providing Real Choices for Real Audiences

In each of the settings, the teachers offered students choices about writing topics within a particular genre. In each of these settings, however, some students resisted because they wanted to write in another genre. Students in the NYC classroom were encouraged to write about personal relationships using personal narrative and were dissuaded from writing fiction, but some students preferred writing about an experience or writing fiction. Students at Hillside School were expected to adopt the perspectives of a character in a response log, but some wanted to write summaries of the books, write about their personal experiences, or write about war. At Valley School, students were limited to writing responses to books or letter writing but had few opportunities to write from personal experience. These examples suggest that it is important for students to have multiple opportunities to write in many different genres with the expectations made explicit. It is hoped that the opportunity for students to learn about and write in different genres will enable them to have the flexibility to write from different points of view or adopt a variety of stances. Like the student Jeffrey, who Hynes (2000) describes and who favored nonfiction over fiction but became a reader and writer when his interests in car repairs were valued, other students can find their voices when genres other than personal narrative are encouraged.

Even as we offer a multiplicity of opportunities in different genres, we need to be aware of how easily students can be shut down. As Lensmire (2000) points out, "The development of voice can, has, and will go in different directions than becoming. In other words, if becoming suggests an opening up of student voices, it also points to the possibility that they can be shut down" (p. 81). Engaging students in deliberations about their writing and about the values of different genres can elucidate the issues and become part of the ongoing discourse.

In addition to deliberation about the values of differing genres, students also need chances to write for broader audiences. The students who appropriated the classroom expectations viewed literacy as a means for meeting classroom expectations, but not as a tool to help them in other arenas. Further, their audience was usually limited to the teacher. Students who resisted the expectations were limited to a narrow audience, themselves, or an audience outside of school, whereas students who could transform themselves viewed literacy as a tool to communicate with an audience, often beyond the assignment. These differences in purpose and audience suggest that if we want students to see literacy learning as an important element in their lives that goes beyond the classroom, we need to provide them with larger audiences than the teacher or themselves. We need to help students see literacy as a tool for their lives beyond school. By engaging students in writing across different discourse communities, we can help students become aware of differences in values and practices of groups at the same time as they situate themselves within particular communities (McCarthey & Moje, 2002).

Providing Opportunities for Exploring Identities

In addition to the types of embedded activities discussed here that value students' cultures and background knowledge, I believe it is important to help students explicitly consider identity as a transitional state, one in which we are always engaged (Giroux, 1988; Hagood, in press). For example, we can discuss with students how they might take on different subject positions depending on the context—while at home they may engage in different types of literacy activities than they do at school. Guiding students to consider how they position themselves in certain settings, whether in or out of school, can help them to consider the contextual nature of who they are (Mishler, 1999).

We can communicate to students that they do not have to sacrifice their ethnic, cultural, or language identities to assimilate into the dominant culture, but that they can renegotiate who they are becoming on a continual basis (Nieto, 2002). Providing opportunities for students to read books about youth who are grappling with their changing identities in a variety of realistic contexts can highlight differences in positions and power. Having students articulate "possible selves" while at the same time attending to the differences in power relations can help them to explore the power of hybrid identities (McCarthey & Moje, 2002). Rather than silencing those students like Anita, Greg, and Lucas, we can engage them in dialogue about the roots of their resistance and help all students consider the ways in which their attitudes and behaviors might be warranted. Dialogue with students about identity and the ways in which our identities are embedded within larger social contexts can help students see literacy as a set of practices that involve analysis, struggle, and, ultimately, transformation.

Conclusion

The suggestions described here have in common the need to value and legitimize students' voices by allowing them to read, write, and talk about issues of importance to them. Rather than imposing views of good reading and writing, we need to guide students in learning different perspectives. Together, teachers and students can move toward creating classrooms that allow more students to take transformative stances.

The analyses of the cases demonstrated the interaction between students' developing literate identities and the classroom contexts. In showing this connection, the cases have provided examples of how identity is embedded within social and cultural contexts and demonstrated that language is key to the process of identity construction (Gee, 1990). The role of teachers' and parents' perceptions in shaping identity also has been shown, providing support for Mishler's (1999) theory that identity is relational. The relationships we develop inside and outside the classroom, influenced by culture, class, and gender (Egan-Robertson, 1998), contribute to the continual process of identity construction.

The stories of the students from three different U.S. settings can encourage educators to realize what a large impact their classrooms can have on students' developing identities as well as understanding the ways in which students play a role in shaping those contexts. Increased understanding of the ways in which students appropriate, resist, or transform classroom norms can remind us of the need to keep students as our primary focus. I believe that the students' stories offer educators a sense of hope that by providing students with many opportunities to express who they are through oral and written language, they will find spaces to create, reconstruct, and share their identities with others.

References

Abbott, J. (1996). *Profiles of fifth-grade children who write avidly.* Unpublished doctoral dissertation, University of Texas, Austin.

Anzaldúa, G. (1999, October). *Nos/otros: "Us" vs. "them," (Des) conocimientos y comprisos.* Presentation at the Conference of Territories and Boundaries: Geographies of Latinidad, University of Illinois, Urbana-Champaign.

Aronowitz, S., & Giroux, H.A. (1991). *Postmodern education.* Minneapolis, MN: University of Minnesota Press.

Athaneses, S. (1998). Diverse learners, diverse texts: Exploring identity and difference through literary encounters. *Journal of Literacy Research, 30,* 273–296.

Atwell, N. (1987). *In the middle: Writing, reading, and learning with adolescents.* Upper Montclair, NJ: Boynton/Cook.

Au, K. (1991). Participation structures in a reading lesson with Hawaiian children: Analysis of a culturally appropriate instructional event. *Anthropology and Education Quarterly, 11,* 91–115.

Au, K. (1993). *Literacy instruction in multicultural settings.* Fort Worth, TX: Harcourt Brace.

Au, K. (1998). Social constructivism and the school literacy learning of students of diverse backgrounds. *Journal of Literacy Research, 30,* 297–319.

Bakhtin, M.M. (1981). *The dialogic imagination.* Austin, TX: University of Texas Press.

Bakhtin, M.M. (1986). The problem of speech genres. In C. Emerson & M. Holquist (Eds.) (V.W. McGee, Trans.), *Speech genres and other late essays* (pp. 60–102). Austin, TX: University of Texas Press.

Belsey, C. (1980). *Critical practice.* New York: Routledge.

Bernstein, B. (1973). Class and pedagogies. *Educational Studies, 1,* 23–41.

Blake, B.E. (1997). *She say, he say: Urban girls write their lives.* Albany, NY: State University of New York Press.

Biggers, D. (2001). The argument against Accelerated Reader. *Journal of Adolescent & Adult Literacy, 45,* 72–75.

Borko, H., & Eisenhart, M. (1986). Students' conceptions of reading and their reading experiences in school. *The Elementary School Journal, 86*, 589–611.

Bourdieu, P. (1977). *Outline of a theory of practice.* Cambridge, UK: Cambridge University Press.

Calkins, L.M. (1986). *The art of teaching writing.* Portsmouth, NH: Heinemann.

Calkins, L.M. (1991). *Living between the lines.* Portsmouth, NH: Heinemann.

Canady, C., & Krantz, S. (1996). Reading and communication: A comparison of proficient and less-proficient fourth-grade readers' opinions. *Language, Speech and Hearing Services in the Schools, 27*, 231–238.

Cazden, C.B. (1988). *Classroom discourse: The language of teaching and learning.* Portsmouth, NH: Heinemann.

Cherland, M.R. (1994). *Private practices: Girls reading fiction and constructing identity.* London: Taylor & Francis.

Cochran-Smith, M., & Lytle, S. (1993). Learning to teach against the grain. *Harvard Educational Review, 61,* 279–310.

Cohen, D. (1988). *Teaching practice: Plus ça change...* (Issue paper 88–3). East Lansing, MI: National Center for Research on Teacher Education.

Cuban, L., & Tyack, D. (1993). *Tinkering toward Utopia: A century of public school reform.* Cambridge, MA: Harvard University Press.

Delpit, L. (1988). The silenced dialogue: Power and pedagogy in educating other people's children. *Harvard Educational Review, 58*(3), 280–298.

Delpit, L. (1995). *Other people's children: Cultural conflicts in the classroom.* New York: W.W. Norton.

Dillon, D., & Moje, E. (1998). Listening to the talk of adolescent girls: Lessons about school, literacy, and life. In D. Alvermann, K. Hinchman, D. Moore, S. Phelps, & D. Waff (Eds.), *Reconceptualizing the literacies in adolescents' lives* (pp. 193–223). Mahwah, NJ: Erlbaum.

Dressman, M. (1993). Lionizing lone wolves: The cultural romantics of literacy workshops. *Curriculum Inquiry, 23*, 245–263.

Dressman, M. (1997). *Literacy in the library: Negotiating the spaces between order and desire.* Westport, CT: Bergin & Garvey.

Egan-Robertson, A. (1998). Learning about culture, language, and power: Understanding relationships among personhood, literacy practices, and intertextuality. *Journal of Literacy Research, 30*, 449–487.

Emerson, C. (1983). The outer world and inner speech: Bakhtin, Vygotsky, and the internalization of language. *Critical Inquiry, 10*(2), 245–264.

Erikson, E.H. (1968). *Identity, youth, and crisis.* New York: Norton.

Evans, R. (1993). Learning "schooled literacy": The literate life histories of mainstream student readers and writers. *Discourse Processes, 16*, 317–340.

Evans, K.S. (1996). Creating spaces for equity? The role of positioning in peer-led literature discussions. *Language Arts, 73*, 194–202.

Faigley, L., Cherry, R., Jolliffe, D., & Skinner, A. (1985). *Assessing writers' knowledge and processes of composing.* Norwood, NJ: Ablex.

Fairclough N. (1989). *Language and power.* London: Longman.

Fairclough, N. (1992). *Language and power.* London: Longman.

Fecho, B. (2001, April). *Literacy, identity, and classroom transactions.* Paper presented at the annual meeting of the American Educational Research Association, Seattle, WA.

Ferdman, B.M. (1990). Literacy and cultural identity. *Harvard Educational Review, 60*(2), 181–204.

Finders, M.J. (1997). *Just girls: Hidden literacies and life in junior high.* New York: Teachers College Press.

Foley, D. (1990). Learning capitalist culture: Deep in the heart of Texas. Philadelphia: University of Pennsylvania Press.

Freire, P. (1970). *Pedagogy of the oppressed.* New York: Continuum.

Gee, J. (1990). *Social linguistics and literacies.* London: Falmer.

Gee, J. (2001). Reading as situated language: A sociocognitive perspective. *Journal of Adolescent & Adult Literacy, 44,* 714–725.

Gee, J., & Crawford, V. (1998). Two kinds of teenagers: Language, identity, and social class. In D. Alvermann, K. Hinchman, D. Moore, S. Phelps, & D. Waff (Eds.), *Reconceptualizing the literacies in adolescents' lives* (pp. 225–245). Mahwah, NJ: Erlbaum.

Giroux, H. (1988). *Schooling and the struggle for public life.* Minneapolis, MN: University of Minnesota Press.

Guthrie, J.T., & Anderson, E. (1999). Engagement in reading: Processes of motivated, strategic, knowledgeable, social readers. In J.T. Guthrie & D.E. Alvermann (Eds.), *Engaged reading: Processes, practices, and policy implications* (pp. 17–45). New York: Teachers College Press.

Gutierrez, K., Baquedano-Lopez, P., & Turner, M.G. (1997). Putting language back into language arts: When the radical middle meets the third space. *Language Arts, 74,* 368–378.

Gutierrez, K., & Meyer, B. (1995). Creating communities of effective practice: Building literacy for language minority students. In J. Oakes & K.H. Quartz (Eds.), *Creating new educational communities* (Ninety-fourth yearbook of the National Society for the Study of Education, pp. 32–52). Chicago: University of Chicago Press.

Gutierrez, K., Rymes, B., & Larson, J. (1995). Script, counterscript, and underlife in the classroom: James Brown versus "Brown v. Board of Education." *Harvard Educational Review, 65,* 445–471.

Hagood, M. (in press). Critical literacy for whom? *Reading Research and Instruction.*

Harré, R. (1984). *Personal being: A theory for individual psychology.* Cambridge, MA: Harvard University Press.

Harris, V.J. (Ed.) (1992). *Teaching multicultural literature in grades K–8.* Norwood, MA: Christopher-Gordon.

Heath, S.B. (1983). *Ways with words.* Cambridge, UK: Cambridge University Press.

133

Holdaway, D. (1986). The visual face of expression and language. In D.B. Yaden, Jr. & S. Templeton (Eds.), *Metalinguistic awareness and beginning literacy: Conceptualizing what it means to read and write* (pp. 79–97). Portsmouth, NH: Heinemann.

Holquist, M. (1990). *Dialogism: Bakhtin and his world*. London: Routledge.

Hudson, S.A. (1986). Context and children's writing. *Research in the Teaching of English, 20*(3), 294–316.

Hynes, M. (2000). "I read for facts": Reading nonfiction in a fictional world. *Language Arts, 77*, 485–495.

Ladson-Billings, G. (1994). *The dreamkeepers: Successful teachers of African American children*. San Francisco: Jossey-Bass.

Lemert, C. (1997). *Social things*. Lanham, MD: Rowman & Littlefield.

Lemke, J.L. (1989). Social semiotics: A new model for literacy education. In D. Bloome (Ed.), *Classrooms and literacy* (pp. 289–309). Norwood, NJ: Ablex.

Lensmire, T. (1993). Following the child, socioanalysis, and threats to community: Teacher response to children's texts. *Curriculum Inquiry, 23*(3), 265–299.

Lensmire, T. (2000). *Powerful writing, responsible teaching*. New York: Teachers College Press.

Levinson, B.A., & Holland, D. (1996). The cultural production of the educated person: An introduction. In B.A. Levinson, D.E. Foley, & D.C. Holland (Eds.), *The cultural production of the educated person: Critical ethnographies of schooling and local practice* (pp. 1–54). Albany, NY: State University of New York Press.

Luke, A. (2000). Critical literacy in Australia: A matter of context and standpoint. *Journal of Adolescent & Adult Literacy, 43*, 448–461.

Mahiri, J., & Godley, A.J. (1998). Rewriting identity: Social meanings of literacy and "revisions" of self. *Reading Research Quarterly, 33*, 416–433.

McCabe, A. (1997). Cultural background and storytelling: A review and implications for schooling. *The Elementary School Journal, 97*(5), 454–473.

McCarthey, S.J. (1994). Authors, talk, and text: The internalization of dialogue from social interaction during writing. *Reading Research Quarterly, 29*, 201–231.

McCarthey, S.J. (1998). Constructing multiple subjectivities in classroom literacy contexts. *Research in the Teaching of English, 32*, 126–160.

McCarthey, S.J., & Moje, E.B. (2002). Identity matters. *Reading Research Quarterly, 37*(2).

McKenna, M.C., Kear, D.J., & Ellsworth, R.A. (1995). Children's attitudes toward reading: A national survey. *Reading Research Quarterly, 30*, 934–956.

McNeil, L. (1986). *Contradictions of control: School structure and school knowledge*. New York: Routledge.

Mead, G.H. (1934). *Mind, self, and society from the standpoint of a social behaviorist*. Chicago: University of Chicago Press.

Merriam, S.B. (1998). *Case study research in education: A qualitative approach*. San Francisco: Jossey Bass.

Michaels, S. (1987). Text and context: A new approach to the study of classroom writing. *Discourse processes, 10*, 321–346.

Mishler, E.G. (1999). *Storylines: Craftartists' narratives of identity*. Cambridge, MA: Harvard University Press.

Moll, L., & Gonzalez, N. (1994). Lessons from research with language-minority children. *Journal of Reading Behavior: A Journal of Literacy, 26*(4), 439–456.

Morson, G.S., & Emerson, C. (1990). *Mikhail Bakhtin: Creation of a prosaics*. Stanford, CA: Stanford University Press.

National Center for Research on Teacher Education. (1988). *Dialogues in teacher education* (Issue paper 88–4). East Lansing, MI: Michigan State University.

Nieto, S. (2002). *Language, culture, and teaching*. Mahwah, NJ: Erlbaum.

Noddings, N. (1992). *The challenge to care in schools*. New York: Teachers College Press.

Patton, M. (1980). *Qualitative research methods*. Beverly Hills, CA: Sage.

Phelps, S., & Weaver, D. (1999). Public and personal voices in adolescents' classroom talk. *Journal of Literacy Research, 31*, 321–354.

Reyes, M.D. (1991). A process approach to literacy instruction for Spanish-speaking students: In search of a best fit. In E. Hiebert (Ed.), *Literacy for a diverse society: Perspectives, practices, and policies* (pp. 157–171). New York: Teachers College Press.

Rodino, A., Gimbert, C., Perez, C., Craddock-Willis, K., & McCabe, A. (1991, October). *Getting your point across: Contrastive sequencing in low-income African American and Latino children's narrative*. Paper presented at the 16th Annual Conference on Language Development, Boston University, Boston, MA.

Routman, R. (1991). *Invitations: Changing as teachers and learners K–12*. Portsmouth, NH: Heinemann.

Sailors, M., Worthy, J., Assaf, L., & Mast, M. (2000, December). *Judging a book by its color: Students' perceptions of participation in Accelerated Reader*. Paper presented at the annual meeting of the National Reading Conference, Scottsdale, AZ.

Sarup, M. (1996). *Identity, culture, and the postmodern world*. Athens, GA: University of Georgia Press.

Sleeter, C. (1995). Curriculum controversies in multicultural education. In E. Flaxman & H. Passow (Eds.), *Changing populations changing schools* (Ninety-fourth yearbook of the National Society for the Study of Education, pp. 162–185). Chicago: University of Chicago Press.

Tatum, B. (1997). *"Why are all the black kids sitting together in the cafeteria?"* New York: Basic Books.

Templeton, S. (1986). Metalinguistic awareness: A synthesis and beyond. In D.B. Yaden, Jr. & S. Templeton (Eds.), *Metalinguistic awareness and beginning literacy: Conceptualizing what it means to read and write* (pp. 293–309). Portsmouth, NH: Heinemann.

Vygotsky, L.S. (1978). *Mind in society: The development of higher psychological processes.* (M. Cole, V. John-Steiner, S. Scribner, & E. Souberman, Eds. and Trans.). Cambridge: Harvard University Press. (Original work published 1934)

Weiler, J.D. (2000). *Codes and contradictions: Race, gender identity, and schooling.* Albany, NY: State University of New York Press.

Wertsch, J.V. (1991). *Voices of the mind.* Cambridge, MA: Harvard University Press.

Willis, A.I. (1995). Reading the world of school literacy: Contextualizing the experience of a young African American male. *Harvard Educational Review, 65*(1), 30–49.

Willis, P. (1977). *Learning to labor: How working class kids get working class jobs.* New York: Columbia University Press.

Yon, D.A. (2000). *Elusive culture: Schooling, race, and identity in global times.* Albany, NY: State University of New York Press.

Young, J.P. (1998). Discussion as a practice of carnival. In D. Alvermann, K. Hinchman, D. Moore, S. Phelps, & D. Waff (Eds.), *Reconceptualizing the literacies in adolescents' lives* (pp. 247–264). Mahwah, NJ: Erlbaum.

Children's Literature References

Conrad, P. (1991). *Pedro's journal: A voyage with Christopher Columbus, August 3, 1492–February 14, 1493.* Honesdale, PA: Caroline House.

Dahl, R. (1961). *James and the giant peach: A children's story.* New York: Knopf.

Jacques, B. (1986). *Redwall.* New York: Philomel.

Key, A. (1989). *The forgotten door.* New York: Scholastic.

Matas, C. (1992). *Adventure in Legoland.* Markham, ON: Scholastic.

Penner, L.R. (1991). *Eating the plates.* New York: Simon & Schuster.

Price, L. (1990). *Aida.* San Diego: Harcourt Brace Jovanovich.

Reeves, N. (1993). *Into the mummy's tomb: The real life discovery of Tutankhamun's treasures.* New York: Scholastic.

Shepard, A. (1995). *The baker's dozen: A Saint Nicholas tale.* New York: Atheneum.

Snyder, Z.K. (1986). *The Egypt game.* New York: Dell.

Soto, G. (1992). *The skirt.* New York: Delacorte.

Spinelli, J. (1990). *Maniac Magee.* New York: Harper Trophy.

Taylor, M. (1976). *Roll of thunder, hear my cry.* New York: Bantam.

Tolkien, J.R.R. (1974). *Lord of the rings.* Boston: Houghton Mifflin.

Author Index

A

ABBOTT, J., 20, 131
ALVERMANN, D.E., 133
ANDERSON, E., 133
ANZALDÚA, G., 12, 122, 131
ARONOWITZ, S., 6, 12, 86, 106, 123, 131
ASSAF, L., 106, 135
ATHANESES, S., 127, 131
ATWELL, N., 25, 88, 131
AU, K., 17–18, 121, 127, 131

B

BAKHTIN, M.M., 12–14, 29–30, 40, 58–59, 84, 95, 103, 114, 123, 131
BAQUEDANO-LOPEZ, P., 15, 133
BELSEY, C., 12–13, 131
BERNSTEIN, B., 17, 131
BIGGERS, D., 106, 131
BLAKE, B.E., 16, 131
BORKO, H., 19, 132
BOURDIEU, P., 14, 109–111, 116, 132

C

CALKINS, L.M., 17, 25, 31–32, 119, 123, 132
CANADY, C., 19, 132
CAZDEN, C.B., 79, 117, 120, 132
CHERLAND, M.R., 16, 132
CHERRY, R., 19, 132
COCHRAN-SMITH, M., 121, 125, 132

W

Y

Subject Index

Page references followed by *f* indicate figures.

B

C

144

G

GAMES, 73

GREG (HILLSIDE SCHOOL STUDENT), 73–79; background, 116; identity, 84–85; journal excerpts, 75–77; literacy practices, 76–78; resistance to classroom expectations, 110–113; teacher relationships, 117–118; as writer, 84–85

H

HABITUS, 14

"HALF TRUTH-HALF FICTION" WRITING, 114

HILLSIDE SCHOOL, TEXAS SITE, 23–25, 63, 122, 128; books and related tasks, 65–68; classroom literacy activities, 64–65; classroom observations, 24; parent interviews, 25; researcher's stance at, 28; student selection and data collection, 24; student work, 25; teacher selection and data collection, 24; teacher-student relationships, 117; writing workshop, 120–121

HYBRID TEXT, 59

HYBRID VOICE, 114

I

IDENTITY, 1–7; blending of, 61; clashing of, 61; construction of, 12–14, 130; definition of, 12–13; importance of, 70; literate, 72, 107–113; providing opportunities for exploring, 129–130; reconsiderations, 11–13; in theory, research, and practice, 9–30. *See also* student identities

IDEOLOGICAL POWER, 15

INNER SPEECH, 13

INSTRUCTION: literature-based, 17–19

INTERNALLY PERSUASIVE DISCOURSE, 14, 30, 58, 103

INTO THE MUMMY'S TOMB'S (REEVES), 81

INVISIBLE PEDAGOGIES, 16–17

J

JAMES AND THE GIANT PEACH (DAHL), 66, 71, 76, 82

JEFFREY (STUDENT), 128

JENNIFER (VALLEY SCHOOL STUDENT), 91–95; appropiation of classroom norms by, 108–109; identity, 104; literacy practices, 93–95; as reader, 104; RR book selection by, 93; teacher relationships, 118; as writer, 104

JOURNAL WRITING, 32, 34; notebook excerpts, 34; questions for, 90; rationale for, 32; response log excerpts, 80–82; student excerpts, 75–77, 102–103

JUSTICE, SOCIAL, 79–84, 102

L

LANGUAGE: in classroom, 15; colorful, 65; as "identity kit," 13; inner speech, 13; power and, 15; role in identity construction, 13–14

LATINO/A STUDENTS, 99; appropiation of classroom norms by, 109; backgrounds of, 116, 121; Hillside School, Texas site, 24; importance of identity as, 70; NYC site, 23, 31; Valley School, Texas site, 26

LE BLANC, MS. (TEACHER), 26, 87–88, 121; assumptions and expectations, 124; concerns about Reading Renaissance program, 91; fifth-grade language arts program, 88–89; goals, 89–90; reading workshops, 88–89; student relationships, 118; views of students, 94, 96, 101, 108

LEARNING: about students, 22

LETTER WRITING: student samples, 55–56, 97

LIMINAL SPACE, 59

LITERACY: assumptions about, 124–126; classroom activities, 64–65; classroom practices, 16–17; communities of effective practice, 121; home practices, 115–116; identity in, 9–30; maternal interest in, 101; student practices, 35–39, 41–48, 51–57, 69–72, 76–78, 80–83, 93–98, 101–103

LITERATE IDENTITIES, 72; students' constructions of, 107–113

LITERATURE-BASED CURRICULUM: teacher enactments of, 119–124

LITERATURE-BASED INSTRUCTION, 17–19

LITERATURE-BASED MULTIAGE CLASSROOMS, 63–86

LUCAS (VALLEY SCHOOL STUDENT), 95–99, 105–106; background, 116; book selection, 97–98; handwriting, 96; identity, 103–105; literacy practices, 96–98; as reader, 103–105; resistance to classroom expectations, 110–113; as writer, 103–105; writing samples, 97

M

MANDY (HILLSIDE SCHOOL STUDENT), 79–84; identity as writer, 84–85; literacy practices, 80–83; teacher relationships, 118; transforming expectations through text, 114–115

MANIAC MAGEE (SPINELLI), 88–89; journal questions for, 90

MARTIN, MS. (TEACHER), 24, 65; reading-response sessions, 67

MEYER, MS. (TEACHER), 31–33; assumptions and expectations, 124; identity of, 60; interviews with, 44–45, 50–51; notes to students, 34; student conferences, 34, 37, 42–44, 51–52; student relationships, 117; student views of, 37; views of students, 108; as "white middle-class gatekeeper," 111

MIGUEL (NYC STUDENT), 33–40, 59; appropiation of classroom norms by, 108–110; background, 116; interviews with, 37–38; literacy practices, 35–39; notebook excerpts, 34; teacher notes, 34; teacher relationships, 117; writing conferences, 37; writing sample, 38–39

MORRIS AND MARSHA, P.I. (ELLA), 49

MULTIAGE CLASSROOMS: literature-based, 63–86

N

P

R

workshop and Reading Renaissance, 87–106; to teacher expectations, 40–49; in writing workshop, 31–61

RESPONSE LOGS: excerpts, 80–82

RETELLING IN ONE'S OWN WORDS, 13–14, 29

RITA (HILLSIDE SCHOOL STUDENT), 68–73; appropiation of classroom norms by, 108–110; background, 116; identity, 84–85; literacy practices, 69–72; portfolio evaluation, 71; teacher relationships, 117; as writer, 84–85; writing samples, 70

ROLL OF THUNDER, HEAR MY CRY (TAYLOR), 88–89, 94, 96, 114

S

SAMPLING: purposeful, 22

SECOND LANGUAGE STUDENTS, 98

SINGLE-VOICED DISCOURSE, 14

THE SKIRT (SOTO), 91

SOCIAL CONTEXTS, 107–130

SOCIAL DISCOURSE, 13–14; assimilation of, 29

SOCIAL JUSTICE, 82, 102; transformation through, 79–84

SPACE INTERESTS, 97

SPANISH: appropriating classroom norms in, 68–73. See also Latino/a students

SPEECH: inner, 13

STUDENT IDENTITIES: construction of, 12; context and, 2–3; developing as writers, 58–61; as readers, 103–106; reconstruction of, 30; as writers, 84–86, 103–106

STUDENT NOTEBOOKS: excerpts, 34; rationale for, 32; response log excerpts, 80–82. See also journal writing

STUDENT SELECTION AND DATA COLLECTION: Hillside School, Texas site, 24; New York City site, 23; Valley School, Texas site, 26–27

STUDENT WORK: Hillside School, Texas site, 25; New York City site, 23; Valley School, Texas site, 27

STUDENTS, 126–128; backgrounds of, 116–117, 126–128; constructions of literate identities, 107–113; fiction writing by, 50–51; interactions with norms and expectations of teachers, 29–30; interviews excerpts, 37–38; learning about, 22; responses to classrooms, 30; social contexts, 107–130; teacher-student relationships, 117–119; views of reading and writing, 19–20

STUDENT-TEACHER CONFERENCES: reading-response sessions, 66–67; writing conferences, 37, 42–44, 51–52, 54–55

T

TAAS. See Texas Assessment of Academic Skills

TEACHER SCRIPTS, 30

THE
RIVER
QUEEN

GILBERT MORRIS

THE
RIVER
QUEEN

A WATER WHEEL
NOVEL

B&H
PUBLISHING GROUP
NASHVILLE, TENNESSEE

Copyright © 2011 by Gilbert Morris
All rights reserved.
Printed in the United States of America

978-1-4336-7320-7

Published by B&H Publishing Group,
Nashville, Tennessee

Dewey Decimal Classification: F
Subject Heading: LOVE STORIES \
STEAMBOATS—FICTION \
MISSISSIPPI RIVER—FICTION

1 2 3 4 5 6 7 8 • 16 15 14 13 12 11

Chapter One

The snowstorm that had taken Natchez by surprise kept the temperatures well below freezing outside the family home of Charles Ashby. Fires bloomed in every room. Upstairs, in Julienne Ashby's bedroom, the logs shifted and sent a myriad of sparks up the chimney. The heat-crackle of the wood made a cheerful sound in the room as it wafted out comforting waves of warmth. Julienne's room was very feminine, full of flower brocades, oval-framed pictures, and mirrors. Three light, comfortable dressing chairs were set about to be both ornamental and useful. A double bed stood in the center of the room made up with clean sheets, a crisp white bolster, and a wine-colored eiderdown comforter that was pillow-thick. Set off in an angle of the room, an ornately carved mahogany washstand bore a delicate French porcelain pitcher and washbowl.

Now, however, a streak of mud went up one side of the satin-covered comforter, leading to a large dirty stain in the middle of the cover, and seated cross-legged in the middle of that stain was ten-year-old Carley Jeanne Ashby. She watched her sister Julienne as she went through the long and tedious process of dressing for a shopping excursion. Carley was a pretty girl, with long, curly red-gold hair, wide blue eyes, and a fresh peaches-and-cream complexion. She was small for her age, but she was energetic and had a strong constitution, which was a good thing since she was an incurable tomboy. Today her frilled dark-blue dress was relatively clean, as she had been wearing a heavy wool cape outside, but her pantalettes were caked with filthy mud, her hands were dirty, one of her pigtails had a dirt clod in it, and there was a streak of mud across one blooming cheek.

"Carley Jeanne Ashby," Julienne said with mild amusement, "you are positively filthy. What on earth have you been doing? Plowing?"

Turning, Julienne huddled close to the fireplace. She had just put on her winter pantalettes and chemise—commonly pronounced "shimmy"—and shivering, she pulled on her heavy wool dressing gown again. She was a lovely woman of twenty-three, tall and slender, but with a womanly figure. Like her sister, she had inherited her gorgeous thick red-gold hair from her mother, but she had wide, very dark eyes and velvety lashes, somewhat startling with her fair hair and complexion. "Where is Tyla?" she asked herself with some irritation. "I can't possibly lace up my corset by myself."

But Carley ignored this and repeated loudly, "Plowing? 'Course not, 'cause I don't have a mule. I've been collecting rocks. Want to see them?" When Carley Jeanne had been six years old, she had taken a straw bag from their cook, Mam Dooley, that was used for carrying vegetables from market. Carley had rarely been without the bag since then, and now it was old and frayed and permanently stained, but still she carried her "treasures" in it. These could be anything from rocks to wildflowers to bugs to fishing worms.

"No, darling, I'll look at your rocks some other time," Julienne answered. "So you escaped from lessons again, I take it."

"Aunt Leah doesn't care," Carley said dismissively.

"You're going to be an ignorant hooligan," Julienne said absently, then went to the door, flung it open impatiently, and started to shout, "Ty—Oh. Here you are."

"Here I am," Tyla said, rolling her eyes. "I just now finished ironing these sleeves, Miss Julienne."

"Oh, yes, I forgot. Lay the dress out, Tyla, and help me get into this corset," Julienne ordered.

Tyla went over to Julienne's bed and sighed as she saw the big dirty spot, and the small dirty child, in the middle of the bed.

"I've been collecting rocks," Carley told her helpfully. "That's why I'm so dirty."

"Could you go be dirty somewhere else, please?" Tyla asked.

"No, I don't want to. I want to watch Julienne dress. When am I going to get a shape like you, Julienne? Darcy said I look like a fence picket."

"Little girls are supposed to look like fence pickets," Julienne said, pulling her corset over her head. The crisscross lacings on the back hung loose. "You won't get a womanly shape until you're older."

"How old?"

"A lot older. Tyla, just lay the dress on one of the chairs and come help me."

"Yes, miss," Tyla answered obediently. Tyla, whose name was actually Twyla, had been brought to the Ashby household when she was a newborn baby. Her grandmother, Old Mam, had been Julienne's and her brother Darcy's nurse. Twyla's mother, Old Mam's daughter, had died in childbirth, and Charles Ashby had agreed to let Old Mam bring Twyla to live with them and raise her with his own children. Julienne, at three years of age, had called her "Tyla" and the name had stuck. Tyla had grown up with the older Ashby children, but when she turned thirteen she became sixteen-year-old Julienne's maid. Now she was a petite black woman of twenty, with a beautiful smile and a modest demeanor.

With one last regretful look at Julienne's filthy comforter, she laid the dress on a side chair and came to tighten the laces of Julienne's corset, while she held onto the bedpost.

"Unh," Julienne grunted. "I knew I shouldn't have eaten that dish of kidneys for breakfast."

"Ecch," Carley said. "Kidneys. You're silly to tie yourself all up tight like that, Julienne. You've already got a shape."

"When you have one, you'll understand and you'll tie yourself all up, too," Julienne retorted. "What's all this talk about a shape, anyway?"

"I was talking to my friend Denise Hopgood about it. Denise's sister is fourteen and she doesn't have a shape yet. We're worried," Carley told her solemnly.

"Carley, find something else to worry about," Julienne said, managing a smile between grunts as Tyla yanked the corset lacings hard. Finally the corset was fastened, and Julienne had a nineteen-inch waist. Quickly Tyla picked up three petti-coats, a linen, a cotton, and a woolen, pulled them over Julienne's head and tied them around her waist. Leaning against the wall was Julienne's hoop underskirt, collapsed into concentric rings. Tyla laid it down on the floor and Julienne stepped into the center ring. Rising, Tyla pulled the crinoline up as it ballooned out, a series of very light steel rings cov-ered with crisp cotton, widening out to a full bell shape.

Carley watched, fascinated. "Why can't I have one of those?"

"Because, Miss Carley, you won't even keep your petticoats on if you can shuck them without your mother or your aunt noticing," Tyla said sternly. "Whyever would you want to wear a hoop skirt?"

"I don't want to wear it," Carley answered impatiently. "I want to put it on and swing it back and forth and play like I'm a big bell. Or I could put it up outside, on sticks, and make a tent. Or maybe I could hang it from a tree and get under it and pretend like I'm in the clouds."

Shocked, Tyla said, "It's underclothes, Miss Carley. You can't have underclothes outside flapping in the breeze for everyone to see!"

"If that's the most shocking thing she ever does, I'll be amazed," Julienne said. "Oh, I do love this new outfit!"

The dress was made of chocolate brown velvet, with the wide skirt gathered so tightly that it was richly voluminous. The bodice had an open corsage, with a blouse front of ecru satin jean with tiny pleats. The high button collar folded down over a string tie of chocolate brown grosgrain. The sleeves were wide, with a wide ruffle of the ecru satin ruffle at the wrist. Her long cape-jacket was triple-tiered, of the same chocolate brown velvet with wide grosgrain trim on the three flounces. Julienne had her milliner make her a deep bonnet of the velvet, with ecru satin ruffles framing her face.

Now she sat at her dressing table, a wide oval table with a ruffled cotton tablecloth covering it, and a hinged mirror atop. Tyla began to brush Julienne's hair and arrange it into a modest chignon so her bonnet would fit over it.

Carley studied the dress crumpled into a corner, thrown carelessly there by Julienne. It was a dark green with a flounced skirt and had a matching tartan shawl, also thrown on top of the dress. "I don't understand why you have to change clothes, Julienne. That dress you were wearing was pretty."

"That's a morning dress, for receiving calls," Julienne told her. "Now that I'm going shopping, I have to change into heavy winter underthings and an afternoon promenade dress."

Carley grinned. "Oooh, receiving calls! Did Archie-BALD come mooning around again?"

"Carley! His name is Archibald, and you know very well that his friends call him Archie. But you're just a little girl, and you're supposed to call him Mr. Leggett," Julienne scolded. "And where did you hear that? 'Mooning around'?"

"You said it," Carley said smartly. "I heard you tell Tyla that yesterday, when Archie-Bald called on you yesterday morning."

"Oh. Well, you shouldn't be eavesdropping on people's private conversations."

"I was sitting right here when you said it. I didn't know I was eavesdropping. Are you going to marry Archie-Bald?"

Julienne gave a careless half-shrug. "He'd like for me to, but somehow I don't think I could bear listening to him droning on and on forever about business. After awhile it's somewhat like having a hum in your ear. HMMMMMMMMM."

Carley joined in. "HMMMMMMMM. That's Archie-Bald. Not like Etienne. Etienne's fun. Why don't you marry him, Julienne? He calls on you all the time too. He must like you a lot."

Tyla finished Julienne's hair, went to pick up her half-boots, and knelt to put them on her.

Julienne was smiling, a dreamy, private softening of her lips. "Oh, Etienne. I know he admires me, but it's obvious that he has to marry a woman with money to support him in his chosen lifestyle, which is extravagant."

"What's estravagant?" Carley demanded.

"EXtravagant. It means that Etienne needs a lot of money for his clothes, his horses, his jewelry, and a fine house."

Carley nodded. "I know, like you and Darcy. But I like Etienne. He always picks me up and swings me around and calls me *cherie*. And he doesn't make me leave the parlor like Archie-Bald does when you come in. I know Etienne likes you a lot, Julienne, because at our last party I saw him kiss you when you went out into the garden—"

"What? What?" Tyla snapped, her eyes wide.

"Never mind that, Carley, you talk too much," Julienne said hastily. "Besides, when you're a little older you'll learn that men like Etienne are not serious suitors. Etienne is just a tease."

Tying up the laces on one half-boot, her head down, Tyla said quietly, "And some people may say such things about you too, Miss Julienne."

"Why, Tyla?" Carley asked curiously. "Who's Julienne teasing?"

"Mr. Leggett, for one," Tyla answered. "And he's sure not the first."

Far from being displeased, Julienne laughed. "Tyla, you prattle on far too much about my reputation. Ever since you had that religious experience, or whatever you call it, you've been so holier-than-thou."

Tyla looked as if she might argue for a moment, but then her expression softened. "I'm so sorry, Miss Julienne, I don't mean to be that way. I just worry about you. I don't want you to be known in town as a light woman. And I know that if you could just draw closer to the Lord Jesus, you'd understand better what I'm saying and why I worry." She pulled the laces on the left shoe tight, and it snapped. "Oh, dear. If you'll wait just one minute, Miss Julienne, I can pull this lace out and repair it."

"No, no. Just take these boots and throw them away, Tyla. Go get me the other boots, the Balmorals. I should be wearing brown leather with this outfit anyway."

Tyla looked up at her with dismay. "But Miss Julienne, these boots cost six dollars! It will be easy for me to fix this lace, and then when we go to town, I'll get new laces."

"No, Tyla," Julienne said with a hint of impatience. "I am not going to town in tatters, it's silly. I like the new Balmoral high boot style better anyway. I'll stop by our bootmakers and order a new pair in black leather with suede uppers. As I said, just throw those away."

With clear hesitation Tyla unlaced the other boot, then stood slowly, staring down at them. They were ankle boots, made of the finest, softest leather, with a small heel.

Eyeing her, Julienne asked, "Do you want them? If they fit, of course you can have them, Tyla. Now, hurry, please, I know Father is getting impatient, waiting for me."

Tyla hurried out of the bedroom and Julienne turned back to the mirror to pat her hair. Soon Tyla returned with the Balmoral boots, which had a higher upper that reached to mid-shin. Kneeling again, she put them on Julienne, then stood and fluffed out her wide skirts.

"Thank you, Tyla, now why don't you go and get your hat and cloak."

Tyla left again and Carley asked, "Why doesn't Tyla have to change clothes to go shopping? She's still wearing the same dress she's had on all day."

"She's just a servant, Carley, they're not like us." Julienne came over to the bed and reached down to take Carley's hand. "Come on up—Oh, Carley, your hand is freezing! Why, your feet aren't just dirty, they're wet!"

"I know. I'm cold."

"Silly girl. Anyone else would catch their death. Oh, Tyla, Carley is chilled through and through. Please go get Libby and tell her that Carley's got to have a hot bath. Then come on out. By that time the carriage will be ready."

NATCHEZ, MISSISSIPPI, IN THIS year of 1855, was the oldest town on the Mississippi River, and could arguably be said to be the most important port on that major artery of American commerce. In the eighteenth century Natchez was the starting point of the Natchez Trace, the old Indian path that led from this city on the river all the way up to Nashville, Tennessee, and the Big Muddy was the cause of all of that traffic. Men from all over the Ohio Valley transported their goods on flatboats to Natchez, sold everything including their rough rafts for lumber, and took the Trace back to their homes, either walking or by wagon. The little town of Natchez began to grow as the port commerce increased, and all of the merchants that bought and sold from the "Kaintocks," as they called the flatboat men, prospered. They began to cultivate the little outpost of Natchez into a tidy, well-ordered middle-class merchant town.

Later, when Robert Fulton invented his steam-powered boat, and through hybridization, cotton transformed from a hard-to-grow crop in the South to King Cotton, Natchez suddenly turned into a gracious, elegant city for rich planters, who built block after block of fine Greek Revival mansions on the high bluffs above the river. By 1855 the population of Natchez was about five thousand, so it was dwarfed by the huge sprawling cities of New York, Baltimore, and Boston; but Natchez had more millionaires by percentage than any other city in America. Natchez was a lovely small city, well-manicured and orderly, and it was strictly for the rich.

The merchant district reflected this refined strata of society, too. As Julienne looked out the window of their fine brougham carriage, she was satisfied to see that all of the sidewalks had been swept of snow, and were immaculate. The seven-block stretch of Main Street that held the shops consisted mainly of dignified brick establishments, with sparkling windows and tasteful displays.

"Father, I have to go to my dressmaker's, Mrs. Fenner's, my milliner's, my shoemaker's, my glover's, and, and, where else, Tyla? I forget," Julienne said.

"Confectioner's," Tyla prompted her. "Remember, that's the only way you could get Miss Carley into a hot bath. You promised her you'd get her some candy."

"Yes, confectioner's. What about you, Father? Where are you going?"

Charles Ashby, seated across from them, looked at Julienne and frowned. He was a handsome man, with thick silver hair and patrician features, tall and with a dignified, erect posture. "I have to go to the bank and see Preston Gates."

"Again?" Julienne said with exasperation. "Papa, you're always so upset after you meet with him. Why don't you two just exchange letters or something?"

"Julienne, I keep trying to tell you that handling our finances is not something you can manage by just exchanging polite notes. And why are you going on this shopping excursion? Didn't you just have half a dozen new dresses delivered yesterday?"

"Yes, and this is one of them," Julienne said, spreading out her rich velvet skirt. "Isn't it beautiful? Don't you like it?"

"I like it very much, and you look beautiful in it, as usual," Charles said with clear affection. "But that's just my point. Why are you visiting every merchant in town when you just got in a lot of new clothes, all of which I know you will look lovely in?"

Julienne laughed, a light, girlish giggle that made even her rather stern father smile. "Silly Papa, I'm not visiting every merchant in town! I just want to do my final fittings for my evening ensemble for the party tomorrow night. And if everything's ready, I want to go ahead and pick them up instead of having them delivered."

Charles's mouth drew into a tight line. "Julienne, I thought we had settled this. This party tomorrow night is not really the sort of thing that you should be attending. It's more of a business engagement, for men. I was under the impression that you understood that."

"I do understand that, but the invitation was for 'Charles Ashby and Family' and besides, Archie is going to come with us and be my escort. He's so staid and proper, anyone with the least hint of impropriety about them would probably freeze solid in his presence."

"So you manipulated Leggett into letting you drag him along for appearance's sake," Charles said. "I give up. Just please, Julienne, try to remember that money is tight. Maybe you don't need any more clothes for awhile."

"Of course, Papa," Julienne said happily. "Just this dress. And, of course, the gloves and matching shoes. Oh, and I simply must have new black leather boots, and I had ordered three new winter bonnets, so they're already done and paid for."

"Not really," Charles muttered.

Ignoring his dour looks, Julienne said, "Here's Mrs. Fenner's, and Tyla and I can walk on down the street to the other shops. Then we'll just come all the way down to the bank and meet you, all right, Papa?"

"All right, Julienne," he said. "Just please don't dawdle, I hope my business with Mr. Gates won't take too long."

PLANTER'S BANK WAS AN imposing two-story edifice of red brick and black shutters on the precisely spaced double-six windows. In previous years, when

Charles Ashby had been in the flush of prosperity, he had thought that the bank looked dignified and respectable. In the last couple of years, however, as his fortunes had steadily declined, he began to think that it seemed forbidding. As he went through the enormous double front doors, of six-inch-thick walnut blackened with age, he felt almost as if he was entering a prison.

Regardless of his true financial status, and his private musings, Charles Ashby was still regarded as one of Natchez's elite, one of the aristocratic cotton planter class, and the president's clerk looked up and recognized him immediately. A small, stooped man with tiny spectacles and thinning hair stood up from his desk, hurried through the swinging wooden gate, and came to greet him. "Mr. Ashby, how good it is to see you again. Are you here to see Mr. Gates?"

"Yes, I am. Is he available?"

"Of course, sir, please just step this way and I'll let him know that you're here."

Charles followed him past the waiting area, and perhaps for the first time, he really looked at the people sitting there. They were dressed poorly, in rough plain clothing, and most of them looked worried. Three women were there, their faces pale and drawn, obviously widows, wearing black clothing and bonnets. One of them looked as if she had been weeping, clutching a worn reticule with gnarled work-ridden hands. A sudden vision of his wife Roseann sitting there, weeping and aged, rose in his mind and filled Charles's mind with black dread. When he went into the president's office, his face was grim.

Preston Gates was a small man, no more than five-six. He dressed as the president of a successful bank should, as his father and his grandfather had, with plain black coats, either a gray or black waistcoat, shiny brass buttons, a gold watch and chain, and iron-creased black trousers. He had black hair, a full beard closely trimmed, and sharp black eyes. Coming around his big oak desk, he extended his hand and said, "Good day, Charles, it's good to see you. Please, come sit down."

Instead of indicating one of the straight chairs in front of his desk, Gates led Charles to one corner of his office, where two comfortable armchairs were drawn up underneath the great windows that looked out over the neat and manicured public square. Between the chairs was a tea table with an Astral lamp with a hand-cut bellflower glass shade, a beautiful wooden box, and a marble ashtray. As they settled into the chairs, he asked, "Cigar? Brand-new investment of mine, imports from Hispaniola. I think you'll find they're much superior to American tobacco."

"No, thanks," Charles said, and shifted uneasily in his chair as Gates lit his cigar.

Gates puffed and puffed and rank smoke filled the air. Squinting through it, he asked, "How's the family, Charles?"

"They're fine, thank you, Preston. But this isn't a social call, it's business, I'm afraid."

Gates nodded as if he knew this. "So what can I do for you?"

"As soon as this last cold spell is over, we're ready to start tilling and fertilizing the plantation. Hopefully we'll be able to plant the first few weeks of March."

"Of course. This snowstorm was a freak of weather. Very unusual for the last of February. But it shouldn't delay planting more than a week or two."

"I hope and pray not," Charles said with grim emphasis. "But the problem is, Preston, that I've gone over and over the finances for both the plantation and my investments, and the returns on neither of them are enough for me to finance the planting this spring."

With deliberation Gates removed the cigar from his mouth, held it between his thumb and two fingers, and stared at it. "I'm not at all surprised, Charles. You know very well that I have tried, in the friendliest manner possible, to stress that you have made some disastrous decisions over the last few years. In fact, what started this decline in your situation is when you freed all of your slaves. With paid labor there is simply no way for you to realize a good profit on your cotton. Your expenses are too high. No other plantation owner has paid field labor."

"I know that," Charles said quietly. "You've been telling me that ever since I freed them four years ago. And you know my answer to that. When the Lord Jesus saved my soul, and I learned about the love of God, I realized that it was very wrong to enslave other human beings. I can't do it, I won't do it. And I believed—believe—that the Lord will bless me for it."

"As a matter of fact, that may be true in the case of your plantation, Charles," Gates agreed. "Your yield is always amazingly high, with little loss to pestilence, and that's very unusual. Though your profit margin is smaller compared to plantations with slave labor, Ashby Plantation is still a wealth-producing enterprise."

"But it's not enough," Charles said worriedly. "Not even with the return on my investments."

"Again, I tried to warn you last winter not to use the principal for household expenses. Your investment account is down to less than a thousand dollars, Charles. No amount of interest on that small sum is going to cover your expenses. And that's the real rub, isn't it? You and your family are accustomed to a very expensive lifestyle. At this point there is nothing you can do except cut down your costs."

Charles rose and went to stand in front of the wide window. He stared, unseeing, down at the spiky sculptures of the old oak, elm, and maple trees surrounding the square. His wide, normally squared shoulders were stooped. "When we had this same conversation last year, I was determined to do just that. To cut down on our expenses, our extravagances. But somehow . . ." His voice trailed off faintly.

A regretful expression flitted across Preston Gate's face, but it was quickly replaced by his neutral professional demeanor. Charles Ashby was a third generation patron of Planter's Bank, and the Gates and Ashby families had been friends for all those years. But business was business. "I understand, Charles. However, this year you have no choice."

"I know. But Preston, the accounts that I have outstanding right now are becoming pressing and I'm completely out of ready cash."

Evenly Gates said, "I'm aware of that."

Charles turned to look at him, his eyes narrowed. "Are you? Then I assume that you've paid more than just a passing attention to my affairs. So you know very well the predicament I'm in."

Gates nodded. "It's my job, Charles."

Wearily, as if he were much older than his fifty-four years, Charles shuffled back to his chair and slumped into it. "Then you know that I've come to ask for a loan."

"Yes, I know, and I know that it will have to be a sizable one, to get you up-to-date on your existing obligations and to finance spring planting. And, of course, enough to tide you over until harvest, hopefully at a smaller monthly outlay than your past expenses. I estimate that you'll need at least twenty thousand dollars."

"That's what I had in mind," Charles said numbly.

Gates stubbed out his cigar, then moved to seat himself behind his desk. It was a clear transition from a friendly conversation to a purely business discussion. He took a folder from the top of a stack on his desk, opened it, perused it for a few moments, then looked up.

"Charles, the Board of Directors will not approve a personal loan for you without some assurance. They will, however, offer you a twenty thousand dollar mortgage on Ashby Plantation, only because of the reasons we were just discussing: it is a highly profitable working plantation.

"The term of the mortgage will be for ten years. We will allow you a monthly draw; we can't offer you the entire amount of the mortgage outright. However, your repayments will not start until October, when you should start realizing the profits on your harvest. But for this consideration we will demand a higher rate of interest. Ten percent."

Charles jumped out of his chair and paced back and forth, his head down. Absently he rubbed his left hand with his right. "Mortgage the plantation? But the Ashbys have owned that land outright for four generations, we've never had to borrow against it!"

Gates merely watched him expressionlessly.

After pacing nervously for a few minutes, he came again to the window and seemed to wilt, his shoulders bowing again, his head drooping. "All right, Preston. I'll take the mortgage on those terms."

Gates's voice gave away the first signs of emotion. "If there's anything at all I can do, Preston, any way that I can help you, please let me know."

Charles turned and came to stand in front of his desk, and Gates rose. "Thank you, Preston, but you've been very helpful already, I realize." He straightened up and stuck out his hand, and Gates shook it heartily.

"The papers will be ready tomorrow, Charles. And the money, of course," Gates said. "Just drop by to see me any time."

Charles nodded and went to the door. "You're a good friend, Preston. I thank the Lord for you. I'll see you tomorrow."

CHAPTER TWO

Julienne stood on a footstool in her bedroom. Sitting on the floor, her mother squinted as she sewed one of the bottom ruffles of Julienne's ball gown. "Now, Julienne, how in the world did this get torn again? Tyla said something about Carley."

"That little monkey was prancing around, pretending to dance with me, and she stepped on the ruffle and it tore," Julienne answered.

Seated in the corner, rubbing one of Julienne's gloves vigorously with sparkling mineral water, Tyla muttered, "And she got black licorice all over your gloves. That child is as wild as a wood squirrel."

"Oh, it's just a spot. I know you can get it out, Tyla," Julienne said carelessly.

"Julienne, you did not buy her black licorice again," Roseann said with distress. "You know how

22

I hate that candy. It makes her teeth and fingers all black."

"It's the only kind she likes, Mother. Besides, you didn't see her with black teeth, did you?"

"No, but just because she hides from me and Leah after she eats it doesn't make it any better," Roseann said. "I just don't know what to do with her, she doesn't pay attention to a word I say." With an impatient gesture she pushed back a lock of red-gold hair that had fallen in front of her eyes. Now forty-nine years old, she retained a youthful beauty, with her fine complexion and abundant red-gold hair. She was a small-framed woman, very feminine and fragile-looking.

"Are you all right, Mother?" Julienne asked. "If you're tired please let Tyla finish."

"No, no, I'm just finishing now." She put in two tiny lock stitches, then fluffed out the ruffle. "There. Not a stitch shows," she said proudly. Roseann was an excellent seamstress and enjoyed all kinds of needlework. With an effort she tried to get up, but Tyla hurried to help her rise.

Stepping down from the stool, Julienne made a little turn and mock curtsey to her mother. "Thank you so much, Mother. Isn't this dress just absolutely delicious? It's the newest fashion from France."

Roseann looked a little doubtful. "It is a wonderful fabric, dearest. That particular bright blue becomes you. But I'm a little confused about the bodice."

"Your shimmy is showing," Tyla said sturdily. "I'm not so sure French ladies are as proper as they should be."

The dress was a smoky blue satin, with such a high gloss that it shimmered brightly in the light. The skirt was wide, of course, with eight tightly gathered flounces, the bottom one (the one that Carley had stepped on) was eight inches long and swept the floor gracefully. Off-the-shoulder, with a low neckline, the bodice was long and pointed, with four cutouts of graduated lengths down past the waist, bordered by satin ruching. Underneath Julienne wore a creamy white satin plain blouse.

"This is called a chemisette, Tyla, and it's made to fit underneath the bodice of the dress," Julienne said. "It's supposed to show."

"It's a shimmy," Tyla repeated with emphasis, "and shimmy's aren't supposed to show."

"Oh, dear," Roseann said softly.

Julienne hugged her. "Don't listen to Tyla, Mother, believe me, I know what ladies of quality are wearing these days. Now why don't you go on downstairs and wait for me in the parlor. As soon as I'm all done, I'll come down and you can see that I'm perfectly respectable."

"I would like some tea," Roseann said. "Please don't make Mr. Leggett wait, Julienne, he's always so very prompt."

"Yes, I know," she said impatiently. Roseann left and Julienne seated herself at her dressing table.

"Make my hair perfect, Tyla. I want to be the most beautiful lady at the party tonight."

"You will probably be the most beautiful lady at the party," Tyla said sternly as she brushed Julienne's hair, "because you may be the only *lady* at the party. Miss Julienne, I know you've got your head set on going, but please, please, just think, for once. This isn't a social gathering with friends that your family has known for years. This is some kind of rabble-rousing bash with a bunch of river men. Your father said that all kinds of men that have to do with the steamers are going to be there, even roustabouts. A party at Natchez-Under-the-Hill! You shouldn't ever go there after dark for any reason, much less to a party!"

And there Tyla had defined the nature of the other, darker half of the city of Natchez.

While the genteel city of Natchez had been built on the high bluffs overlooking the river, the port itself that provided the riches for that city was the shantytown of Natchez-Under-the-Hill, strung down along the muddy shores of the Mississippi. It was the most notorious port on the river. All along the docks, where hundreds of steamships came and went every single day, were saloons, gambling dens, brothels, filthy shacks with rusty tin roofs that served as flophouses for drunks and whores, and meager stores with armed guards. Every night there were fights that ranged from drunken scuffles to murderous knifings and shootings. The regular Natchez police would not dare go there. It was policed, after a fashion, by a brutal gang called the Big Bosses, a group of the roughest, most dangerous men. They ran a protection racket, charging the saloon owners and pimps and merchants to keep them from being robbed, to break up fights, and, when necessary, to haul off the bodies and make them disappear.

"Don't be so dramatic, Tyla," Julienne said disdainfully. "Ladies go to Natchez-Under-the-Hill all the time, since it's the only way to board a steamer. You know we've gone down there to take three trips to New Orleans, and nothing at all happened. And it's not as if I'm going to a saloon. We've known the Moak family for years, and they always have fine parties, with all the highly-regarded families."

"But this is not a Moak family party," Tyla argued. "Mr. Moak is wanting to sell that riverboat, and so he's invited all the men from the river to come tour it. I'll bet Mrs. Moak, or Felicia and Susanna, aren't going to be there."

"Father is going to be there, so it will be perfectly proper for me to go."

Stubbornly Tyla shook her head. "It's not proper. Not with all the riffraff that's going to be there. Roughnecks and bad women, I'd imagine. And there you'll be, right in the middle of them. It's no place for a Christian lady."

"But I am a Christian lady and you know it, Tyla. I go to church, I pray. Besides, you're always fussing at me about being a snob. You should be glad that I'm going to a social function with people that are beneath me."

Tyla sighed deeply. "There's a world of difference between being charitable to those less fortunate than you, and partying and carrying on with riffraff."

She went over to retrieve curling tongs from the grill over the roaring fire, licked her finger and snapped it on the red-hot rod, and nodded with satisfaction when it sizzled. Then she carefully wound a long gold strand of Julienne's hair around it and held it for a few seconds, to make a perfect ringlet. Julienne sat very still, she didn't even speak, as Tyla made four ringlets. Once Carley had jostled Tyla's arm while she was doing this, and the hot iron had badly burned Julienne's neck.

When she finished Julienne picked up the conversation. "Again, we're not partying and carrying on. There's going to be a late supper in the Grand Salon, then fireworks and dancing. It's going to be so much fun. I don't understand you any more, Tyla. You've gotten so religious, so disapproving, that you never have any fun."

"Miss Julienne, didn't we have fun this afternoon, picking out your jewelry to wear? I'm not all sour, it's just that I know that you really are a virtuous, kind lady, but not everyone knows you like I do. People can be mean gossips, and if you keep ignoring the rules of polite society you're going to get a reputation as a loose woman. It would grieve the Lord for that to happen."

"I'm not grieving anyone but you, dear Tyla. Let it go, will you? I'm tired of arguing about it. You're harder on me than even my mother and father.

I want to look pretty, I want to have fun, I want to dance. I might even meet some new exciting people!"

Picking up the thick gold headband with pearl droplets adorning it, Tyla placed it just so at the crown of Tyla's head. She wore gold earrings with teardrop pearls that matched the tiara, and a three-strand pearl bracelet. "You may meet some new people, all right," Tyla grumbled. "When they cut off your head to get this gold."

FINALLY JULIENNE WAS READY and went downstairs to the parlor, a formal room with heavy velvet draperies, sofas, loveseats, and recamiers in the elaborate French rococo style, urns full of aspidistra, vases of peacock feathers, and gilt-framed paintings of seventeenth-century shepherdesses and maidens and princesses frolicking in dreamy woodland settings filled with golden light. Julienne was surprised to see only her mother, seated in a wingback chair by the fire, and Archibald Leggett sitting across from her. When Julienne entered he bounded to his feet.

"Miss Ashby! You look beautiful, just beautiful," he said, beaming at her. He was an average-sized man, with a compact figure, two inches shorter than Julienne (or four, as she was wearing two-inch heeled ball slippers). His hair was a nondescript brown, but it was always groomed perfectly in the style of the day, parted on the side with waves and brilliantine tendrils framing his face. Though his hair was thick, and he had bushy sideburns, he was somehow unable to grow adequate facial hair, as was all the rage. Once he had tried a mustache, but it was as faint and silky as a newborn baby's hair, and Julienne had teased him so unmercifully about it that he had shaved it off.

"Archie" had a small nose, large round brown eyes, and short full lips. They were almost like a cupid's bow. In fact he was a nice-looking man, but to Julienne he looked too boyish and a little femi-nine. She preferred lantern-jawed masculine men with a commanding presence. Archie was formal and very proper, unassuming, and she thought that he was not very intelligent.

To his enthusiastic greeting she replied, "You're too kind, Archie. Thank you very much." Julienne had long called him Archie even though they had never gone through the convention of agreeing to call each other by their given names. To her it seemed silly to call this nondescript young man "Mr. Leggett." He, of course, had always called her "Miss Ashby."

"Not at all, you do look stunning this evening," he replied, leading her to sit on the sofa. "And you come by it honestly, as you so closely resemble your lovely mother."

Although Roseann Ashby was close to fifty years old, and she had been married for more than thirty years with three children, she still had an air of innocence and naiveté. "You're very kind, Mr. Leggett," she said with pleasure.

With some impatience Julienne asked, "Where is Papa? I know I'm running a little late but I did think he'd wait for me."

Archie Leggett cleared his throat. "Er, I persuaded him to go ahead, Miss Ashby. I've got my carriage, and I thought you wouldn't object to going down to the *Columbia Lady* with me."

"Of course not," Julienne said, rising. "Shall we go, then?"

Magically Tyla appeared with Julienne's shawl. Her new ensemble was indeed stunning. Her blue satin dress shimmered richly, her over-the-elbow white gloves were spotless (as Tyla had been able to completely remove Carley's licorice smudge), her hair was dressed perfectly, complimented by the gold tiara and gold-and-pearl earrings, and she had ordered a lavish cashmere shawl, dyed the same azure blue as the dress, with a twenty-two-inch-long silk fringe. The blue brought out the golden highlights of her hair, and made her eyes dark and mysterious. Archie Leggett's compliments had been both right and wrong; she was an extraordinarily beautiful woman, but her slender height, her erect carriage, and her athletic grace was much more mindful of Charles Ashby than Roseann's fragile prettiness.

Archie offered her his arm and escorted her to the waiting five-glassed landau. The day had been cold and clear, and the previous day's blanket of radiant snow had remained. The night sky seemed to mirror the frost-spangled earth, with millions of stars twinkling cheerfully. Julienne inhaled deeply. Though the air was freezing, she loved the exhilaration of cold weather when there was such a spectacular snowfall. It was unusual for a city in the Deep South. "Oh, don't you just love snow?" she asked as Archie handed her into the carriage.

"It makes such a mess in the streets, it's quite an inconvenience," he replied.

Wryly Julienne thought that his answer was so typical of the man. Then again, she had been extremely surprised that Archie had apparently asked her father if he could escort Julienne alone. It was a measure of impropriety that she never would have expected from Archie. In fact, he had objected to Julienne going to the Moak's revelry, but when he found out that she had persuaded her father to allow her to attend, he agreed to go with them.

Archie went to the other side of the carriage and started to climb in, but he hesitated halfway inside. "I wouldn't want to muss your dress, Miss Ashby," he said.

Reflecting that Archie was so timid that he wouldn't even dare to gently push aside the folds of her skirt, she pulled the wide hoop skirt closer around her. "Get in, Archie, you couldn't ruin this wonderful dress if you were trying to."

He climbed in, timidly stepping to avoid the hem of the skirt, seated himself across from her, then knocked on the window behind him, a signal for them to go. The carriage started down the long drive.

Delighted, Julienne stared out the wide window at the snowbound landscape outside. The Ashbys had two carriages but both were sturdy barouches, with shutters to keep out the weather. A glassed carriage was a luxury indeed. The Leggett family was very wealthy. "Just beautiful," she murmured quietly.

"Yes, you are," Archie said, staring at her. Then, to Julienne's shock, he jumped up, trod on her dress, threw himself on the seat beside her, and grabbed her right hand. Clutching it with both of his, he said with an uncharacteristic warmth, "Miss Ashby, I mean, Julienne. You must know how I feel about you. I've been calling on you for a year now, you must know how much I esteem you. Will you allow me to speak to your father?"

"What? Speak to my father?" Julienne repeated in a slight daze. "Archie, you are the only man I know that can take every hint of romance out of a marriage proposal!"

"What? What do you mean?" he asked blankly.

Julienne took a long deep breath and gently drew her hand out of his grasp. "Archie, you are a very nice man. But this is not at all how I envisioned that a man who is deeply in love with me would ask me to marry him."

His eyebrows went up in surprise, but then his face settled into a look that Julienne knew very well. It was an expression of condescension, of conscious superiority, that he always assumed when he talked of business matters and Julienne didn't respond enthusiastically. Julienne had always been secretly amused at this pretension, but just at this moment she realized how very much she disliked it. With a hint of disdain he said, "Yes, I'm aware that genteel young ladies sometimes have foolish and silly daydreams about romance. But, Julienne, you know very well that my family is not only wealthy, but we move in the highest circles of society and the Leggetts are one of the first families of Mississippi. I believe I am regarded as what is somewhat vulgarly termed as a 'fine catch.' And if I may take the liberty, I will remind you that you are twenty-three years old. I'm aware that you have turned away at least two eligible young men, but surely you realize that such things change as a woman grows older."

Anger had risen in Julienne as he spoke, but the sting of truth of the last two sentences deflated her. Though Julienne was careless and her life was somewhat shallow, when forced to she could face facts squarely. Most of her friends married between the age of sixteen and twenty, and after that a woman was considered to be "older." She was well aware that because of her unusual beauty, and the Ashby's place in Natchez society, she was still much sought-after. *But surely Archie-bald isn't my last chance!* she thought rebelliously.

Her thoughts were tumbling one after another, and Archie was watching her with that same supercilious expression. Finally she said with a diplomacy unusual for her, "Archie, I do appreciate your attentions and it is an honor for you to pay your addresses to me in such a respectful manner. But even though we've been seeing each other for a year, to be honest I hadn't come to the point of considering marriage. Would you please give me some time to think about it?"

He frowned. "How much time?"

"I'm not sure, Archie, but I do need some time to consider. It is a big decision, you know."

"I don't understand your hesitation, but then again I suppose women are the weaker gender, and you're not really capable of being strong and decisive," he said with an air of generosity. "You may have time to consider, Julienne. That is, I assume that now I may call you 'Julienne.'"

For a moment the somewhat devilish side of Julienne wanted to say, *No, you may not assume that*. But then the more commonsense, and even cautious, side of Julienne took over and she replied, "Of course you may. I would like that, dear Archie."

CHAPTER THREE

Sighting the lights of the grand steamboat ahead, towering over the other boats at the dock, Julienne's eyes glowed. "You know, I heard that Mr. Moak was spending entirely too much time going back and forth to New Orleans on the *Columbia Lady*, and that's why Winnie Moak is forcing him to sell her."

The Moak family had been the Ashby's neighbors for years. Elijah and Winnie Moak were close friends of Charles and Roseann Ashby. Their son Stephen was one of Darcy Ashby's best friends, and their two daughters, Felicia and Susanna, were long-time friends of Julienne's.

Elijah Moak had built the *Columbia Lady*, one of the biggest and most luxurious steamers on the river. Its home port was in New Orleans, where

Stephen Moak lived and managed the *Columbia Lady* and two other mail packets the Moaks owned.

But Elijah Moak had to sell the *Columbia Lady*, and he had decided to have a grand party on board the steamer to show her off to possible buyers. The businessmen that were considering buying the riverboat wanted their captains and pilots to have a look at her, and the captains and pilots wanted their engineers and first mates to have a look at her, and so the guest list included a strata of society from the highest to the lowest. This is what so scandalized Tyla, that Julienne would be mingling with roustabouts. And there had been rumors for weeks that because of the unusual nature of the guest list, there would be saloon girls, card room hostesses, and prostitutes attending.

"I hadn't heard such," Archie replied to her observation with interest, "but I'm not at all surprised. All of their money was from Winifred Tannehill's family. When the Married Women's Property Act passed, old Ambrose Tannehill made Mr. Moak put everything in his daughter's name. And Winnie Moak rules that money with an iron hand."

Archie Leggett's father, in addition to having one of the biggest and most profitable cotton plantations in the South, was on the Board of Directors of Planter's Bank, so Archie often had inside information about people's finances, which he gleefully shared with all and sundry.

"I can't believe this line of carriages," Julienne said impatiently. "It looks like everyone in Natchez is going to the *Columbia Lady* tonight."

They were crawling down the crazily crooked old path, now named Silver Street, that went from the high bluffs of Natchez proper down to the docks, and Natchez-Under-the-Hill. Ahead of the long lines of carriages Julienne could see the steamer, a grand mountain lined with red and green lanterns. It took several minutes for them to reach the *Columbia Lady*, but at last Archie was handing her out as she stared, her dark eyes wide and glowing.

The *Columbia Lady* was indeed a *grande dame*. She had four decks instead of the more prosaic three, and all four decks were brightly lit with lanterns every three or so feet. Her black smokestacks were sky-high, and topped with elaborate floral wrought-iron crowns. As Julienne and Archie walked across the landing stages to board the boat, they saw that the main doors of the main deck were wide open, and the cargo hold had been emptied and cleaned and turned into a ballroom, though it more properly might be called a dance hall. The only instruments were a loud piano and a shrill trumpet. Obviously this deck was for the lower classes, for tough-looking men in rough clothing were dancing with underdressed women with garish makeup and wild hair.

Meanwhile, a steady stream of people were mounting the mahogany and brass stairwell up to the second deck, in river parlance called the boiler deck because it was above the boilers, but when the steamers had started carrying well-to-do passengers, the owners changed the name of this somewhat superfluous deck to the Ballroom Deck. The people mounting the stairs were dressed in evening dress, the women in every shade of silks and satins, the men in tailed coats with starched white shirts, neat white bow ties, slender-cut black breeches, white gloves, and tall black satin hats. Archie and Julienne followed them, greeting acquaintances and admiring the boat. "It's so luxurious," Julienne said. "Like a home of royalty."

"I've heard it said that the best steamers are sometimes called floating palaces," Archie told her. "Personally, this is the first one I've seen that would qualify."

They reached the double doors of the enormous room that was alternately a dining room or a ballroom. Two tall sturdy Negroes stood on both sides of the door. The *Columbia Lady*'s colors were red, blue, and gold, and they were dressed in a sort of matching livery, with blue coats and trousers and red waistcoats. One of the men took all of the gentlemen's hats and gloves, and placed them precisely in lines on a long table with a white tablecloth. The other Negro man bowed and offered each lady a fan, a lovely cream-colored silk with a design worked in it in gold thread with a gold tassel. Along one edge was printed in gold thread *Columbia Lady*.

"Come on, Archie, let's go find our seats," Julienne urged him. He was already starting to head off toward a group of men standing at one wide window, all of them dressed in evening clothes and talking with animation. Julienne never had to worry about Archie being over-attentive at parties; he always found a group of men to talk about his favorite topic, business, whether it was banking or the price of slaves or the crops or the Cotton Exchange.

"Hm? Oh, all right, Julienne," he said absently and allowed her to pull him by the arm toward the front tables of the dining room. She saw her father standing behind the head table, talking to Elijah Moak and several other men. Many women had already been seated and deserted. They admired their fans and drank red punch. The head table sat across the top of the room, but all of the other tables were round, each with blinding white ruffled tablecloths and four candlesticks in a circular silver holder. The place settings were of china with a blue morning-glory pattern, gold napkins, and gleaming silverware.

"Julienne!" she heard a sweet voice call. "Here, Julienne, you're seated with us." At a table located in the center-front of the head table were Julienne's friends, the Moak sisters, motioning to her. She hurried to the table, pulling Archie mercilessly by the hand. "Felicia, Susanna, how glad I am to see you! From the talk around town I thought I might be the only lady here, surrounded by persons of doubtful morals and low reputation!"

Archie held her chair and she sat down by Felicia Moak, who laughed and said, "Leave it to Julienne to come right out with it. Mr. Leggett, after so long it's plain that you haven't succeeded in taming Julienne."

"But I will," he said with his customary seriousness. "Good evening, Miss Moak, Miss Susanna."

"Good evening, Mr. Leggett," Susanna said with particular emphasis, staring up at him in what might only be termed longingly.

Julienne was amused, for she had known for a while that Susanna Moak had a crush on Archie Leggett. It seemed that Nature had played a rather unkind trick on Susanna Moak, for her older sister Felicia had inherited their mother's beauty. She was a dark-haired, velvety-eyed, curvaceous woman of a lively and delightful charm. Susanna, on the other hand, didn't really resemble anyone in the Moak family. She was nondescript, with medium-brown hair, brown eyes, unremarkable features, and a frame so thin that she had virtually no figure at all. Her eyes were weak, and she required eyeglasses to read even large print, but she refused to wear them in public. Unfortunately this gave her a tendency to squint. Tonight Felicia wore a dark green that made her look like a woodland goddess, and Susanna wore a deep coral shade that was lovely in itself, but unfortunately it made her complexion look sallow.

Archibald Leggett never seemed to notice Susanna beyond the formal greetings he gave her at social gatherings, and now as usual he forgot her and turned to Julienne. "As you're in excellent company, Julienne, I'm sure you won't mind if I join some of my associates over there."

"Certainly, Archie, go ahead."

With an awkward bow to the ladies, Archie hurried back to the group of men standing close to the entrance of the dining room. Susanna watched him, then with a start turned back to her sister and Julienne with an air of exaggerated carelessness.

Felicia was saying, "He called you 'Julienne.' This is an important step, especially for Archie. It only took him a year to come around to it."

"If you only knew," Julienne said mischievously.

Felicia's winged eyebrows shot up. "Knew what? Bigger news than that Archie has taken such liberties as to call you by your given name? What is it? Tell, tell!"

"Yes, tell," Susanna echoed with much less enthusiasm.

The three girls huddled close together and Julienne murmured, "He asked me to marry him tonight. That is, I think he did. You know him, it took him a paragraph or two, and it ended with something about talking to Papa."

Susanna looked downcast, but Felicia smiled delightedly. "Of course he proposed! That's just Archie's way. So when is he going to speak to your father? When can we expect the big announcement?"

"Mmm, not any time soon. I told him I had to think about it."

Felicia sat up straight again and burst out, "Not again! What is this, the third time?"

"I suppose it would be the fourth, if you count Rich Darden," Julienne said, concentrating. "Of course, he never actually proposed, but—"

"That's because out of nowhere one day you tossed him over for Jonathan Nesmith, and he didn't last six months," Felicia interrupted her.

"Four marriage proposals," Susanna said wistfully. She looked so woebegone that her sister reached over and patted her hand.

"Don't worry, Susanna, you'll find a man perfectly suited to your tastes and that's as smart as you are, so you won't be bored," Felicia said. The hard truth of the matter was that no man would pursue Susanna while Felicia was unmarried. But the Moaks were so wealthy that one day it was inevitable that young men would be lining up for Susanna's hand too.

As they talked about the grandeur of the *Columbia Lady*, Felicia confirmed that her father was indeed having entirely too much fun on his excursions to New Orleans and her mother had put a stop to it. Julienne admired the dozens of Negro servants lining the walls, all in livery, and the china and silverware. "And I am so excited about the dance and fireworks!" she gushed.

"We'll probably set fire to ourselves and half a dozen other boats too," Susanna said glumly.

"Of course we won't," Felicia said, then turned to Julienne. "Wait until you see the promenades. Father brought all the children from the plantation and dressed them up in livery. There are over a hundred of them, and they're lining the decks, tending to the lanterns, and each of them have a bucket of water in case any sparks land on the deck. They're so cute!"

After about half an hour, the two Negro butlers simultaneously struck three *tings* on small silver bells as a signal for dinner to start, and everyone began to take their seats. Archie was seated by Julienne. Felicia's current admirer, a fine-looking, easygoing man by the name of Terrell Catlett, and whom everyone called "Lucky," came in from the card room and was seated by her. To Julienne's surprise her brother Darcy was with him and joined them as Susanna's dinner partner.

"Hello, Jules. Good evening, Miss Moak. Miss Susanna, I see I have been chosen to be your dinner partner this evening, it's an honor." He seated himself and smiled at Susanna winningly. She blushed deeply and dropped her head. He was a very handsome young man, with thick dark hair and blue eyes, his features clean and striking. He was of average height and build, but he had a lean, sinuous grace. Susanna always blushed when she was around him, partly because he was so good-looking, but he also had a somewhat cruel streak and teased her sometimes. As in his greeting to her, he idly pointed out that she had no escort.

"Evening, Leggett," he said shortly.

"Mr. Ashby," Archie said stiffly. The two men despised each other.

"I didn't know you were back," Julienne said. "How long have you been back? Why haven't you been home?"

Darcy shrugged carelessly. "Living on the *Columbia Lady* is like living in a grand hotel. I'm staying until she's sold."

"I would imagine that paying a stateroom fare every night would be a much more exorbitant cost than staying in any fine hotel," Archie sniffed.

"Yeah, you just go on and imagine that, since it's not really your concern, is it, Leggett?" Darcy said coolly. The truth was that Elijah Moak, and in particular Winnie Moak, didn't know that Darcy was on the *Columbia Lady* every time she sailed. He had been staying in New Orleans with their son Stephen, and Stephen indulged Darcy and let him go on the cruises without paying the fare. The *Columbia Lady* had an elegant card room, always filled with wealthy men, and Darcy loved gambling.

The first course was served, a bowl of steaming turtle soup, followed by the fish course, a specialty of the house, a casserole called Peppered Oysters Gruyere. The main course was a steak filet with a thick, rich cognac sauce, with bacon-wrapped asparagus spears on the side. Dessert was Italian brandied pears with heavy cream.

As they finished up Julienne told Felicia and Susanna, "I believe this has been one of the most sumptuous meals I've ever had. You must tell your father, and thank him for me."

"You should thank him yourself, Julienne, I know he'll want to say hello to you," Felicia said.

As the diners had finished, most of the men had again stood and gathered in groups, and Elijah Moak was surrounded by men, including Charles Ashby. Julienne said, "He's so busy, but perhaps I will get a chance to speak to him this evening."

Darcy rose and gave a cursory bow. "If you'll excuse me, ladies and gentlemen, I'm sure I'll see you all later." He left, weaving his way between the tables to the door on the starboard side of the dining hall. Julienne knew that led to the card room and the smoking room, which was also a bar. She sighed, but then her attention was caught by a man standing in the group with Elijah Moak and her father. He was very tall, well over six feet, and as brawny as a bare-knuckle boxer. But he was dressed elegantly, and as he talked he gestured with one thick hand that had a large twinkling diamond pinky ring.

"Who is that gentleman that's talking to your father?" Julienne asked curiously.

Felicia turned to take a discreet look, then answered, "His name is Lyle Dennison. He lives in New Orleans, but he's moving here. He's a widower, I understand, I believe his wife died four years ago. Father says he is the most likely buyer. He's very wealthy."

Seeing Julienne's intent expression, Archie said with ill humor, "He's nothing but a slave trader. He owns the second-largest market in New Orleans, and he's buying into the Forks of the Road. He has no people, he comes from nothing, Julienne. He's not our sort at all."

"I just wondered who he is, Archie," she said impatiently. "I wasn't going to go ask him to buy me a drink and give me a cigar."

"Of course not," Archie said, shocked. "It's not seemly to even joke like that, Julienne."

"You sound like my maid," Julienne retorted.

Felicia stood and everyone else stood up with her. "You two argue all the time, you're like spoiled children. Everyone come along, it's time for the fireworks up on the hurricane deck. While we're all up there, they'll clear the tables out and set up the musicians, and then we'll dance!"

THE FIREWORKS WERE MAGNIFICENT, and luckily none of them managed to set fire to any steamers, though they were, as always, close-packed at Natchez-Under-the-Hill.

When the crowd returned to the ballroom, Julienne was surprised to see that quite a few men, obviously not of the wealthy planter class, were standing around. Some of them wore evening dress, but in some indefinable way they looked flashier, more vulgar than the men in the highest circles of

society. Intently Julienne tried to define the difference and decided that it was for several reasons.
Generally they had much more brilliantine on their
hair; Julienne noticed that first because in fact the
ballroom had that sweetish odor wafting about.
Their waistcoats were in garish colors and loud
patterns, and she saw with disdain that they wore
heavy, ostentatious watch chains. A man of quality
didn't wear a watch and chain with formal evening
wear. Their voices were louder and somehow more
coarse than the men of her acquaintance.

And there were several other men, too, that were
not wearing white tie and tails at all. They wore
plain long coats, black, gray, or dark blue, with white
shirts and thin black ties. Their trousers were not
cut to a perfect fit, and often seemed to be plain
wool, which did not retain a knife-crease.

In particular she noticed one of these men,
standing in a group of men talking animatedly. He
was tall, with very broad shoulders, and a bronzed
strong face with longish thick brown hair. He was
staring at her with unabashed admiration. Quickly
she looked away, but then she sneaked a look back
at him, and he was still watching her just as avidly,
but now with an expression of slight amusement.
She lifted her chin and turned to Archie. "Felicia
said they're going to open with a quadrille. I don't
suppose you want to dance the first dance?" Archie
was not a very good dancer, and he continuously
complained that learning to dance was a frivolous

waste of time and he couldn't see any enjoyment in it.

"No, I don't want to, but it is my duty since I escorted you," he said with ill humor.

They took their place in a square with three other couples, and began the slow ceremonious steps of the ancient quadrille. Archie missed a turn and once took the wrong lady's hand, and Julienne could barely contain her impatience. He danced as if it were a chore, like chopping wood, and he was never embarrassed when he danced poorly. He truly thought it was beneath him.

At last the first dance ended, and the next two were lively polkas. Acquaintances claimed Julienne for both dances, and as she whirled around the gleaming dance floor she occasionally caught glimpses of the man she had noticed before. He stood alone now and never took his eyes off her. It made her uncomfortable, at the same time she was flattered. His expression, though very intent, just seemed to be one of deep admiration. Instinctively she knew there was nothing threatening about his regard.

The next dance was the varsouvienne, a stately, slow dance with precise steps. To her delight, Etienne Bettencourt appeared and claimed her.

"Alors, cherie, vous semblez magnifique ce soir," he said admiringly.

"Merci, Etienne," she replied. "Don't speak any more French. I seem to have completely lost the language." Etienne was a Louisiana Creole from one of the first French families to settle in New Orleans.

"Then I must speak to your father and offer my services as a French tutor," he said, his blue eyes alight. "Ladies of the *haute ton* must always be able to speak the most beautiful language in the world."

Julienne laughed. "Somehow I can't see you as a tutor, Etienne. *Non, non, c'est impossible.*"

"There, you still speak French with an impeccable accent, Julienne. You're just too lazy to practice it as you should."

"To please you, sir?" she asked merrily. "No more than we see each other you can hardly blame me for dedicating myself to your language."

"Ah, I see you're displeased with me," he said with mock gravity. "I haven't been to call on you for awhile. But that's because you have broken my heart, *cherie*. You won't marry me, and I am *désolé, tres désolé.*"

"You are not desolated. You would be horrified if I took your silly proposals seriously," Juliette said mischievously. "I happen to know that you talk such foolishness to practically every woman you meet. You'd better watch out, Etienne, someday some innocent little girl will actually think you're sincere and then you'll be in big trouble with her family."

"And then we must fight the duel," he said with a theatrical sigh.

"You wake up every morning trying to think of someone to duel," Julienne teased. "I would think that, since you had to leave New Orleans because of that last duel, you wouldn't be quite so eager for that particular pastime."

"In matters of honor a gentleman cannot be denied his right to a fair and just settlement," he said grandly. "It just seems that somehow I have always been involved in quite a few matters that had to be settled that way."

"Yes, so I hear," Julienne said. "It's a wonder you can afford that many bullets."

His fine face brightened. "If you would just marry me, *cherie*, I would have plenty of money for bullets."

Julienne was still laughing when the dance ended. Etienne was taking her back to Archie, when suddenly the man who had been watching her stepped between them, put one arm around Julienne's waist, took her right hand in a dance position, and positively swept her off in a stately waltz. The waltz was definitely the favorite dance of the time, so the floor filled up so quickly that she immediately lost sight of Etienne.

Julienne danced automatically, so surprised that for long moments she was speechless. She had placed her left hand on his shoulder, and now she became aware of the hard muscling of his arms and chest, and the strength in his hands. She stared up at him. He had strange eyes, a hazel color that had deep brown-green depths. He stared back.

Finally he said, "Hello, ma'am. My name is Dallas Bronte. I think you're the most beautiful woman in this room. In fact, I'm pretty sure you're the most beautiful woman I've ever seen."

"Th-thank you, but-but, you're very forward, sir," she said, managing to dredge up some indignation. "I don't dance with men when we haven't been properly introduced."

"But you are," he said, grinning. He had a crooked smile, with perfect white even teeth. Julienne now noticed a long red scar that ran from his right jaw down his neck. He was roughly handsome, his deeply tanned features masculine and hard. His cheekbones were high and jutting, and he had a strong jawline.

"I didn't exactly mean to," she finally answered. "But since I obviously am dancing with you, I suppose I'll have to introduce myself. My name is Julienne Ashby."

"It's a pleasure to meet you, Miss Ashby. And it's a pleasure to dance with you too."

"You're a very good dancer, Mr. Bronte," Julienne said with surprise.

"I like to waltz. But I don't know any of those other fancy assembly dances. I had to wait a long time before I could waltz with you."

Again, he stared down at her with such an intensity that Julienne was uncomfortable. "If you can waltz, you can polka, sir. There have been two polkas."

"No, for you only a slow waltz," he said in a deep voice.

They danced in silence for a few moments. Dallas Bronte seemed to be drinking her in, looking at her hair, deep into her eyes, searching her face.

Julienne's awkwardness increased, and she blurted out, "Bronte, I don't believe I've heard the name before. Who are your people, Mr. Bronte?"

"I don't have any family. My parents are dead, and I never had any brothers or sisters," he said bluntly. "But I know what it means when a lady like you asks about my 'people.' My family were poor farmers in Tennessee, that's all. I'm a nobody."

Julienne was embarrassed, and it made her speak sharply. "Obviously you're not a nobody, Mr. Bronte. You're here, and nobodies don't generally attend Moak parties."

"Oh, really? Have you seen that bunch of nobodies down on the main deck? It's a bunch of river men, which is the only reason they're at this party. Just like me. It's because Mr. Moak is selling the *Columbia Lady*, and he knows that when the river men see her, they'll be able to tell the buyers the truth about her."

"Yes, of course. So you're a river man?" Julienne hinted.

"I'm a pilot," he said shortly.

She brightened. Pilots were the kingpins of the men who worked the river. They were considered, in the river's particular hierarchy, even more important than captains. But that was about the extent of her knowledge of the workings of a steamer. "A pilot, that's a very difficult job, I understand. Knowing how to guide a boat on the Mississippi River. What boat, or ship, or whatever you call it, are you on now, Mr. Bronte?"

"We call them boats. And I'm between jobs right now. Can we talk about something else? Tell me about yourself," he demanded.

"What? What do you mean?" Julienne asked, mystified.

"I mean, tell me about yourself," he repeated slowly, as if she were an inattentive child. "How do you spend your days? What do you like to do? What's your favorite pastime? Things like that."

Julienne was nonplussed. In her experience with men, she had found that they liked very much to talk about themselves and had very little interest in anything she might have to say, or the things that she was interested in. She was confused, and to her consternation she found that her mind had gone blank. "Well, I and my mother receive visitors in the early afternoon. Sometimes I go shopping. In the evenings there are balls, cotillions, dinners given by friends, sometimes the theater. My family has a very active social life."

He looked puzzled. "But what do you like? What do you do when you're not receiving callers or shopping or at a party?"

She stared at him, and again noticed the deep green-brown depths of his eyes. "I–I–don't—"

At that moment the dance ended, and Etienne Bettencourt popped up in front of Dallas Bronte like a toy jack-in-the-box. "You, sir, how dare you snatch Miss Ashby and waylay her in this insufferable manner."

Dallas Bronte looked down at Bettencourt, for he was a full half a foot taller than the hot-tempered Creole. "I didn't snatch or waylay Miss Ashby. I waltzed with her. And who are you, anyway?"

"I am a friend of Miss Ashby's, and I am a gentleman, and so I must protest this callous manner of yours. I find it insulting to the lady, and that I cannot, and will not, excuse."

The merest hint of amusement twisted Dallas Bronte's mouth. "I don't think the lady was insulted, and I think that she has excused me for my manners, and so you should, too, little man."

Etienne Bettencourt drew himself up to his full five feet, eight inches, and his blue eyes sparked hotly. "I am not a little man, how dare you, sir? I demand satisfaction for this offense!"

"Etienne—" Julienne began.

Dallas Bronte ignored her. "Oh, you want satisfaction, little man? I'll shoot you at dawn any place you decide!"

"Mr. Bronte—" Julienne tried.

"I will have my second contact your man!" Etienne shouted.

Archie Leggett, who had been lurking about on the edges of the crowd that was steadily growing around the three, timidly tapped Etienne on the shoulder. "Mr. Bettencourt, perhaps you should think this over. I happen to know that Mr. Bronte is nothing but a roughneck. He is certainly not a gentleman."

Etienne's eyebrows shot up. "What? *C'est ça?* You're just a common laborer? *Non, non,* I wouldn't lower myself to duel with you, Bronte. Julienne, come with me. I'll keep the riffraff from bothering you for the rest of the evening." He grabbed her arm and hauled her off much more roughly than Dallas Bronte had swept her away in the waltz.

She turned around to look at Bronte, who was staring after them darkly. She met his eyes and saw none of the warmth that had been so plain when he had looked at her before. Turning on his heel, he stalked to the nearest door and disappeared out on the promenade.

Somehow Julienne had lost the sense of excitement she had during the party. Though Etienne gave a highly colorful and dramatic description of the events to Felicia, Lucky, and Susanna, and they laughed heartily, Julienne didn't feel that it was very funny. Surreptitiously she kept looking for Dallas Bronte, but she didn't see him again.

Finally Archie sidled up to her and asked her if she was ready to go home. It was only a few minutes after midnight, and the dance floor was still full. Normally Julienne wanted to stay until the dancing was over, as Archie was content to talk endlessly with his cronies, and she never lacked for partners. But now she answered dully, "I believe I would like to go home, Archie. I admit I'm tired."

He took her out to the main deck stairway, and to Archie's horror, and Julienne's amusement, they saw that some of the roustabouts had lifted one of the great planked landing stages, and three women were astride it, shrieking with laughter. They were coarse-looking women, and one of them had such a loose bodice that it was about to slide completely off one shoulder. Archie averted his eyes and hurried Julienne so much that they almost ran to the carriage.

After they tumbled in Archie said breathlessly, "What a disgraceful display. I knew something like this would happen. No ladies should have been attending that rout."

"That's just silly, Archie. Ladies see those kind of men and women on the streets down here all the time. We're not ignorant little kittens, you know."

Archie replied in a lecturing tone, "Real ladies of quality take no notice of such things, through a desirable sense of propriety and modesty. Sometimes you are wanting in those qualities, Julienne."

"What do you mean?" she demanded.

"Well, for example, you laughed out loud when that ignorant, drunken piece of river trash came stumbling into the ballroom with a lit cigar. Imagine! A man actually smoking a cigar in the presence of ladies! It's an outrage. And you laughed, Julienne!"

"I was laughing at that silly goose of a girl who pretended to have the vapors. I suppose when she sees those women riding the landing stages with their clothes falling off she'll just drop dead of shock," Julienne said brazenly.

Archie's eyes widened in outrage. "There. That's what I mean, Julienne. Such a lack of ladylike

modesty! Listen to me, you simply must stop exhib-
iting yourself in such a manner. It invites common
louts like Dallas Bronte to take liberties."

Ignoring his criticism, Julienne asked, "How do
you know about Mr. Bronte? He told me he was
a pilot. They're not exactly ignorant roustabouts,
Archie."

"He may be a pilot, but he's connected with some
kind of scandal, and the details are so sordid that
I have no intention of inflicting it on you. There's
no need for you to know about it, Julienne. He is no
concern of ours. When we are married you'll have
to curb this inappropriate curiosity about people
that are beneath your notice. Particularly men," he
added nastily.

Julienne merely sighed, leaned back against the
velvet padded seat, and stared out the window.
Somehow the immaculate snowscape outside
didn't seem nearly as inviting as she had thought.
By the hard winter starlight it looked impersonal,
uninviting, and cold.

And she remembered the warmth in Dallas
Bronte's voice.

CHAPTER FOUR

Julienne slept until just after noon the next day. When she awoke she felt sluggish. Tyla placed her breakfast tray on the bed as Julienne sat up, yawning and rubbing her eyes. "Don't do that, Miss Julienne, you'll make your eyes red and look like a Saturday night drunk," she admonished her. "Come down to it, I smell liquor. You weren't a Saturday night drunk, were you?"

"Of course not," Julienne said indignantly. "I just had two glasses of champagne."

Tyla drew open the heavy draperies and Julienne squinted in the glaring afternoon sunlight. "What's it like outside?" she asked idly as she poured her cup of tea from the small silver teapot.

"Messy," Tyla answered succinctly. "It's warmed up a lot, and the snow's melting fast."

"Fine with me. Now that we've had a pretty snow, I'm ready for winter to be over and for a lovely warm spring."

Tyla turned to eye her knowingly. "Spring, that's for weddings, isn't it?"

"I guess," Julienne said carelessly. "But I was thinking more about my visit to New Orleans to see Simone, the middle of next month. I hope it's sunny and warm and blooming by then!"

"That's only in a little over two weeks, you know."

"It is?" Julienne said blankly. "What day is it?"

"Sunday, Miss Julienne. It's February 25. Your passage is booked for March 12, that's fifteen days away," Tyla explained patiently.

"Good heavens! I guess it was snowing and freezing and February and I was just thinking of wintertime. I didn't really realize it's almost spring. And I haven't even started thinking about my spring wardrobe, much less ordering it!"

Tyla's mouth tightened, and she asked, "So we're going to Mrs. Fenner's today?"

Julienne hesitated, then shrugged and sipped her tea. "No, I'm still tired, I don't feel like going out. And no, ma'am, it's not because I drank too much last night, I told you, it was just two glasses of champagne. And you were wrong about the party on the *Columbia Lady*, Tyla. There were a lot of people of good family there."

"Mm-hm," Tyla said noncommittally. "And I heard there were some from not-so-good family too."

"But those river people weren't really at the Moak's ball," she argued, but then she hesitated. A vivid image of Dallas Bronte's roughly handsome face staring down at her as they waltzed rose before her eyes, and abruptly all the memories of the eventful night flooded her sleep-muddied mind. She turned and stared out the bright window.

Tyla eyed her knowingly, then went into Julienne's massive closet to get her an at-home dress, underclothes, petticoats, and shoes. She came out and began laying the items out neatly at the foot of the bed, then sat on a side chair to brush the soft suede slippers.

After awhile Julienne turned to watch her, then said, "Come take this tray, Tyla, and sit down with me for awhile." She patted the bed.

Tyla set the tray on a side table, then took her place sitting by Julienne. All of their lives they had done this. Despite Julienne's constant protests that Tyla was holier-than-thou, she had always confided in her. Since they were children she had always trusted Tyla with all of her secrets, and her maid had never betrayed a confidence, nor did she really act judgmental toward Julienne. Deep down Julienne admired Tyla's steadfast faith, and often wondered how it was that some people seemed to be so much closer to the Lord than others, including herself. When she had these doubts, she always managed to shrug them off with the excuse that it was just that Tyla was "low church" while Julienne was "high church."

Now, however, her thoughts were on men. In particular, she was thinking about Archie Leggett and his proposal, and how she felt about that. Somewhat confusingly, Dallas Bronte's question to her kept interfering with her train of thought. *It seems like a silly question, but is it really? What is it that I really like to do? What is my life made up of? And if I were to marry, what would that mean?*

She began to talk to Tyla, telling her about Archie's proposal and skirting around the deeper questions in her mind. "I suppose Archie is suitable," she said with disdain. "But that man is such a crashing bore. And he's a prig. He's already presuming to tell me how to behave! And I haven't even agreed to marry him yet! He has no right to dictate to me, even if I do get involved in a-a-stupid, embarrassing situation!"

Quietly Tyla asked, "What situation was that, Miss Julienne?"

"It wasn't my fault," she answered plaintively. "There were some river men, some pilots and captains, that attended the dance in the ballroom. I was dancing with one of them, and Etienne Bettencourt got all upset and said that he had offended me, and then this man called him a little man, and then Etienne wanted to fight a duel. All this happened right in the middle of the dance floor, and I suppose it was sordid. Usually gentlemen do these things when women aren't around, and I wish Etienne would have thrown his little fit outside. But

I suppose that's what I get, dancing with a low, common riverboat pilot."

"Excuse me, but it sounds to me like Mr. Bettencourt caused that sordid scene, and he's supposed to be a fine gentleman," Tyla said evenly.

"Hm? Oh, yes, I guess I see what you mean," Julienne said reluctantly, but then she smiled. "But Etienne is different. He's so dashing, and everyone knows he's got that fiery Creole temper."

Tyla cocked her head slightly to the side. "You admire him. You're very attracted to him."

In a low voice, Julienne said slowly, "You know, Tyla, I do admire him. He is an extremely attractive man. I think—I think I may even be in love with him. I think about him a lot. A lot more than Archie."

Tyla sighed, then, in an unusual gesture for her, she reached out and took Julienne's hand. "Let me tell you something, Miss Julienne. What you're feeling for Mr. Bettencourt is not love. There are other names for it, but I'll just say it's passion. It's a physical attraction, and that's all."

Julienne jerked her hand away. "How do you know? And what do you think, that I'm actually in love with Archie Leggett?"

Tyla shook her head. "No, I know you're not in love with him. Believe me, I know what love for a man is. A strong, godly love that's meant to last for a lifetime. And I know you. You don't have that kind of love, Miss Julienne. Not for Etienne Bettencourt or Archie Leggett or anyone else."

"But how do you know all this, Tyla?" Julienne demanded. "You're three years younger than I am, and you're talking like you're some ancient wise woman!"

"I do have some wisdom, thanks to the Lord Jesus and His Holy Spirit in my heart. And I know about loving a man. I've been learning about that for years now."

"You have?" Julienne asked in shock. "Do you mean you have a man, Tyla? That you're in love with someone?"

"Yes, I am," she said, and smiled, her wide dark eyes soft and luminous. "The Lord has blessed me so much. I've been in love with a good man, a fine man, since I was seventeen years old. And he loves me."

"Well, who is this lucky man? And why doesn't he grab you up and marry you?" Julienne joked.

The smile faded from Tyla's face. "His name is Matthias. He belongs to the Moaks. He's one of their stablemen, and he drives their big landau with the four-horse team."

Julienne looked blank, and Tyla added, "You've seen him before, Miss Julienne, plenty of times. And you saw him last night. He and his brother Thaddeus served as butlers at your party."

Then Julienne remembered the two big fine-looking Negro men who had been at the door receiving guests. "Oh, yes, I remember now! I have seen Matthias, several times, when I went out with

Felicia and Susanna. He is a very handsome man, Tyla. So when are you two going to get married?"

"Don't you understand, Miss Julienne? Matthias is a slave. He can't just get married," Tyla said grimly. "Mr. Moak would never let one of his slaves marry a free woman of color."

"Oh, pshaw. Then I'll just tell Father to buy him, and manumit him like we've done with all of you, and then he can come here and be our stableman and driver and he can move in with you. Whyever haven't you told me this before, Tyla? It's so simple, and you would be so happy!"

"No, ma'am, it's not that simple. Miss Julienne, haven't you been listening to your father for the last year? Money is real tight in this family, it's been hard for your father for a long time now, and it's getting worse. And Matthias is what white people call a 'prime buck,'" she said grimly. "He would cost a lot of money, even if Mr. Moak had a mind to sell him. Which he doesn't."

Julienne stared at her. "But this is awful, Tyla. I didn't think, I didn't realize that you were in this terrible situation. Aren't you angry? Don't you just hate Mr. Moak?"

"No, I don't hate him, or anyone else. Yes, sometimes I get angry, but I always pray, and the Lord fills me with love," Tyla answered softly. "Miss Julienne, I know you can't understand that, and I'd give anything if you would come to the Lord Jesus, and ask Him to save you and give you peace. I'm no better than you, I never was, we're all sinners. It's just that you have to realize, like I did, that having good manners and going to church and not breaking society's rules doesn't mean that you're righteous in the Lord's eyes. We're all of us terrible, hopeless sinners. When I realized that, I fell to my knees and begged forgiveness, and asked the Lord Jesus to come into my heart and save me from my sin. And when He did that, He also saved me from bearing the hurt of other people's sin. He gave me love, and He gave me peace."

"But how can you have peace? How, when you can't be with the man that you love?" Julienne cried.

"Because I trust in the Lord Jesus, and my Father God. I know that He will bless me, no matter what happens. Who knows what will happen tomorrow, Miss Julienne? No one does, anything can happen, we may not even live through this day. But I know that every minute I walk and breathe is right alongside my Lord Jesus. And there's no earthly comfort that can compare with that."

She rose then and went to pick up the breakfast tray. "I'm going to go get you some more hot tea, Miss Julienne. You just please think about what I've said."

"I am thinking about it, Tyla," she said, throwing aside the covers and climbing out of bed. "I'm going to wash up and dress and then I'm going to go talk to Papa. I know he's been poor-mouthing for awhile now, but that's just Papa. And I can't believe that he can't talk Mr. Moak into selling Matthias.

They've been friends forever, and I know if Papa just explained the situation to him, an arrangement could be made."

Julienne was still talking when Tyla left the room, her face filled with sorrow.

WHEN JULIENNE WENT DOWNSTAIRS, still bubbling over with her plans to unite Tyla and Matthias, she found only her Aunt Leah in the family sitting room. "Good morning, Aunt Leah. Where is my mother? And Papa?"

"It's afternoon in this hemisphere, my dear. Your mother is resting before dinner. Your father has gone to the plantation. He thinks he may have to stay for a few days." She answered calmly, never looking up from her knitting. She was much like her brother, Charles Ashby, a slightly older feminine version of him. She was tall, with thick white hair and brown eyes. Although her proud posture was forbidding and her demeanor was stern, she was actually a good-humored woman with a dry sense of humor.

Julienne threw herself onto the sofa, slumped back, and crossed her arms. "Why does he have to go out to that silly plantation all the time? I need to talk to him."

Aunt Leah glanced up, a mere flash of her dark eyes. "Julienne Rose Ashby, I hope never again to see your back touch the back of a seat. You look like one of Carley's rag dolls, and that is unfortunate, considering they've all been buried, or drowned, or used for fish bait, or hung by the neck until dead. Now, your silly plantation is your family business, and your father is needed there. In fact, I was going to go with him except that he asked me to stay, and the reason I need to stay is because I must look after you."

Julienne, now sitting up straight in a ladylike manner, asked, "Me? Why should I need looking after?"

Dropping her knitting and gazing at Julienne directly, she replied, "Because your father knows you're going to New Orleans in two weeks, and he said you were talking away about your spring wardrobe. Listen to me, Julienne. The family is going through a very difficult time financially right now. Though I suppose he's tried, Charles hasn't seemed to be able to make you understand. Or Darcy, or even Roseann. There is no money, Julienne. You cannot order an entire new spring wardrobe."

"What! What in the world am I supposed to do?" Julienne said petulantly.

"That's why I've stayed. Tyla and your mother and I will all be able to rework your clothes from last spring. By the time we're finished you'll think you have a brand-new wardrobe."

"I don't understand," Julienne complained. "Why, all of a sudden, is there no money? We still have the plantation, don't we? We've always had money."

"Less and less of it for some time now."

"But I can still go see Simone, right?" Julienne asked suddenly. "Papa promised!"

"Yes, you're still going to New Orleans, though we really can't afford it," Aunt Leah answered, "but you are going because your father did promise, and he's a man of his word."

"That's one good thing, anyway," Julienne said. "Even if I am going to look ridiculous in last year's fashions."

"You will look beautiful as you always do, and Simone won't know the difference," Aunt Leah said sturdily.

Maybe not, but I will, Julienne thought sulkily as she flew back up to her room to drag out all of last year's dresses.

She had completely forgotten about Tyla and Matthias.

MARCH ARRIVED IN A fit of temper, with thunderstorms roaring, pounding rains, and great sky-bursts of lightning. It stormed day and night the first days of the month. On Sunday the eleventh, the day was bleak, with lowering clouds, but it didn't rain. Monday dawned, still dark and threatening.

"We're going," Julienne said stubbornly. "I've been looking forward to this trip for months. And for the last two weeks I haven't been to a single party or even paid any visiting calls, and I've been so bored, and New Orleans has the grandest spring season. We're going."

"All right, Miss Julienne," Tyla said resignedly. "It just seems dangerous, is all. Big storms for days, and that cruel Old Man River."

"It's just a storm on a river, not a hurricane in the north Atlantic," Julienne retorted. "Don't be afraid, Tyla, the steamers go every single day, no matter what the weather. It really doesn't affect them, you know."

"I guess not," Tyla conceded. "All right then, sit down and let me fix your hair and put your bonnet on while Caesar's loading your trunks."

After the freakish late snow in February, it seemed that the Deep South had decided to abruptly shift into spring. It was still cool for the South, in the upper forties at night and the fifties and sixties during the day, but already the trees and wildflowers had started blooming. Julienne had read that morning in the New York newspaper that they had had a two-foot snowfall. *I would hate to live in the North*, she thought happily. *I really do love my home.*

In spite of her complaints, Julienne really was happy with the way her clothes had been freshened up and redesigned by her aunt and her mother. This traveling ensemble was very attractive, a crisp poplin dress of dark green and gold stripes with a matching floor-length hooded cloak of green. Her mother had completely redone the bodice of the dress and had fashioned the cloak from the skirt of another dress, lining it with a durable green cotton jean to make it water resistant.

She went downstairs to say goodbye to her family. Her mother was nervous and begged her not to go; even Charles said, "Julienne, I can change your passage until later on, you don't have to travel in this wicked weather."

"Please, Papa, I'll be fine, you know that." She kissed his cheek, then bent down to hug Carley. "Be good, little monkey. Don't drive Mother crazy, and stay in your lessons with Aunt Leah."

"I don't want to," she said darkly. "I want to go with you."

"No you don't. I'm not going fishing," Julienne answered, smiling.

Finally they were in the barouche and winding slowly down Silver Street. Out of nowhere, a long, deafening roll of thunder sounded over their heads, forked lightning spears struck near, and the rains began.

"Oh dear," Tyla said faintly.

The carriage stopped, and Caesar, the Ashby's man-of-all-work, yanked open the door. He held a big black parasol, and rain dripped dismally from each point in a steady stream. "We're here, Miss Julienne. This is your boat, I guess."

Julienne stepped out, and immediately her boots filled with mud and water and the hem of her wide hoop skirt was sopping at least eight inches up. Blinking, she looked at the steamer rocking on the uneasy river.

"But that's so little," she said. "Are you sure that's the *Missouri Dream*?"

"Yes, ma'am, saw it plain as plain painted on the side when we drove up," Caesar answered. "Can't see it through this soup, I know, but that's her."

The *Missouri Dream* was a sturdy steamer, carrying both passengers and freight. She was fairly new, and so wasn't at all worn or shabby, for her owners kept her up very well. But she was small. At least, to Julienne, she looked tiny and scruffy, and that was probably because the last steamer she had seen had been two weeks ago, the queenly *Columbia Lady*. In fact, she had had a vague notion that she was sailing on that grand ship. Felicia Moak had told her that Lyle Dennison had indeed bought the *Lady*, and being reminded of it she had mentioned it to her father and told him that she wanted to go on that boat to New Orleans. But then she vaguely recalled that he had said something about the *Columbia Lady* being prohibitively expensive. Still, Julienne was irritated.

"Oh, very well. Come on, Tyla, let's get in out of this downpour. I'll see if I can get one of the crewmen to fetch my trunks." Loaded on top of the carriage Julienne had two great steamer trunks, two traveling cases, and eight hatboxes. Tyla had one humble carpetbag.

Caesar, blinking and spluttering in the rain, shielded Julienne as she stepped smartly on the landing stage. Tyla pulled her shawl over her head and hurried behind her. When Julienne boarded, she looked helplessly around for a crewman, but none were there.

"I'll start bringing the trunks up, Miss Julienne," Caesar said. "But you'll have to find your stateroom where I'm to bring them."

"All right," Julienne said uncertainly. She looked around. The big double doors that led to the cargo area and the firebox were just ahead of her, and over the din of the storm she could hear snatches of shouting and cursing. Julienne had no desire to go sashaying up in there. Ruefully she decided that she'd better go up to the pilothouse and see if she could find the captain or at least the first mate.

The stairs leading up to the hurricane deck, where the pilothouse was perched, was outside. Without a word Julienne threw her hood up, bowed her head, and hurried out to run up the stairs, followed by Tyla. When she reached the pilothouse, she couldn't tell if anyone was in there, because the rain smeared the windows. She threw the door open and practically ran in.

Two men were there, and they whirled to stare at her, startled.

"I apologize for the intrusion, but there is not a single crewman to be seen down on the main deck," she blurted out angrily, pushing back her hood and brushing rain away from her eyes. "I am a paying passenger and I require assistance. Where is your crew?"

Still the two men were speechless. Julienne stared at them irately, but suddenly her dark eyes widened and her mouth even opened slightly with astonishment. "Mr. Bronte? Dallas Bronte? You? What are you doing here?"

He quickly recovered. "Nothing useful, apparently. This is the pilot of the *Missouri Dream*, my friend Kip Herrin. Kip, I had the pleasure of making this lady's acquaintance a few weeks ago. It's my honor to introduce you to Miss Julienne Ashby."

"It's a great pleasure to meet you, Miss Ashby," he said, bowing over her hand. He was a young man, with bright eager eyes and a wide smile.

Julienne was surprised but pleased at Dallas's fine manners, but she now felt ridiculous, standing there dripping and bedraggled. "So kind," she said automatically. "I apologize for bursting in on you like this, but I really didn't know quite what to do."

"I'm so sorry, Miss Ashby, but we had stacked our wood outside and when this storm came up all hands were called to bring it into the cargo hold," Herrin explained. "Even Captain Wynans is down there, shifting cotton bales, to make room. That's why no one was there to greet you."

"I'll take care of it, Kip," Dallas said easily. "She's in the Texas, I imagine. I'll get her all settled."

"Thanks, Dallas, but hurry back, would you? I want to go over Point 142 again," Kip said.

Dallas sketched a salute, then took Julienne's arm. "This way, ma'am, right over here is the hatch to the inside stairwell down to the Texas deck. Oh, hello, ma'am. Are you Miss Julienne's maid? Here, step right down here, careful now." He lifted a heavy hatch in the deck, and helped Julienne and Tyla down the steps, then followed them. "Right ahead, down the hallway, the last one of the left. The Texas stateroom. It's one of the biggest, so I'm sure that's where you're booked, Miss Ashby. You ladies go on in, and I'll go see about your luggage."

They went into the stateroom, and Dallas disappeared.

Julienne looked around, dismayed. The room had two small bunk beds against one wall. A single straight chair was underneath a small window. On the other wall was a chest only eight inches deep, to give room to squeeze between it and the beds. It held the smallest water jug and pitcher Julienne had ever seen, along with two white towels.

"Good heavens, this is smaller than my closet," Julienne said with disgust. "What was Papa thinking?"

"He did the best he could, considering," Tyla said. But her voice was weak, and she gripped the side of the bunk bed so tightly her knuckles were bloodless.

Julienne turned to her. "You're ill, Tyla. Why didn't you tell me you were getting sick?"

"I didn't want to complain, but I really haven't been feeling myself today," she answered weakly. "And I guess you've forgotten, Miss Julienne. I never have traveled on water too well. And sure even you've noticed that we're rolling something fierce."

Julienne felt a wave of shame. Always before, Tyla had either had her own little compartment connected to her stateroom, or had been in some other part of the boat where the servants bunked. She hadn't really been aware that Tyla got sick when she traveled. "Yes, well, maybe this storm will pass, and Old Muddy will be back to its lazy self," she said with forced cheer. "Anyway, you go ahead and get comfortable and lie down, Tyla. I'm perfectly capable of seeing to the trunks. No, don't you dare, you take the bottom bunk. I insist."

Despite Tyla's weak protests, Julienne took off her jacket and loosened her blouse buttons, removed her shoes, noting that they were her old half-boots that she had thrown away. Julienne practically forced her down on the bottom bunk, and covered her up securely. "Rest now," she said sternly. "I'll be back soon."

She went to the door and Tyla asked weakly, "Miss Julienne? Is that nice man, that Mr. Bronte, the same man you met at that party and you said was no gentleman?"

"That's the man himself."

"He's sure a fine-looking man," Tyla murmured softly. "A man you could depend on, a man that would take care of you."

"What? But how—?" But Tyla's chin had sunk down and she closed her eyes wearily.

Julienne closed the door quietly and went to find Caesar and Dallas Bronte. She found them on the main deck. All of her luggage had been brought on board but they were stacked just inside the double doors, barely out of the rain. As she neared them she could hear Caesar saying in distress, ". . . has to have her things. She can't have her nice things piled down here with dirty cargo, and all these rough-necks shoving them around."

"I understand, Caesar, but—oh, there you are, Miss Julienne. I would guess that now you've seen your stateroom you can understand that you can't have your luggage in there. I was just trying to explain to Caesar that they'll have to be stowed down here," Dallas said patiently.

"It's true, Caesar, there's barely enough room for me in there, much less any trunks," Julienne grumbled. "Don't worry, Caesar, it's only about ten or twelve hours to New Orleans, they'll be fine down here for that time."

"May be a little longer than that," Dallas said gravely, "but I'll help you if you need to get some things, maybe rearrange some clothes and put what you'll need in one of the traveling cases."

"I don't know about all that," Julienne said uncertainly. "Tyla takes care of things like that for me. But she's sick. I guess, Mr. Bronte, maybe I should get you to help me look in one of my trunks and see if I might need to repack a case for overnight." She turned to Caesar. "Thank you so much, Caesar, but get home now and get Libby to fix you some nice hot soup. You're soaked through. Don't worry, get on now."

Reluctantly he left, and Julienne turned to the mass of trunks and boxes piled by the door. "So you're volunteering to help me, Mr. Bronte? I must admit I've never had to deal with a problem like this."

"No, I'm sure you haven't," he said dryly. "What I'm going to do is take them over in that corner over there, see? Stack 'em up and secure them with a stout line. They'll be safe, they won't take up much room that way, and I can get to them easy if you need to get something out of them."

"That sounds good, I guess. If you would please take this trunk first, and let me look in it and get some things I may need. So you do think we may be traveling all night?"

"Maybe," he said. "Depends on the storm. Can't see a blooming thing when it's raining steady like this, it's hard to spot your points and landmarks. A good pilot slows down, a lot, when he can't see too well."

Julienne nodded. "Then I'd like to pack a small case for me, and take Tyla's bag. I think they'll fit under the bunk, won't they?"

"Sure." Gamely Dallas bent and picked up one of the trunks. It was massive, two feet deep, forty inches high, and two feet wide, and it was packed to the brim. With a small grunt he picked it up, walked to the corner, and gently set it down at an exact angle to fit into it.

Julienne admired this obvious show of strength, but she said nothing except, "Would you mind bringing me that small case?" She walked to the trunk, took a key out of her reticule, unlocked it, and opened the top. Dallas stood there holding her small black leather case. He looked down and a delighted grin lit his face. The boyish expression sat oddly on his tough features.

Julienne's eyes widened. The top of the trunk had a shallow fitting that set on top, divided into compartments. Julienne's most delicate pantaloons, lacy chemises, satin corsets, and sheer underslips lay in them. She slammed the top back down and stared at Dallas accusingly.

"You weren't supposed to see those," she snapped.

"I know," he said. "But I did. They're real pretty."

Julienne's cheeks flamed. "You—you are so impertinent! How dare you?"

"How dare I what? Say your underthings are pretty? Should I have said they're ugly?"

"This is not funny," Julienne said between gritted teeth. "Just secure my trunks as you said, Mr. Bronte." She whirled and thought she had made a fine, dignified exit, but he called after her.

"Miss Ashby?"

She turned slowly. He stood there, his arms crossed, his chin tilted upward. "I'm not your slave like poor Caesar," he said. "I don't even work on this boat. I was just trying to help you out, but I'm not taking orders from you, ma'am."

Julienne's eyes narrowed and she drew herself up to her full height. "Excuse me. I thought you were being a gentleman."

"Maybe if you acted more like a lady, I'd act more like a gentleman," he drawled.

"Ooh! You're insufferable!" Julienne almost shouted.

"Okay, then, if you can't stand me so bad, I guess you don't want my help. Be seeing you, Miss Ashby." He turned to walk toward the double doors.

But just before he disappeared Julienne said, "Wait. I mean, please wait, Mr. Bronte."

"Yes?" he said, turning.

"It seems I require some assistance with my trunks," she said in the politest tone she could manage. "Would you please help me, sir?"

"I dunno. What about your little French pet he-goat? He gonna show up and try to butt my shins again?" he asked, his strange greenish eyes alight.

Julienne gritted her teeth. "Mr. Etienne Bettencourt is not my—oh, never mind. I'm asking you, as a gentleman, to please render your assistance to a lady."

"Of course, ma'am." He went back to the trunk he'd placed, and Julienne thought he was going to lift the top again. She bolted to it and slammed her hand against the top, looking at him accusingly.

"I was just going to see if you locked it back, ma'am," he said. "Stored down here, it better be locked."

"Oh. Well. No, I suppose I didn't. You confused me. Here, I'll lock it now." She bent to insert the key and lock the trunk securely again.

Dallas Bronte went to the other trunk, which was slightly smaller, and brought it to the corner. When Julienne finished, he set it on the top of the other one. "It was kinda funny, you know," he murmured, "you showing me your pretty underthings."

"It wasn't. And neither was the pet goat."

"Yes, it was," he said, grinning at her.

She looked rebellious, then her mouth twitched. "Maybe. Maybe it was just a little funny. Not very funny."

"I dunno. Seemed pretty funny to me."

They argued the entire time as Dallas walked her back to the stateroom. As he left she was still smiling.

AT MIDNIGHT JULIENNE MOST definitely was not smiling. The storm had fought them all evening and night, with great deafening peals of thunder, wild wind, and rain that spattered hard against the shuttered window. The steamer rocked and pitched as the Mississippi River fought the fierce elements.

Still, Julienne was unafraid. She could feel the comforting great *throck, throck* of the sternwheel paddle, steady and secure. The little steamer was tight and well-built, for they had had no leaks, no water sloshing along the decks, not even dribbles from the single window in the stateroom.

But Tyla was deathly ill. Her normal rich cocoa-colored skin looked an unhealthy yellow, and her eyes were dull and feverish. As the night had worn on, she had developed a cough with thick congestion. Her coughing had gagged her, and she had vomited until she could bring up nothing else, but still she heaved. Julienne knelt by her bunk, holding her head, keeping the two blankets tucked securely around her. Tyla had grasped her hand in a death grip, gasping that she was scared they were going to wreck, that the storm would kill them. Julienne held her hand and stroked it, telling her in a soothing, soft voice that the boat was fine, that Tyla was just imagining things because she was ill, that Julienne would take care of her and not let anything happen to her. Finally Tyla had fallen back, seemingly senseless.

Julienne continued to kneel by her and hold her hand, and she felt it grow hot. She pressed her wrist against Tyla's forehead. Tyla was going into a fever. *This isn't seasickness*, Julienne thought uneasily. *I wonder if she's got the influenza? Oh, Lord, no, please not that!*

Influenza had spread among the field hands at Ashby Plantation, and three men, eight women, and eleven children had died. That was why her father had been spending so much time there the last weeks. Aunt Leah, insisting it was her Christian duty, often went out to the plantation with him, nursing the sick men, women, and children. As Julienne thought of this, she wondered if Tyla had gone to the plantation too. It occurred to her that she knew very little about Tyla, that she really had no idea what she did when she wasn't waiting on Julienne.

Tyla opened her eyes, and Julienne saw that tears welled up in them. "No, no, please don't cry, Tyla. If you cry I'll cry and you know how much I hate to cry. It makes your eyes red, like a Saturday night drunk."

Tyla managed a weak smile. "I know you're no Saturday night drunk, Miss Julienne. You never could be, you're too strong for such nonsense. I just feel so bad, so awful, being so helpless. I'm so sorry, Miss Julienne, I'm ashamed for you to have to take care of me like this."

"No, no! Don't!" Julienne said harshly. "How many times have you taken care of me, Tyla? All of my life. That's how much you've helped me. So stop it, stop apologizing, it's embarrassing me. I thought you were crying because you were still scared. Are you, Tyla?"

She sighed, a weak shuddering intake of breath. "I was awfully scared, yes. But I've been praying, and I feel the Lord's presence real close to me now. Who could be afraid when the God of all the earth is holding your hand? Who could fear when the Lord Jesus whispers comfort to you? *Though He slay me, yet will I trust Him . . .*"

Julienne didn't know that verse. She thought that Tyla was just delirious with fever. She watched her for long moments and saw that her chest rose and fell rhythmically, and felt some of the heat lessen in Tyla's hand. Wearily Julienne laid her head down on their clasped hands and fell into an uneasy doze.

She awoke with a start, unable to tell how much time had passed. Tyla slept peacefully, and her forehead felt a little cooler, Julienne thought. Gently untangling her hand, she stood. Or at least she tried to. She had been in an awful position, for how long now she had no idea, seated on the floor with her legs tucked under her. When she straightened them, sharp jolts of pain shot all the way up to her hips, and she would have groaned except she was afraid that she would awaken Tyla. Like a frail old woman that has fallen, she slowly pulled herself up by the bedpost. It seemed to take a long time. Then she threw her head back, massaged her burning, aching neck, and tried to straighten her back to work out the spasms.

It was only then that she noticed that it had stopped raining. The wind still groaned and beat against the wooden shutter, and long deep rolls of thunder sounded ominously. She threw open the shutter and then she saw the lightning, far off now, but splintering the sky continuously. There was a storm ahead of them, all right, but Julienne didn't know if the one they had been in had passed over, or if this was more of Nature's fury ahead.

The sharp cool wind blew through the stateroom, and Julienne realized how stuffy and close the room had become. And it stank of illness. Reluctantly Julienne regarded the bucket in the corner, the only bathroom facility available on the *Missouri Dream*, apparently. Because Tyla had been so ill it was almost full.

No, I can't. I won't. I don't have to do things like that, she thought with a sudden ugly burst of anger.

But Julienne had a streak of practicality, and though she was shallow she was not a weak woman. She was strong, and right then she realized that not only could she do this chore, but she should do it. Besides, she really did want to walk, to move around, to get some blood moving back in her half-paralyzed limbs. With dark amusement she realized that she still wore her hoop skirt. It was even wider than the space between the chest and the bunks. Yanking up her heavy skirts, she untied the steel cage and dropped it, kicking it carelessly under the bunk. Because the air had been chilly, and the wind strong, she decided to wear her cloak and pulled it on quickly. Then she put the top on the bucket securely, picked it up, and gave Tyla a quick cautious look.

She slept quietly, and in the dim light Julienne even thought she saw a small smile on the girl's face. She breathed deeply and evenly. Julienne slipped outside and walked quietly down the hall. She went up the staircase that led up to the hurricane deck, but to her disgust she couldn't lift the hatch. Either she wasn't strong enough, or it was locked. Climbing back down, she went down the narrow hallway outside the staterooms, carrying her stinking bucket.

"How do people do things like this?" she muttered to herself. "Why isn't there at least one sanitary room? Or maybe there is, and I just don't know where it is. This is so stupid!"

At last she reached the end of the hall, and the door that led out to the stairwell going down to the main deck. As she opened it the wind shrieked wildly and threw it open, banging against the wall. Julienne struggled to close it behind her. As soon as she was out on the stairs, she leaned over the railing, judging the wind, and when there was a lull she quickly emptied the bucket over the side. With relief she snapped the top back on and set it down just inside the stairwell door. She wanted to walk, to stay outside and breathe in some of the cold clean air.

Her heavy cloak flapping about her, she made her way down the stairs and to the main deck. She stood by the ornamental railing, holding onto it securely, trying to make sense of the wild night. Low black clouds scudded by, veiling the stars and an uncaring cold white half moon. Lightning still raged ahead of them, and the far-off thunder never stopped. She looked down, and the river was a raging black torrent. Instead of the ship steaming along it, Julienne thought it was more like it was riding a dangerous runaway horse.

A shadow loomed beside her, and Dallas Bronte said, "Good evening, Miss Ashby. Hope I didn't scare you, I tried to make noise walking up but you probably couldn't hear it with all this racket out here."

"No, I didn't hear you, but you didn't frighten me," Julienne answered. "I don't scare easily."

"Guess not. You're not scared right now? River's wild tonight."

"Not really. It's just a storm. We have them all the time, and all the steamers don't sink."

"No, they don't." He grasped the top railing and looked out, his eyes searching the distance in front of them. He was quiet for so long that Julienne began to wonder.

"Mr. Bronte, you are a riverboat pilot, correct?" she asked.

"I have my pilot's license, yes," he answered cautiously, still looking far away. "I don't have a boat right now."

"But still, you know the river. You—you aren't trying to tell me that I should be worried, are you?"

Julienne hoped that he would immediately dismiss her doubts, but to her dismay he frowned and considered her face for a long time. "Let me tell you something, Miss Ashby. Pilots are a special breed, and not one of us is any more knowledgeable than another. Every pilot has to know this river better than he knows his own home. And he does, or he would never get his license. And so no pilot would ever presume to second-guess another pilot."

"I didn't want a lecture on how special pilots are," Julienne said, turning to glance up at the pilothouse. It was not lit, of course, as the pilot inside couldn't possibly see the darkness outside if he stood in a lit room. But she thought she could see the outlines of

Kip Herrin in the lurid light of the lightning flashes. "I was just asking a question, Mr. Bronte. I thought you might know something I don't know."

He shook his head, a short sharp movement, and watched the vague glimpses of the landscape sliding by. Julienne stared toward the shore, too, though all she saw was a blur of black with some lighter gray splotches. She wondered what Dallas Bronte saw.

Oddly, the silence between them was not awkward. It stretched out, and they both watched and listened to this fierce world. But they were acutely aware of each other. Without consciously realizing it, Julienne moved closer to him, and at the same time he took a step toward her, looming over her as if he were shielding her.

Unbidden, suddenly, an overpowering desire to touch Dallas Bronte rose like quickfire in Julienne, and she drew in a sharp ragged breath. His strong hands were close to hers, and she wanted to grab them and pull them around her. She wanted to turn to him and press her lips against his and run her hands through his thick hair and feel the heat of his breath on her. She wanted—

The sky split, the river exploded, the world burst, or at least that's what the next few moments seemed like to Julienne. As if she were moving in slow motion she turned to look, to see what the frightfully loud noise behind her was. But then her whole body was falling and in this slowed time she realized that Dallas Bronte had pushed her down and had thrown himself on top of her. He covered her head with his hands and forced her to press her face to the deck, and he laid his head on top of hers. She heard loud groans of metal, another explosion, then another, and things started falling out of this insane sky, crashing all around her. Through Dallas's body she could feel at least two heavy hits on his back. Still he forced her head down.

This seemed to go on for a long time, the frightful noises, the crashes around them, the ship beneath them tilting crazily. Dallas lifted his head and let go of Julienne's head, then grabbed her shoulders and hauled her up. To her horror she saw fire everywhere, the glass windows bursting out of the staterooms and the pilothouse, and she saw that the boat's nose was tilting upward and she and Dallas were sliding down toward the black raging water. Before she could say a word, she was deep under, the water roiling around her and over her head. She panicked and began struggling helplessly, her heavy clothing dragging her down. She opened her mouth to scream but it filled with water and she began to choke.

A strong hand grabbed her shoulder and pulled, hurting her badly. Then she breathed air, and coughed. Roughly Dallas rolled her over onto her back and crooked one arm under her chin. "Be still," he commanded her.

He began to swim, hauling her along like a heavy sack. His strokes were awkward, one-armed, but unbelievably strong. Julienne just lay there, concentrating on breathing, making herself relax because she realized that if she struggled the yards and yards of her dress, petticoat, and cloak would again pull her down like anchor weights. After awhile Dallas stopped and stood in hip-deep water that still swirled so fast and deep around them that Julienne couldn't stand up. He scooped her up into his arms and waded to the shore. Gently he set her down, then stood and turned back to the river. All Julienne could see now were flames, and even in the chaos of her mind she knew that the fire was low, too near the water. The *Missouri Dream* was sinking fast.

Dallas took a long, deep breath, cupped his hands to his mouth, and shouted, "Anybody there? Anybody need help?"

Julienne couldn't hear a thing except the far-off thunder and the rushing of the river. Still Dallas waded out and started swimming toward the ship. She could see his head outlined against the flames, searching this way and that, striking out to swim a few strokes one way, and coming back.

And then the flames disappeared, and the darkness closed in. Julienne sat there, her mind dulled as if she had been given a strong drug. She began to shiver. Then Dallas was standing there and he said in a deep, painful voice. "She's gone. No one else made it."

Julienne looked up at him, her face white and bloodless, her eyes stretched painfully wide with shock. "No—no!" She scrambled to her feet and ran, stumbling to the water's edge. "No! Tyla! Tyla!" she screamed and started to wade out.

But Dallas was there, and he pulled her back, and wrapped her in his arms. "Shh, shh, Julienne, don't, don't. They're gone. They're all gone."

She clung to him and began to sob.

CHAPTER FIVE

Slowly the darkness Julienne was in lessened. She thought her eyes were opened but she wasn't sure. The harsh blackness dissipated to a dismal gray, and sound—noises—started sounding in her ears.

She took a deep, gasping breath, and then with an effort opened her eyes. They were instantly stung with icy rain; the wind shrieked and tore at her soaked heavy skirts; and by a lightning flash she saw Dallas Bronte's grim face above her. He was carrying her, and now against her side she could feel his harsh grunts as he struggled through the thick woods.

She reached up to touch his face and was startled by how very weak she was. "I can walk," she tried to say, but the sound was lost in the tempest.

He looked down at her and searched her face. Her cold fingers pressed against his cheek, and gently he set her on her feet. She stumbled but didn't fall. He leaned down close to her ear. "Are you sure you can walk?" His voice was deep and strong, so he didn't have to yell at her. She nodded.

Still half-carrying her, they worked their way through the woods. Vines tore at her, and she felt as if she were fighting through deep, cold water. Realizing that she was about to faint again, Julienne made herself take deep, long breaths as they toiled.

After what seemed like an eternity, she could tell there was a clearing ahead. She took a step, dimly aware that Dallas was yanking her back, but then her shin hit a big log and she sprawled in the cold mud. He picked her up quickly and carried her again. Julienne was at the end of her strength. She clung to him, burying her face in his chest.

They came into a clearing where there was a tall chimney, but the farmhouse had burned. "Barn," Dallas grunted. "At least a roof."

He carried her into the small deserted barn. The doors had long ago rotted at the hinges, and sagged. Lying Julienne down on the mound of dirty hay left behind, he worked and worked to drag them so that they closed enough to keep out the driving rain.

Julienne struggled to sit up. "Where are we? What happened?"

Dallas turned to her, stripping off his sodden leather coat. "That chimney's a landmark on the river. We're nine miles south of Natchez. The boilers exploded."

"Tyla," Julienne whispered and began to weep. She was shivering helplessly.

Dallas came to her, grasped her upper arms, and lifted her up. "Julienne. Julienne. Listen to me. You're freezing cold, and your clothes are soaked, and I'm afraid you're going to faint again, and then I don't know if you'll live through this night. Do you understand?"

She stared up at him, tears rolling down her cheeks. But her mind was clear enough to see the sense in what he was saying. "Y-yes, I understand."

His face grew dark and stern. "You have to take this ton of clothes off, and I'm stripping down too. The only way you're going to get warm enough is from my body warmth."

"No, no," Julienne said automatically. "Can't you—can't you light a fire?"

"There's no wood, only hay, and if I set that on fire, the smoke would just choke us and we wouldn't have a good warm fire anyway. Julienne, you have to trust me. This is the only way."

Julienne stood there, looking down, shuddering so hard her teeth rattled. With the force of a blow she realized that ever since that terrible moment on the boat, her life had literally been in this man's hands. He had saved her then, and he would save her now.

She lifted her chin and tried to unclasp her cloak fastening, but her fingers were so cold she had no feeling in them. "Will you help me, please, Dallas?" she asked pitifully.

Quickly he undid the clasp and slipped off her cloak. Then he turned her to unbutton the twenty-two buttons of her dress, which he did quickly. Then, leaving her dress resting on her shoulders, he undid the tight laces of her corset. Turning her back around as if she were a child, he gave her one reassuring, warm glance, and slipped her dress off her shoulders. "Th-thank you, I can do the rest," she said.

He nodded, then made a half-turn so he wasn't looking at her. He pulled his shirt over his head and wrung it out, then quickly shed his trousers, so all he was wearing was his ankle-length felt under-pants. He picked up Julienne's cloak, which must have weighed ten pounds, and wrung it out as best as he could.

Julienne felt numb and stupid, as if she were in a troublesome dream. She took off her corset and her four petticoats, so all she was wearing was her chemise and pantalettes. They too were soaked of course, but they were of such thin material that she was sure they would dry quickly.

The hay was piled into a corner of the little barn, and Dallas pulled on it and worked with it until there was a bed. "Come on, Julienne," he said quietly. Obediently she lay down, and he pushed piles of hay around the bed. He lay down beside her, pulled a thick layer of hay over them, then spread her cloak on top of it. Without a word he turned to her, put his arms around her, and pulled her close.

She shivered and shivered, and she thought perhaps her brain might be frozen, too, because it seemed that she wasn't thinking at all. Images darted through her mind, flashing through in brief moments like the lightning, of the boat burning, of Dallas's grim face above her, of Tyla coughing, of Dallas's desperate calls out over the raging river, of Tyla, lying in the bunk, of water crashing in. Her breaths grew shallow and distressed and Dallas murmured, "Don't faint again, Julienne. Stay with me, stay with me." He began to stroke her back, softly and gently, a comforting caress that a mother might give a sick child.

Julienne made herself think, made herself concentrate on breathing, on trying to relax and let the heat from Dallas's body warm her.

Finally, dreamily, she lay pliant in his arms, savoring his breath on her face, the closeness and radiant warmth of him. She was, perhaps, more aware of her own body than she had ever been, and she felt a stirring in herself that slowly turned in a burning heat that she had never known. She felt the hard muscling of his chest, his flat stomach, the bulky strength of his arms. She made no conscious choice; she only did what she wanted to do, what she felt compelled to do. She reached up, put her hand on the back of Dallas's neck, pulled his head down, and pressed her lips to his.

As he kissed her, Julienne felt the soft, wild half giving and half receiving in her own body. Everything for that moment was unreal: the sinking of the ship, the desperate fight to stay alive, and the wind howling outside their cocoon, but his warmth was real, and the touch of his lips on hers was real. She felt that his caress kept loneliness and fear away. Though Julienne was innocent, she became aware that Dallas's growing passion made a turbulent eddy around them both, and she knew that he was not alone in his desires. She returned his kiss with a fierceness that shocked her.

At that instant Julienne was helpless and open to his strength. All she wanted in that moment was love and assurance and security and hope, and they all seemed to lie within his arms.

Suddenly Dallas jerked, took a deep breath, and turned his head away. Then he halfway sat up and moved away from her. His desertion stunned Julienne. "What's the matter?" she whispered and tried to pull him back.

Dallas caught her hand, pressed it to his lips, and didn't answer for a moment. When he did his voice was hoarse. "This isn't right, Julienne. You've had a bad shock, and you're not yourself."

Julienne could not believe what was happening. She had offered herself to him as she never had to a man, and he was refusing her. She cried, "Don't you want me?"

Gutturally he said, "Of course I do, you're a beautiful, desirable woman. But not like this. You would hate yourself, but you'd hate me more. No, Julienne."

Julienne was devastated. He had rejected her! Shame crawled through her like a sickness. Turning over quickly she curled up into a defensive ball, her eyes tightly shut. For long moments she grimaced, fighting desperately not to weep again.

"I'm sorry," he said, his voice desolate. "But you're still too cold. I'll try—I won't—" He put his arm across her and started to pull her close, but Julienne was like a stone.

"Don't touch me," she said between gritted teeth. "Don't ever touch me again."

He sighed deeply, piled more hay over her, then doubled her cloak to cover her with it. He lay back, staring at the filthy roof of the barn.

Julienne could hear his breathing and knew he wasn't asleep. Even though she was so stiff and tense she was almost paralyzed, as the moments passed she knew she was drifting off to sleep from utter exhaustion.

He turned me away! He rejected me! And he's nothing but a roughneck, a man so common and beneath me that he shouldn't even be able to look at me!

The last thought she had before she drifted off into the now-welcoming darkness was that she thought she now knew what true hatred was. She hated Dallas Bronte.

JULIENNE BECAME AWARE OF Dallas stirring, and even though he wasn't touching her she knew that he had gotten up. She turned over and managed to push herself up to a sitting position. A dreary gray light came through the cracks of the barn, and a steady rain beat on the tin roof. It was a dawn most miserable and cold. Hurriedly she grabbed her cloak and held it to her chest.

Dallas wasn't looking at her anyway. He already had his breeches on, and he was pulling his shirt over his head. Even through the thick fog of her mind Julienne admired the breadth and deeply wrought muscles of his chest, but swiftly the memories of the night overtook her, and she turned her head away. "What are you doing?" she asked hoarsely.

"I know the Landers plantation is two miles upriver from here," he answered. "I'm going to walk up there and bring back help."

His words sent a cold shiver through Julienne, and she realized that she desperately did not want him to leave her, no matter what had happened between them. He was her tenuous hold on life, and sanity. Without him, she thought, she would sit in this horrible wreck of a barn and cry and hope that she would die. "No. I mean, I'm coming with you," she said, struggling to rise. She was so weak, and her entire body was as sore and pained as if she'd been beaten with a club.

He watched her gravely, then came forward to help her stand, still clutching her cloak like a shield. "Do you really think you can walk that far? It's two miles *by river.* I don't know how far the river road is from here. You've been through a very bad time, and you're sick and weak."

"Stop telling me how I feel," Julienne said angrily. She clung to her anger, welcoming it, for it was her only defense against the miserable shame hovering in her mind like a cruel cloud. "You don't know anything about me. I'm coming with you, and don't worry, you won't have to carry me."

"I wouldn't mind," he said, trying to lighten the ugly tone.

She glared at him, then waded through the hay to where he had hung her petticoats and dress on the low wall of the horse's stall.

Defeated, he said, "I'll wait outside."

It took her a long time to dress. Her clothes were still wet and heavy and she had so little strength. But Julienne had made up her mind that she could do this; she had to do this, because being left alone terrified her. Somehow she summoned her strength and began to try to dress herself. Immediately she realized that it was impossible for her to tie up her own corset; in fact, she couldn't even button her dress. *I can't even dress myself! Oh, Tyla, Tyla, whatever am I going to do without you?* she thought, and deep desolation threatened to overwhelm her. But after a moment she fiercely fought it off. Throwing her corset carelessly aside, she pulled on her dress and considered her petticoats. She had two thick cotton ones and a wool one, and they were all still wet. The woolen one stank. With disgust Julienne put on her cloak over her loose dress, pulled it close around her, and walked out of the barn.

Dallas stood there, searching the threatening sky. At the moment it wasn't raining, but from the lowering clouds even Julienne could tell it might start again at any time. He pointed to a path that led to the east, up a gentle incline. "I'm sure that leads to the river road. Are you ready?"

"Yes." Without looking at him she started walking. The path was ankle-deep in mud, and she hadn't gone very far before she could barely lift her feet, and sometimes she slid precariously backward.

Dallas appeared at her side and gently took her arm. "I know I don't have to carry you," he said hastily. "But at least let me help you, Julienne."

Ungraciously she grabbed his arm and leaned on him. "I haven't given you permission to use my name, Mr. Bronte," she said coldly. In the circumstances it was absurd, and Julienne knew it. But the bitterness and anger that she was nourishing inside her pushed all calm thoughtfulness aside.

"Yes, ma'am," he bit off, matching her frigid tone.

They reached the top of the little hill, and there they found the road, running straight north. Julienne was relieved, but it was short-lived. The road stood in water, with wagon ruts at least a foot deep, now filled with gummy mud. As she struggled along, even with Dallas's help, she began to grow treacherously exhausted. He put one arm around her and held her arm with his other hand. He seemed strong and unbowed, walking straight and tall, but taking small, slow steps to accommodate Julienne.

They came out of the woods and on either side as far as they could see were empty fields, ready to be planted with cotton. "This is Landers' fields," Dallas said. "With any luck at all there will be some field hands out plowing."

"In this weather?" Julienne said wretchedly.

Dallas made no answer.

But just a little farther on, they saw a man on horseback, far out in the middle of the field on their right. He had dismounted, and he walked slowly down the still-visible rows, occasionally kneeling and reaching down to the earth.

Dallas narrowed his eyes and Julienne saw now that they had turned into a bright deep green. "That's Kinsey, their overseer. Stay here." He disentangled himself from her, though she was loath to let him go. Ignoring her clinging hands, he took off running and shouting toward the distant figure. Hazily Julienne wondered how he could possibly have recognized the man, who was so far off that to Julienne he just looked like a rather absurd man-shape.

Hugging herself, she realized that her knees were trembling. She wasn't shivering with cold; the hard walk had warmed her up. But Julienne's body had sustained some horrible shocks in the last hours, and she felt so small, so vulnerable, and so weak that she barely could comprehend that it was her own body betraying her. Looking around she tried to find something, a log or even a little rise to sit down on, but there was nothing. Her head hurt, and she grew dizzy and nauseous, and murkily she decided to just sit down on the road. But then she knew only blackness, and she fainted dead away.

JULIENNE WAS DROWNING, AND she knew she was going to die. Though her body struggled and fought, and she felt as if her head was bursting from trying to hold her breath, her mind was strangely calm. "I'm sorry, Dallas," she told him. "You were so right and honorable. I was wrong, I was awful. Please help me." Though only choked garbles came out of her mouth, he seemed to understand. Serenely he floated beside her, his thick hair waving gently. He nodded.

"Please help me," she said again. But the vision of his face faded. Julienne fought to breathe, and she flailed wildly, trying to scream.

"Julienne, darling, calm down, it's all right, you're safe," a blessedly familiar voice said. Soft hands took her own, and Roseann gently pressed her back down. "Lie down, darling. Don't struggle so. Just be calm and rest."

Julienne realized that she was home, in her own bed, and her mother was there. She fell back, and in her bewilderment wondered why she felt so hot and why her bed seemed to be wet. "It's because I was drowning," she murmured drowsily. "Can't go into the water again." Again the darkness closed down upon her.

Later she opened her eyes and looked up. Her Aunt Leah and Carley were kneeling by her bed, their hands pressed together in prayer, their eyes closed. As if from faraway she heard Aunt Leah saying, ". . . give her strength, Lord Jesus, lift this terrible darkness from her heart and mind. Heal her spirit, Blessed Lord . . ."

Julienne wandered back into the blank formless shadow world that surrounded her again, and their faces and Aunt Leah's quiet voice faded away.

It seemed she wandered there a long time, hopelessly sad and bitter. Sometimes she caught glimpses of Dallas Bronte, but it was as if he was a ghost, insubstantial, that appeared before her eyes and then quickly turned into dust. Once her brother Darcy was there, and she could hear him but only in a faint distant whisper: *Don't do this, Jules. Stay here, sweet sister, stay here.* She saw Tyla, far off, smiling sweetly at her, and she tried to wave to her and call her, but no matter how hard she struggled, she couldn't make a sound, and Tyla turned away and walked off, disappearing into the gloomy mist.

But then, somehow, she started feeling her body again. She slowly became aware of her arms, her hands folded across her stomach, her legs, the weight of her head against a cool pillow. Her face was warm, and the heat felt tender and welcoming. She opened her eyes.

Her bedroom was flooded with light, and as her mind grew aware she knew that it was late afternoon. She heard birds singing outside. By her bed sat her Aunt Leah, reading the Bible.

"Hello, Aunt Leah," she said, and was surprised by the almost inaudible croak that came out of her mouth.

Leah's head snapped up and instantly she was standing by Julienne's bed, pressing her hand against her forehead. "Oh, thank You, God, thank You, Father," she murmured. Smiling down at Julienne she said, "Hello, dear. I'm so glad you're awake at last. Are you thirsty?"

"Oh, yes, please, some water," Julienne whispered.

Leah went to the washstand and filled a glass with water from a crystal pitcher that had ice shards floating in it. Cool droplets streamed down its gleaming sides, and Julienne was amazed how pretty she found this simple sight.

"Don't gulp," she warned Julienne as she slid one arm behind her to help her sit up. "Just small sips."

She held the glass up to Julienne's face, but with determination she took it. "If you would just fix my pillows, Aunt Leah, I can do this myself," she croaked.

Leah plumped up two pillows to support Julienne, and obediently she settled back and took three small sips of the cool water. She thought that it was the most delicious taste of anything she had ever known.

Settling back in her chair, Leah watched her carefully. After many tiny sips Julienne finally felt that she had soothed her raging thirst, and her throat didn't feel as raw. By herself she managed to set the glass on the table by her bed. Her aunt watched her and seemed to nod with approval. "You've been very ill, Julienne. I'm surprised you have this much strength."

Confused, Julienne asked, "I've been ill? For how long?"

"For five days. You've had raging fevers, and you've been mostly unconscious. Julienne, do you remember what's happened?"

"Happened?" she repeated dimly. "I remember . . ." She fell silent, her face working. Then she closed her eyes tightly. "Oh, no," she said faintly. "Tyla. Tyla's dead, isn't she? She—there was an explosion, and the boat sank. But Dallas—Dallas—"

She fell limply back onto the pillows and pressed her hands to her eyes. They felt grainy and inflamed, but no tears came. She remembered all about the wreck, how Dallas had saved her, how he had literally carried her to safety, but looming large and lurid in her mind was how she had thrown herself at him. And he had turned away from her! A common nobody like him, and he didn't want her!

She groaned, a wild painful sound.

Leah said quietly, "I'm sorry, Julienne, but it's best that you remember right now, if you can. You've been—lost, somehow, and for a while it seemed you didn't *want* to come back and we were all very afraid. But you're a strong woman, Julienne. You have to face this, and with God's help, deal with it, and go on."

Julienne drew in a deep ragged breath, then dropped her hands and opened her eyes. Staring at the ceiling, she said, "I remember, Aunt Leah. I remember it all, unfortunately. Well, maybe not quite all. The last thing I remember is Dal—Mr. Bronte running to some man that was out in a cotton field. I tried to wait for them to come back, but I—I—that's all I remember."

"You fainted," Leah told her. "It was the Landers' overseer that was riding their fields. He rode to the house, fetched their carriage, and then he and Mr. Bronte brought you home."

"I don't remember any of that," she said dully. "Oh, Aunt Leah, it was horrendous. Tyla died, and I thought that I was going to die too."

Leah sighed deeply. "It was such a terrible tragedy, twenty-three people died. Everyone, crew and passengers, except for you and Mr. Bronte. And from what I understand, you very well may have died had it not been for him. He saved your life, Julienne, more than once that terrible night."

"More than once? What do you mean?"

"I mean he saved you from the boiler explosion, he saved you from drowning, and if he hadn't found shelter and a way to keep you warm, you might have died from exposure to the elements," Leah answered gravely.

"He told you all that?" Julienne demanded in such a sharp tone that her aunt looked at her curiously.

"Very reluctantly," she answered. "He had to explain how you two had survived, and Charles finally managed to drag the entire story out of him."

"The—entire story?" Julienne repeated with dread. "Oh, no," she whispered bleakly.

Leah frowned. "Julienne, I think you must be still confused. Mr. Bronte saved your life. But he appears to be a very humble man, because it was only with extreme difficulty that he explained about the wreck and having to swim and finding that deserted farmhouse, out in the middle of nowhere, in that raging storm. You were a very lucky woman, Julienne, that he was able to make a fire to warm you up. By the time you got here, you were so thoroughly chilled and your blood was so thin that you were literally half dead. If he hadn't taken such good care of you, you probably would be dead."

Julienne kept staring at her for so long that Leah thought she might be going into a stupor again. "Julienne? Are you all right?"

She roused, then said in a coldly bitter voice, "A fire. A deserted farmhouse. That's what he told you."

Leah cocked her head to the side. "What's the matter, dear? The Lord blessed you mightily by having Mr. Bronte there to save your life. And though I would think that going through such a terrible thing would make you grateful to the Lord Jesus and also to Mr. Bronte, you sound as if you're angry. Is it because of Tyla?"

"No. Yes. I don't know," Julienne said wearily.

"I think it's time for you to lie back down," Leah said sternly. She stood and poured a brown liquid from a heavy crystal decanter into a small glass. "Drink this, dear. Then you should be able to rest quietly."

Obediently Julienne drank and shuddered as the harsh warmth from the brandy spread down her throat into her stomach. Leah rearranged her pillows and Julienne lay back down. Catching Leah's hand, she asked, "Where is Mr. Bronte now?"

"I don't know, dear. Charles begged him to stay with us for a few days, but he flatly refused."

"Good," Julienne said in a stony voice. "I don't want him here. I don't ever want to see him again."

"Oh, really?" Leah asked gently as she settled back into her chair and picked up her Bible. "That's odd. Because you've been asking for him, Julienne. For the last five days, you've asked for Dallas Bronte again and again."

CHAPTER SIX

Cruel winter was gone, and late April in Natchez was gorgeous. It seemed as if Nature was trying to make up for the desolation of the cold season, for the spring had been balmy and pleasant.

The barn was dark, but slanting rays of light filtered through the cracks, falling on Carley's face. Industriously she worked a shovel into the soft ground of half manure and half dirt. In the nearest stall, their horse Reddy seemed to watch her with disapproval. When she saw a group of huge earthworms wiggling, she let out a cry of joy. "I gotcha!" With both hands she scooped up the dirt and worms over and over again, dumping all of it into her ever-present straw bag.

Caesar came into the barn and, sighting Carley, crossed his arms and said sternly, "Here you are.

Your Aunt Leah sent me to find you and fetch you back to your lessons. And just look at that dress, and your pantaloons, Miss Carley! Your poor mama might faint dead away when she catches sight of you!"

"I'm digging worms, Caesar. Fishin' worms," she said, ignoring his chiding.

"You've got no call to be down at that pond by yourself. You could fall in and drown. Then where would you be?"

"I'd be dead."

"There. That's just what I said."

"Silly, Darcy's going to take me. If I fall in, he can pull me out. He can swim."

A small look of regret creased Caesar's face, and he spoke more gently. "Mr. Darcy, he's poorly today. I don't think he's going to feel like taking you fishing."

"But he promised," she said, straightening to look up at Caesar. Then her face fell. "He got all liquored up last night again, didn't he."

Uncomfortably he replied, "Miss Carley, little girls don't need to know things such as that. All you need to know is he's feeling poorly."

"He promised," she said dully. Dropping her bag, she stalked out of the barn, her hands down at her side in stiff fists. Running upstairs to Darcy's room, she knocked and called, "Darcy! Darcy, wake up!"

She heard his muffled voice inside, "Not now, Carley. Later."

Stubbornly she opened the door, and there Darcy lay, fully dressed in the middle of the bed. Carley could smell the sour reek of alcohol in the air. She shook his shoulder, very gently. "Please, Darcy, please get up. You promised to take me fishin'."

Darcy groaned and rolled over to turn his back to her. "No, Carley, I can't today. Tomorrow."

"You always say that," she said angrily.

"Carley, just go away. I'll take you fishing some other time," he mumbled. "I promise."

She repeated bitterly, "You promise. You always promise, but you never do."

But he didn't hear her, so she left, slamming the door behind her, and ran back to the barn. She decided to re-bury the earthworms. Maybe in a couple of days Darcy would take her fishing, and she would dig them back up.

DARCY STAYED PASSED OUT for most of the day. At about two o'clock he suddenly sat up and grabbed his head with both hands. He had a blinding head-ache. For a long time he sat there trying to pull his mind together, then slowly and carefully he rose, walked over to the pitcher and bowl on his wash-stand. Picking it up, he drank deeply straight from the pitcher, and the tepid water soothed his burning throat. Searching his face in the shaving mirror on the chest, he groaned. His eyes were so bloodshot they seemed more red than blue, his thick shiny auburn hair was standing up all over his head and looked greasy, and his complexion looked sickly yellow.

Pouring the rest of the water into the bowl, he splashed water into his face until he finally began waking up. As he dried his face with a clean towel, he smelled the fresh cottony smell of the towel and realized that he stank of stale liquor and sour sweat. Mentally he cursed their lack of servants, for he would have given anything to have a hot bath. Instead he picked up an amber bottle, pulled the cork, and made a disgusted face. "Bay Rum, how could I have ever put that sickening stuff on myself?" He slammed it back down and picked up a small deep green bottle, uncorked it, and sniffed it. Relieved, he emptied a few drops into the water left in the washbowl. Royal Lyme, imported from England, had a lighter, bracing scent. Stripping, he scrubbed himself all over with the freshened water, and immediately he felt better. Rubbing his scratchy jaw with regret, he thought, *Draw the line at shaving with cold water. I just have to convince Father to get me a body servant, that's all there is to it.*

He dressed quickly in a clean linen shirt and comfortable black breeches. Though he felt better, his head still throbbed, and he had a familiar subtly nauseous feeling in the pit of his stomach, a sure aftereffect of drinking too much.

It was too warm to wear a coat, so he grabbed some papers out of the coat he'd been wearing the previous night and went downstairs. No one was in the parlor, so he went out the back door and down the bricked path to the freestanding kitchen. Inside, their cook and maidservant Libby looked up at him. "Well, hello there, Mr. Ashby. You look awful, just purely awful."

"Just say whatever you're thinking, Libby. Don't worry about hurting my feelings," he said sarcastically.

"I won't," she said sassily. "Sit down, I'll get you some coffee. And it's a pancake day, if I'm not mistaken."

"It's a pancake day," Darcy said. "Please." He always begged Libby to make him pancakes when he had a hangover. He had no idea why, but they seemed to make him feel better.

He took his seat on a stool at the waist-high oak worktable. It was old and scarred, and for at least the thousandth time he smiled a little at the crudely etched letters in the corner: a crooked angular "D" and the first downstroke of an "A." Their butler back then, a dignified old slave named Eli, had caught him carving them when he was eight years old, and had stopped him. Darcy had never finished the "A."

Libby set down a thick old mug in front of him and poured hot, fresh coffee from a blue-speckled tin coffeepot into it. He looked up at her and managed a ragged grin, and she made a face at him.

Libby was thirty-five years old, but she looked younger. She and Caesar made an odd couple. Caesar was average size, average height, and his looks were unremarkable except for the dark gleam of his ebony skin and his somber manner. Libby was short and curvaceous, and she had warm golden skin and delicate features. She was lively and bright-eyed, a complete contrast to her husband in every way. When he had reached his teen years, he had realized that Libby had a lot of white blood, and he wondered about it, for she had been born a slave at Ashby Plantation. But in a thousand years he couldn't imagine his father, or his grandfather, com-mitting such a sin. Both of them were men of deep Christian faith and high moral scruples.

Dryly Darcy reflected that it seemed he didn't take after any of the men in his family.

With quick efficiency Libby made Darcy a stack of pancakes and set them down, along with a dish of melted butter and a small tin pitcher of Vermont maple syrup. "You're about as spoilt a boy as I ever saw in my life," Libby said as she served him. "I swear I don't know why I baby you like I do. But I guess all women do," she added slyly.

"Guess so," he agreed. "I'm glad, too."

"Brat," she muttered as she went back to the fire-place, to continue turning an enormous roast on a spit.

"Sass," he retorted. It was an old ritual between them.

He ate hungrily and polished off two more cups of coffee. When he was finished he felt much bet-ter, as he knew he would. He stood and stretched. "Where is everyone, Libby?"

"Miss Julienne's making her calls, your mother is resting, and Miss Leah was in the library, and the Good Lord Himself only knows where Miss Carley is," Libby answered. "Caesar found her just after breakfast, but he lost her again."

"What about Father? He didn't go out to the plantation again, did he?" Darcy asked.

Libby shook her head. "He's been in his study all day."

Darcy headed to the door. "Thanks, Libby. Your pancakes have mystical healing properties."

"I should sell 'em," she grumbled. "Libby's Mystical Hangover Remedy."

Ignoring her parting shot, Darcy finished off the coffee, left the kitchen, and went to his father's study. The door was closed, and Darcy knocked. "Father?"

"Come in," he heard faintly.

Darcy found his father sitting at his desk, staring at the mass of papers before him. When he looked up, with a slight shock Darcy thought that his father seemed to have aged. All of a sudden, he looked old, his face gray with strain, small spectacles perched on his nose, his normally square shoulders stooped.

Darcy sat down in an armchair in front of his desk and lounged back. Idly he asked, "Do you feel all right? You don't look too well."

"I'm fine," Charles answered rather shortly. "I'm just really busy, Darcy."

"Sorry to interrupt," Darcy said unrepentantly, "but I have to talk to you." Throwing his papers down on Charles's desk, he continued, "Guess I overspent my allowance again, Father, so I need some more money. And there's these."

Slowly Charles picked up the papers and perused them with a pained look on his drawn face. Appalled, he said, "Three hundred dollars? You gave out three hundred dollars in I.O.U.'s to Stephen Moak and Lucky Darden?"

Darcy shrugged. "Started out on a streak, but it fizzled out. And Lucky Darden's name fits him all too well."

Charles leaned back in his chair, took off his spectacles, and massaged his temples. Looking down, he said quietly, "I don't have any more money to give you, Darcy. And I can't pay these markers."

"What! But they're debts of honor! I have to pay them!" Darcy almost shouted.

Wearily Charles looked up at him and said, "Then pay them."

A long heavy silence stretched out. Finally Darcy muttered darkly, "I can't pay them, and you know it."

"I can't pay them either, and now you know it," Charles snapped. "What were you thinking, Darcy? Haven't you paid any attention at all to what I've been telling you for months? *We do not have any money!* I told you that I doubted I'd be able to give you your allowance, maybe for the next several months! I told you that, son!"

Darcy jumped out of his chair and began to pace. "You've been saying things like that for years, that we have to cut back and do without some things. But we didn't. Julienne keeps getting enough clothes to dress the county, Mother got her new barouche, and you even tried to get Julienne to replace Tyla with a new maid! And here I am, with no body servant, and she's had a maid all of her life! If we've got no money, where were you going to get the money to buy a maid?"

Charles's dark eyes sparkled angrily when Darcy started speaking, but as his son's rant went on, Charles seemed to wilt. Faintly he answered, "I wasn't going to buy a slave, Darcy, you know that. There's a girl at the plantation that I thought might do, and her pay would only be a little bit more as Julienne's maid. I just thought, since she lost Tyla, that she would want another girl. But it seems she doesn't."

"But my point is that you're willing to spend all kinds of money on Julienne, but you're cutting me off," Darcy complained. "It's not fair."

Charles started to speak, but then he seemed to think better of it, and shook his head. "Son, I mis-spoke before. I'm not feeling well, not at all. And I had already decided that we're going to have to have a family meeting tonight after dinner. We'll discuss all of this then."

"I'm going out tonight," Darcy retorted.

"I know I can't stop you. But I am not giving you any money, Darcy, and I'm telling you right now that I won't honor any more of your debts, so don't try to borrow any money from your friends. Anyway, I would like for you to stay and have dinner with us tonight," Charles said with evident weariness.

"I suppose I have no choice," Darcy said, yanking the door open. "I'm going back to bed until then."

THE ATMOSPHERE AT DINNER was strained. Charles and Leah were silent, and Darcy was in a foul humor. As usual, Roseann was quiet, seeming not to notice the strain on the conversation.

Julienne was oblivious to everyone else's discomfort, as she talked about her calls that day. Since she had recovered from the accident, she had stayed ostentatiously busy, making calls every day that someone wasn't calling on her, going to town almost every day, even when she couldn't beg her father for any money to spend, accepting every invitation offered to her. In the springtime there were many parties and balls and barbecues, and she was out almost every night.

She said with artificial brightness, "I was calling on Felicia and Susanna, and Stephen was there, and we were having a wonderful time. And then Mary Nell and Sadie Stanford came driving up in that awful black landau that looks just like a hearse. Of course the Moaks have to receive them, even though they are such dreary women, with faces like puddings. And Sadie has gained so much weight that I swear I could see the seams splitting in her bodice. It really ruined my visit."

No one said anything for long moments. Finally Julienne went on, "I suppose Archie will call tomorrow. He missed today."

"No, he didn't," Aunt Leah said deliberately. "He did call, but you missed him because you left so early."

"Oh. Well, he'll live."

Carley had been subdued, but now she giggled and said, "Archie-Bald calls every day, Julienne. He's sooooo in looooove with yooooou!"

Julienne laughed. Leah glanced at Roseann and Charles, who seemed not to hear Carley. She said quietly, "Carley, children shouldn't make fun of adults. You should be more respectful."

"Aw, it's just ol' Archie-Bald," Carley said with disdain. "Even Julienne calls him that sometimes."

"Could you people stop talking so loud?" Darcy said ungraciously. "It makes my head pound."

"Darcy got liquored up last night," Carley announced. "Darcy's got a hangover, Darcy's got a hangover," she went on in a singsong voice.

Grimly Darcy turned to his mother. "That child is a disgrace, Mother. I think she needs a good spanking and to be sent to bed without supper."

Roseann's eyes were downcast and she said nervously, "Please, Darcy, don't be so harsh. She's just a child."

Aunt Leah's mouth drew into a straight harsh line, but of course she couldn't discipline Carley when her parents wouldn't. And in spite of Darcy's outburst, he and Julienne indulged her shamefully. That was why Carley would never sit through her lessons, she always ran out of the schoolroom the moment Leah's back was turned. No one in the family ever tried to correct her, and Leah felt that it wasn't her place.

Little was said the rest of the meal. As they were finishing up, Charles sighed deeply and said, "All of you please come into the sitting room. I need to talk to you."

"Even me?" Carley piped up.

He hesitated, then finally said, "No, no, Carley. Libby will take you upstairs and you can get into your nightdress. I'll come up later to read to you."

He was so grave that Carley took Libby's hand and left the dining room without protest. Charles went down the hallway to the family sitting room, a less formal, and more comfortable room than the parlor, and they all followed him. Though the night was warm and the windows were opened, Caesar had laid a small fire in the fireplace. Charles took his place standing in front of it, his hands behind his back. The others seated themselves on the plump sofa and rather worn armchairs.

Timidly Roseann said, "Are you sure you want to do this tonight, dear? You look as if you aren't feeling well."

"I'm all right, dear. No, I'm afraid this can't wait any longer." Absently he massaged his left hand with his right. "I wish I had been a better husband, Roseann, and a better father to you, my children."

"Don't be foolish, Charles," Roseann said worriedly. "You are a wonderful husband and father."

"I love you all very much," he said quietly. "But that's just not enough. I haven't been the head of my household, I haven't led you in the right ways, I haven't protected you, and I'm so very sorry."

"This is about money, isn't it," Julienne stated. "You're really worried about money."

Darcy looked stubborn. "Father, why can't you explain, really, what's going on? I mean, we all know you've been talking about our lack of money, but I for one don't understand what the problem is."

"I'm the problem," Charles said regretfully. "For at least three years now, we have been living beyond our means. I thought I was managing our affairs, I kept thinking that I would really force you all to stop spending so much money. But I didn't. I just let things go, I was just too weak to face the problem and make the sacrifices required to fix it. Sometimes in my mind I blamed all of you for being too extravagant, but that's wrong. This is all my fault. I should have taught you all better, and I should have made a way for us to have a good life without spending so much money."

Julienne looked very unhappy and said in a low voice, "You did try to tell us, Papa. We just didn't listen. But you sound so very somber. How bad is it?"

"It's bad," he said bluntly. "I had to mortgage the plantation, and in fact the bank made me a very good deal. But those storms the first of March . . ." His voice trailed off, and he grimaced with pain. Again he grabbed his left hand with his right, then rubbed his left arm.

Leah said, "This is ridiculous, Charles, sit down. You're clearly ill. We can deal with this problem, but we don't have to put you through this right now, tonight."

He shook his head stubbornly. "No, Leah. I've been making excuses to myself for years now. I'm not excusing myself any more." Setting his jaw, he continued, "The storms in early March, they flooded four hundred acres of the lower fields. For days we thought that the Mississippi had carved a new course, and that the acreage would be permanently underwater. But just this week the waters receded and went back to the regular course before those spring floods."

Frowning, Darcy said, "So? What's the problem?"

Charles answered sardonically, "Aside from the fact that I had to mortgage land owned free and clear by the Ashbys for almost a hundred years? Anyway, the problem is that those fields had been underwater too long, the soil is soured. They're going to have to lay fallow this season." Looking around the room, he could see that his family, except for his sister Leah, looked bewildered. It only reinforced his guilt, that he had allowed them to be so ignorant of how to manage a home and finances in an appropriate manner.

The pain in his arm increased, and he was short of breath. But Charles was so focused on trying to

manage this crisis that he ignored these dire warn-
ings. With difficulty he went on, "That means that
we can't plant four hundred acres, so we won't
have the profits on those acres, and the plantation
is going to make much less money this year. When
the bank realized this, they changed the terms of
the mortgage. The monthly draw I'm going to be
able to make against the plantation has been dras-
tically reduced. And that means that we'll have
much, much less money every month. All of us are
going to have to—"

It was a spasm of pain so severe it drew his left
arm up into a painful cramp, and then his chest felt
as if he had been struck by an iron weight, crushing
all the breath out of him. He gasped, then crumpled to the floor.

Roseann, Darcy, and Julienne were all frozen,
their eyes wide with shock. Leah jumped up, knelt
beside him, then looked up and said in a sharp
voice, "Julienne! Tell Caesar to go get the doctor!
Right now!"

Julienne jerked upright as if she had been
shocked, then, her face white with fear, she turned
and ran out of the room.

DR. JEROME RANKIN HAD been the Ashby family
doctor ever since Julienne could remember. He
was a balding, short, stout man with a kind manner. When he arrived, Julienne felt completely

reassured, because she believed that Dr. Rankin could do anything.

But her heart sank when he returned to the sitting room from her father's bedroom. His face was grim, and he shook his head. "I'm so sorry, but I have to be honest with you. Charles is dying."

He waited for it to sink in. Roseann's face drained of all color, and she dropped her head and burst into tears. Darcy looked as if he were in shock. Leah took a sharp indrawn breath, then went to kneel beside Roseann and put her arms around her.

Julienne felt stunned, as if she had received a sharp blow to the head. Swallowing hard, she said faintly, "But . . . surely there is something you can do?"

"I'm sorry," he said again. "But he's had heart trouble for some time now. He instructed me never to tell any of you, and of course I held that confidence. I know this is a terrible shock to all of you, but I must tell you that Charles knew it was going to happen. It was just a question of when."

"But how could he not tell us!" Julienne said shrilly. "He should have told us!"

He looked at her with his sweet expression. "Maybe so, maybe not. Charles believes that all of us are called home by the Lord in His time. He trusted in the Lord to take him when He was ready. And now Charles knows that it's his time."

"That's right," Leah said, lifting her head. Roseann's sobs subsided, and she looked up. Standing up, Leah went on, "I knew that Charles was ill, and I suspected it was his heart. But any time I asked him about it, he just smiled and said, 'The Lord Jesus gives me breath and life. When it's time for me to go home to Him, then I'll go.'" She stared hard down at Roseann, then Darcy, and then Julienne. "But I know my brother, and I know that even though he trusts the Lord with all his heart, he's probably fighting hard."

"Good!" said Julienne. "He's strong, he could live!"

"Maybe," Dr. Rankin said quietly. "But if he did, he'd be sick and crippled for whatever's left of his life. He thinks it's his time, Julienne, and I agree with him. But your aunt's right. I've seen it so often before. It's hard for good people to feel like they can let go of their responsibilities, they feel guilt, they worry about their loved ones. I know that you all know me and trust me. So I'll tell you I think you should let him go."

"No!" Julienne said vehemently.

Darcy still looked bewildered, and muttered, "No, no . . ."

Roseann stood up and wiped the tears from her face. "Dr. Rankin is right," she said in a surprisingly strong voice. "Charles trusts the Lord with his life, and he'll trust Him with his death. If he believes it's time, we have to let him go. Both of you come with me now, and you, too, Leah. It's time to say good-bye."

They went up to their father's bedroom and went inside. Immediately Roseann went to sit on the bed, while Darcy, Julienne, and Leah stood on the other side. Julienne saw how small her father looked, how sunken and gray was his face, and she could tell he was wracked with pain. The last bit of hope that he would live faded away.

Roseann traced his cheek with her hand and said, "Charles, my love? Can you hear me?"

He opened his eyes and looked up at her. "Oh, Roseann, my dearest love, I'm sorry, so—"

"No," she said sternly. "Never be sorry. I'm so proud, and so blessed, to have you as my husband. You're a wonderful father, a kind, loving, patient man. Listen to me, my love. Don't worry. Don't even think about us any more. The Lord is coming to take you home, and there you will have joy and rest and comfort forever. Please just close your eyes and look for Him, because I know He is very near to all of us right now."

His dull eyes stayed riveted on her face as she spoke, and then he seemed to sag, his entire body went limp, and his face became peaceful. Roseann smiled and took his hand.

He turned and looked at them on the other side of the bed. "I always loved you, my children, and I'm so proud of you. Please tell Carley I'm sorry I couldn't read to her tonight."

Choking back a sob, Julienne said, "It's all right, Papa. I'll read to her from now on. I—I've always loved you, Papa. So much."

He nodded slightly. "Darcy, take care of your mother and your aunt and your sisters."

"Yes, sir," Darcy said bleakly. "Father, I—I love you very much."

"I know," Charles said. Very little life was in him as he looked at Leah. "Thank you, sister."

"No, thank you for giving me a family when I lost mine, beloved brother," she said. "The Lord will bless you for it."

He turned back to Roseann. "Love you, Roseann. Love you."

"I love you, my darling," she whispered. "I'll see you soon."

They all stayed there, watching him. He gazed at Roseann for a long time, and miraculously she just looked back into his eyes, smiling. His eyes fluttered, closed; his breathing became shallow, very light breaths, each one farther apart from the other.

And then Charles Ashby went home.

CHAPTER SEVEN

Julienne left her mother's bedroom and went to the sitting room. She sat down on the plump sofa and slumped down, letting her head rest against the back of the sofa. A grim smile played on her face when she recalled the last time her Aunt Leah had seen her with her back touching the back of a seat. But she knew her aunt wouldn't catch her this time, for she and Leah were taking turns caring for Roseann, and Leah had just gone up to let Julienne rest for awhile. She was exhausted.

Carley came in to sit by Julienne. "Are you too tired to take me for a walk?" she asked. Ever since Charles's death she had clung to Julienne and Leah. Though Roseann had been magnificent in Charles's last moments, and had borne the two days aftermath and then the funeral with her head held high, immediately after that she had collapsed, and had been virtually bedridden ever since. But though she was Carley's mother and Carley loved her dearly, she had always been closer to Julienne and her Aunt Leah, and even Tyla.

"I'm so sorry, Carley, but I am just exhausted. Maybe if I could just rest for about an hour, I'll be able to take you out for awhile before dinner. Will that be all right?" Julienne said.

"I guess so. Would you—could you please let me take a nap with you?" she pleaded. "I promise, I won't fidget, I'll be quiet and still."

Julienne put her arm around her and hugged her close. "Of course you can. I'd like that. Just let me sit here for a minute, then we'll go upstairs."

They sat for a few moments in silence, just hugging each other. Then Caesar came in and stood just inside the door, his head dropped. He and Libby had grieved over Charles Ashby's death almost as much as the family had. "Miss Julienne, I'm awful sorry to bother you, but me and Libby thought we'd better tell someone."

"Go ahead, Caesar," Julienne said, sitting straight up as ladies should, and folding her hands serenely on her lap.

He fidgeted, then looked up with a woeful expression. "The butcher, he won't sell us any more meat on account. And this morning the dairyman told us that after this week we'll have to go on a cash paying basis."

Julienne blinked, her mind reeling. After an awkward silence, as Caesar refused to meet her eyes, she managed to say calmly, "All right, Caesar, I'll take care of it. Would you please get the buggy ready to go to town? I'm going to write a letter, and I'll need you to take it to Mr. Preston Gates at Planter's Bank."

"Sure, sure, Miss Julienne," he said. "I'll just go hitch her up and bring her around. You send Libby out with that letter when you finish."

"Thank you, Caesar." He left, obviously relieved.

Troubled, Carley asked, "Julienne? Can't we have steak any more?" Aside from black licorice, beefsteak was Carley's favorite foods.

She turned to her and took her hand. "Of course we will, Carley. It's just that since Father passed away, it has sort of confused the shopkeepers that we buy from. I know that Mr. Gates is taking care of things right now, and he hasn't called because we're in mourning. But don't worry, I'm going to send a note asking him to come talk to me and Aunt Leah, and we'll get this all straightened out."

THE NEXT AFTERNOON CAESAR showed Preston Gates into the parlor, where Leah and Julienne waited for him. He bowed over their hands and said sincerely, "Please accept my deepest condolences for your loss. Charles was a good man, an honorable man, and I counted him as a friend. He will be sorely missed."

"Thank you, sir," Julienne said. "Please, sit down."

He took his seat on a wingchair across from them and glanced around. "Is Mr. Darcy Ashby here?"

"No, I'm afraid not," Julienne answered evenly. "Mr. Gates, I appreciate that you are hesitant to discuss business with us, considering that we are in mourning. But already some questions regarding the family's finances have arisen. My aunt and I will be responsible for managing our affairs from now on, so I'm sure you understand that we need you to help us figure out our financial situation now."

He nodded, and his sharp features reflected a deep uneasiness. "I wish I had good news, but I'm afraid I don't." He shifted uncomfortably in his chair.

Leah said quietly, "Mr. Gates, we already knew that the house is mortgaged, and Charles was just telling us about some of the plantation business, including the fact that he had mortgaged it, when he fell ill. I just want you to understand that we both understand that we're in some financial straits, and you are not going to cause us to have the vapors by what you tell us."

"I don't think that," he said. "I think that both of you ladies are smart and capable. It's just that—Charles's early death is so tragic, and not only for the obvious reasons. You see, Ashby Plantation is a highly profitable enterprise, and the bank had no problems with mortgaging it, because we know that we would be paid back, that the risk was very low. But now, you see, without Charles, that risk has suddenly become very high. I'm afraid that the bank is going to be obliged to foreclose the mortgage."

Both Leah and Julienne grew utterly still. Gates sat forward, rested his elbows on his knees, and looked down at his restless hands. After long moments Julienne said in a choked voice, "Are you—are you saying that we're losing the plantation? That the bank is taking it away from us?"

Without looking up, he murmured, "We don't have a choice. A little over ten thousand dollars is owed on a twenty-thousand-dollar mortgage, Miss Ashby. The bank couldn't possibly extend the rest of the money to your family, because there is no one to run the plantation. And so we will have to foreclose."

Now even Leah looked shaken. Julienne's face worked, as she struggled to control the tremendous anger rising in her as his words sunk in. She swallowed hard, took a deep ragged breath, and said in a voice so hard it barely resembled her own, "If I understand what you are saying, Mr. Gates, it is that the bank is getting a rich plantation for about ten thousand dollars. You will sell it, I know, for at least six times that much. The Ashbys will lose what has been their home for almost a hundred years, and you knew this, and *you let me bury my father there!* How could you! How dare you!"

Leah said sharply, "Julienne, be quiet. This is not Mr. Gates's decision alone. He has to answer to his Board of Directors, and they make these decisions, not him. Your father knew this when he did business with them, and that's what it is. It's business."

Julienne's anger waned, then her face crumpled and she buried it in her hands.

Gates looked up and looked at Leah gratefully. Then regretfully he said, "I am so very sorry, Miss Julienne, Mrs. Norris. I know it is cold comfort, but I did try to get the Board to approve signing the mortgage over to your mother, because everything was left to her, you know. But they wouldn't even consider it."

Julienne looked up, her face ashen. "Please accept my apologies, Mr. Gates. Of course I know my aunt is right, and I know that you are—were a good friend to my father. I'm so very sorry for speaking to you the way I did."

"Please, please," he said uncomfortably, making an awkward waving gesture with one hand. "I understand, and I don't blame you, Miss Ashby. In fact, I agree with you, because I still feel responsible. The whole situation has grieved me terribly."

Leah sighed deeply. "That's very kind of you, Mr. Gates. So, where are we now? I mean, what is the whole situation?"

"The problem is that the payments on the mortgage are three hundred dollars a month, and the family expenses have been running about eight hundred dollars," he answered gravely.

"Over a thousand dollars a month?" Leah blurted out. "Oh, no, Charles confided in me some, but I had no idea it was that bad!"

Julienne frowned. "I don't understand. How are we to live? What can we do?"

"You have no choice, Miss Julienne. In fact, this is what your father was considering doing anyway. You're going to have to sell this house and sell the carriages and horses, and find a smaller place to live. From now on I'm afraid you're going to have to learn to make do with much less."

Stricken, Julienne was silent, so Leah asked, "And will that give us enough income, sir, to perhaps invest a principal and live off the interest?"

"I'm afraid not, Mrs. Norris," he answered. He seemed to have made up his mind to stop trying to spare their feelings, for he went on somberly, "I have already taken the liberty of doing some research to find out how much the house might sell for, and even at the best price we can expect, it will barely cover the mortgage and all of your outstanding debts.

"There is some good news, however. About five years ago, your father put five thousand dollars in an interest-bearing investment account in your mother's name. Right now the balance is around sixty-one-hundred dollars. Supposing we might clear around two thousand dollars on the sale of the house, and if you withdrew a thousand dollars from this account, with three thousand dollars you should be able to buy a small cottage and have money for food and other necessities for quite awhile. And you would also have the interest from the investment account."

"How much would that be?" Leah asked sharply. "You said the principal was five thousand dollars?"

"Yes, and it's invested at five percent. That would give you an interest income each month of a little over twenty dollars."

Julienne gave a short hysterical laugh, a harsh sound. "Twenty dollars? When we've been spending over a thousand dollars a month? That's impossible!"

"With God all things are possible," Leah said quietly. "We'll do whatever we have to do, Julienne, and the Lord will bless us and watch over us, always."

Julienne looked rebellious but didn't answer.

Gates rose and said, "Mrs. Norris, Miss Ashby, I've told you what I think your options are, in my best opinion. I know you'll need time to think about all this. I know that Charles kept very good records, and if you can't find what you need here, just ask, and the bank will answer any questions you have and supply any records you may require. And please, if there's any way that I can help you, any way at all, please don't hesitate to let me know."

Leah and Julienne walked him out, and Leah thanked him profusely, while Julienne was merely polite.

"This is worse than I ever could have imagined," Julienne said as they closed the front door.

Her aunt managed a smile. "We'll get through it, dear, and we will be a good, strong, happy family again. I know it. The Lord will bless us and watch over us and protect us and even prosper us, if we are faithful to follow Him."

"That I'll leave up to you," Julienne said grimly. She turned on her heel, swept down the hall to her father's office, went in, and locked the door.

LATE THAT NIGHT, AFTER Roseann had gone to sleep and she had put Carley to bed, Leah went to the sitting room and sat in front of the fire she had instructed Caesar to build. "My old bones are cold even in warm weather these days," she murmured to herself. "A home fire is comforting anyway, dear Lord, thank You for it." She took up her Bible and began to read.

Julienne came into the room and sat in the chair beside her, staring at the fire. "I'm sorry I've been so horrible all day," she said in a low voice. She had locked herself in her father's study and had refused to come out for dinner, or even to read to Carley and put her to bed.

"We all know that you're so grieved, Julienne, and that the burden of all this trouble has fallen on your shoulders," Leah said. "We're your family. We love you, and no one is going to be angry with you."

"Thank you," Julienne said softly. Then, rousing herself, she said, "Yes, I understand now that I don't have the luxury of throwing temper tantrums any more. It's clearly up to me to manage things from now on. But, Aunt Leah, would you help me, please? I know I'm smart enough to figure out all of this money business, but you've been through it."

"Of course I'll help you, Julienne," she answered warmly. "Charles let me help him some, you know, so I think I know more about the household than you do. And you know, I loved my husband very much, and we were happy, but we were poor. I learned how to manage a household, the hard way." Barry Norris had been in the U.S. Army, and he had died in Oklahoma, fighting Indians.

Julienne smiled a little. "And I need you to teach me, the hard way, it looks like. But there's something that I wanted to talk to you about. Would you come into the study and look at some papers with me? I mean, truly, Aunt Leah, I want you to go over everything with me, just like I've been doing all day, but there is one thing that I especially wanted you to see."

"Let's go," she said.

They went into the study, settled themselves into two comfortable armchairs, and Julienne handed Leah a sheaf of papers. Perusing the top sheet, she murmured, "A title—oh, of course, I had completely forgotten about this. Charles bought a steamer— let's see, this title is dated 1848, that's right. The *River Queen*. Now I remember. She hauled our cotton for a couple of years, but then there was some sort of mishap, and Charles had to dock her."

"That next paper said the boiler blew up," Julienne said somewhat fearfully. "But I don't understand, it didn't sink?"

"No, I know it didn't sink," Leah answered quickly, shuffling through the papers. "Here, let me see . . . no, this report said that the boilers burst, Julienne, but she was towed to Natchez-Under-the-Hill. That was three years ago."

"Oh," Julienne said with relief. "When I saw that, I just thought that—that—well, you know what I thought."

"Obviously they didn't explode," Leah said kindly. Thumbing through the papers again, after a few moments she said, "There's no record that she ever traveled again. But here, look here. Charles wrote notes to himself that he had the carpenters and some workmen drydock her and scrape her and revarnish her every winter. And here's the harbor-master's receipts. We're still paying dock fees every month!"

"So we have a steamer?" Julienne asked in confusion. "But what does that mean?"

"It means that the Lord is showing us a way to deliver us," Leah said solidly. "And I'm going to believe it's a miracle."

"But we don't know anything about steamboats," Julienne complained. "At least, I don't."

"Neither do I. But Captain Silas Plank does."

"Captain Plank, Captain Plank," Julienne repeated in an undertone. "I recall that name. Yes, yes, now I am remembering something about Father being so excited to have a steamer, and having Mr. Plank as captain. But when I found out it was only for freight, I paid no more attention to it. Do you think Captain Plank would help us?"

"I know he would. I remember him well. He's a fine man, a good Christian man, and he was close to your father. He was at the funeral, though he didn't address the family since Charles and I were the only ones who ever met him. There are several letters in here from him. The last one was just last month."

"Does it have a return address?"

"Oh, yes."

Julienne nodded. "Then I'll call on him tomorrow. I know this is not exactly gold coins raining down from heaven, but I do feel better, Aunt Leah. I'll even say a thank-you prayer to God tonight. It may be a short one, and maybe not the warmest prayer I've ever prayed, but you've influenced me, Aunt Leah."

"I'm praising Him right now, and believing for a miracle," Leah said happily. "Julienne, I know that you're bitter, maybe even angry, toward God right now. But He is just and true and He will never forsake us. In time you'll come to see that, I know."

CHAPTER EIGHT

"Why, I'm glad to see you, Miss Julienne. My, you've grown up." Silas Plank was a hale old man of sixty-eight years. The outdoors life had given him a ruddy complexion, and his hair was snow white. But still there was a life in his eyes, and he leaned forward toward her where he had placed her in a chair and fixed her a cup of tea. "I was so sorry to hear about your daddy. He was a good man. Good to me."

"He thought a lot about you, Mr. Plank."

"I've thought about those days on the *River Queen*. If those two boilers hadn't cracked, I think he could have made a lot of money with it."

"That's what I want to talk to you about," Julienne said quickly. "I didn't quite understand what happened to the *River Queen*."

"She was a good, hardworking boat," he said solidly, and glanced at her questioningly. "Do you have any idea about how a steamer works?"

"I'm afraid not."

"You seem like a sharp young lady, so I think I can explain it to you. See, you build a fire into these big barrel-like things filled with water, and they have pipes coming out of them. They make steam, it goes through the pipes to the engine, and that's what powers the boat."

"I see that," Julienne said thoughtfully.

"The thing is, see, is that these boilers get real, real hot, and they keep boiling off the steam, and the engineer has to keep adding water to them all the time. But sometimes you can bust up a boiler good. In winter, when the river water you pump in to add to the boiler is freezing cold, and the boiler itself is hot, it cracks the boiler. And that's what happened to the *River Queen*. Busted two of her boilers wide open, and we figured the other two would go too. So we just shut her down and had her towed back to Natchez. See, it didn't explode through the bottom, or blow anything up off the boiler deck roof. It just ruined the two boilers, but then that caused some of the gears and pulleys to jam up and break, and then the paddle wheel stops turning."

"Captain Plank, do you think that the *River Queen* could be repaired and put back in service?"

"You know, Miss Ashby, I've thought of that, I sure have. And your father and I talked about it.

I think it could be done. At least it could have three years ago." He eyed her shrewdly. "I've heard that she's still anchored down at Under-the-Hill."

"We think so, though none of us has been down to look at her. But we do know that for the last three winters my father has sent down the carpenter and some workers to drydock her and work on the hull. So we hope she's still afloat, at least."

"I'm not too surprised, your father loved that sweet little boat, and I always thought he hoped he could get her going again. Well, I'll tell you, Miss Julienne. It would be a long shot. It would cost a lot of money to restore that boat, but if it could be put together, and you could get some good help, there's a lot of money to be made on the river."

"And we need to find a way to make money, Captain Plank. My family is in a very unfortunate way right now, financially. I really hate to ask you, sir, but would—could you possibly help us with the *River Queen*? Agree to captain her, figure out what she needs, help us find the parts and the crew to get her on the river again."

"I wish to goodness I could," he said vehemently. "I would, in a minute. But what you don't realize, Miss Ashby, is that you don't need a captain. A captain's job is to manage the crew. What you need is a good pilot, that knows a good engineer, and that can get together a crew that not only can manage hauling freight but can make repairs and renovations on the boat."

"Then can you recommend a pilot? I know that even though you're retired, you still know everything about the river."

"It was my life for fifty years. Guess it'll still be a big part of my life from now 'til I'm gone," he said with a smile, but then it faded. "But Miss Ashby, did you know that pilots are the highest-paid men on the river? They can demand much, much more than a captain."

"No, I didn't know that. How much would a pilot's wage be?" she asked hesitantly.

Steadily he answered, "Right now they're making anywhere from one hundred fifty to two fifty a month. It's real hard to find one for less that two hundred."

"Two hundred dollars a month!" she exclaimed. "Oh, my goodness, I had no idea." Her face fell. "Then it's hopeless. My family can't possibly afford that."

He nodded. "I was afraid maybe that was the way it was. I know the bank's probably not been your best friend since your father passed."

"No, they haven't," Julienne said dully.

"I might know a man, though," he said quietly. "A pilot. He's a good pilot, a tough man that knows this old river as good as it can be known. He's got friends, too, and I think he'd be able to get a crew for you. He's going through a rough patch right now, so I think he'd help you out for a whole lot less than a pilot's wage."

"Really?" She brightened. "Tell me about him."

Plank's mouth tightened. "He was piloting a boat when it hit a brand-new snag, one that no one had come up on yet. Tore the hull in two like it was made of canvas. Now, that happens, you know, and usually there's no blame put on the pilot, especially a good one. But somehow rumors started flying around, and people talked, and word got out he'd been drunk when he was piloting the boat. The owners fired him, and he's never been able to get past it. He's been taking jobs here and there as a fireman, maybe just a roustabout. But I think it might help him—and you—to take on the *River Queen* and get her going again."

"But is he a drunk?" Julienne demanded.

"I'll never believe he was drinking when he was piloting," Plank said with emphasis. "I've known the man for years. He's a river man, he takes a drink, I know. But he's honest. Dallas Bronte would never take a boat out if he'd been drinking."

"What! Dallas Bronte!" Julienne repeated with horror.

Captain Plank narrowed his still-sharp blue eyes. "You've met him, I take it."

"Yes, once. Twice. Anyway, he—no, I couldn't ask him for—for anything. It's just not possible," Julienne said in confusion.

"I see," Captain Plank said, though he didn't. "Well, then I'm sorry to say that right now nothing else comes to mind, Miss Ashby. I can't think of another pilot right now that would be in a position to help you."

For several moments Julienne sat still, confused and upset. *I can't do this! I won't!* But then, as it had so often happened since her father died, she came to the hard realization that she could indeed do it, and she would do it, because she had to. She had no choice.

"Perhaps I was too hasty," she said to Captain Plank, who nodded knowingly. She continued, "Although Mr. Bronte and I have had some unfortunate disagreements, I can see that really I must at least ask him to help us."

"And he'll say yes," Captain Plank said. "Because it'll help him too."

WAKING UP LONG BEFORE daylight, Julienne tossed in her bed. She had slept but little, and now as she finally threw the cover back and began to dress, she found herself as disturbed as she could ever remember. She dreaded the thought of going to find Dallas Bronte and asking him for help.

After putting on undergarments, she found herself staring at her dresses and thinking about what would be appropriate. She had no old out-of-fashion dresses for she gave them away as soon they lost favor. Finally she chose a blue and gray striped, polished taffeta skirt with a white silk blouse, lace ascot with a small stickpin, and a tight-fitting gray jacket. As she sat down before the mirror and began brushing her hair, a memory came of the many times that Tyla had done her hair so well. It was a poignant memory, for she had grown genuinely fond of the young woman. She found the tears rising in her eyes and, picking a handkerchief from her dressing table, she wiped them away and finished fixing her hair, parting it down the middle and putting it into a modest bun at the back of her neck. She couldn't decide between her blue bonnet or her gray, but then she realized that she didn't have to be meticulous about her dress, not for meeting Dallas Bronte.

CAESAR DROVE THE BROUGHAM down to Natchez-Under-the-Hill. The only decent looking building down there was the harbormaster's office, a small dusty brick building with muddy windows. "Wait here for me, Caesar, this shouldn't take but a few moments," she instructed him.

She went inside to a musty-smelling cluttered room with two desks piled with papers and books. Through the windows she saw hundreds of dust motes floating daintily in the air. A man with his sparse hair parted down the side, a long nose, small close-set eyes, and sleeve garters looked up and then jumped up when he saw Julienne. "Ma'am? Are you lost?"

"No, I'm not lost. I'm looking for a pilot, and a captain friend of mine said he may be registered here."

"Likely he is," the man said in a fawning tone. "The pilots always notify us where they are, on what boat, and who is available."

"I believe this man is available. His name is Dallas Bronte. Has he registered an address with you to be contacted by owners?"

"Well, yes, ma'am," he said. "So you are an owner? A steamboat owner?"

"I am," she answered shortly. "I recently inherited a steamer, and if possible I would also like to know where she's docked. But Mr. Bronte first please, if you could look up his address."

He gave her a furtive grin. Obviously he had lost some of his awe of her. "I don't have to look up Bronte's address. He's where he always is between jobs. At the Blue Moon." At her mystified expression he said with a slight leer, "The Blue Moon Saloon and Gentlemen's Rooms. Right down the street."

"I see," she said frostily. "Thank you for that information. Now, my steamer is the *River Queen*. Can you direct me to where she's docked?"

"The *River Queen*? That wreck? She's all the way down at the end, you'll have to walk, I'm afraid. Silver Street ends, but the shore goes on around a little corner, and there she is."

"Thank you," she said shortly, and turned to leave.

He called, "Why don't you let me walk you down there, Miss—Miss—" he hinted.

"I hardly think that's possible, sir. I haven't been introduced to you, and so therefore I don't know you. And I don't believe that I want to. Good day."

She hurried out and practically jumped into the buggy. "Drive until you see the Blue Moon Saloon," she called to Caesar.

"What?" he said incredulously.

"Just drive, Caesar. Blue Moon."

It was only about a hundred feet down. On Silver Street it was a typically busy day, with riverboat men swaggering, ill-dressed women staggering along, calling out to the men, dirty street urchins running, and mules hauling freight, their drivers whipping them and cursing. Steamships were lined up at the shores with barely enough room between them to reverse out and pull away.

"We're here," Caesar called down mournfully. "Miss Ashby, you can't go in there. Please tell me you ain't going to."

"I am going to," she said evenly, climbing out of the buggy without his assistance. "You just sit right there, Caesar, and if anyone tries to touch the horse or this buggy you give them a smart crack with that whip." Under her breath she added, "Wish I had a whip to crack."

The Blue Moon Saloon was a shabby two-story wooden structure with an overhanging tin roof. Two windows in the front had so many years' grime, and so much river mud, that she could see nothing at all behind them. The sound of a tinny piano blared, and men's coarse loud voices, mostly profane. She hesitated for a moment at the door, which was sagging wide open. Behind her Caesar called, "Miss Ashby, wait! You just gotta let me come with you."

Wordlessly she pointed to a dusty, faded sign beside the door. In crude letters it read: *No Negroes.* Caesar could read, and he said nothing else.

Gathering her courage, she went inside and looked around, blinking in the semidarkness. A crude wooden bar along one side took up the entire wall. There were several tables scattered through-out the place. It was not large, and there were only half a dozen men there and one blowsy-looking woman with wild black hair. They all fell silent instantly when she entered. Then one of the men, with only a few black teeth and a limp slouch hat pushed far back on his head said, "Well, looky looky here. A fine lady visiting. Pretty one, too."

"Shut up, you. Can I help you, miss?"

Julienne looked up to see that a man wearing a semi-clean apron had come wiping his hands on it. He was a big man with steely gray eyes and a huge mustache.

"Please, sir. I'm looking for Mr. Dallas Bronte."

Surprise leaped to the man's eyes, and he said, "Well, he's here."

"Could I see him, please?"

"Reckon that'll be up to him. You go up those stairs there and he'll be in the second room on the left. Just knock on the door." He saw her hesita-tion and said in a more kindly tone, "I am Otto, and

I run this place, miss. It's rough enough and really no place for you, but no harm will come to you. Just call out if you have trouble. I'll be right there."

"Thank you, sir." Leaving the man, Julienne was aware that she was being watched. She crossed the floor, and the rickety stairs creaked under her weight. They were caked with mud and dirt, and when she reached the second story she saw that the hallway had a carpet runner that had once been blue but was now a leprous gray.

She heard a woman's laughter coming from somewhere, and to her dismay when she went to the second door on the left she heard the woman's loud laugh again. Straightening her shoulders, she knocked on it loudly. A murmur of voices sounded inside and then the door opened, and Julienne found herself facing a skinny young woman wearing a skimpy, low-cut dress. The woman looked her up and down incredulously, then muttered, "What do you want?"

"I'm looking for Mr. Dallas Bronte."

The woman stared at her then turned and pulled the door open wider. "Dallas, this woman wants you."

Through the half-cracked door, she saw Dallas Bronte wearing a pair of brown trousers and an undershirt, sitting at a rickety table that held an ashtray with a half-smoked cigar and a worn pack of cards. He had a glass in his hand, and when he looked at her his eyes widened. "Well, well, well.

Look at this. Welcome to the Blue Moon, Miss Ashby."

"You know this woman?" the young woman asked.

"Yes, I know her. Surprised to see her is all." Julienne did not know what to do. She simply stood there and finally Dallas got to his feet and came to the door. "What could I do for you?"

"Please, Mr. Bronte. Could I talk to you—alone?"

He shrugged. "Guess so, got nothing else to do. Lulie, go take a break will you? I'll see you tonight."

"You'd better." The woman almost shoved her way past Julienne, her back straight, and she shot one withering glance at her.

"Don't mind Lulie. She's a friend of mine. You just kinda have to get to know her to appreciate her." He still stood in front of her, puzzled.

"I apologize for coming without letting you know," Julienne said with some discomfort.

"Yeah, you should have sent your calling card, and I would have let the butler know to expect you," he said sarcastically.

Julienne started to retort angrily, but then she looked down for a moment. When she looked back up, he was still watching her warily. "Could we please start over again? I need to talk to you, Mr. Bronte, and it's very important. Maybe we could take a walk?"

After a slight hesitation he said, "All right. Give me a minute." He half-closed the door, then reappeared almost instantly with a pullover tan shirt and a somewhat threadbare and shapeless brown coat. Settling a wide-brimmed brown felt hat on his head, he pulled the door closed and motioned for Julienne to go on down the hallway and the stairs. He followed her closely, and no one said anything as they left the Blue Moon.

When they got outside, Dallas immediately looked up and said, "Good day, Caesar. How are you?"

"Very well, sir, considering."

"And your pretty wife?"

"She's pretty as ever."

"Pretty as a rose and can cook like a dream. You hang on to that one, Caesar."

"I tries my best, sir, I sure do."

"I'm going to take Miss Ashby for a walk, Caesar. You just wait here, will you? If anyone bothers you, tell them they'll answer to Dallas Bronte. You hear that?"

"Yes, sir, I hears you, Mr. Bronte," Caesar said with ill-disguised relief.

They turned and Dallas offered Julienne his arm. The crazy-quilt planks of the boardwalk were so unsteady, she took it, though with some misgivings. He looked down at her, and the sight of his face brought so many memories flooding back to her—some good, some painful, some horrible—that she couldn't gather her wits enough to speak.

But Dallas seemed not to notice her confusion. He said in his distinctive low voice, "I'm so sorry about your father, Miss Ashby. He seemed like a very good man, a good husband, and a good father."

Bewildered, she asked, "How do you know so much about my family? And about Caesar and Libby?"

He grimaced. "I did spend one night and the next day at your house after we brought you home. It didn't take long to see that you have a great family."

"Oh, yes, of course. I was ill at the time, so I hadn't really realized . . ." Her voice trailed off.

"Yes, you were sick, Miss Ashby. So sick your family was scared you might not make it. And then your father passed away. I know you must be in some terrible trouble." He left it unsaid: that Julienne would never have come to him for any reason unless she was desperate.

"I am," she sighed. "We are. My family. And I— I thought that maybe you might consider helping us. Captain Silas Plank recommended you for a— a project, you might call it."

Dallas nodded. "Captain Plank, he's a good man, a fine captain. I had the pleasure of working with him twice. Wish it could have been more." A shadow of regret darkened his face, then he turned to Julienne. "So what is this project? How can I help the Ashby family?"

"It seems that the Ashby family owns a riverboat," she said with an attempt at lightness. "It's been out of service for three years, but we thought, and Captain Plank also thinks, that it may be possible for it to be renovated and put to work again."

"Really?" Dallas said with surprise. "Where is she? What's her name?"

"The *River Queen*. And she's here. If I understood that little toad down at the harbormaster's office, she must be right down at the end of the shoreline, around that bend." Julienne pointed. They were making their slow way along the boardwalk fronting the saloons and gambling houses and brothels. It ended abruptly about fifty feet ahead, and some ancient steps led right down to the shore of the river. It curved around into a point, and Julienne thought the *River Queen* must be past that point.

"I've seen her," Dallas said with quiet wonder. "I never boarded her, but I've seen her before, and wondered about her."

Excited, Julienne said, "You have? How very odd! Would it be possible for us to go see her now?"

He frowned down at her skirt. "The bottom of your skirt would get filthy, and even though the shore has dried out some, you're bound to have to wade through some stinking mud."

"Not the first time," she said in a low voice. His head whipped around to search her face, but she looked straight ahead and went on, "But that's the only way, isn't it? It's too narrow, the buggy couldn't get down there. Please, Dal—I mean, Mr. Bronte? You just have no idea how important this is to me."

"Okay," he relented. "It's not far."

They went down the shaky stairs carefully and stepped onto the shores of the Mississippi River. At this point the shore was about ten feet wide.

Dallas was right, it didn't have standing water, but Julienne's heeled boots sunk about three inches into the ground with each step. Wordlessly she worked her way, keeping up fairly well with his long stride.

They rounded the point, and sure enough, the *River Queen* was moored right there. Julienne stopped in her tracks to look her over, and Dallas stood by her side, his arms crossed, his eyes narrowed, as he too searched the boat.

She had three decks, the main deck, the Texas deck, and the hurricane deck. She was midsized, with her stacks reaching about forty-eight feet high. Her paint had long ago peeled and faded. Once she had been a gleaming white with red trim, black stacks, and a bright red paddle wheel. The Texas deck and the hurricane deck had the remnants of a fence of white picket railings and gingerbread trim on the top, but many of the slats were missing and the white paint had faded to a leprous gray. Many of the stateroom windows were broken. Atop the hurricane deck the pilothouse was a plain square, but the roof was high-topped with curlicued corners and had once been painted red.

After Julienne had searched her for awhile, she thought that the *River Queen* looked shabby, neglected, and somehow sad. But she wasn't the frightful wreck that Julienne's mind had taunted her with. Curiously she looked up at Dallas.

Aware of her scrutiny, he said, "She doesn't look too bad, actually. She's not listing at all. That's kind of surprising, considering that she's been laid up for three years."

"My father had some work done on her during the last three winters," Julienne said. "He brought in some of the people from the plantation, and there was something about drydocking her to work on her hull."

Dallas nodded. "Smart of him. Must have sanded her and varnished her and replaced any wood that might have been starting to rot." He looked down at her. "But I can't tell anything until I see the firebox and the engine."

"The firebox? What's that?"

"It's just the boiler room; we have names for stuff just so people will think we're real smart. Wait here." He took off his coat and threw it on the ground.

Before Julienne could say a word, and to her amazement, he started wading out into the water to the boat, fully dressed. It was chest-high before he reached the tip of the main deck. Easily he pulled himself on board, then went to a stanchion and began loosening a rope.

"What are you doing?" Julienne called. "Decided to take a swim?"

"Only because I had to," he answered. After the slack in the rope had been loosened, he started to slowly unwind the rope, wrapping it around his back and leaning back for leverage. Bit by bit he let the rope slip, and one of the long planks standing upright on the main deck—the landing stage—started lowering. "Stand back," he warned her with gritted teeth.

Cautiously Julienne took a few steps back, and when the stage was about three feet above the shore, Dallas let it fall. It splashed mud everywhere, including on Julienne's skirt. "Sorry," he said. "It's kinda heavy."

"Never mind." Picking up his jacket, she made her way across the landing stage onto the boat. It seemed steady enough. Handing his coat to him, he shrugged it back on. "Thank you. I wasn't looking forward to wading out here," she said.

"That's not going to happen," he said, then turned to go to the double doors that led into the main deck. There was a generous cargo bay, with four small windows on each side. "Have to fix those," he murmured. Quickly he went to the far doors into the boiler room and threw them open. Julienne followed him and looked around. He was already peering closely at things, running his hands over pipes and drums and rubbing the dirt off some gauges. He paid special attention to two of the boilers. They were the only things that Julienne knew. They were big metal drums, with furnaces underneath and pipes coming out of them. Dallas muttered to himself, disappearing around behind the boilers and pipes.

Julienne supposed he had gone on to the farther engine room, but she really didn't want to follow him. Everything in the room was filthy, with black oil, with crusted dirt, with black ash.

"I'm going upstairs," she called.

He said something unintelligible.

Going to the side door, she went through it to the outside stairwell that led up to the Texas deck. The door there led into a big empty room, which Julienne knew must be a combination ballroom and dining room, such as had been on the *Columbia Lady*. Of course, there was no comparison. It was about a third of the size of that grand room. No double doors led out onto an exterior promenade. The windows, except for one, were broken. She smelled the sour, musty odor of mold and mildew, and looked down. The floor was black. She turned her shoe and dragged the edge across it for about an inch. Underneath she could see a yellowish wood, but the mildew was at least an inch thick.

Sighing, she went through the door at the back of the room on the left-hand side, into a galley that was not large and roomy, but was practical. An icebox, two cook stoves, and floor-to-ceiling shelving surrounded a long high worktable. Here, too, everything was the same dirty color of green-gray, even the walls.

A small side door led out toward the center of the boat, and Julienne went through it. It led into the hallway in the middle of the staterooms. Going to the first one and holding her breath, she went inside. Looking around, she was immediately depressed.

It was slightly larger than the one on the *Missouri Dream*. But it was absolutely filthy, and there was not a stick of furniture in it. The window was broken, and, peeping outside, she saw that the shutters were gone. The walls, floor, and especially the ceiling was solid black with mold.

She checked a couple of the others, and saw that they were in the same condition. Dully she counted; the *River Queen* had twenty-four staterooms, twelve on each side. At the end of the hallway, where the stairs led up to the hurricane deck, she paused. It seemed that the last two stateroom doors were much farther away from the stateroom doors before them. Curiously she opened the one on the left and saw with surprise that it was much larger than the other staterooms, though it was in the same squalid condition. Checking across the hall, she saw that the last stateroom was of the same generous size. For some reason this cheered her up a little.

Finally she went up on the hurricane deck and went to the pilothouse. The enormous wheel was there, long idle. Always there was a small bench in the back of the room, and Julienne sat down there, staring at the buttons, the levers, the bell pulls hanging from the ceiling. Staring out the wide window, she saw the river. On this difficult day it seemed kind, lazily flowing along, the late afternoon crimson sun glinting orange sparkles on the brown water. It was the first day she had seen the river since the wreck, and somewhat to her surprise it didn't frighten her, or even make her sad. In a way watching it seemed to bring her some peace.

After what seemed a long time, Dallas came into the wheelhouse. Immediately he went to the wheel and laid his hands on it. Looking around, he said, "Amazing. All the bells and whistles on this little boat."

Turning to Julienne, he answered the questions in her eyes. "It can be done. She's a well-built boat, tight and snug. Two of the boilers will have to be replaced, and some of the machinery, but the engine itself is sound. But it's going to take some money. How much do you have?" he asked bluntly.

Thoughtfully she answered, "We have some, but there are some decisions that we have to make about how exactly we can spend it. Right now my Aunt Leah and I are pretty much making all those kinds of decisions." She looked up at him earnestly. "Ordinarily I couldn't imagine letting a stranger know about our personal business. But as I told you, Mr. Bronte, this is a different time, and my family is in a completely different situation than we were a month ago. So I'm asking you, would you please come meet with my family? Talk to them, explain to them about the *River Queen*? And then, Aunt Leah and I will try to work out an agreement between us. But until you've spoken to my family, I'd prefer not to discuss details yet."

Harshly he said, "I have to tell you, Miss Ashby, that I have a reputation on this river, and it's not a good one. People say I'm a drunk, and that I'm the worst kind of pilot there is because I'm irresponsible.

Maybe even criminally irresponsible. Your family needs to know that."

"They do," Julienne said quietly. "As do I. Will you come speak to them, please?"

He looked surprised and pleased, and instantly said, "I will. And I'll tell you right now, Miss Ashby. I feel like I owe you, and your family. No, no, please don't argue, and I know you don't want to talk about our past, and that's fine. All I'm saying is that I can help you, and I will."

CHAPTER NINE

The family sat staring at Dallas, who was still wet. His clothes were rough, and his hair needed cutting. Julienne had called them all in. For once, Darcy was home. After he had found out that they were losing the house and the plantation, he had generally stayed out getting drunk every night, and sleeping all day. But since Leah had told him about the *River Queen*, he had hung around, waiting to find out about it.

Julienne didn't waste words. "Mr. Bronte has looked at the boat, and he says it can be fixed. If it can be fixed, it can be put into service again. But I'll let him tell you about it."

Dallas rubbed his jaw, and because he hadn't shaved that day, the whiskers bristled. "The *River Queen* is sturdy, and she's always been fast. With some work she can be a tough, hardworking boat, hauling freight. And there's money to be made on that. Every boat that hits Natchez can fill it up with cotton in harvest time. Other seasons, there are other things, you can pick up mail freight, tools, farming equipment, cattle."

Darcy frowned. "I don't remember much about it when Father had it, but I thought the *River Queen* had staterooms, and a dining room. What about passengers?"

Dallas shrugged. "It would take a whole lot more money to get her into shape for passengers. Right now you'd do much better to fill up that ballroom with freight."

"And there's another thing about the staterooms," Julienne said with determination, glancing at Leah, who nodded encouragingly. "If we invest in the *River Queen*, we won't have enough money to buy another house. Aunt Leah and I think that we should live on the boat, and we've explained to Mother, and she agrees with us. There are plenty of staterooms, and though they're in bad shape, they can be cleaned up."

Darcy's cloudy blue eyes widened. "Live on a boat? Are you insane, Julienne? The Ashbys live on some rotten little tub on the river?"

Her mouth tightened. "Aunt Leah and I have discussed this, Darcy. Both of us think that for right now, at least, it's the best possible solution."

"Well, I don't think it's any solution at all!" he almost shouted. "It's ridiculous, and embarrassing.

What are our friends going to think? We'll just be river rats!"

"Our real friends will be friends, no matter where we live," Leah said. "And if they don't like where we live, then they probably aren't our real friends anyway."

"I don't care," Darcy blustered. "I'm not going to do it. I refuse to live on some rundown stinking riverboat."

A short silence followed this, but finally Julienne said in a tight voice. "Very well. We have to be out of the house in two weeks. I suggest you find some lodgings before then."

"You know I don't have any money. All this money you and Aunt Leah are talking about, how is it that I'm not seeing any of it? If you would be fair, and give me my share, I'd be out of here so fast all you could see is my tailcoat flapping out the door," he said sulkily.

Julienne let out a dry laugh. "If I gave you a fair share, Darcy, all you would get is thousands of dollars worth of debts. You've taken no part in helping me and Aunt Leah trying to figure out what to do, so you've no right to criticize the decisions we make. We can offer you a home, and food, and the love of our family. That's what all of us are getting out of this. It's your decision whether to stay with us or not."

"Not much of a choice," Darcy said, then looked away.

Carley piped up, "Darcy, it'll be fun! We can fish all the time! I want to live on the *River Queen*. Maybe I can learn to be a pilot like Dallas!"

"You probably could, you're a pretty smart little girl," Dallas said.

"And a good girl," Julienne said. "Most of the time. Now, there are about a hundred details that Mr. Bronte and Aunt Leah and I need to work out. Mother, are you all right?"

"Yes, dear," she said. "I'm feeling so much better now that things are settled. And, Mr. Bronte, I'm so very grateful to you for helping us. It's such a comfort to me."

He looked embarrassed and said, "I need the work, ma'am. So it's helping me too."

THE NEXT TWO WEEKS were dizzying to Julienne, she was so busy. But she welcomed it. The full days, often stretching into working evenings, kept her mind occupied and she was able to push back so much of the sorrow she felt from the loss of Tyla and her father, and the lingering shame that still burned her when she dwelt upon Dallas Bronte too much.

But his attitude, his helpfulness, and the particular care he had taken of her entire family—except for Darcy—had raised her spirits immensely. Every time he came to the house he took time to sit with her, tell her funny little stories about the river, ask about her needlework, and admired whatever it was she was making. He tried to make time to go outside with Carley, so she could show him rocks or bugs or the flowers that were blooming, and a couple of times he let her climb high up into a tree, then fetched her down. He showed Aunt Leah the highest respect, and often deferred to her, along with Julienne, about the dozens of decisions that must be made about the *River Queen*.

And mostly when he came, he met with Julienne and Aunt Leah about business. After they had explained to him about their finances, he had worked hard to get estimates on replacement parts and equipment for the *River Queen*. They had finally agreed that they must spend at least two thousand dollars to get her steaming again. When Dallas understood what a hardship this was for them, at first he had refused any payment at all, insisting that if they would let him have room and board on the *Queen*, that was all that he needed. But both Julienne and Leah insisted that he at least take a wage that was comparable to a farmhand, which was forty-six cents a day. Reluctantly he agreed. Later they found out that he spent almost all of it on food, or some gadget for the *Queen*, or, more often, treats for Carley.

Preston Gates had found a buyer for the house, and almost shamefacedly he added that the buyers were interested in the furniture. The parlor furnishings were imported from France, the paintings in the parlor were also French, and many of the fine accessories. The dining room table was Spanish and was two hundred years old, and still had all fourteen of the matching ornate plush-seat chairs. All of their sideboards and side tables were of fine walnut, and many of the side chairs were of maple and cherry, made by American craftsmen. Carley's, Darcy's, and Julienne's beds were relatively new, all spindled four-posters of oak. All of these things Julienne gladly sold, to Gates's surprise. The buyers offered them one thousand dollars for the lot, and though Charles had paid much more for them, she was glad to get it so simply, without trying to barter off piece by piece. The only things she kept were her parents' bed, chest, and armoire, which had been Julienne's great-great grandfather's.

Now Julienne, Leah, Roseann, Libby, and Caesar were packing up their belongings and gathering up the few pieces of furniture, mostly from the sitting room, that they had decided to keep. Julienne was packing Carley's books.

"Can I take this chair, Julienne?" Julienne looked down and saw that Carley had picked up a small chair. Once it had been painted bright blue, but it had faded to a dull grayish-blue with age.

"It won't fit you very long," Julienne said. "It's for little children."

"I don't care. I want to keep it because Tyla gave it to me. It was hers, you remember?"

And there, the pain struck Julienne again. Every day, it seemed, something happened to hurt her, to bring to the forefront of her mind the pain and sorrow she had suffered. But she reflected that each day, each time, the pain lessened just a little. Now she managed a smile and said, "No, I had forgotten that. Of course you can take it. We can set your dolls in it."

"Maybe Dallas will teach me how to paint," she said happily. "I want it to be blue again. Where is he? I'm going to go ask him."

"He's gone for a few days, Carley. He heard about some things that we needed for the *River Queen*, and they're up in Cairo. So he's going to go try to buy them for us."

"I know where Cairo is," Carley said proudly. "Illinois. I've been studying my maps with Aunt Leah."

This came as a big surprise to Julienne, who was about to question her more, when Libby came in. "There's some men at the door, Miss Julienne. One of them said Mr. Bronte sent them."

"I'm coming," she said, and hurried downstairs. Three men stood awkwardly in the foyer, fidgeting with their hats. As Julienne neared them, one— a husky, tanned man with sad hound-dog eyes— stepped forward. "Are you Miss Ashby? Dallas sent us to help you move onto the *River Queen*, ma'am. My name is Ring Macklin, this here is Willem Hansen, and that's Jesse Allgood." Hansen ducked his head. He was a tall, thickly built Swede with thin blond hair and light blue eyes. Jesse Allgood was a giant Negro man.

"Thank you so much, gentleman," she said courteously. "If you'll come upstairs, I'll show you the bedroom furniture to be loaded. Those pieces will be the biggest and heaviest that we're taking. The rest is small chairs and parcels and some trunks."

"Yes, ma'am," Macklin said. "Dallas rented us a couple of wagons. We'll fill them up, and if we can't get it all, we'll make two trips."

Loading the wagon did not take long, for the three men were strong and worked hard and quickly. Even Darcy helped some, though with ill humor. Caesar and Libby carried smaller things. They had staunchly told the Ashbys that they were their family, and they were staying with them. Although after Charles freed them, he had always paid them a laborer's wage of seventy cents a day, they flatly refused to take any pay for now, insisting that if they could live on the *Queen* and have board, they wouldn't think of going anywhere else. It had touched Julienne's heart.

The wagons were loaded, and the men, along with Caesar and Libby, headed out toward Silver Street and Natchez-Under-the-Hill.

The buyer of the Ashby's open buggy had allowed them to keep it, along with one of the horses, until they got settled onto the *Queen*. Now Aunt Leah, Roseann, Julienne, and Carley put on their bonnets and climbed into the buggy for the last time. Darcy drove, as he was an excellent horseman and driver. Snapping the whip lightly, he muttered "Hup," and the buggy moved off down the drive.

Roseann looked back at the house and tears filled her eyes. Carley, who was sitting beside her, put her arm around her and said, "Don't cry, Mama. I'll take care of you."

Julienne felt much like crying herself. She had learned, however, that she could not show such weakness any more. Her mother was helpless, and depended on her, and so did Carley. And Aunt Leah's courage and unceasing good humor encouraged Julienne and strengthened her. She looked at her and said, "What a journey we're on!"

Leah smiled. "Yes, a journey. Just like the Israelites left Egypt for the Promised Land. And just to show that our Father God is full of surprises—who would ever have thought that Dallas Bronte could be Moses and Natchez-Under-the-Hill could be the Promised Land?"

Even Roseann laughed.

JULIENNE LEANED OVER AND drew a deep breath. She was absolutely exhausted and filthy. It was late in the afternoon, and they had all been working all day long to try to clean up their staterooms. Julienne had managed to make hers somewhat presentable, but she knew that Caesar was working alone in the nightmare of the galley, and she felt she had to help him. He had stubbornly refused her help.

"Caesar, all of our foodstuffs and pots and pans and dishes are still stacked down on the main deck.

I'll clean if you'll bring all of that stuff up and try to get it in some order. Some of those packing cases are too heavy for me."

"Yes, you're right, Miss Julienne. Now, I've got those shelves pretty clean, and I cleaned out that icebox. Seems like Mr. Bronte got us a nice big block of ice for it too. I sure do need to get that stuff up here." He left, muttering to himself.

The big four-top cook stove was covered with grease so old that it had turned into rock, Julienne thought. Gritting her teeth, she started scrubbing with a rough canvas pad and vinegar. They had been cleaning everything with vinegar, because it had sanitary properties and Julienne knew that it was the best thing for cleaning sickrooms.

Ring Macklin came in and said, "You can't scrub that stuff off, Miss Ashby, not when it gets like that. I'll bring a chisel up and knock it off, and I can scrub it down real good then. Why don't you go see your mama? I just talked to Caesar, and we're going to get this kitchen going. We'll have a fine supper in an hour or two."

"That would be so kind of you," Julienne said, wiping her brow. "Libby is a wonderful cook, and I know she and Caesar would appreciate any help you can give us. And of course, please make sure that we have enough for everyone."

"Yes, ma'am. You go along now," Ring said. "Give us a little time and we'll all feast like kings."

Julienne went to check on her mother, who was lying down. She was in one of the larger staterooms, with her own furniture and her own bed linens, and Julienne was so glad. She had bought small beds and washstands for everyone else, and they had salvaged enough of their wooden side chairs that each room had at least one chair.

She sat down beside her. "Mother, you are too tired. You did too much."

"I hardly did anything, Libby did almost all of it. And I know that she needs to be working on her and Caesar's room," she fretted. "Are you and Carley and Leah settled?"

"We're all fine," Julienne said soothingly. "And we're going to have a nice supper in an hour or so."

Roseann nodded. "Where's Darcy?"

Julienne wanted to say, *He's drunk and laid out in his filthy room because he didn't clean one inch of it.* But she knew this would only grieve her mother, so she said, "He's fine, he's resting. He'll be at supper. Why don't you try to sleep a little? I'll come get you when we're ready to eat."

"I think I can nap," Roseann said and closed her eyes.

She left her mother's room and went to find Leah, who was scrubbing the floor in her stateroom. Together they sat on the bed while Julienne told her about her mother and supper. "And I don't know when Mr. Bronte will be back. He was a little vague about what exactly it was he was going to go see about."

"What good would it do for him to explain it to you?" Leah asked with amusement. "I know whenever he tries to tell us about the equipment and things he needs for this boat, it sounds like he's speaking Chinese. Tiddle-de-diddles and boggledy-geegaws and such."

Julienne giggled. "That's true. If he had told me, I wouldn't have known anything anyway."

Leah's light expression sobered up and she said, "Julienne, he is working very hard to help us. You believe that, don't you?"

"Yes."

"And we have to trust him. No, that's wrong, no one is forcing us to, least of all him. But I trust him. Do you?"

"Yes," Julienne said slowly, "yes, I do. You really like him, don't you, Aunt Leah?"

"Ever since the first time I met him, when he brought you home. He reminds me of my husband. Barry Norris was a wonderful man, and I think Dallas Bronte, when he truly finds himself, will be every bit as wonderful too."

TWO DAYS LATER IN late afternoon, Julienne was sitting with her mother and Aunt Leah, trying to sew curtains. She wasn't a very good seamstress. For the third time she pricked her forefinger and stuck it in her mouth.

Carley came running in and said, "Dallas is back! And he brought a whole bunch of stuff!"

At once Julienne put her sewing down and hurried outside with Carley. She saw four wagons filled with what looked to be enormous pieces of junk. She and Carley went down the landing stage, and Dallas jumped down from the wagon and smiled at them. "Did you think I ran off with all your money, Miss Ashby?"

"No," Julienne smiled. "It wasn't enough to tempt you. What is all this?"

"Well, these are the boilers. These are parts of the engine. These are the pipes we need to replace."

"Is that everything we need?" Julienne asked.

"Just about. Still need to replace a couple of gauges, and some of the lines have rotted so bad they can't be spliced. We'll have to replace those. But this is the bulk of it."

"Good, I'm so glad you found these—things," Julienne said. "I think Ring and Libby are working on supper. Don't you want to come inside and rest?"

He laughed. "No resting on a riverboat when she needs work done. I'm going to round up this crew and we're hauling all of this stuff inside right now. We'll grab some supper, but we'll be working tonight."

At midnight Julienne could still hear the men on the deck below, banging and talking, sometimes swearing. She had not yet undressed, so she pulled on a shawl and went down to the boiler room. Ring, Willem, and Jesse were all working there, but she didn't see Dallas. It was a few moments before they saw her, then they all stopped working and almost came to attention. Each man was literally black from head to toe, with their eyes shining out eerily.

Her mouth twitching, Julienne said, "Thank you, gentlemen, but under the circumstances I think you're going to need to stop jumping every time I or my mother or my aunt appear. You're working men, not our butlers. Please, just go on with what you're doing. Where is Mr. Bronte?"

"He's back in the engine room, Miss Ashby, I'll fetch him," Jesse offered.

He disappeared, and soon Dallas came in. He too was completely black, and his grin looked a mile wide, with big shining teeth. "Evening, Miss Ashby. Are we keeping you awake?"

"No, not at all," she said hastily. "I just was curious and wanted to see how the work is going."

He nodded. "Why don't you come outside with me for a minute. I'd like to breathe something besides soot and oil for a change."

He kept his distance, so he wouldn't brush up against her and soil her dress. They walked out to the railing on the main deck and Dallas took a deep breath. "She's fine tonight, isn't she?"

Julienne understood that he meant the river, and she looked around. It was a warm night, with a light haze that softened all the lights on the boat and make them look like round fuzzy globes. The river was serene, with only occasional gleams of starlight on the quiet waters.

"You love this river, don't you?" she asked.

"I do. Always have. It was the best thing that ever happened to me, when I realized I could be a pilot and live on this river. It's all the home I've ever really wanted." He turned to her. "What about you, Miss Ashby? Can you ever love this old river, after everything that happened?"

"I don't love it as you do, but I am beginning to understand how you can. No, I don't fear the river, and I certainly don't hate it. I guess you might say I'm learning to like it a little."

"Like me," he said with a half-smile.

"Maybe," she said. "Maybe a little. No joking now, though, Mr. Bronte. I want to thank you, for all my family. Words don't seem enough—"

He put up a hand to stop her. "You and your mother and your aunt have thanked me so much, it makes me want to crawl under a rock. I want you to understand something. You gave me a job, as a pilot. I just told you how much that means to me. And no one else would give me a chance. I owe you as much gratitude, if not more, than you could ever owe me."

"A pilot," she sighed. "Of a grounded boat."

"Not for long," he said happily. "Miss Ashby, in two days we're going for a ride. We're going for a ride on the *River Queen!*"

CHAPTER TEN

Julienne, Roseann, and Aunt Leah were seated on the "lazy bench," the bench in every pilothouse where everyone sat except the pilot, who never sat. Carley was supposed to be sitting with them, but she was so excited that she kept hopping up to yank on Dallas's arm and ask questions. Even Darcy lounged in the doorway, the interest plain on his face. Dallas had been overly optimistic; it had taken the crew five days to get the *River Queen* ready. By now they were all nervous and eager, watching as the first thin streams of smoke started threading from the smokestacks.

Carley was so keyed up she started jumping up and down, pointing, and demanding, "What's that? What's this thing over here? Can I pull this rope? Can I turn the wheel?"

The last request was funny, because it was absurd. The *River Queen*'s wheel was midsized; it was ten feet in diameter. They could range up to thirteen feet. So that a man could even reach the top of the wheel, the floor directly underneath the wheel was countersunk four feet. The top of the wheel reached Dallas's shoulders. The pins were eight inches high, and about three inches thick. When a pilot had to make a hard turn, or if the ship were going downstream and a current pushed the rudder hard up against the hull, the pilot may have to stand on a pin or one of the spokes to get her to turn. Little Carley could have hung from a spoke all day long and the wheel would never have moved.

"Can't turn the wheel, Miss Carley Jeanne, that's my job, and I wouldn't want you to steal my job away from me," Dallas said gravely.

"But I want to be on the crew," she said, propping her tiny—and for once, clean—hands on her hips. "Ring said you have a skinny crew, and you need some deck hands, and he said a word that Mama told me never to say."

"He did, did he?" Dallas asked, his eyes glinting. "Well, he was telling the truth, even if he did say that word. I'll have to have a word with him about that. Sorry, Mrs. Ashby."

Roseann sighed. "I'm sure Carley was hiding and Mr. Macklin didn't know she was listening. She does that a lot."

"But I want to be on the crew," Carley insisted again.

"Tell you what," Dallas said. "How about if I make you second mate?"

Suspiciously Carley said, "I know Ring is first mate, Jesse's the fireman, and Willem's the engineer. What does a second mate do?"

"She does whatever the first mate and the pilot tell her to do," Dallas said. Then, to her delight, he scooped her up and held her high underneath a big golden ring suspended by a cord from the ceiling. It was next to a trumpet-like tube that ran into the floor. "Okay, mate, pull that ring for me. That's an order."

"How many times?" Carley asked. Her face was lit with perfect bliss.

"As many as you want."

Carley pulled hard on the bell pull three times, and very faintly below they could hear it ring. After a moment, Ring Macklin's deep voice sounded through the tube. "Here, sir."

Dallas held Carley over the tube, because at four feet tall she couldn't speak into it. "Ask him if we're fired up and ready to go."

In her shrill little voice she yelled, "This is Second Mate Carley! Pilot Dallas wants to know if we're fired up and ready to go!"

"Ready, Miss Carley," Ring answered.

"No, it's Second Mate Carley!"

"Oh, sorry. Tell the pilot we've got plenty of steam, mate!"

"Okay. 'Bye, Ring."

Now Dallas held her under another brass ring and said, "Now, pull that one time."

"Is that another one that only Ring and Jesse and Willem are going to hear?" she demanded.

"That's right, it's called the backing bell, so they'll know to start backing us out."

"Can't I pull that one?" she pleaded, pointing to the largest ring, just above the wheel. "That's the huge outside bell, isn't it?"

"You're right, Second Mate. Sure, we need to alert the crew that orders are coming. When we ring the big bell, we call it 'tapping.' So give it two taps, mate."

Carley reached up and pulled the ring twice. It was hard for her, so Dallas had to help. They all heard the great two-hundred-fifty-pound brass bell out on the fore of the hurricane deck sound its grand gong.

"Now ring the backing bell," Dallas said, watching her.

"You have to put me over there," she said impatiently, pointing to it. "I can't reach it from here."

"You remembered which bell pull, that's good, Second Mate," he said, moving to the left, or port side, of the pilothouse.

"That's my job," she said gravely, and pulled it one time.

They felt the ship begin to tremble, and Dallas set Carley down to take the wheel. Immediately she ran out the door, to the stern, and looked over to watch. They heard her high, excited voice, the words unintelligible, but they knew she was watching the big paddle wheel start to turn.

Very slowly the *River Queen* started backing in a mild curve. The movement of the boat seemed choppy and hesitant to Julienne. Finally the ship was pointed almost straight downstream, and Dallas reached up and pulled another bell cord. Heavily she waded to a sluggish stop, then, almost by inches, she started moving forward.

"Now we'll see," Dallas muttered. "If we do have a queen, or if we've got a mud crawler."

She gathered speed, the paddle wheel beginning to make a solid rhythmic beat of a drum. Underneath their feet they heard the engines, a low cadenced hum. Her gait smoothed out, and within minutes she was moving smoothly and effortlessly down the old river. Carley came running back in, breathless. "She's going! The *River Queen* is going! HOOORAAAAYYY!!"

The others got excited and stood up to line the windows. Carley said, "I can't see, I can't see." Darcy picked her up and held her so she could watch out the starboard windows. The deep forests and rust-red clay banks slid by.

Julienne went to stand by Dallas. "Well, Pilot, what's the verdict?"

He grinned down at her. "Oh, we've got a queen, all right. She may not look like it on the outside, but she's got heart, and she travels like a dream. Light, smooth, and graceful. A real river queen."

JULIENNE HAD BOUGHT A big old rectangular pine table with indifferent varnishwork, and twelve mismatched armless straight chairs, and this served as their dining table. During the first few crazy days on the *River Queen*, they had no place to sit and eat, and Julienne, Carley, and Darcy had sat on the floor in Roseann's stateroom while she and Leah sat in straight chairs with wooden trays to hold their meal. A dining room table had been one of at least a hundred things that Julienne had never thought she would have to go out and buy. Finally she had found the table and chairs in a junky, filthy little shop on the boardwalk and put it in the ballroom, close to the galley door. She also used it as a desk, struggling with the myriads of papers that had become her most burdensome daily chore. She hated it even worse than scrubbing.

After the *River Queen* had steamed for about an hour, they had returned to Natchez-Under-the-Hill, and to Julienne's surprise they had pulled in right in the middle of the docks, instead of a half-mile downriver. "Surprise," Dallas said to them, grinning. "New berth. I talked the harbormaster into charging us the same fee as down there in the wilderness." Julienne was elated, until she looked up at the boardwalk. They were docked right in front of the Blue Moon Saloon.

After their cruise Julienne had asked Leah to help her with the accounts. To her surprise, her mother had said she would join them. All of them, even Darcy, had been immensely cheered up from the *River Queen*'s maiden voyage.

Now she and Leah and her mother sat at one end of the old scarred table, going over the details of running their home—a steamship, with a crew. "We can't afford to keep buying all the kinds of food we're eating right now," Julienne was saying. "I've decided it would be best if we made out separate weekly menus and two shopping lists, one for us and one for the crew. They eat like ravening wolves, and it's just impossible for us to keep buying meat for them."

"What do you mean, Julienne?" Leah asked, frowning.

"It's simple. We can't afford as much meat as we've been buying, and such things as butter and sugar and fresh fruits and vegetables are expensive too, and we have to cut back. I think we should supply the crew with hardtack, rice, and potatoes— they're pretty cheap—and eggs, though we'll have to limit them, because I've seen Jesse eat six eggs at one sitting. Libby could make stews with our leftover vegetables, and maybe add tripe or chitlings. She told me that aside from being a bread or cracker or whatever hardtack is, it thickens stews nicely. And she said that sometimes the butcher has oxtails, and they're cheap. Maybe every once in awhile the crew could have oxtail stew."

Leah was staring at her incredulously, and even Roseann had dropped the embroidery hoop she

was working to listen to her. Julienne grew uncomfortable. "What's the matter? Both of you know
what kind of shape we're in. All of the things
Mr. Bronte has had to buy for the *Queen* have
cut way into our ready cash. We're ready to haul
freight, but we don't have anything to haul yet, and
he doesn't know when we might get a load. Right
now we have to skimp everywhere we can."

"If I understand what you're saying, the only ones
skimping here are going to be the crew," Leah said
stiffly.

"Well, yes, Aunt Leah," Julienne said, obviously
mystified at her aunt's testiness. "They work for us.
They're like our servants."

"And so you're putting Caesar and Libby on this
hardtack stew diet too?" Leah demanded.

"No, of course not. They're practically family,"
Julienne replied impatiently. "But this steamboat
crew is not. Mother, I apologize, I don't really want
to burden you with these things. But surely you
agree that those men are not like us. Willem goes
to the saloons or gambling or I-don't-know-what
every night. Ring's not quite as bad, but it's only
because I don't think he actually goes every single
night."

"But Jesse is a good Christian man," Roseann put
in gently.

"But he's still not on our social level, and I don't
just mean because he's black. I'm talking about the
entire crew. They've been brought up in a world
that we have nothing to do with, their lives are

completely different, and their understanding of what life is. They know they can never be like people of our social status."

Impatiently Leah made a wide circle with her hand, indicating the still-filthy empty ballroom, the broken windows, the scarred and rickety old table. "Do you really have any idea how ludicrous you sound, Julienne? Look at us! We're not wealthy any more. We have to depend on the Lord for our daily bread, just like most everyone in the world."

"But we're different," she protested. "People like us are different."

To her surprise, her mother said strongly, "No, Julienne, we are not better than anyone else. I know that Charles and I brought you up encouraging that sort of thinking, but we were very wrong. I've been so sheltered all of my life, and it made me ignorant. I had no idea what the real world was like, and I knew nothing of people beyond my own small, insular circle. But those days are over for us, Julienne. We must stop being so criminally ignorant, and let the Lord teach us how to live with grace and charity toward others."

Julienne fell silent, her mind whirling.

Leah spoke up, "And what about Mr. Bronte? After all he's done for us, and in his behavior toward us, he has definitely shown that he is a gentleman and honorable, even though he's not of our exalted circle of Splendid Persons. Are we putting him on bread and water, too?"

Julienne's eyes narrowed and she started fidgeting with the stub of a pencil she held. "You don't know him, Aunt Leah, not really. Besides, our deal was that we offered him a wage and room and board. Evidently he's not boarding here, and I'm assuming he's getting other—necessities—wherever it is he's living."

"Mr. Bronte certainly is living here, and he eats what we provide," Leah said vehemently. "I'm surprised you know so little about him, and the crew. Do you know where he sleeps? Down on the main deck, behind the engine room, in the stifling hot crew quarters, in one of those narrow bunks. Have you even seen that horrible cranny they call their quarters? And he eats down there with them, on a board set on two sawhorses, and they pull up old empty crates to sit on."

Julienne's eyebrows winged upward, and her dark eyes widened. "What? But we offered him the captain's cabin, across from Mother's stateroom, and he turned it down! I thought—I thought—" She stammered into silence.

Roseann looked confused and upset, but Leah was watching Julienne knowingly, and asked, "You do know why Mr. Bronte turned down the stateroom, don't you? Because he doesn't have the money to buy a bed. And no, he didn't tell me that. It only makes sense, because I know what we're paying him. And I know what he does with that money too. He's bought a fishing pole and hooks for Carley, and he bought a couple of extra lanterns for the crew so they could have more lights in the quarters at night, and maybe it escaped your attention but he's the one that bought those peaches yesterday."

Julienne stared at her. *He's not been staying at the Blue Moon? But I was so sure! What's wrong with me? Do I always want to think the worst of him because he—he—No! I'm not even going to think about that again! I've just got to forget about that awful night we were together. It's making me act like a crazy woman!*

Finally she shook her head a little to clear it, then said in a subdued voice, "No, I didn't know all of that. But still, Aunt Leah, everything I've said about trying to figure out the food budget is true. We really do have to cut back."

Roseann said, "I understand what you're saying, Julienne, but I believe we can figure out menus that we can all share. I know I may not have much practical experience, but you and Leah are smart. You can think of how we can all have good, nourishing food. Including the crew."

"But how? I don't see how we can afford good food for eleven people, not with the amount of money we have to spend," she grumbled.

"That's because you know about as much about a kitchen and cooking as I do about flapping my wings and flying," Leah said tartly. "You and I will work together to get a figure to spend weekly on food, and then Libby and I will work on the menus and do the shopping."

Picking up her embroidery hoop again, Roseann said sweetly, "I think Leah's right, dear. Just think of it as one less thing that you'll have to worry about."

Oh, good, Julienne thought with bitter sarcasm. *Now I'll have much more time to worry about what Dallas Bronte is doing.*

THE NEXT DAY NO one knew where Carley was at dinnertime, so Julienne went looking for her. She found her sitting at the back of the main deck, fishing. Julienne went to sit beside her. Carley's feet were bare, and she dangled them over the side. "Aren't you hungry?" Julienne asked. "We've got some soup and some ham."

Carley made a face. "Yech, pea soup. It's green. I don't like it. Ham's okay, but I decided to catch some catfish. I'm real hungry for catfish."

"I see," Julienne said gravely. "But since it may be awhile before you catch your fish and Libby gets it fried, how about if I go make you a ham sandwich? You can stay here and fish and eat."

"Did Libby make some tomato catsup today?"

"I'm sure she did, since you ask for it no matter what we're eating."

"Then if you put some tomato catsup on my ham sandwich, that would be good."

"All right, be back in a minute." Julienne went into the galley and made what, to her, was a disgusting sandwich.

When she returned to where Carley sat, she saw that Jesse Allgood had come out on deck and was squatting down beside her. When Julienne walked up, he jumped to his feet. "Good evenin', Miss Ashby. I was just talking to Carley about fishing."

Julienne took her seat beside Carley again and handed her the sandwich. "It's fine, Jesse. Maybe you have some fishing tips for her?"

Carley said, "I was telling him that I'm using chicken liver for bait. Darcy said it might be good to catch catfish with. But I'm not catching anything."

Jesse said, "That there's good bait, but you're fishing at the wrong time, Miss Carley. You gotta fish nights for catfish."

"At night? Don't they sleep at night?"

"No, they eat at night. And the best way to catch a whole mess of 'em is to use throw lines."

"What's a throw line?"

"You tie a hook on the end of a line. You tie something heavy to make it sink, then you cut off a piece of it for a long tail end. It sinks down to the bottom. Pretty soon old mister catfish, he come around. He grabs it. You see your line jerking around, and you grab hold, and you pulls it in."

"Will you show me how, Jesse?"

"I surely will, Miss Carley. But best time for cat-fishing is around midnight. You're gonna have to ask your mama if you can stay up that late."

Carley turned to look appealingly up at Julienne. "Can I please, Julienne? If you say I can, Mama won't care. Please?"

Julienne smiled. "You know what, that sounds like a lot of fun. How about if we both let Jesse teach us how to fish for catfish about midnight tonight?"

Carley's big blue eyes widened. "You mean it? You'll fish with us?"

"I mean it," Julienne said, rising. "I'm going to go right now and finish up my work so I can rest some this afternoon. And you need to rest too, Carley. Finish eating, wash up, and go take a nap. Okay?"

"Sure!" she said, yanking her pole out of the water and hopping up. "I'm going to go into the galley and get a pickle. A pickle would be good with this sandwich. Oh, boy, we're going to have so much fun! And maybe we'll catch lots and lots of catfish."

"We will," Jesse promised. "You just wait and see." He took her fishing pole and went back through the main deck doors, and Carley scampered up the stairs.

Julienne was about to follow her, but then she saw Dallas coming up the gangplank and went to meet him. She noted that he had on his best clothes, a black frock coat, a white linen shirt with a high collar, a black tie, black-ironed trousers, and a black felt slouch hat. It was a warm day, and as she joined him he touched the brim, then took it off and wiped his brow.

"Hello, Mr. Bronte," she said. "Rather warm today, isn't it?"

"Yes it is, Miss Ashby," he said, matching her formal tone.

Slowly they walked up to the railing on the main deck. "May I ask what's bothering you, Mr. Bronte?" she asked hesitantly.

Dallas looked at her. "What makes you think something's bothering me?"

"You don't keep your thoughts secret very well. Your face gives you away."

"I guess that's why I lose money at poker," he said glumly. "I've been to everyone I can think of on this river, but I haven't been able to find us any freight."

"You mean no one needs anything hauled right now?" Julienne asked with surprise.

A slight breeze stirred one of the damp thick curls on his forehead and he lifted his head as if to welcome it. Then he replied distantly, "No, it's because of me, Miss Ashby. They don't trust me because of my reputation."

"But that all happened over a year ago, didn't it? Surely all that scandal is old news. And you didn't lose your pilot's license."

He said bitterly, "But everyone thinks I'm a drunk. Nobody wants to trust a drunk."

"Oh, I see," Julienne said faintly.

Wearily he said, "Maybe I should go get Carley to pray for me. She thinks God will do anything for her."

"No, don't stir her up now, I just talked her into taking a nap," Julienne said hastily. "Apparently Jesse has special secret knowledge about catching catfish, so we're going fishing at midnight tonight. That's the only reason Carley agreed to take a nap."

"'We'?" Dallas repeated with surprise, staring down at her. "Don't tell me you're going to go fishing?"

"I certainly am. Why shouldn't I?" Julienne said with a hint of temper.

"You just never struck me as a fishing kind of girl," Dallas said, his eyes alight. "In fact, you never struck me as a doing-anything-outdoors-kind of girl. But anyway, do you suppose I could wrangle an invitation to this fishing party?"

"Of course," Julienne said with only the tiniest hint of stiffness. "I'm sure Carley would love for you to fish with us."

"Carley would, huh," he repeated under his breath, then turned to go through the main deck doors. "See you at midnight, ma'am," he said. "Betcha I catch more fish than you, Miss Ashby."

"You most certainly will not!" she called after him.

"Bet I will," she heard him say just before he passed through the doors.

Realizing she would have to shout to answer him, and ladies never raised their voices in public, Julienne was content to say to herself, "Bet you won't. And you just wait, Mr. Bronte. I'll get the *River Queen* some freight!"

AT MIDNIGHT THE WIND was moaning softly over the waters of the Mississippi, and the small laps against the side of the *River Queen* made a sibilant sound. Dallas, Julienne, Jesse, and Carley sat along the back of the main deck, their legs dangling. All of them were barefoot. It had taken a lot of persuasion for Julienne to remove her shoes, but at last she had done it and had been pleasantly surprised at how good dunking her feet in the tepid water felt. Several throw lines were strung out by each of them, and they had been sitting there for several minutes.

"What'll we do now?" Carley asked.

"Why, we don't do nothing but sit and wait," Jesse answered.

"Tell me about the biggest fish you ever caught, Jesse."

The others listened as Jesse talked about a mammoth catfish he had caught once, and even as he spoke, one of the lines close to Carley began to twitch. "You got something there, Miss Carley," Jesse said. "Grab that line!"

Carley let out a yelp and grabbed the line. She pulled at it and said, "Blatherskite, he's heavy! He must be a whale!"

The grown people watched her, smiling at her excitement. She tugged and tugged at the line, and finally Jesse had to help her. They pulled a big fat catfish. "How much do you think it weighs, Jesse?" Carley asked, her eyes shining.

"'Bout a ten-pounder, I'd reckon."

"I knew it! I prayed and asked God if He would send me a ten-pound catfish. See, Dallas? All you have to do is ask!" she said with elation.

"Wish it were that easy," Dallas murmured.

The fish bit well that night. They wound up with some half dozen good-sized fish. Jesse was going to clean and fillet them, and Julienne knew that Carley was so wound up she probably wouldn't sleep for hours, so she let her stay with Jesse. She and Dallas started walking along the deck.

Dallas looked up at the indigo sky, where they could see the Milky Way so clearly that it looked like a woman's spangled veil above their heads. In a low voice he said, "You know, I keep a little room, a special little room, in the back of my mind. I put all the good things in there. When I'm feeling low, I go in there and I sort of go through them all."

"What do you mean?" Julienne asked curiously.

"I always thought it might be like how a lady goes through a box of her jewelry. She picks up those jewels, feels of them, admires them, remembers the times she's worn them. And that's what I do with the things in that room. I slowly go over them, savor them all again. And this night is one of those things that I'm going to put in that room. Watching Carley pulling that catfish in."

It was a tender side of Dallas Bronte that Julienne had never seen. "I don't have a room like that," she said lightly. "But maybe I should."

He nodded but his voice was far away. "I need all those good things, times like this. It's a comfort, somehow."

He sounded very lonely, and on impulse Julienne laid her hand lightly on his sleeve. He looked down at her with surprise. She smiled and said, "Please don't worry, Mr. Bronte. We'll get some freight."

The hazy starlight made her look otherworldly, like a nymph floating by in a dark forest. He swallowed hard, and said, "Thank you, Miss Ashby. Thank you for giving me this chance. I won't let you down."

"You never have, Dallas," she said, then turned and slipped away.

Chapter Eleven

Julienne thought that she had never been so frustrated in her entire life. Gritting her teeth, she stood on Carley's little chair, the one that Tyla had given her. Pushing the tin bracket against the wall, just one inch to the left of the window, she took a small nail out of her mouth, stuck it in the hole at the bottom of the bracket, and tried to push it hard enough to stick in position, but she couldn't do it. Grunting, she held the bracket with her pinky, ring, and middle fingers, pinched the nail with her forefinger and thumb, and banged the hammer against the head of the nail. It ricocheted across the room, she hit her forefinger, and jumped so hard she almost fell off the chair. "Blatherskite!" she muttered, Carley's current favorite word.

Caesar appeared at her stateroom door and stared at her with reproach. "Miss Julienne, you ought not be doing that! Any of the crew would do that for you, or I will!"

"No," Julienne said moodily. "You all have enough to do, too much. I can learn how to put up a curtain rod and hang a curtain, I'm not an idiot." At one time the *River Queen* staterooms had had curtain rods mounted, for the nail holes were still there. Dallas had told her that they had probably been brass and had long ago been looted. He had found six sets of brackets and rods in one of the junk shops, and Julienne was determined to replace the canvas they had tacked up against the windows with cotton curtains.

Caesar had opened his mouth to argue with her, but she brightened and asked, "Is that the mail?"

"Yes'm, it's why I'm here. But Miss Julienne, if you'd just let me—"

"No, Caesar, thank you, but I've made up my mind to hang our curtains. Thank you for bringing the mail," she said, hungrily taking the envelopes from his hand. Defeated, he left.

Julienne saw Felicia Moak's flowery script and eagerly tore it open as she sat on her bed. As she read the half-note, her face slowly changed from eager expectation to perplexity, and then she grew very somber. Laying it aside slowly, she picked up another letter, saw the return address, and opened it. This letter was a full page, written in a small tidy script. When she finished the letter she looked up, out her broken stateroom window. All she could see was the steamer that was next to them, a cheap, gaudy packet. After long moments tears started rolling down her cheeks. Vaguely she thought, *I haven't cried since Papa's funeral . . .*

She didn't know how long she sat there, feeling the hot tears rolling down her face, staring blankly out the window. She started when she heard a voice at her door. Caesar had left it open.

"Julienne, your mother and I were wondering if there might be some way that Mr. Bronte could— Oh, Julienne! What's wrong, dear?" Aunt Leah hurried to sit by Julienne and put her arm around her. Taking a handkerchief out of her pocket, she softly wiped Julienne's face. "Please tell me, dearest, let me help you," she said softly.

"Oh, Aunt Leah, I've been such a fool! Such a stupid, proud, shameful fool!" she said bitterly, taking Leah's handkerchief and scrubbing her face harshly.

"Everyone on this earth is, at some time or another," Leah said calmly. "But please tell me what's affecting you this way so suddenly, Julienne. I had thought that you seemed to be dealing with our situation better, especially since the *Queen* is on the river again."

"I had been doing better, but it's not just because of that. I think—I think, Aunt Leah, that in the back of my mind I just thought that this was just a temporary thing, just an event that would soon be over, and we could go back to our lives again. I know that sounds stupid, but I wasn't really *thinking* that way. I guess you could just say I was *feeling* that way."

"I understand," Leah said. "And that's not stupid, Julienne. After you receive a deep shock, it often takes a long time before we really see things, and comprehend things, clearly."

"Maybe. But that's not all. I really thought that my old life was right there, just waiting for me to pick it up again," she said bitterly. "But I was wrong. I was wrong about so many things.

"Yesterday, when Mr. Bronte came back and he hadn't been able to find any freight, I felt so superior to him. I thought, with my friends and contacts, I'll be able to ask their help to find work for the *Queen*. So—so I sent a note to Felicia Moak, telling her that I would call on her today. I was sure that Mr. Moak would be able to recommend us to haul freight to any number of people. Anyway, this is the note I got back." She thrust the pink scented half-note into Leah's hands.

Leah scanned it quickly and looked up. "I hate to say this, Julienne, but I'm not at all surprised. At any time, didn't you wonder that the Moaks haven't called on us, or at least written us?"

"No, I didn't," Julienne answered bitterly. "I just told myself that we were in mourning—supposedly, though we've been working like field hands—and that of course they wouldn't call on us here. But it's been over a month since Papa died, so I thought that that was a suitable mourning period, and they would welcome a call from me. That is honestly how stupid I was."

"Stop saying that, Julienne, you are not a stupid woman. This was just a blindness on your part, and that is not unforgivable, under the circumstances. You and Felicia have been friends for, what? Fifteen years?"

"Not friends, obviously," Julienne said shortly. Some of the color was coming back into her cheeks and the tears had stopped.

"I do have a question," Leah said in a lighter tone. "She says that she couldn't join you on your ride today? What did you mean by that?"

"When I got this idea, I realized, of course, that since we don't have a buggy or carriage any more, I had no way to call up in Natchez. So I asked Caesar about renting a buggy, but he told me that the only thing you can rent in Natchez-Under-the-Hill is a freight cart with a driver and a mule. Well, I thought that it might not be appropriate for me to ride in a mule cart to call on the Moaks," she said with a straight face, and stopped, because Leah had begun to laugh.

In a moment she continued, "And besides, a mule cart costs fifty cents, and I don't have fifty cents. So I asked Ring if he knew of anyone that had a saddle horse I might borrow for an hour or two, and he did. So I wrote Felicia that I was going riding and asked her to join me."

Still smiling, Leah said, "It's probably a good thing they're leaving town, and she couldn't go with you. Felicia rides like a flour sack, she always did."

"Leaving town, I'm sure you believe that as much as I do," Julienne rasped, picking up the note again and reading: *"And I'm so utterly sorry, dear Julienne, but we are all going to be gone for an undetermined period of time, so I'm afraid if you should chance to call we likely will not be at home.'* Never at home, to me, I guess."

"I'm sorry you've been so hurt, my dear," Leah said sympathetically. "It's a sad thing to learn, but people are weak, and they will let you down."

Except Dallas flitted through Julienne's mind like a bright butterfly, and she managed a mischievous smile. "Well, you've had the bad news, Aunt Leah. Now for the good news. Archie-Bald Leggett wouldn't marry me if I was the only woman left in America." She waved his letter.

"Oh, Julienne, please do not tell me that you were crying because of him," she said disdainfully. "You weren't going to marry that silly little man anyway."

"I don't know, the thought has crossed my mind a few times in the last weeks. Don't look at me that way, Aunt Leah, I'm baring my ugly dark soul. There were times that I thought that if I married him it might at least mean the end of our money troubles. And we would have a nice home. You know, he kept calling on me even after Papa died. Since his father was on the Board of Directors of the bank, he must have known that this was going to happen, that we were really poor, but he did call and he seemed to be just as ardent as ever. I know he hasn't called down here, but as I told you, somehow I excused all of that, thinking that we would be back to our lives soon, and everything would be like it used to be."

Leah's mouth tightened. "My dear Julienne, if you think that Archie Leggett would have provided a nice home for your mother, for Carley, for Darcy, and particularly for me, you really have been doing a magnificent job of blinding yourself, and also of making yourself utterly deaf. He would have a nice home, and you as his wife would share it, but there is not a chance he would have lifted a finger to help any of us.

"And as for him calling on you and pressing his suit after your father died, I think I know why," she said shrewdly. "I would imagine that Preston Gates was exerting all the pressure he could on the Board to turn the mortgage on Ashby Plantation over to the family, and I'll bet Archie's father was doing the same. Don't you see? Instead of leaving everything to Darcy, Charles left everything to Roseann. So whoever controls her controls the plantation. If he had married you, he would definitely have had control over our family.

"That way, Archie would have gotten the plantation, the house, everything. For very little money, I might add. All he would have had to do was pay the creditors and that pittance owed on the plantation.

Those sums were a fraction of their worth, and the Leggetts carry that much around in their pockets."

Light dawned on Julienne's face. She stared at Leah, her dark eyes now clear and even bright. "Do you mean to say," she said in a somber voice, "that Archie-Bald was not helplessly, fervently, passionately in love with me? That's it! I'm never falling in love with a man again!"

"You weren't any more in love with him than my pinky finger," Leah said. "And don't joke about such things, Julienne. The Lord has a strange way of bringing our words back to us in odd ways. Now, if you've stopped mooning over Archie-Bald, would you please come help me and your mother with a couple of things?"

"I'll be glad to," Julienne said, rising and brushing her skirt. "As long as it's not hanging curtains."

TWO MORE DAYS WENT by, and Dallas spent each day going up and down the docks, hunting for freight. Both days he came back empty-handed and discouraged. But now Julienne took pains to encourage him. Carley stoutly assured him that she had prayed for a "really good haul that weighs a lot so we'll make a bunch of money" and so it would certainly come to them any day now.

On the third day he left and didn't come back in time for supper that evening. Julienne anxiously awaited him and couldn't decide whether his lateness was good or bad. One minute she told herself it was good news, he must be working out some kind of complicated deal to make up a good cargo. The next minute she scolded herself because she was certain that he was at the Blue Moon Saloon, drunk and partying riotously with Lulie.

They were at supper, and they were talking and laughing. Even Roseann had cheered up considerably. Julienne and Leah had put an absolute stop to her doing any cleaning or manual work, for she was still of fragile constitution and required rest each day. Julienne, recovered from her shock at her friends' letters, had decided to talk about it to the family. She had made a mock-somber announcement that Mr. Archibald Legget, Esquire, had begged to be excused from his proposal. "It was too precipitate, he feared, for his mother and father had been long asking him to wait for a year or two before considering marriage," she said, her mouth twitching.

Carley's brow wrinkled. "What's precipate?"

"It means too soon. His mummy and da-da said so," Julienne answered tartly.

They started laughing, and Dallas came in. They all, except Darcy, called out greetings to him and told him to sit down.

"You've got a big silly grin on your face," Julienne said with amusement. "It must be good news."

"It's double-good news. I've got a contract for a trip, and we're loaded both ways. We'll be loading the *Queen* tomorrow and taking our cargo to New Orleans!"

Everyone began to talk at once, asking questions, Darcy talking about New Orleans, Julienne wondering what to wear. Finally Leah said sensibly, "Mr. Bronte, it's late and you must be hungry. Would you like some supper?"

"I'm close to starving," he said good-naturedly. "Thank you, Mrs. Norris, I would appreciate something to eat."

She rose and went into the galley. Carley said, "It's oxtail soup! And it's so-so-so good! Except I never could find the ox's tail in it."

"That's probably a good thing," Dallas said. "But I like oxtail soup too. Do you, Miss Ashby?"

To Julienne's guilty mind he seemed to be eyeing her with particular meaning, but then she realized he couldn't possibly have known about her conversation with Aunt Leah and her mother. "As a matter of fact, I thought I would despise it, but it's really very good. Of course, Libby could cook Mississippi mud and it would taste wonderful."

Libby came out with a steaming bowl, and Leah cut him two thick slices of bread and buttered them for him. Giving him a chance to eat, the others kept talking for awhile, about New Orleans, and what they might buy if they made any money. Dallas watched them and listened as he ate, and he looked happy.

Finally he finished, pushed back his bowl, and leaned back in his chair. "That was fine, Miss Libby.

And I do mean fine. Thank you very much. If there's any left over, I know the crew would love some of it, even if it's just a little cupful."

"That's what they had for supper too," Libby answered as she cleared plates. She shot a meaningful look at Julienne, who dropped her eyes. "Oxtail, it don't cost much, but it sure makes a thick hearty stew. Lots of people like it, even white quality folks, you know."

Dallas looked puzzled at this declaration, but Julienne quickly said, "All right, we've been polite to let you eat. Now, what are we hauling? To and from?"

"And how heavy is it?" Carley demanded.

"Oh, it's heavy, all right," Dallas said. "A big, fat haul."

His answer puzzled them, and, glancing at Roseann, he went on hurriedly. "It's livestock downriver. Farm equipment back."

Darcy asked warily, "Livestock? What kind of livestock?"

"Er—cows. Some cows. And pigs."

A silence fell across the room, and a look of astonishment came to every face.

"Pigs?" Julienne repeated blankly. "Pigs?"

"Yes, pigs," Dallas answered. "You know, four-legged things with long snouts that go around saying *Oink! Oink!* Pigs. You must have seen a pig or two in your time."

Carley clapped her hands. "Oh, boy, pigs! Maybe there'll be some babies, and I can keep one for a pet!"

"No!" Leah, Roseann, Darcy, and Julienne said in unison.

Darcy said with disgust, "Pigs. I can't believe it. Can't you do better than that, Bronte?"

"No, I can't, because it's a real good job, Ashby," Dallas said defensively. "I just happened to see an old friend of mine right before he went into the harbormaster's office, and I figured he was looking for a steamer. I grabbed him real quick, talked to him, told him about the *River Queen*, and about our—my—situation. He not only asked me to take this livestock haul, but he spent half the afternoon sending telegraphs back and forth to shippers in New Orleans, and he found us this good load of farm machinery for the trip back. It took him a long time, that's why I was so late coming back, and he sure didn't have to go to the trouble. But I guess that's what good friends do."

Leah glanced at Julienne, who gave her a rueful half-smile. Then Julienne said, "He's right, Darcy. Pigs have to be transported too. We're not the only steamer on the Mississippi River that has hauled them. We owe Mr. Bronte, and his friend, our gratitude."

"And to God," Carley put in. "'Cause pigs are fat, so they'll be really heavy, and that's what I asked for, a heavy load so we'd make lots of money."

"Yeah, what about that, Bronte? What about the money?" Darcy asked with sudden interest.

Dallas glanced at Julienne, and she said quietly, "Darcy, I'll have to go over the details with Dallas, and make calculations on our expenses, and exactly how much we'll be able to clear. What we get paid isn't all our money, you know."

"That again," Darcy said, his fine mouth twisting. "When you Big Bosses figure out my allowance, you let me know, would you? I've got to go, I've got an appointment. Good night, Mother, Aunt Leah." Savagely shoving back his chair, he left. Carley looked crestfallen, and seeing it, Julienne could have strangled her brother. But then she realized that when her father had been alive, she herself had been little better. She wasn't sulky and rude like Darcy, but she manipulated her father constantly to give her things and money that he didn't have. And though she treated Carley good-naturedly, she largely ignored her. She sighed deeply.

Eyeing her, Dallas said, "I stand by what I say, that it's a good haul, but I am sorry about the pigs. I know it's not going to be easy for ladies to be on a pig boat."

They all immediately protested. Finally Roseann said softly, "Mr. Bronte, we are so grateful, to you, to your friend, and as Carley said, to the Lord. This has been an answer to prayer. Don't even think of any regrets, because this freight is a blessing from God."

"Even pigs, ma'am?" Dallas asked with curiosity.

"Even pigs," she repeated. "We will thank the Lord for them."

"Especially," Carley said piously, "big fat pigs."

DAWN BROUGHT A FUROR of activity, for the livestock had been driven by two Negro men all the way down Silver Street right to the dock. Everybody was staring at the sight, and since they left quite a mess behind, they made their feelings known. All up and down the docks the noise of hoots of derisions, disgusted shouts, catcalling, and eloquent profanity sounded. The berth where the *River Queen* was docked swarmed with pigs squealing and snorting. Eight cows stood staring and gravely chewing cud.

Ring and Jesse lowered one landing stage, while Dallas and Willem lowered the other. Julienne had always been fascinated at this, because she remembered the first time she and Dallas had come to see the *Queen*, and he had lowered the gangway by himself. But always, she had noticed on the docks, it took at least two, usually more men, to do it. Now, however, she was much distracted—as was much of Natchez-Under-the-Hill—with the pigs. They were a squirming, lively, vocal crowd.

Dallas's friend, the owner, rode up on a fine horse behind the livestock. He was a short rotund man in his middle fifties, balding, with bushy side whiskers. His clothes were well-tailored and of good quality, but he dressed very plainly, in a black frock coat, waistcoat, and trousers. His tall hat was felt, not silk. Dallas went to meet him. "Good morning, Mr. Fender. The *River Queen* is all ready and rarin' to go."

Fender dismounted and watched as his drovers and the crew started herding the pigs onto the boat. "Dallas, it's a big comedown for a pilot like you to be driving a pig boat. It's not going to help your reputation one bit."

Dryly Dallas said, "Mr. Fender, those pigs have a better reputation than I do right now. Thanks again for helping me out. I won't forget it, and somehow one day I'll pay you back."

"Just business, Dallas," he said, shaking his head. "Besides, if the new *River Queen* is as fast as the old one was, you'll be making a quick, clean trip, and that'll be good for both of our reputations."

"This is our shakedown trip," Dallas said. "So we'll see if she's the fast *Queen* she used to be. I'll tell you, she may not look like much on the outside but her firebox and engine are top of the line. I think she's gonna steam as good and fast as a clipper."

"I sure hope so, Dallas. I feel for the Ashbys. I wasn't acquainted with them, but I heard what happened to that family when Mr. Ashby died. Big scandal, I'm sorry to say. Anyway, you remember the terms, right? I'm paying you half the money. You collect the other half from Pike at the other end when you deliver." He took an envelope from his breast pocket and said, "It's cash. Easier for you and the Ashbys. You can count it if you want."

"No, sir," Dallas said, tucking it into his trouser pocket. "Thank you."

Fender hesitated and said, "Be sure you get the money before you let Pike have the livestock, Dallas. And if I were you, I wouldn't take a bank draw."

Dallas nodded. "That way, is it?"

"I don't know anything for sure against him; as far as I know he's always paid his freight. You just hear things. If I were you I'd get cash."

"I'll make sure of that. Thanks again, Mr. Fender."

Dallas went back to the boat. The animals made a horrendous racket. The cows were bawling now and the pigs sounded like an undulating screech. The boat shook as they herded them on board.

Pushing pigs aside, Dallas made his way along with the animals up the gangplank and saw that the men were having trouble driving the cows into the wooden pen they'd built overnight for them. He took off his hat and started whacking them, calling, "Hup, hup, git along, little dogies! Git on in there, c'mon, git!"

Finally the pigs were happy and already wallowing in the hay covering the cargo deck, and the cows were happily snorting and snuffling from a trough filled with mash. The crew brought in the landing stages, and men on the docks and on the nearby steamboats called out to them.

One squat river man with his mouth covered by a fierce black beard and mustache yelled, "Hey, Dallas, I got a load of snakes I got to ship down river. You want to take them? I can get you a good price."

Dallas said, "You bring 'em right on board. We'll take anything that flies, crawls, swims, or hops."

When they finished he told Ring, Willem, and Jesse, "Let's blow outta this joint. We got a date in New Orleans." Grinning, they went back toward the firebox and the engine room. Dallas climbed the stairs and saw the family lining the rail on the Texas deck, watching. He gave them a quick wave and called, "We're on our way! Miss Carley, blow me a kiss for good luck!"

With enthusiasm Carley kissed her hand and threw the kiss at him.

He hurried to the pilothouse, relieved because Carley hadn't followed him to insist on ringing all the bells. It had been fun, when they had been just trying out the *River Queen*, but this was serious business and it would have been very inconvenient for him to have Carley—or anyone else for that matter—in the wheelhouse while he was pulling out of the crowded docks. It was still early morning, and dozens of steamers, flatboats, barges, and rafts were crowding the waters at the busy port.

And also, Dallas admitted to himself, it was the first time in over a year that he had stood in a wheelhouse, the pilot, taking a valuable load of freight on a good tough steamer. He was elated, and it was not something he wanted to share right at that moment.

Ring's voice sounded up through the listening tube. "She's ready to go when you are, Dallas!"

Grinning like a little boy, he reached up and rang the backing bell.

CHAPTER TWELVE

At about ten that night Dallas heard a timid knock on the pilothouse door behind him. "Am I disturbing you?" he heard Julienne ask.

"Not at all, come on in."

She came in and stood beside him, but not too closely, giving him room. A perfect half moon shown down on the old river, and it lit her face with a gentle ghostly light. "Beautiful," she whispered.

"It's a good night on the river," he said quietly.

The water-moon bobbled along the smooth black water, always before them, teasing them along. The *thunk-thunk-thunk* of the paddle wheel was a comforting background timpani. They were traveling along a stretch where the river blossomed out to over a mile wide, and the dark blur of the woods along the shore seemed to be floating fast past them.

They were, it seemed to Julienne, far on the right side of the stream. Even as she reflected on this, Dallas eased the wheel over slightly, and the *Queen* obediently slid over, closer to the center of the river. They slid along, then soon he turned back and they hugged the starboard shore again. "Why are we kind of jiggling along all on one side?" she asked curiously.

"Because along this stretch, on the port side, the river is shallow for a little over a mile, and then there's a sandbar. You have to stay on this side until we get past the sandbar."

"So you know the river that well? Even how deep it is over there and about that little sandbar?" she asked with interest.

He never took his eyes from watching alertly straight ahead. "Miss Ashby, I know every sandbar, every snag, every current, every hole, and every bend and loop of this old man. Every pilot does. We have to."

"Are you telling me that you actually *memorize* this river?" she said in amazement.

"Four times," he said evenly. "Upriver, downriver, day, and night."

She digested this for awhile. Ahead she saw a soft yellow light, and as it grew closer she could see a little river shanty, with two windows in the front. "Do you know the people that live there?" she asked curiously.

"No, but we call it Jameson's point. It's a land-mark for a pilot. I see that shack, and I know that just about a mile ahead is the big landing for the Jameson plantation, so I have to be ready to pull out around it."

"But does that mean you know exactly how many miles per hour we're traveling? And you calculate one mile, and then you know when you're coming up on the landing?"

"No, not really. You just know, you just feel it. It's kind of hard to explain. But anyway, I do know that we're going about thirteen miles an hour, under easy steam. That's fast, Miss Ashby. That's real fast. I'm proud of the *Queen*."

"Me too," she said. "She's giving us a lovely ride. Except for the scent, of course. But I'm not com-plaining," she said hastily. "I—I just wanted to tell you that I've changed, Dal—Mr. Bronte. I'm deter-mined to be grateful for all the wonderful things that you're doing for us, and the good things that we have to look forward to, now that the *River Queen* is giving us some hope for the future. And—and in spite of—everything, I like the river. I can see the day when I might even love it."

His face became alert when she almost called him by his first name. Now he said intently, "You know, Miss Ashby, this river has tried to kill me four times, but I still love it. I'm glad that that wreck didn't ruin everything for you, forever."

It was the first time they had ever spoken one word about the wreck. Julienne swallowed hard and said with difficulty, "Mr. Bronte, about that night—that night, in the barn—"

"Please stop," he said harshly. "That was not you, Julienne. I know you now. That was a woman that was in shock, that had lost her best friend in an awful death, that was frightened, and was already half dead. And I don't want to talk about it any more, except to tell you that I'm so sorry for everything. I would not hurt you for all the money on this earth," he finished vehemently.

She dropped her head and furtively wiped tears from her eyes. "I don't want to talk about it any more either, except for this: Thank you for saving my life. Thank you for bringing me home safe. And thank you for your care of me and my family."

"You're welcome, ma'am," he said.

She turned again to watch the river. He rested his hands on the wheel, as the *River Queen* glided sweetly along. After awhile Julienne said, "If you'll let me call you Dallas, I'd like for you to call me Julienne."

"I'd like that," he said. Staring straight ahead, he smiled.

THE WHARVES AT NEW Orleans were not a place that Julienne wanted to linger. Always before she had landed there and had immediately been whisked quickly away in fine carriages to where rich people ate and drank and lived. She stood on the Texas deck, watching the teeming masses of people, carts, horses, and herded livestock below. It was, of course, no better than Natchez-Under-the-Hill, but somehow Julienne felt more vulnerable, even frightened, by the crowds of riverboat men. *I suppose Natchez-Under-the-Hill is the devil I know, she thought glumly. Who would have thought that I'd feel some bizarre sort of security there?*

They made the turn into the docks. She saw a big man with a bright red waistcoat strained over a large belly, smoking a stub of a cigar, watching them as they nosed into Slip Number 86, which was on their shipping orders. She felt the paddle wheels stop and the engines slow to silence. Soon Dallas came down the stairs to help lower the landing stages. To Ring he said, "Keep 'em in until I say so."

"You bet, Dallas," Ring said. "But hurry up, would ya? I won't be sad to see these critters go."

Dallas shrugged. "I've had human beings that gave more trouble. Some of 'em even smelled this bad." He walked out onto the dock, and the big man wearing the scarlet vest came at once to see him. "You Bronte?"

"Yes, sir, pilot of the *River Queen*. Are you Mr. Pike?"

"That's me, here's my bill of sale from Fender, you can take a gander at it. I brought my drovers, they'll help you unload."

"Sure, Mr. Pike. Here's the bill of lading. As soon as you pay your freight, we'll get to it."

"I'll get you paid after they're offloaded," Pike said impatiently. "I know my cows are thirsty, and those pigs are losing weight every minute. I'm in a hurry."

Dallas pulled himself up to his full six foot, two inches. "That livestock has been well-tended. They can wait until I've got my money, sir."

Pike's face grew flushed. "You don't trust me?"

"It's not a matter of trust. It's business. I've got your cattle. You got my money. You give me the money. I'll give you the cattle. Simple business transaction."

Pike stuck the dead chewed cigar in his mouth and growled, "Maybe I'll just leave them with you."

"Fine with me. I got half pay for this trip from Mr. Fender. I'll just sell them myself, which will cover the rest of the freight, and make me a nice little profit on the side."

"You can't do that," he said, but now with much less bravado.

"You just watch me, Mr. Pike."

He stared at Dallas and for a moment, it seemed, he would argue more. Then he muttered a curse under his breath, reached into his pocket and pulled out a bankbook. Quickly Dallas said, "We're not going to be here long enough to go to town and get your draft cashed, Mr. Pike. But I need fuel money for the trip home. It's going to have to be cash."

"Cash!" he cried, his face reddening again. "My draft is perfectly good! I could just leave that bunch of pigs on that boat, you know!"

"You already said that, and then we decided that you're not going to do that," Dallas said with elaborate patience. "Cash, Mr. Pike."

Muttering darkly, he pulled a rolled wad of cash out of an inside jacket pocket, licked his thumb, and started flipping bills out of the wad. Dallas watched him closely. He started to gather them up, and Dallas said politely, "Twenty more dollars, Mr. Pike, I see you've miscounted. Must have been an accident. Yes, I see that twenty right there, that'll do it." As soon as it had been added to the pile, Dallas yanked it out of his hand. "Thank you so much, Mr. Pike, it's been a pleasure doing business with you. You can have your pigs now."

"That would be ever so kind of you, Mr. Bronte," Pike said, his voice dripping with sarcasm.

Dallas turned and walked back up the gangplank, followed by two of Pike's four drovers. The other two stayed on shore, for Pike had a long line of wagons with high sides to carry the livestock.

On the Texas deck above him, he saw the Ashby family lining the rail, watching the goings-on. He noticed that Darcy Ashby was dressed to the nines, with a blue cutaway frock coat, silver satin waistcoat with a gold watch chain, iron-creased black trousers, and a black silk top hat. He and Julienne were arguing; at least, he looked angry, and she seemed to be pleading with him. But he had much more important things to attend to, as he came to the main doors of the cargo deck he shouted, "Let 'er rip, Jesse! All the little piggies are going home!"

The doors opened, and all of the *River Queen* crew helped the drovers herd the pigs onto the landing stages. It was all going just fine, until it seemed that one fat pink sow with black blotches seemed to lose her senses, and as soon as she came out the main doors she ran right by Jesse, squealing, and launched herself off the boat. She landed right by the side, of course, in the shallow water. But she was heavy, and immediately sunk about six inches, so that the ripples ran over her broad back and lapped up against her chin. She lifted her head and began wailing, a loud squeal that sounded almost like a human cry. Everyone was laughing at the ludicrous sight, including Dallas.

But then, even through the spectacular ruckus of the docks, he heard Carley screaming. "Dallas! Dallas! She's drowning, she's drowning!"

Quickly he looked up and saw her leaning precariously far over the rickety rail, and her face was wrinkled up with such fear and distress that his heart melted. He looked at the screeching pig; he looked at the crew and drovers. The pig was in no danger, of course, and he knew that Pike's men would get the pig, she was valuable. But they were all working hard, herding the rest of the pigs on shore and into the wagons. Carley kept screaming that the pig was drowning, and then she started crying.

Muttering to himself, he stepped off the boat into the filthy water. Wading over to the pig, he bent down, wrapped his arms around her, and tried to jerk her up out of the mud. She struggled but still didn't come free. "Now listen here, pig," he growled. "I'll get you out of this predicament but I'm not carrying you all the way to shore. So shut up and pull!"

The only thing slipperier than a wet pig is a muddy pig, and this pig was covered with slimy Mississippi mud. Dallas pulled and yanked, using every bit of his considerable strength. Finally, with a mucky sucking sound, she worked free. He let go, and she scampered up the shore, and seemingly with relief ran up the ramp into a waiting wagon.

"You saved her!" Carley shouted gleefully. "Dallas, you saved her! HOOOORRRRAYYY for Dallas!"

Julienne and Leah were grinning widely, and both of them lost their respectability enough to join Carley and shouted, "Hooray, Dallas! You saved the pig!"

Dallas pulled himself back onto the deck of the *Queen*, and as soon as he was out of sight and earshot of the ladies, he muttered a lot of those words that Carley wasn't supposed to hear.

Finally the pigs were loaded onto the wagons. With very little trouble they got the cows offloaded, and with relief all around they watched Mr. Pike and his wagons driving off.

Dallas turned to Jesse, who was grinning so widely he looked as if his face would split in two. Dallas's breeches were caked with slimy mud up to his thighs, his shirtfront and sleeves were filthy, and he stank horribly of pig and the disgusting

centuries-old muck in the water of the port of New
Orleans.

"Don't say a word," Dallas growled.

"No, sir, I won't."

"All right, I want you to go get Caesar and Miss
Libby for me, since I'm not fit to go up to the Texas,"
he said with exasperation. "I'm going to send them
to town—" He stopped short, his eyes widened, and
he slapped his hip. "Oh, no," he grunted, and yanked
the money out of his trouser pocket. Miraculously,
it hadn't gotten wet and muddy.

Darcy Ashby called, "Bronte! There you are." He
tiptoed across the soiled deck, taking little delicate
steps so as not to soil his mirror-shined boots. When
he reached Jesse and Dallas, he said to Jesse, "I want
you to sweep a path out of this wretched hole, and
also sweep off the gangplank. This garbage is going
to ruin my boots."

Jesse, his smile now gone, looked at Dallas uncertainly. Dallas said evenly, "Go and find Caesar and
Libby and tell them to dress to go to town, Jesse."

With a furtive glance at Darcy, Jesse hurried off.

Darcy turned to Dallas and said furiously, "Just
who do you think you are? The Ashbys own this
boat, and all of you work for us—for me!"

"You're wrong about that," Dallas said, his eyes
glinting. "I don't work for you, I work for your
mother and your sister and your aunt. I even work
for Carley, as you can see. But I don't work for you,
and I never will. And these men are not your servants. They're the crew of the *River Queen*, which

means they work for me. Don't you ever try to order them around again."

"I won't because I'm leaving," Darcy said sulkily. "I'm going to stay with a friend until this stupid boat starts making some real money so I can get my own flat. Now, give me my share of the money for this haul."

"No," Dallas said flatly. "Until we've picked up our return load, and have gotten back to Natchez, we're not going to know exactly how much we cleared. Your sister told you that. You want some of this money now, you go talk to her."

He made an ugly face. "You can't talk sense to her, she's gone barking mad. It's all your fault too, Bronte. I can't think why she puts so much trust in a river rat and a drunk like you. Well, I'm out of it. Just try to keep from getting drunk and wrecking my boat and killing my family." This vicious triumphant exit was definitely diminished, however, as he daintily tiptoed out of the cargo hold.

Dallas watched him, a mixture of disdain and relief on his face. As far as he was concerned, the *River Queen* would be a much happier boat without Darcy Ashby. Since the day the Ashbys had moved onto the boat, Darcy had done absolutely nothing except sleep all day, demand food when he woke up, dress, go out and get drunk, and come back at all hours of the morning.

Jesse returned with Caesar and Libby. Dallas asked them, "Do you two know New Orleans? Town, I mean?"

"Oh, yes, sir," Caesar said. "The Ashbys have lots of friends here. We've visited plenty of times."

"Good," Dallas said. "I want you to go to the nearest apothecary and tell him you need three barrels of boric acid salts. If he doesn't have that much, find out where you can get it. And then go to the nearest hardware store and buy a hip bath. And I mean a nice one, a big wide one, a brass one lined with porcelain. And buy two ten-gallon copper pots. Here's plenty of money. Rent a good sturdy cart."

"Yes, sir," Caesar said. Tucking the money securely in his inside coat pocket, he offered Libby his arm and the two headed for the doors. After a thought, Dallas called after them, "Caesar? You and Libby get you some dinner, or ice cream, or whatever you want. And oh, yes. Get some black licorice."

THE CREW, INCLUDING DALLAS, began shoveling the soiled straw from the main deck and loading it into wheelbarrows, then dumping them into a refuse cart. "I don't want to dump this mess into the river in case I have to go swimming again," he said dryly.

"Sure hope no pigs fall in a-drowning again," Ring chortled.

It took them three hours of hard work, but they got every piece of straw shoveled up. "We can't wash it down and clean it good until Caesar and Libby get back with the boric acid salts," Dallas told them. "So go ahead and take a break. You can go on up to the galley, Libby said she left stuff for dinner. Bring me a plate down, would you?"

Ring, Willem, and Jesse all went up the stairs. Dallas went out to the deck and leaned against the railing. It squeaked and was loose, and he thought, *I'll sure be glad when we've got the old girl fixed up nice again. She deserves it.*

Julienne came to stand beside him. "Hi. Why don't you come up? The men are eating in the dining room. I've decided that it's silly for you to have to take your food down to that little hole you sleep in. From now on, you eat at the table."

"That's good," Dallas said warmly. "Thanks, Julienne, I know the men appreciate it. But even I can't stand the way I smell, that's why I'm outside. I'm hoping for any little breath of breeze to carry the stink downwind."

Julienne giggled, a youthful, carefree sound that Dallas had never heard from her before. "I must admit that you are—fragrant. But it was all in a good cause. You saved the pig from drowning, and though Carley always thought you were the 'bestest river man she ever saw,' now she wants to marry you."

"Huh. Getting a good woman should be so easy," he grunted.

She looked up at him curiously. "You know, I've always been meaning to ask you—I mean, it's really none of my business, I know, but—that is—"

He turned around, leaning back with his elbows on the rail, to look down at her. "You want to know about Lulie, don't you?"

A delicate blush stole over her cheeks, and she quickly looked down. "I have wondered."

"It's not what you think, Julienne," he said quietly. "I just feel really sorry for her. Did you know that she's only twenty years old?"

Jullienne's head snapped up. "What? But I thought she must be much older than that!" To Julienne, her worn face had looked like a jaded woman of at least thirty-five.

Dallas shrugged. "She was orphaned, and her aunt and uncle took her in. Her uncle started abusing her when she was thirteen years old. She ran away, and she's been at the Blue Moon since she was fourteen."

"But surely—surely there's some other way—" Julienne said haltingly.

Dallas's face hardened. "A servant? No one would hire a fourteen-year-old without family, without references. Besides, slaves are cheaper. A schoolteacher? She can't even read. Life is messy, Julienne, and sometimes you can't fix it. Most prostitutes don't wake up and decide on that as a career. Lulie sure didn't."

Julienne sighed. "Sometimes I regret the days when I wasn't aware of such things. I know it's shallow and selfish, but it's so hard to understand the evil in this world."

"I don't get it either," Dallas agreed. "I wish I could find comfort and peace in God like your mother and your aunt and even Carley do. Never have, though. Maybe it's just not for me. Anyway, Julienne, I just want to tell you one more thing. I never was anything but friends with Lulie. I've known her since she was fifteen, when I started going to the Blue Moon. Whenever I rent a room there, I let her stay, because all of those girls sleep in a little windowless stinking room on filthy mattresses behind the saloon. She sleeps on the bed, and I sleep on the floor in my bedroll."

She looked up at him then, her dark eyes shining, but then her gaze went beyond his shoulder and she whispered, "Oh, no. I was so afraid of this."

He looked behind, and Darcy was stamping up the gangplank. His face was red, and his expression was full of rage. Julienne ran to meet him and laid her hand on his arm. "Oh, Darcy, I'm so sorry. I tried to tell you how the Moaks treated me. I was so afraid Stephen—"

Furiously he muttered, "Just shut up, Jules!" and yanked his arm away from her so hard that she stumbled a little.

Dallas Bronte was right behind her and put his arm around her to steady her. Quickly he stepped to the side and took a wide stance, blocking Darcy's way. His eyes were flashing dangerously and his jaw was clenched. "Julienne, go up to the Texas. I need to talk to your brother."

With one wide-eyed look at him, she gathered up her skirts and hurried away.

Darcy looked up at him angrily, but then his high color faded and he licked his lips nervously. "Get out of my way, Bronte," he said, his voice now low and uncertain.

"You are not boarding this boat until we get some things straightened out," Dallas said in a tone of clear warning. "Libby and Caesar aren't cleaning up after you any more. Your aunt and sister aren't washing and ironing your clothes any more. No more getting drunk every night and sleeping all day. You want to stay on this boat, you work."

"Work? What does that mean?" Darcy said sulkily.

With grim humor Dallas said, "I'm not a bit surprised that you don't know the meaning of the word. You're going to work, Ashby. Not only are you going to clean your own stateroom and wash your own clothes and bed linens, but you are going to help on this boat. You're going to start in just a few minutes, when we get the cleaning supplies and we have to swab out this deck. You're going to be swabbing right along with the rest of us."

Outrage washed over Darcy's handsome face, making it ugly. "You can't make me do that! You can't make me do anything at all!"

"Let me put it this way," Dallas said slowly, the menace in his voice returning. "If you don't work, you don't eat."

Darcy stared up at him, and his face drained of all color. Finally in a choked voice he muttered, "My mother and sister would never agree to that."

To his confusion, Dallas nodded. "I know. But I just want you to realize that you're just a pathetic, spoiled, whining brat hiding behind your poor mama's skirts. I know this, and the crew knows this. See, we're real men. I have to tell you that, because I don't think you have any idea what being a man is. Real men look down on you. You just chew on that, Ashby."

Darcy stared up at him, his face pale, his blue eyes wide with shock. His mouth moved, but no words came out.

Dallas watched him for a few moments, and then his voice dropped to a feral growl. "There's just one more thing I want to tell you, Ashby, and if you have any sense left in your empty head you better listen to me. If I ever hear you speak to your sister, or any other lady, like that again, I will beat you to a bloody pulp. If I ever see you handle your sister, or any other lady, like that again, I will beat you to a bloody pulp. Do you understand?"

"Y-yes."

"Good," Dallas said, stepping aside to let him pass. "I'm very glad we've come to an understanding, Ashby. Just make sure you don't forget what I said."

CHAPTER THIRTEEN

"And after you finish cleaning all the mud out of the pipes and pumps and boilers, you gotta oil and tighten up those safety valves," Dallas said to Ring. "They're squeaky, and they're clattering. And I don't know what's wrong with the rods, but they're wobbling. It's got to be either the reach rod or the pendulum rod, but I can't see a thing wrong with either of them."

Ring's tough face wrinkled. "Dallas, you know I don't know no more'n a mule about an engine. Wish I did, but guess I'm just dirt-dumb. It's just too bad that Hansen left us in the rub like this." Willem Hansen, their engineer, had left to take a job on a bigger boat that paid twice as much as the Ashbys were paying him.

Dallas sighed. "Yeah, I know, Ring, but I can't blame the man. And you're not dumb, either. It just takes an engineer to know an engine. I'm no engineer either, or I'd know what's wrong with the—" he hesitated, glancing at Carley squatting at his feet. "With the blamed thing," he finished lamely.

Julienne came in then, holding her skirts closely around herself so as not to brush up against the greasy machinery. She walked up to Ring and Dallas and stared at the floor in front of them. A man's booted feet were sticking out from underneath a maze of pipes. Carley squatted by the feet. Jesse was bent over, looking underneath the pipes. He bobbed up to touch his forehead to Julienne and then bent back over.

A muffled voice said, "What I want to know is how Hansen ever squeezed underneath here, the big ape. Carley, hand me that monkey wrench."

Julienne's mouth opened, and she blurted out, "Is that my brother?"

Ring and Dallas exchanged amused glances, and Dallas said, "Yes, ma'am."

"You mean that's my brother? Lying on the floor? What's he doing lying on the floor?" she asked, astounded.

Though his voice was still muffled, he said loudly, "You know, I can hear you, Jules. I'm crazy, not deaf. I'm trying to open a valve down here so a bunch of stinking Mississippi mud can pour out onto my face." Carley giggled.

Julienne just stood there gaping, so Dallas finally asked, "So, what are you doing down here, Julienne?"

"What? Oh. I was looking for Carley. Carley, what are you doing? Repairing a piston or something?"

"No, Dallas won't let me fix anything yet," she said with disgust. "I'm helping Darcy. Then we gotta oil the valves and reach for the rods."

"That ain't the right valve, Mr. Ashby," Jesse said helpfully. "It's that one just up above your right eye."

"Yeah, that's great, so all the muck'll go right in my eye," Darcy grumbled.

Julienne was so distracted by this strange phenomenon of her brother that she forgot Carley. Taking her arm, Dallas said, "C'mon, I've got to head out. I'll walk you out."

She allowed him to lead her out on deck, and he said soothingly, "You know, Carley's going to be fine. She actually likes messing around down here, and she's got a curious mind. She really pays attention to this stuff. And it's a lot better for her to be occupied. Did you know Jesse caught her skipping down the gangplank yesterday by herself? She said she was going to go dig crawfish for catfish bait."

"Oh, no," Julienne groaned. "Whatever are we going to do? I guess we'll just have to keep the landing stages up all the time."

He gave her an odd look. "No, I don't think so, Julienne. That doesn't make any sense."

"What? Why not?" she demanded.

"Because Carley is a child," he said patiently. "And she's an obedient child. She's never failed to do one thing I've told her to do, and she's never gotten fussy when I've forbidden her to do something she shouldn't. I'm sorry to say it, but you and even your mother have let her run wild, and it's only because of that lack of discipline that she does foolish things like thinking she can go wandering around Natchez-Under-the-Hill by herself."

Julienne's eyes narrowed with annoyance. "Just a minute, Dallas. Who do you think you are, telling me how to raise my sister, and criticizing my mother?"

"I don't mean to," Dallas said quietly. "It's just that in the world you live in now, letting Carley run around on her own isn't just an annoyance. It's dangerous. And my crew cannot be responsible for watching her."

"Who asked you to?" Julienne said angrily. "Carley's just headstrong, and she will have her own way or bust. There's nothing else to do."

"Sure there is. Just talk to her, Julienne. She's a smart little girl, and she understands a lot of things better than adults do. I think that if you just explained to her that things have changed, and she has to obey you and your mother and your aunt, and you tell her plain and simple what she can and can't do, she would obey you."

"Fine, Mr. Great-Kingpin-Pilot Know-It-All! I guess that's how you cowed my poor brother into

working!" she snapped. "By having a 'plain and simple' talk with him."

"Pretty much," Dallas said, shrugging.

"I doubt that, you probably threatened him, you
big bully!"

Dallas said nothing.

He was right about Carley, and Julienne knew it,
and deep down she had known it for a long time.
But it stung, coming from a man who was unmarried, had no children, had never had brothers or
sisters, and who shouldn't know anything about it.
She stormed, "You know what? I may need your
help with this boat, but I don't need you to tell me
how to take care of my sister. Suppose you just leave
that to me and my family!" With that she turned on
her heel and stalked off.

Dallas watched her, frustrated, then he walked
down the gangplank and up to the boardwalk.
*Blasted women! One minute they're all honey-sweet
and the next they're sinking their fangs into you! No
wonder I never got married!*

It was a long, fruitless, discouraging day for Dallas.
They had returned from their round-trip haul to
New Orleans five days previously, and though he
went out looking every day, he still hadn't found
another load. All day he went back, again, to each
warehouse manager, each shipping office, the harbormaster's office, with no offers for loads for the *River
Queen*. Then he went down to the docks, going from
boat to boat, talking to everyone he knew to ask if
they knew of an engineer that was available. No one

could think of a single man. He went up again to the boardwalk and started asking at the flophouses, the brothels, the gambling dens, and the saloons, and couldn't find a single engineer in all the river men holed up in Natchez-Under-the-Hill.

Finally he stood just past the foot of Silver Street. On his right was the *River Queen*. On his left was the Blue Moon Saloon. He stood there for a long time, scowling down at the filthy, splintered board-walk. Then he wheeled and stalked into the Blue Moon.

Walking over to the bar, he cocked his foot up on the brass footrail and plunked down a half dollar. "I'll have a whiskey, Otto."

"Sure, Dallas." The bartender, a fat man with a handlebar mustache, poured him up a shot glass full of the brown liquid and asked, "No business for the *Queen* yet?"

"Not yet."

"Well, if I hear of anything, I'll be sure and send 'em to you. I know you need to put the *Queen* to work."

"I'd appreciate that, Otto. And now I've lost my engineer. I've been searching this town and can't find a man anywhere."

Otto stood polishing a glass with a dingy towel, nodding. Half of his job was pouring whiskey, and the other half was listening. "Can't think of any right now, but I'll keep my ear to the ground. Never know, one might just walk in here and ask you for a job tonight."

Dallas stood propped up against the bar for some time. Men came in, the girls woke up and started coming in from the back room, scratching and yawning. By nightfall the place was packed, the air was blue with smoke that almost choked a man to breathe it. Two poker games were going on, and there was a roulette wheel and a blackjack dealer, but he had no inclination to gamble. He ordered more drinks, and Otto doubled up on them at no charge. Eventually he realized that the noise was growing muffled, as if he had rolled cotton in his ears. Idly he picked up a nickel on the bar and spun it on its end. At least, he tried to do it, but his fingers felt like fat sticks. The coin fell on its side and he noticed idly that he saw two coins. *"I'm getting drunk. That's what I'm doing. What do you think about that, Miss Julienne Snippy-Snoot Ashby?"*

He downed the last of his drink and dizzily waved to Otto for another. As Otto poured it, he heard a man say, "Are you Dallas Bronte?"

Dallas turned and saw a tall young man about his height. He was young, no more than twenty-one or twenty-two, Dallas guessed, lanky and boyish-looking, but wiry, the kind that had more strength than one might suspect. He was plain, not handsome at all, but he had a pair of quick, alert, brown eyes and a broad smile. Dallas said, "Thass me. Dallas Bronte."

"My name's Revelation Brown, Mr. Bronte. I hear you're the pilot of the *River Queen*?"

But Dallas had gotten stuck on his name. "You tell me that? What kind of a mama would name her baby 'Revelation'?"

"She loved the Lord, and she loved that book. Revelation, you know."

"Huh. Must be hard to get along with a name like that."

"Not bad. People just call me Rev, usually. Mr. Bronte, are you born of the Spirit?"

The bluntness of the question and the cheerful face of the young man struck at Dallas. "No, I don't think so. This is no place to be talking about things like that."

"Why, of course it is! Any place is good to share the gospel. Matter of fact, that's what I do everywhere I go."

"It could get you thrown out of a place like the Blue Moon."

"I've been thrown out of saloons before," he said cheerfully. "But what I wanted to talk to you about was, I heard around that you've lost your engineer."

Dallas's brain cleared a little and he answered, "Yes, I did. Have you worked on boats?"

"Yes, sir, I ran the engines of the *Mandley H. Chapman*."

"She was a good old boat. Yeah, I heard she got docked a coupla months ago. But you look kinda young for an engineer."

"I left home when I was just fifteen. I got a job as cabin boy on the old *Tennessee Birdsong*, my first boat. Wasn't long before I found out I have a knack with engines, and I've been working on them ever since. The *Chapman* was my first tour as an engineer, and I did pretty good, if I say so myself."

Dallas nodded, "She was an old girl, you must have been good to keep her running for the last couple of years." He looked Rev up and down, squinting his eyes to narrow it down to just one man he was seeing instead of three. "I need a man all right, but the trouble is, Brown, I can't pay much. Probably nowhere near what you were making on the *Chapman*."

"That's all right. All I need is a place to sleep, a little grub, an engine to work on, and a nickel or two for an ice cream every once in awhile. I love ice cream."

Dallas studied him and saw a sincerity in him that impressed him. Dallas may be a dead loss at a poker face, but he could tell a liar across a crowded room. "All right then, Brown, let's have a drink and we'll talk." He motioned to Otto.

"Call me Rev," the young man said.

The bartender hurried up and asked, "What'll it be, gents?"

"Another whiskey for me. 'Fraid they don't have ice cream here at this fine establishment, Rev, so what you drinking?"

"I'll have a sarsaparilla. Bartender, are you saved?"

Otto blinked his eyes. "No. I'm a bartender."

"Well, bartenders need God too, don't they?"

Otto grinned good-naturedly. "Does he talk like this all the time, Dallas?"

"It's starting to look like it. Get the man a sarsaparilla."

"Sure."

When the drinks came, Rev sipped his and said, "So tell me about the *Queen*, Mr. Bronte."

"If you can stand being called Revelation, I can take being called Dallas." He went on to tell Rev about how the *Queen* had been laid up for three years, and how they had very little money to get her on the river again. He told him about the one haul they'd had. Then he told him about the problems he'd noticed with the engines.

Rev listened carefully, nodding from time to time. "Dallas, I know you don't know me, but I'm telling you I know without even having to look what the problem is, and it's an easy fix, which means cheap. Give me a chance. I'll show you what I can do. After I pray over those boilers and that engine, your *River Queen* will run better than she ever has."

Dallas stared at the young man and found himself smiling. "You read the Bible a lot, Rev?"

"All the time. Do you?"

"I used to."

"Why'd you give it up?"

Dallas twirled the glass in his fingers, drank the last few drops and said, "It made me feel bad. I knew all that stuff about sinners would just aim right at me."

"But you do believe in God, then?"

"Do you take me for a fool, Rev? Of course I believe in God. Any man with sense knows that the world couldn't have made itself. Anyway, you got the job, if you want it, Rev. I'll pay you fifty cents a day to start, and that's with room and board. But there's something I gotta explain to you," he said, frowning. "The owners sail with the *River Queen*, see, so that's why I have to tell you. There's this sister, well, there's two sisters, but this one sister I gotta explain to you about."

Rev was grinning at him. He looked about fifteen years old. Dallas stopped running on and demanded, "What?"

"I know all about the Ashbys and their problems, Dallas. It's hot talk on the river, the scandal and all. I thought it was pretty big of you not to gossip about them, and then try to poor-mouth me into taking less money. And I gotta tell you, when I heard about them, and figured out it was the *River Queen* that lost their engineer, I just knew the Lord was sending me to you. And I promise you won't be sorry."

The two stood there talking, but they were interrupted when Lulie showed up. Dallas was pretty well hazy by this time, and his lips were numb, but he managed an introduction. "Lulie, this is Revelation Brown. Don't cuss in front of him."

"Glad to know you, Miss Lulie. Are you saved, Spirit-filled, and sanctified?"

Lulie stared at him, mystified. "No, I'm pretty sure not. Is Revelation your real name?"

"Just call me Rev. But, ma'am, saloon girls, they need God just like bartenders and riverboat pilots do," he said slyly, glancing at Dallas.

"Aw, wet your whistle again, Wev. I mean Rev. More sarsaparilla for Rev and whiskey for me and Lulie," Dallas called out to Otto.

They stayed for awhile, but slowly Dallas found it harder and harder to pronounce his words. Finally he mumbled, "Got to go, Lulie." He pushed away from the bar and stood up straight, but his legs suddenly seemed to be made out of rubber. He sagged, and Revelation put his hands underneath Dallas's arms. "Come on, Dallas. Let me give you a hand."

"Get me back to the *Queen*, Rev."

"Yes, sir. Miss Lulie, I'll come back, and I'll tell you how to get saved."

Lulie laughed. "If you're looking for candidates to preach to, this is the right place. Come back, Dallas, when you've sobered up."

The June air was warm, but Dallas was too drunk to appreciate it. He was disgusted with himself and mumbled all the way back to the ship. He kept tripping over his own feet, but each time Revelation pulled him upright. When they got to the gangplank he tripped on a loose board, stumbled, and went down to his hands and knees. He tried to get up and found he was too dizzy.

Rev reached down, set him up straight, then grabbed him around the lower legs and hoisted him over his shoulder. "Up we go," he said. Dallas thought, *He must be stronger than he looks.* With interest he watched behind him. The world looked different, but he couldn't quite work out exactly why.

They got to the main deck and he felt Rev bend his knees a little bit and ease him off his shoulder. His legs almost buckled, and Rev threw Dallas's left arm around his own shoulders and put one strong arm around his waist. Dallas squinted his eyes, trying to make out the shapes in front of him. He saw three or four person-looking things.

He heard Revelation say, "Good evening, ladies. My name is Revelation Brown, and I'm your new engineer. Would you be so kind as to direct me to Mr. Bronte's sleeping quarters?"

Dallas focused enough to see Julienne eyeing him with disgust, and Aunt Leah looked somber. "I bet you think I been drinking," he said, trying to muster some dignity. "Well, I guess I have been, but just a wittle. A little."

Julienne shook her head. "He has a stateroom up on the Texas deck. Would you like some help? I could ask one of the crewmen."

"No, ma'am, I think me and Dallas can make it just fine, thank you ma'am." They started toward the stairs, and Julienne didn't want to watch in case both the stranger and Dallas came tumbling down them headlong.

She went to the back of the main deck and looked out over the river. Late that evening storm clouds had begun moving in, and the errant breeze on the Mississippi River had transformed into wild rushes of wind from all points of the compass. Julienne and Leah had taken two of their brand-new rocking chairs out to the main deck to watch the storm come in, fanning themselves against the hot southern night, enjoying the occasional odd cool drafts that swept over them.

It was a black night. An eerie quiet lay over the river, the sure prelude to a storm. After awhile Julienne could even hear the soft swish of her aunt's skirts, and Leah came to stand by her side. "It seems that Mr. Bronte is comfortably ensconced in his new quarters. I would imagine that he's going to be a little confused when he wakes up in the morning."

With the money that they were to realize from their haul to New Orleans and back, before they left, each of them had decided on one reasonably-priced thing that they wanted most. Julienne had demanded a hip bath. The Texas deck had two sanitary rooms, but no bathtubs. They were scarce in Natchez and exorbitantly high. Dallas knew that they would be much cheaper in New Orleans, which was why he had sent Caesar and Libby to search for one. And, of course, for the black licorice, which was what Carley had asked for.

Darcy had demanded cash, and though Julienne tried to explain that they wouldn't know exactly how much they would clear until they finished the haul and returned to Natchez, he kept insisting. Finally she had given him five dollars from her very small emergency fund. He had said that would be a down payment and had sashayed off to see Stephen Moak.

As soon as they got back to Natchez, Roseann had ordered three bolts of muslin: black, gray, and blue, to make all of them new skirts, including Libby. She had never been able to do any of the hard work on the ship; she didn't know anything about cooking; she couldn't possibly get down on her knees and scrub; and she simply wasn't strong enough to wash and iron. But she could sew, and she loved it, so she mended and patched and sewed on buttons for everyone, even the crew.

Surprisingly Aunt Leah had asked for a bed, a chest, and a washbowl and pitcher. When Julienne had questioned her about it, she merely said, "When we are not hauling freight, Mr. Bronte works all day looking for freight, and half the night he works on the engines. When this boat is on the river, Mr. Bronte has to stay at that wheel for hours and hours at a time. When he can rest, he deserves a nice, quiet room. I want him to have the captain's stateroom, and I don't want any of you to say anything about it to him."

Julienne had felt a little ashamed at her thoughtlessness at the time. But she certainly wasn't now. "So it's true what everyone said about him," she said bitterly to her aunt.

"He's drunk," Aunt Leah retorted. "He's not *a* drunk."

"What's the difference?"

Leah sighed. "You've been so sheltered, maybe you really don't understand. But when Barry was in the army, I saw what real drunks are. They drink when they wake up and drink until they pass out. They can't possibly work. They drink instead of eat, they're usually violent, and for most of them, when they get to a certain point, that poison is so riddled throughout their bodies that it finally kills them. Now we've been living on this boat with Dallas Bronte for over a month. Until tonight, have you ever seen him take a drink?"

"No," Julienne said sulkily.

"No, you haven't," Leah said with satisfaction.

"But he's so arrogant," Julienne blustered. "Today he tried to tell me how to take care of Carley! How dare he!"

"What did he say?" Leah asked curiously.

"That Jesse had caught her leaving the *Queen* by herself, saying she was going to go dig crawdads for bait, of all things! And Dallas said it was because we—me and mother—haven't been bringing her up right!"

Softly Leah said, "And he's exactly right, Julienne."

"What!" she said with outrage. "How can you say that, Aunt Leah? How can you agree with *him*?"

Again she said, "Because he is right, Julienne. Please calm down and listen to me. I'm not at all surprised that Carley thinks she can just go where she wants, and do what she wants. To her, going to dig for crawdads is no different than going out to the barn to dig for worms. No one ever stopped her from doing that. And no one has explained to her why she can't do it now."

Julienne stared at her. As the truth of her aunt's words began to dawn in her mind, she dropped her head and rubbed her forehead. "She never would stay in her lessons with you. So many times I've thought that Carley was growing up so ignorant, so uneducated. But I just passed it off, thinking that you should make her do her lessons."

"It's not my place. It's never been my place. Just like it's not up to this crew to teach Carley right and wrong and to discipline her. We're just so blessed that Mr. Macklin and Jesse and Mr. Bronte love that child. You don't realize how much time they spend with her, and how carefully they look after her."

Julienne lifted her head and said bleakly, "He was right. Dallas was exactly right. I've spent this whole day, since we had that fight, thinking horrible things about him."

"I wondered why you were in such a foul humor," Leah said with some amusement. "But then I should've known that you crossed Dallas Bronte. Somehow he has a way of locking horns with you and Darcy."

Julienne turned to her and asked, "Darcy? You know what's happened to him, don't you, Aunt Leah? Why he's been working—and sober—for the last few days?"

She nodded. "He came to me in a blue-faced fit, after he came back from trying to see Stephen Moak in New Orleans. He blurted out this entire—I'll call it a conversation, though it seemed to me to be fairly one-sided—that he had with Mr. Bronte. Darcy thought that I would excuse him, would pet him, maybe give him some money. But just like I've done with you tonight, Julienne, I told Darcy that everything Mr. Bronte had told him was right. That I completely and totally agreed with him."

"What did Dallas say to him?"

Leah's mouth twitched. "One of the topics they discussed was that Mr. Bronte was not going to let Darcy eat if he didn't work."

"What! But that could never happen!" Julienne said, irritated again. "You know that we wouldn't let Darcy go without food, as long as we have a morsel!"

"Of course not, and Dallas Bronte is not a fool, he knows that too. It's just that Mr. Bronte used that as an example to teach Darcy that he was subject to certain rules, just like all the rest of the civilized humans on this earth. In effect, he was teaching Darcy a lesson. And it worked too. I realized that as soon as Darcy came to me, instead of to you or to Roseann. He knew, deep down, that Mr. Bronte was right. And he wanted me to listen, and to tell him the truth, and to reassure him that even when we do bad things our family still loves us. And then the next day he went to work."

"I didn't even know until today," Julienne said in a low voice.

"We haven't been talking much about it," Leah said quietly. "We just want Darcy to find his way, without all of us beating him over the head."

"That's probably what Dallas threatened to do to him," Julienne said disdainfully.

"Mm, no, Mr. Bronte didn't say that at all," Leah answered with amusement, remembering that Darcy had said Bronte had promised to "beat him to a bloody pulp."

Julienne let out an exasperated sigh. "All right, Aunt Leah, you're right, and Dallas is right, and I'm wrong. I've been wrong all along about Carley and Darcy. But surely you aren't defending him getting drunk tonight."

"No, I can't defend that," Leah answered somberly. "But neither can I condemn it. And neither can you. Jesus Christ is the only man who has the right to condemn us for our sins, because only He is sinless. And when they asked Him to stone a woman who had committed a sin, the terrible sin of adultery, He said, 'He that is without sin among you, let him first cast a stone at her.' Are you going to be the one that casts that first stone, Julienne?"

Leah's words were almost like a physical shock to Julienne. She actually felt slightly nauseous, and the headache that had been threatening her all day flooded in with a vengeance. Forgotten was Carley, forgotten was Darcy. Her thoughts were like big angry roiling red clouds in her mind.

I am that woman, she thought with a desperation she had never known. *With Dallas, I wanted him so badly, it was almost as if I couldn't control myself. And he stopped me . . . Dallas Bronte, that I've always looked down on, thinking that I was so much better than him, that he was low and common and had no honor. But he's the one who's acted unselfishly, and honorably, and with true charity. And I'm the woman who should be stoned.*

Sensing her distress, Leah put her arm around Julienne and asked softly, "Julienne? What's wrong, dearest, are you ill?"

"No, no, Aunt Leah," she answered, though it was true that she was heartsick. "But would you do something for me?"

"Anything, Julienne."

"There are some things that I need to tell you, and some things that I need to talk to you about, to ask your advice. But mostly I would like it if you would come back to my room and pray with me."

"That would make me happy above all things," Leah said. "No matter what has happened or what is to come, the Lord will save us, will keep us from harm, and will bless us. Always and forever."

DALLAS OPENED HIS EYES and did not know where he was. Then, with the sharp sense of a pilot, he realized he was on his boat, and in the captain's cabin. *Someone must have fixed this up for me*, he thought warmly. Then, with the memories of the day and night before starting to crowd in on him, he reflected irately, *Bet it wasn't Julienne.*

With a groan he sat up on the side of the bed, dropping his head and holding it with his hands.

What a head-pounder! Feels like someone's driving a spike through my head. And it serves me right too. Acting like an ignoramus roughneck! Seems like Julienne might be right about me after all.

Pushing the unwelcome thoughts away, he got up and found that his clothes had been brought up from the crew quarters, washed, ironed, and folded neatly into the little chest. Quickly he washed, shaved, and dressed and hurried down to the main deck.

In the boiler room he found Darcy, wearing new workingman's clothes, a plain gray shirt and rough linsey trousers. Dallas saw he was oiling the valves. Darcy smirked when he saw Dallas's wan face, and he said, "Morning, Bronte. I recommend Libby's pancakes."

Dallas didn't know what kind of insult that might be, but he just grunted, "Morning," and went into the engine room.

Jesse and Ring were standing there talking to a young man. He looked vaguely familiar to Dallas, but finally the liquor cloud cleared a bit and he remembered it all. He was an engineer, Dallas had hired him, and to top it all off he had had to carry Dallas to the boat. And Dallas couldn't remember his name.

The man came forward, his hand stuck out, and automatically Dallas took it, surprised that it was like a rough paw, as big as his own. "Good morning to you, Mr. Bronte," he said. "I've already introduced myself to your crew, and to the Ashbys.

I know you were a mite under the weather last night, so maybe you can't quite get ahold of my name. It's Revelation Brown."

"Yes, yes, sure," Dallas said hastily. "Good morning, Rev. And call me Dallas. I see you've been looking the old girl over?"

He grinned, and he looked about sixteen years old. "Mr. Bronte, this is no old girl. This is the prettiest, spryest, most delightful lady I've ever seen."

"You must be talking about the engine," Dallas said dryly. "We haven't had the money to pretty her up. I kinda hate that too. She deserves better. So you think the engine's in good shape?"

"The best," he answered succinctly. "Ring showed me that little jog in the rods, and I've already fixed it. This engine is as good and solid as I've seen on a floating palace. Whoever put it together bought the best parts money could buy."

Dallas said with a tinge of sadness, "Yeah, it seems like Mr. Ashby loved to have the best. And four boilers, on this little boat! No wonder she's the fastest on the river. And wait 'til you see the pilothouse; it's got every bell and whistle and speaking tube anyone ever thought of. Now all we need is some freight, and I haven't been able to scrounge up a thing to haul."

Rev sucked his lower lip, then said, "You know, I've already prayed for these engines and the boilers and the paddle wheel and all the parts, and for the decks, and for the Ashbys, and for you and the crew. But somehow I forgot to pray for some freight.

Don't you worry, Dallas. I'm going to have this girl full up to the Texas and running down this old river like a thoroughbred!"

CHAPTER FOURTEEN

Dallas couldn't believe it, but he had to believe it. That very afternoon Jacob Fender came down to the *River Queen*.

"I don't have a load myself, Dallas," he said after Dallas's welcoming greeting. "But Lamar Inman is a good friend of mine."

Dallas's smile faded. "Yes, I know Mr. Inman. In fact, I talked to him just yesterday, and he told me he didn't have anything for the *Queen*." Inman & Sons were perhaps the busiest shipping agents in Natchez. Every single day Dallas went into their office to ask about freight, and they always told him there was nothing for the *River Queen*. But Dallas knew very well what they meant: There was nothing for Dallas Bronte.

Fender nodded. "I know, because I'm just coming from Lamar's office, and he told me. But

I recommended you, Dallas, and I told him about the fast clean trip you did for me to New Orleans. Now, he's got a load going to Cairo, all kinds of household supplies and equipment. Everything from tinware to ovens. He's willing to give you the load, if the *River Queen* can carry it. It's not so much the weight as it is the square footage. He can't break up the shipment, so it's either all or none."

"We'll carry it," Dallas said with determination, "if I have to sit on crates of dishes to pilot her." He stuck his hand out, and Fender took it, and they shook hard. "How can I ever thank you, Mr. Fender? We've known each other for several years, and I consider you a friend, but just in a business sort of way. I never would have expected you to vouch for me personally."

Fender pushed his hat back on his head and said steadily, "You know, I used to be a wild man, when I was younger. Paid a heavy price for it, too, and took some beatings that I really didn't deserve. People aren't fair. But now I know the Lord, and He is just and He is fair. So whenever I see an injustice that I can do something about, I do it."

Dallas grinned. "You know what, sir, I really need to introduce you to my new engineer. Because it just so happens that he agrees with you, and he knew you were coming."

"What?" Fender asked with some confusion.

"When you meet Revelation Brown, you'll understand exactly what I mean."

Dallas proudly showed Fender the *River Queen* and introduced him to the crew. When he told Rev about Fender bringing them a haul, he whooped, "Hallelujah! You're an answer to prayer, Mr. Fender!"

"Told you, sir," Dallas said. Fender's normally somber round face was split in a wide grin.

Dallas introduced him to the Ashbys, and their gratefulness seemed to embarrass him deeply, so Dallas brought him away quickly, saying he had to get to Inman & Sons. Fender left, and Dallas hurried to the shipping agent.

They concluded their business and all of the documents quickly, so Dallas wasn't gone long. When he came back, Roseann, Leah, Julienne, and Carley were still up on the hurricane deck. Jesse had found half a dozen very light balsa wood folding chairs with cane seats and backs for coolness. They made wonderful deck chairs. Dallas had bought a small lightweight tent that they rigged up as a pavilion, so the chairs were shaded. Leah had started giving Carley lessons every morning there. Roseann loved to sit up there, sewing or just dozing. Jesse had brought her an empty shipping crate that served as an ottoman, and she seemed to be very comfortable. Julienne had worked all morning but had joined them after dinner.

"We're headed for Cairo day after tomorrow," he announced jubilantly. "And the money's good!"

"Is it pigs?" Carley asked.

"No ma'am, not this time," Dallas said with perhaps more vehemence than necessary. "It's going to be all kinds of stuff for kitchens. And the *River Queen* is going to be full up to the hurricane deck. This haul is so big we're going to even fill up the ballroom." Since they weren't carrying passengers, they had simply boarded up the windows of the ballroom so it would be watertight.

"How long will it take?" Julienne asked eagerly.

Dallas's odd green eyes shadowed. "Well, it's about 750 miles to Cairo. The *Queen* could run straight through in about three days. But I'm sorry to say that we—I can't do that. I'll only work twelve hours without a rest, any more than that and I endanger the boat. So it's going to take us about six days, maybe seven, depending."

"I'm glad," Carley said happily. "I love riding the river. Can I be the second mate again? I promised Julienne I wouldn't bother you the first time we went out, but could I maybe this time ring at least the big bell?"

"You bet," Dallas said, and bent and held his hands out to her.

She flew to him, and he swung her around and around until she gasped, "Oh! I'm so dizzy! It's so much fun!" He set her down.

"Funny how it's not so much fun when you're grown up," Dallas grumbled under his breath with a furtive glance at Julienne. She smiled at him.

After Carley stopped staggering around, she tugged on Dallas's sleeve. "Can you stop working for just a little while, so we can celebrate?"

"What exactly did you have in mind?"

"Digging for crawdads? Please?" Carley answered. "And then maybe Jesse will put us out some throw lines tonight, and maybe I can catch another big ol' catfish!"

"You know, I think I might just take me a little break this afternoon," Dallas said thoughtfully, and Carley's face lit up. "I know a good place right down close to the end of Silver Street where we can probably find enough crawdads to catch a mess of fish. And besides, I saw back up the hill there's a whole field of pretty yellow daffodils blooming. I might even pick a flower and put it behind my ear."

"Would you? Would you pick one for my ear too?" Carley exclaimed.

"I sure will, Miss Carley, ma'am. You'll look a lot prettier than me with a flower behind your ear."

"That's the truth," Julienne said, rising. "I have to see this. And I would love to pick some daffodils to put in our staterooms, they look so nice and cheery. So if I may, Mr. Bronte, I'd like to accompany you."

"Miss Ashby, I would be honored," he said, bowing elaborately. "I'll even let you put the flower behind my ear."

THEY WALKED DOWN SILVER Street in high spirits, with Carley between them, holding their hands. Julienne had threatened to lock her in her room all the way to Cairo if she got excited and ran off.

Silver Street ran down a snaky course from Natchez proper, and it basically turned into the docks and boardwalk. However, it wasn't the only street in Natchez-Under-the-Hill. The little shanty-town was actually eleven blocks long and four blocks deep. At the south end, the farthest away from Silver Street, the buildings lining the shore were warehouses, with dismal shanties behind. As they came to the end of town, Julienne shuddered as she looked back behind the warehouses. She wouldn't venture down one of those cross streets for the world. They were little more than mud paths just wide enough for a wagon, with the warehouses brooding over them, making them shadowed and evil-looking. The thought of Carley blithely skipping down one of those dark alleys made Julienne doubly grateful to Dallas and the crew for watching out for her.

They were nearing the end of the path, and ahead Julienne could see the field of flowers, thousands of them, blooming on the sides of the hilly bluffs. Dallas pointed. "Now just up there, where you see that dogwood tree? There's a whole bunch of crawdad holes there. We'll have a bucketful of them in no time."

They turned off the shore path to the right and started angling for the dogwood tree. On their right was the last warehouse, an ancient crooked barn with the windows and loft door boarded up. As they passed it, they heard a scream.

All three of them stopped, frozen. Then they heard a woman's voice, "Please help me! Please, they've locked me in here! Two men have locked me in here, and they're going to come back and kill me!"

Dallas dropped Carley's hand and ran so fast that Julienne barely saw him move. The double barn doors had a thick plank set on iron brackets to lock them. He started to lift the plank, but it didn't budge, and he saw that someone had driven three nails halfway into it to secure the plank. Behind the door he could hear the woman crying, "Please, please hurry, please hurry."

Furiously he looked around, and in the piles of junk surrounding the barn he saw a hammer head with no handle. Quickly he picked it up, popped out the nails, and heaved the plank. As soon as it cleared the brackets the barn doors burst open. A woman flung herself into Dallas's arms.

"Good heavens!" Julienne said, grabbing Carley's shoulders and pulling her close.

The woman wildly pushed Dallas away, ran back into the darkness of the barn, and came out with a canvas sack. Dallas took her arm and led her over to Julienne and Carley. Even though she was dirty, her face smudged, Julienne could see she was a beautiful young girl, much younger than she had thought. For some reason from the hoarse scream, and the situation alone, she had expected a mature woman. This was a pretty blonde girl with wide terrified blue eyes.

"What in the world is happening?" Julienne asked.

Grimly Dallas replied, "This lady says that two men kidnapped her and locked her in the barn, and she's afraid they'll harm her when they get back."

"I've got to go," the girl said desperately. "I've got to run."

"Wait just a minute, ma'am," Dallas said. "I'm going to help you. I'm sure not going to let any men hurt you. Now, why don't you just come with us—"

At that moment two men came staggering down the alley by the barn. Both of them were clutching gallon whiskey jugs. When they saw the four of them standing there, they came to a sliding stop that would have been funny under other circumstances. With care they set their jugs on the ground, and then they both started running, and the bigger one yelled, "Hey, you! What are you doing? Robbie, you git back in thet barn right now or I'm gonna whip you like a stuck mule!"

Dallas stepped in front of the women and waited, arms crossed.

The two men stopped running a few feet from Dallas. They were sorry-looking sights. One was obviously older, a tall skinny man with an enormous bobbing Adam's apple. The younger one was shorter and though he too was skinny, he had a round pot belly. A scraggly greasy long black beard rested on it. Both of them were wearing clothes so soiled that the only color one could see of them was dirt-brown. Dallas eyed them and saw the bulge at their sides under their long canvas coats. His face grew dark and dangerous.

They hesitated, then with ill grace the older one said, "I'm Milt Meacher, and this here's my brother Zeke. You got our girl there, and we'll be a-taking her back now."

"No, I don't think so," Dallas said calmly. "She doesn't want to go with you."

"Well, that don't matter none, now does it?" Milt sneered. "'Cause she's ours, we own her. Her mama sold her to us, fair and square. Cost us a whole fifty dollars, that girl did, and mean as a snake she turned out to be too. Never woulda paid that much for her if we'd-a knowed it."

"You don't own me, you stupid sniveling son of a skunk!" the girl yelled. She actually started around Dallas, but rolling his eyes he held her back.

"I never heard of any white women slaves," Dallas said slowly. "I don't know where you're from, but that bird's not gonna fly down here."

With an air of superiority Milt said, "I didn't say she was no slave. She's our denture servant. All fair and legal, denture to us for seven year."

"That's 'indentured' servant, you moron," Dallas said. Then frowning, he looked down at the girl. "I guess that indentured servants are still legal, ma'am, but if these men are any threat to you, then me and them are gonna have a problem with it, legal or not."

"It's not legal," she cried. "I'm eighteen years old, my mama couldn't sell me legally! And besides, I told you they're going to kill me!"

"Eighteen year old? Kill you? You're gonna get struck down for lying, girl!" This time it was the younger brother Zeke that spoke, and, swaggering forward a half-step, he shoved one side of his coat back so it hung behind the holster on his hip.

Julienne murmured, "Oh, Lord, no," and clutched Carley even closer.

The whites of Milt's eyes flashed when he saw how his brother was showing out, but he only swallowed, his Adam's apple bobbing rhythmically. Zeke continued, "That there girl is sixteen year old, just look at her, you kin tell she's just a girl. Kill her? Why, that would be stupid, for me and Milt to kill her. We told you we done paid fifty dollar for her. Kill her and lose that money for nothing? That'd be stupid!" he repeated.

As he spoke Dallas's face had darkened until he looked as if he might simply swat the man down like a worrisome gnat. But by the time Zeke finished, he couldn't help a sort of desperate amusement from coming over him. When he spoke, though, it was still in such a quiet, dangerous tone that Milt took a half-step backward and ducked his head. Zeke held his ground, resting his hand on the butt of his holster.

Dallas said, "Now, listen, uh, what's your name? Meat? Listen, Meat. This girl isn't going anywhere with you. In about ten seconds you're going to see her for the last time."

Zeke seemed to swell up; at least, his gut inflated out rounder than ever. "Are you threatenin' me, mister? Are you blind *and* dumb? Cain't you see I got a gun here?"

"Funny. So do I," Dallas said, and pulled his coat back. A pistol was stuck in his trousers, at his side.

"Now wait just a minute here, Mister," Milt said in a much weaker voice, and holding up his hands in surrender. "Ain't no call for us to go wavin' around no guns."

"You shut up, Milt, you ain't never had no sand," Zeke snarled. "Whatcha gonna do, Big Man? Gun me down dead right here in front of your pretty wife and daughter?"

"No, I wouldn't do that. But if your fingers so much as twitch on that gun, I'm going to shoot your toe off," Dallas said in a death-knell voice.

The brothers were a little slow on the uptake, so it took some time for them to work through what Dallas had said. Then Zeke looked back at Milt, and Milt looked at him, and they started laughing. "Didja hear that? Scairt me bad, it did," Zeke said in a jolly voice. Then he turned and said, "You're not just blind and dumb, you're crazy. I'm through messin' around with you, I want you to git outta my way, and—"

He clasped the butt of his gun, and Dallas shot his foot.

It happened just like that, as if the man had suddenly been struck by a bolt of lightning. Dallas stood there holding the smoking gun, Julienne and Carley stopped breathing, and the girl's red full mouth made a round O. Milt's eyes were so big and round they looked like they might pop out of his head and his Adam's apple hopped up and down crazily.

Zeke's mouth fell open, he looked down at his foot, and then he sat down heavily. Reaching down, he grabbed his foot and pulled it up onto his lap. He howled, "OOOOOWWWW! You shot my toe off! Clean off! My big toe!"

"Tried to tell you," Dallas said regretfully. Unhurried, he went to Zeke and bent down, and Zeke flinched. But Dallas simply gently removed the gun from his holster and turned to Milt. His hands shaking, carefully with two fingers he took out his gun and handed it to Dallas. "I'm going to throw these in the river right down there," he said. "You can swim for them." He tucked them into the waistband of his trousers.

"You shot my toe off! OOOOOWWWW!" Zeke bawled, and then started a low monotonous moan.

Dallas turned back to them, took the girl's arm, grabbed Carley's hand, and said gently, "Carley, take Julienne's hand."

Carley reached up and took Julienne's hand, and all together they walked off. The girl kept looking behind her with hatred, but after a few moments she said, "Thank you, mister."

"You're welcome. My name is Dallas Bronte. You can call me Dallas. This is Miss Carley, and this is Miss Ashby."

"I'm Robbie. Robbie Skinner," the girl said, as if she were in a dream. "Thank you, Dallas."

"You're welcome," he said again. When they got to the river, he stopped and tossed the two guns far out into the water.

They reached the boardwalk and climbed the steps. Silently they made their way along, and all of the human traffic of the port started passing them, slave women carrying goods on their heads, male slaves bent over with big boxes strapped to their backs, river men shoving and cursing, children running in and around the adults, catcalling to each other, prostitutes sashaying along in a cloud of scent of old sweat and rose water.

Suddenly Julienne stopped short, let go of Carley's hand and threw her own hands up, palms out. "Stop! What are you doing? Where are we going?"

"Back to the *Queen*, Julienne," Dallas answered, surprised.

Julienne stared at Robbie. "We can't take her back to the *Queen*!"

Dallas's mouth tightened. "She can stay on the *Queen* until we get this all sorted out."

"Sorted out? How? Why? She's not our responsibility! Even though you did shoot a man over her!" Julienne snapped.

"He only shot his toe," Carley said in a small voice.

Robbie stepped forward, between Julienne and Dallas. "Ma'am, Miss, I'm so sorry but I forgot your name. If you could just help me out a little, please, Miss. I don't have a nickel, I had a little bit of money but they took it from me. But I can work. I can cook, and clean, and sew, and I'm strong. I work hard, I'll do anything, you don't have to pay me. If I could just have somewhere to sleep, and something to eat, I'll work harder than two women."

"You? You lied. You said that those men were going to kill you," Julienne said between gritted teeth. "We thought your life was in danger."

Robbie's eyes dropped to Carley's interested face, and she murmured, "And would you have been so eager to help me if I had screamed that some men were going to try to kiss me? I could see you all, through the cracks. I could see her," she said, nodding downward.

When the meaning of her words sunk in, Julienne hesitated but then she turned back to Dallas and continued her conversation with him. "We can't do this, Dallas. We can't take this girl in, it's impossible!"

"Why?" Dallas asked simply.

"Because—because—" Julienne stuttered.

"So what do you think I'm going to do with her? Drop her off at the Blue Moon?" he said evenly.

Her mouth shut, and then she sighed. "All right. But just until we can find her a suitable situation."

"Fine," he said, shrugging. "Don't worry too much, Julienne. She's kinda little, I doubt she eats much. She can always have oxtail soup."

Julienne shot him a deadly glance and they fell in step together, unconsciously, walking along and talking about the details of what they could do with Robbie.

She fell into step behind them, and Carley took her hand. Looking up at her, she said, "I like your name, Robbie."

"It's really Roberta, but no one ever calls me that," she said, but she looked worried.

Shrewdly Carley said, "Don't pay any attention to my sister. She usually ends up doing what Dallas says. She just always has to argue with him first."

"He sure is handsome," Robbie said appreciatively. "Is he your sister's man?"

"Dallas? Oh, no. I'm going to marry Dallas," she said confidently. "Besides, Julienne doesn't like him. Well—I don't know. Sometimes I think she does, and then sometimes it seems like she doesn't. But he helps us, see. On the *Queen*, he's our pilot."

"Oh," said Robbie with interest. "So your family has a riverboat, and that's where we're going?"

"Yes, the *River Queen*. That's where we live now. And you're coming to live with us. Your room is gonna be really dirty," she said, her face wrinkling with distaste, "and you're going to have to clean it, because my Aunt Leah says that cleanliness is next to godliness, so we all have to scrub a lot, except my mother, because she's a lady." A worried look came over her pixie face, and she asked, "Robbie? Is that true, what that man Meat said? That your mother sold you to them?"

"I'm awful sorry you had to hear that, Carley," Robbie said in a low voice. "But you just don't worry about it. You and your sister and Dallas came along, and you're helping me, and I'm going to help you, I promise."

Carley nodded. "I'll pray and thank Jesus that we found you, and that Dallas shot Meat in the toe, instead of having to shoot him down dead."

Though Robbie said nothing, privately she wished that Dallas had shot him down dead.

They got back to the boat, and Dallas gathered the family at the old dining table, and the explanations began. Robbie stood the entire time as if she were a prisoner in the dock, her sky-blue eyes darting to each of them.

It stunned Julienne that neither her mother nor her aunt seemed to be as utterly horrified as she had thought they would be. They were shocked and seemed upset for Robbie's plight. When Dallas finished the story, her aunt took over and said, "Robbie, you've had a terrible time, I'm sure. Come along with me, and I'll take you to one of our staterooms. I'm afraid you'll find it in sad shape, and all we can offer you right now is a cot mattress, but my feeling is that you should rest awhile, and then we can talk about how you can help us out here on the *River Queen*."

"Oh, but, no, ma'am! I want to work, I feel fine, I can work right now!" She sounded panicked.

Leah studied her for a few moments, then took her arm, threaded it through her own, and patted it. "Listen to me, Robbie. You're safe now. No one is going to do you any harm here, nothing bad is going to happen to you from now on. So stop worrying, and just get some rest. Come along," she said firmly. Obediently Robbie followed her through the double doors to the stateroom hallway.

Roseann said, "That poor child. She looks scared to death. She'll be all right in a few days, I'm sure. Dallas, would you be so kind as to ask if someone could set up my chair and the pavilion? I'd love to sit up on the hurricane for a while."

"Can I come with you, Mother?" Carley asked. "I'll be quiet and let you rest, I promise. I'll look at my geography book." She pronounced it, "jog-gerphy," and she loved to study it, to everyone's surprise.

"Of course, dear," she said. "I'd love to have the company."

"I'll set up the chairs and tent for you, Mrs. Ashby," Dallas offered, and she and Carley followed him out to the stairwell.

Julienne and Darcy looked blankly at each other. Julienne said, "I can't believe it. Has this noxious air driven us all insane, or something? How did we just la-di-dah adopt a girl, for heaven's sake?"

Darcy grinned, his old devilish grin that had been so subdued after his and Dallas's "talk." "She's a real looker, and I do mean a prize. No wonder Dallas wanted to bring her home."

Julienne stiffened. "That's ridiculous, Darcy. He couldn't see her when she was having that screaming fit in the barn and he galloped to her rescue."

Darcy looked puzzled. "What's the matter with you, Jules? I mean, I guess I was kinda making a joke, but it doesn't seem like saying she was 'having that screaming fit' sounds very kind. She was in a real bad situation, and I don't blame her for screaming."

"I didn't say that," Julienne said impatiently. "You misunderstood me. I just—I just—don't know how we're going to support another mouth to feed, that's all."

Darcy grinned again. "She can always have oxtail soup."

"Nobody is *ever* going to let me forget that, are they?" Julienne groaned. "But I do not think this situation is funny at all. Mother's just fine kiss-me-hand with a strange woman moving in with us, Carley's already her best friend, Aunt Leah has adopted her, you think she's pretty, and all Dallas can think about is taking care of the poor little helpless gorgeous girl! I'm tired of this whole mess already!"

"Tired of it? Funny, you don't sound tired of it. That's not what you sound like at all."

"Oh? What do I sound like, Baby Brother?" Julienne said sarcastically. Darcy hated it when she called him that.

He stretched, and then said lazily. "You sound jealous, Jules. Especially of Dallas Bronte. That's it. You're jealous."

"I most certainly am not! Oh, I'm going back to work," she said indignantly, and marched back to her stateroom. *Jealous, how ridiculous!*

But a tiny voice somewhere in her busy mind asked—*Is it?*

ALL OF THE ASHBYS' belongings, including all the clothes that they didn't have in the tiny chests in their staterooms, were stored in trunks on the main cargo deck. Because the haul to Cairo was not only going to take up every inch of the main deck, and also the ballroom on the Texas deck, Dallas decided to move the Ashbys' belongings into one of the empty staterooms and told Caesar and Libby that they had better sprinkle the boric acid salts all around the baseboards of the room they were going to use for storage. It was a very effective insect repellent.

They got the trunks and boxes organized, and Dallas strapped the biggest trunk, which was Julienne's, to a small, wheeled cart and pulled it up the steps. To his surprise, when he reached the stateroom, he saw that it was spotlessly cleaned, even the ceiling. Two heavy layers of canvas had been neatly tacked over the window. Robbie Skinner was down on her knees, rubbing a white paste onto the floor along the baseboards. She looked up and said, "Boric acid works a lot better if you make a paste and mix in some pepper."

"Really? Didn't know that," Dallas said, dragging the trunk into the corner and unloading it. Resting his hands on his hips, he watched her for a moment as she laboriously rubbed the paste into the wood. Her hands were fiery red, and he knew it must be from the pepper, for boric acid was not abrasive. Ruefully he said, "You know, the Ashbys are real nice people, for the most part. They wouldn't expect you to start in doing hard work today."

"I know," she said without looking up. "And I did try to rest for about an hour. But I need to work. I'd feel bad if I didn't."

"Okay," he said, shrugging. Then he turned at the door and said, "I admire you for that, Miss Skinner. Shows your true colors."

She didn't answer.

They worked to get all of the trunks strapped up and hauled up, and then they started carrying boxes. Robbie came in without a word and started carrying the smaller boxes. The crew was kind to her and let her carry the boxes without comment. Dallas noticed that even Rev was subdued with her, merely smiling at her and not starting in asking her about the state of her soul.

When they finished, all of the crew started working in the firebox and the engine room. Dallas wanted the *Queen* to be in absolutely perfect working order for their run to Cairo.

They had a fine dinner of cornbread and beef stew with big juicy chunks of meat, brimming with carrots and potatoes. For dessert they had a peach pie, hot from the oven. Caesar and Libby served; they had never joined the Ashbys and the crew at meals, saying it just wasn't right. There was no sign of Robbie Skinner.

Finishing up his pie, Darcy pushed his plate back and said, "Libby, you outdid yourself tonight. Your cooking's always good, but that stew and especially that pie were top notch."

She made a face at him. "Thank you so much, Mr. Ashby, since you just picked out the two things I didn't cook. That little Robbie made the stew and the pie. I only made the cornbread, of which I noticed you didn't compliment. And now she's in the galley, scrubbing it like it was a king's kitchen."

The crew went back to work, and finally at about ten o'clock, Dallas said, "Let's call it a night, boys. I've always been proud of the *River Queen*, but right now she's shining like gold. We're as ready as we're ever going to be."

He went out on the main deck and back toward the stern. He had splurged and bought himself a cigar, an imported cigar from Hispaniola that cost a whole dollar. Dallas hadn't bought himself one thing since he'd been on the *Queen*, and with only a slight twinge he had ducked into the liquor and tobacco shop that was next to Inman & Sons freight office.

Was that just this morning? he mused. *Blatherskite, it's been a long day!* He grinned at his mental grab of Carley's word.

Robbie Skinner came up to stand beside him, and he jumped a little. "I don't care if you smoke that," she said in a low voice. "Believe me, I've seen a whole lot worse than a lit cigar."

Dallas hadn't lit it yet, and he tucked it back into his shirt pocket. "I guess you have. But it's a matter of respect for ladies, you see."

She turned to look up at him. It was a moon-less night, but the stars shone as bright as diamonds, and he could clearly see her face. She was a very beautiful woman, with a heart-shaped face, a full mouth that made a man want to kiss her, perfect almond-shaped blue eyes with long dark lashes. Her hair was waist-length, a glowing yellow-gold, thick and curly. When they found her, it had been all down and tousled, but that day she had pulled it back into a tight demure bun. She wasn't tall, only a few inches over five feet, and she had an hourglass figure that most women would kill for. Dallas was so bewitched that he almost missed her next words.

"That's what I can't believe," Robbie was saying. "That you think I'm a lady."

"As far as I'm concerned, all women are ladies, until they prove otherwise to me," he said lightly. "So far you seem like an honest, hardworking, sweet lady."

She laughed, a delightful trilling sound. "The Meacher brothers sure didn't think I was sweet. You heard what Milt said, that I'm as mean as a snake."

"I don't put much stock into what Meat and Meat Junior said," Dallas said dryly, leaning over to rest his elbows on the rail. "They didn't have enough sense between them to fill a frog's brain."

"No, they didn't," she said vehemently. "And I wish you had let Zeke draw that gun, so you could have shot him dead. If I could've gotten my hands on a gun, or even a knife, they both would be worm food."

"Can't say I blame you, Miss Skinner," he said gently, "but it just didn't play out that way."

She nodded, a short angry bob. "I know. And don't think I'm not grateful, Dallas, I am. And I want to explain all this to you."

"You don't have to do that."

"But I want to." Her face twisted and she said, "I saw the way you were looking at me just now. I know you can't help it. Men have been looking at me like that since I was thirteen years old. And my mama made sure I stayed like this, pretty and with soft hands and skin, so men would keep on looking at me like that."

She turned, gripped the railing, and stared out over the river. "You see, even when I was born, my mama knew I was going to be pretty. I don't look like her, I don't look like my daddy, and I don't look like a single one of my eight older brothers and sisters. My mama pampered me, never made me work, made me stay in school when my brothers and sisters had to work. We had a farm, just out-side of Vicksburg, see. But I never had to do one pinky finger's worth of work. Mama taught me to cook and clean and sew, because she said I'd need to know how to do all that, even though one day we'd all have our own slaves to do such things for us.

"Anyway, from the time I was little, my mama made me bathe every day, wash my hair every other day, she taught me how to use a curling iron, she made me pretty clothes that we couldn't afford. And then, when I turned twelve and started filling out, and my daddy saw for sure that I wasn't his, he just picked up and left."

She hesitated, so Dallas said, "I think I've got an idea of what's happened, but I think you need to talk, ma'am. So you just go right ahead and talk it out."

Without looking at him, she murmured, "Please stop ma'am-ing me. And call me Robbie, please, Dallas."

"Okay, Robbie."

She took a deep breath and continued, "I guess there's no need to tell you what my mama was all about. She explained to me when I turned fourteen that some rich man was going to want to take care of me, and I would take care of him, and he would give us all kinds of money. She paraded me all over Vicksburg, took me to every town meeting, took me to the playhouse when she had the money for tickets, walked me up and down the main street, where the shops were, even when we didn't have any money to buy anything. Pretty soon all kinds of men were talking to me, following us around, but mama wouldn't have any of them. She said they weren't rich enough."

Dallas looked confused, and she gave a brittle laugh and looked over to him, her expression twisted with disgust. "I know, you're thinking of the Meachers. See, my mama fiddled around and fiddled around; she really thought that some rich planter was going to take me as his mistress, she called it, but I call it a whore. Anyway, Mama started drinking, and she got to where she didn't haul me all over town any more, trying to auction me off. She just woke up at noon, started drinking rotgut whiskey, and drank until she passed out. I started working on the farm, which we were about to lose."

She shrugged and finished, "And then one day a couple of weeks ago, we went to town. I had to get some supplies, and because I wouldn't buy Mama any whiskey she came with me to go buy it herself. She was half-drunk already, and she went into a saloon. When she came out, the Meachers were with her. And I found out she had sold me for fifty dollars."

He stared at her. Her voice was hard and bitter. He had thought anyone would weep at such a betrayal, but Robbie only seemed angry.

"I pretended to drink with them," she said, "so they'd pass out and leave me alone at night. During the day I'd fight them, hard, and then I'd tell them that I needed to have a drink to—to—"

It was the first time she had faltered, and Dallas quickly said, "I understand, Robbie. I know what you're saying, that you're still a pure woman. You don't have to tell me all the filthy details about those two, and in fact, you didn't even have to explain to me at all. I figured you hadn't been raped, and I knew you hadn't had a man."

"How did you know?" she asked, mystified.

"You can tell, most of the time," he said quietly. "A man can be fooled, but if he's sharp enough, and pays attention, he can see innocence."

Now her big eyes filled with tears, and she moved close to him and clasped him around the waist. He turned and hugged her comfortingly. She whispered, "Thank you, Dallas. Thank you for everything. You've given me a real life, all with one bullet, in one day!" She looked up at him, now smiling through her tears, and he searched her face.

She reached up, put one tiny hand behind his neck, and pulled him down to kiss her. And he did, gladly. He didn't think about the right or wrong of it; he didn't think about her vulnerability, or the fact that he might be taking advantage of her. He just wanted to kiss her. But he let her control the situation, and after a long lingering sweet kiss, she pulled back and then whispered in his ear, "I've never even been kissed, Dallas. I never wanted anybody to. But I wanted to kiss you. Thank you again, from my heart."

Standing above them on the Texas deck, Julienne Ashby's face turned ashen as she watched them kiss. She hadn't heard anything they'd said. She had just that moment come out to see if Dallas was on deck. And she hadn't heard Robbie's whisper of pure gratitude.

Silently she turned, went into her stateroom, taking care to close the door quietly, and flung herself onto her bed. Staring up at the ceiling, she muttered through gritted teeth, "That good-for-nothing river rat! Maybe he's no worse than any other man, but he sure isn't any better! I'll never, *never* trust him again!"

CHAPTER FIFTEEN

Julienne had an awful night. She could not make herself fall asleep. She was hot, the room seemed horribly stuffy, and she developed an acute headache right behind her eyes. She tossed and turned and tried three times to light the lamp and read. But she couldn't concentrate, and, besides that, it made her head hurt more. Finally at about dawn she slipped into an uneasy doze.

A timid knock on her door woke her up. Groggily she said, "Yes? Carley?"

"No, ma'am," she heard a soft reply. The door opened, and Robbie Skinner brought in a tray. It held a tin teapot, a mug, sugar, cream, and three slices of dry toast. For a moment Julienne's throat constricted. It was exactly the breakfast that Tyla had always brought her when she didn't feel well. But how did this girl know that?

Before Julienne could speak, Robbie said, "Miss Libby told me that she thought she heard you in the night and said to let you sleep late. She said she thought you might like tea and plain toast." Remembering the previous night, Julienne thought, *Then why didn't Libby bring it to me?*

It wasn't the sort of tray that set on a bed, so Robbie carefully placed it on the small chest. Then she turned, folded her hands in front of her, and said, "I know you really don't want me here, Miss Ashby. But I promise you that I'll work hard and earn my keep."

Julienne nodded rather curtly. "Thank you, Robbie."

"You're welcome, ma'am. Do you need anything else?"

"No, that will be all," was Julienne's automatic response. Despite the fact that she hadn't said it for over a month, she had indeed said those same words to Tyla and other servants thousands of times.

Robbie left the room, and Julienne slowly got up and fixed her tea. It was hot and strong, just like Julienne liked it. Chewing thoughtfully on her toast, she thought, *Earn your keep? Yes, I'm going to watch and see just exactly how you earn your keep, Miss Skinner. I'll see just exactly how much rescuing you need from Dallas Bronte.*

It was a busy day, for Leah, Julienne, Libby, and Caesar had to go to town to purchase enough supplies for a trip that could last anywhere from ten days to two weeks. When they returned, Robbie had already done all of the washing and had the clothes in baskets ready to be ironed. She had then set about scrubbing the ballroom. They had cleaned the corner where their dining table was, after a fashion, but no one had ever had the time to try and clean the rest of the big room, and there was mold and mildew all around the baseboards and windows, and the floor was black with it. She worked on it all day, and then put boric acid paste all around the room. She was still working when Julienne went to bed, exhausted. She had not seen Dallas all day.

Early in the morning they started loading their freight. Dallas came up while Julienne was still brooding over her breakfast, sitting alone in the galley on a stool at the worktable. They had to take the dining table out of the ballroom because the freight was going to take up the entire Texas deck, except for the staterooms.

"I've got good news," he told her, "I think. Inman & Sons has a return load for us, textiles out of Cairo. But we can only grab it if we can get there in six days."

Julienne's brow wrinkled. "Is that a problem? I thought you said you could make it in six days."

"I said in about six days." He shook his head. "Wish I had even a cub pilot, there's three or four long straight stretches that a cub could handle, easy. Anyway, I think I've got our wood stops and my rest times down so that we should be able to make it in a little less than six days. *If* nothing goes wrong with the *Queen*, or the crew."

"Why should anything go wrong with the crew?" she asked. Her tone was abrupt because she was still extremely angry with Dallas for kissing Robbie Skinner.

He knew nothing of this and looked at her curiously, but he answered her patiently. "Julienne, I can't even call what we've got a skeleton crew. When this boat is moving, the crew is working, and it doesn't matter if it's for two hours or for twenty-six hours. It's hard, dangerous work. Men can get hurt, or they can just break down and get sick. And the *River Queen* is a good, solid boat, but engine breakdowns happen all the time, and that means stopping the boat to fix the problem."

Impatiently she said, "So are you saying that we can't do this? So what are we even doing on this stupid river then?"

"I didn't say that we couldn't do it," he answered, now in a sharp tone. "I'm just trying to explain to you, in case everything doesn't go perfectly."

"Fine, you've explained, thank you," she said with ill humor.

"Fine," he said, turned on his heel, and stalked out of the galley.

"Fine!" she said loudly to his back. He didn't reply.

JULIENNE DIDN'T SEE DALLAS for six days. When they stopped and she knew he would come to the galley to eat, she made sure she was in her stateroom or out on the deck sitting in her rocking chair. Dallas wouldn't allow them to sit out on their deck chairs on the hurricane deck, stressing that it was far too dangerous. Often Leah, Roseann, Julienne, and Carley stayed most of the day in Roseann's stateroom. Carley did her lessons, Roseann and Leah sewed, and mostly Julienne read.

The reason they had so much leisure time was because of Robbie Skinner. She had taken it upon herself to be their personal maid, even for Carley. She brought them all trays for breakfast, she made up their beds and cleaned their rooms, she helped Leah and Roseann to dress, and after a couple of days Julienne found herself letting Robbie help her too. Every morning Carley was fresh-scrubbed, her hair shining in two perfect pigtails, her dresses and petticoats clean and ironed. Even the ruffles on her pantalettes were starched and crisp.

Julienne, though she was avoiding Dallas, watched Robbie relentlessly. The thought once entered her mind that she was literally spying on the girl, but she was so consumed with trying to figure out if Robbie was falling in love with Dallas Bronte that she didn't care.

To her surprise, she never saw Robbie with Dallas. At least, she didn't go into the galley during the few minutes that Dallas was eating a hurried meal before taking a nap. Begrudgingly Julienne had to acknowledge to herself that she knew that Robbie wouldn't go into Dallas's stateroom when he was sleeping. That would be entirely too blatant.

But to her surprise, she did see Robbie with Rev Brown. The crew crowded into the galley on Dallas's breaks, and Robbie would serve them. She rarely smiled, and her behavior was modest and quiet. But often Rev would stay after the meal, when the others had gone down to their quarters to rest. Julienne passed by the galley several times, and Rev would be helping Robbie clean the galley. They talked in low voices, and once she saw Robbie smiling up at him.

They made it to Cairo in less than six days, pulling into their berth at the port on the early morning of Wednesday, June 27. Leah, Carley, Roseann, and Julienne gathered on the deck to see the port. They had never been to Cairo, Illinois.

The deafening steam whistle blew twice, and Carley looked up at the pilothouse, beaming. Then her eyes widened and she pointed. "Look! Look, Mama! Dallas is letting Darcy bring her in!"

Julienne looked up with shock to see Dallas standing by the port windows, waving and grinning at Carley. Darcy was behind the wheel. She turned back to her mother and Aunt Leah, but they didn't seem surprised at all. They waved and smiled. "What is going on here?" Julienne demanded. "Since when is Darcy a riverboat pilot?"

"Of course he's not a pilot, dear," Roseann answered complacently. "But he's been in the wheelhouse with Dallas this entire trip, and Dallas has been teaching him the river. Darcy seems to enjoy it."

"Good heavens," Julienne said faintly.

"It's no wonder you're so surprised, Julienne," Aunt Leah said sweetly. "You've been in such a fog this whole trip."

"You've been really, really grumpy," Carley asserted.

"I have?" Julienne responded. She knew she had been "grumpy" with Dallas, but she had been completely unaware that anyone had noticed.

"Yes, you have, dear," Roseann added. "I hope you'll get over this depressing humor soon, it's so bad for the system."

"I hope I get over it soon too," Julienne muttered.

As soon as they got docked and the engines wound down, Darcy and Dallas came out of the wheelhouse. Julienne still didn't want to talk to Dallas, so she hurried back to the doors to go back to her stateroom. But she heard them arguing, with Darcy saying, "Ring and I can handle this unloading, Dallas, go ahead and go see about that return load we've got."

"You know, you've done good, Ashby," she heard Dallas say. "I'm real proud of you."

For some reason this irritated Julienne beyond measure, and she fled into her room.

They loaded up their textiles that same day, and left the next morning. Julienne, as before, kept to herself, avoiding Dallas Bronte assiduously. In the six-day return trip she became certain that Robbie Skinner had no designs on Dallas Bronte. She also admitted to herself that Robbie was the perfect servant, quiet, efficient, quick, and smart. The fact that she was so much prettier than Julienne was hard for her to take graciously. Robbie took great pains to minimize her looks, continuously fighting her long blonde hair, pinning it back severely into a tight bun. She wore men's shirts that were much too big for her, so her figure wouldn't be outlined. When the crew, including Darcy, were around, she kept her eyes modestly downcast, rarely speaking. None of that mattered, however, for she was quite simply the prettiest woman Julienne had ever seen, and she struggled to keep from resenting Robbie because of it. However, she did still resent her for kissing Dallas.

By the time they got back to Natchez, Julienne was emotionally drained. She had been angry, resentful, remorseful, jealous, spiteful, and finally she grew exhausted, battling with herself. They came into Natchez just at sunset. It was a gorgeous time of day, with a great red sun very slowly inching down to the land. It tinted the landscape with crimson beams of light, making the dirty old port look almost inviting. Julienne was so weary that she hadn't even come out on deck as they came in. She sat in her stateroom, staring out the window.

Then Carley, who rarely knocked, came bursting in. "Julienne, you've got to come see! The *Columbia Lady*'s in, and she's docked here! And she's lit up like the stars, and she's the grandest thing I've ever seen!" They had seen the magnificent boat coming and going on the river from her home port of New Orleans, but she hadn't stopped at Natchez-Under-the-Hill in the last couple of months.

Without much enthusiasm, Julienne took Carley's hand and let her lead her out on deck. The *River Queen* was just beginning to pass the *Columbia Lady*. Julienne, Roseann, Leah, and even Caesar, Libby, and Robbie had come out on deck for their homecoming. With wide eyes they all stared up at the mighty *Columbia*'s golden decks. Music wafted from the grand ballroom, and with a jolt Julienne recognized the waltz, the same waltz that had played when Dallas Bronte had walked into her life and swept her away in that very ballroom. That had been a world away, a lifetime ago, it seemed to her. The fact that that carefree night had been the last one she would ever have, pressed down hard on Julienne's heart. Here she was, crawling by that gorgeous, elegant, lavish steamer on the shabby little *River Queen*. She didn't want to see the *Columbia Lady* any more, and she didn't want to hear that haunting waltz. Bitterly she turned and went back to her stateroom, which she now viewed with a hostile gaze. Her room looked, to Julienne, like a miserable hovel.

SHE DIDN'T COME OUT of her room for the rest of the day and evening. After the *Queen* was unloaded and Dallas had concluded all the business with Inman & Sons, he had knocked on her door and called, "Julienne? Are you okay?"

Naturally, in the mood she was in, it annoyed her that he had the nerve to knock on her door. He had done it many times before, in fact, but suddenly Julienne decided that it really wasn't proper. Yanking the door open, she replied shortly, "I'm fine, thank you."

He searched her face for long moments, and she dropped her gaze. Quietly he asked, "What's wrong, Julienne? Either you're ill, or something's really bothering you. Can't you tell me?"

"No, I can't," she retorted. "I just really want to be left alone."

Slowly he said, "Oh. Okay. But I just thought you'd want to go over the money. We made enough this time that I thought you might want to open a small bank account, get started on establishing credit."

"I really don't want to deal with that right now," Julienne said dully. "Maybe tomorrow. Or better yet, why don't you go talk to Aunt Leah. She can handle these things as well, or better, than I can." Even though he was starting to reply, Julienne shut the door and threw herself back on her bed.

The next morning Robbie brought her tea and a full breakfast, a perfectly-boiled egg, bacon, jacket potatoes, buttered toast, and peach preserves. She laid the tray on the chest and turned to Julienne, showing no sign of surprise that Julienne had slept in her clothes. "We're heating up water, Miss Ashby. You can have a nice hot bath after breakfast."

"That sounds wonderful," Julienne said wearily. "I'm sure that will make me feel much better."

Robbie nodded and said, "Miss Ashby, Caesar knows you haven't been feeling well, and so he wondered if you want the morning mail, or if he should take it to Mrs. Norris."

"No, please have him bring it to me," Julienne said. "I'll go over it while I'm having this nice breakfast. Thank you, Robbie."

She curtseyed, to Julienne's mild amusement. Carley had taught her how to curtsey, and now she did it at exactly the right times that the best-trained British maids did.

Caesar brought the mail, and immediately Julienne was struck by a handsome thick envelope of rich parchment, addressed to the Ashby Family, c/o the *River Queen*. On the back was printed in gold letters: *Lyle Dennison, Natchez, Mississippi*. She remembered Lyle Dennison, who had bought the *Columbia Lady* from Elijah Moak. When she had seen the steamer the previous night, she had remembered seeing him that night, a tall, muscular, commanding man who seemed to dominate the conversations among the men that night.

Eagerly she tore it open and read:

*Mrs. Ashby, Miss Ashby, Mr. Darcy
Ashby, Miss Carley Ashby, and Mrs
Norris:*

*When I saw the River Queen come
in last night, I realized with regret that
it has never been my honor and privilege to be introduced to you. Considering
that unfortunate circumstance, of course
I realized that I may not simply send you
my card and then call.*

*It is my sincerest hope that you will
consider this missive as my attempt to
introduce myself to you with all the propriety I can muster, and that you will
forgive me for being so forward. In the
hope that I may be received, I enclose my
card, and would be very pleased if I may
call on you tomorrow.*

Until then, I remain,
Your most faithful servant,
Lyle Dennison

The riotous mix of emotions that this polite note
produced in Julienne was almost funny. First she
was elated to receive a note worded in the stiff but
elegant phrases that she had been accustomed to
her entire life, until she had moved onto the *River
Queen*. Then she was horrified when she tried to
picture how—and where—they would receive
Dennison. Down in the engine room? In one of
their miserable staterooms? Following this, she read

the note again and was wildly happy that a prominent man such as Lyle Dennison was calling on them, since none of their "friends" had ever done so, except for Preston Gates, who came by the boat at least once a week. Then, perhaps most disturbing of all, she wondered what she would wear, if Robbie could get one of her nice dresses presentable by tomorrow after being folded up and stored for two months, if they could find her hoop skirts, and particularly her gloves, as Julienne's hands were as worn and rough as a field hands.' Now panicked, she ran up to the hurricane deck, where Roseann, Leah, and Carley were. Dallas was bent over Carley's chair, pointing out stops on a map of the river.

As soon as Julienne caught sight of them she waved the note and said, "Mother! I can't believe this wonderful news! Mr. Lyle Dennison is calling on us! Tomorrow!"

She didn't notice Dallas's face darken, and he slowly stood up straight and crossed his arms.

Roseann said mildly, "That's nice, dear. Now, tell me again, who is Mr. Dennison?"

"He owns the *Columbia Lady*," Dallas answered her darkly, "along with some other things in Natchez-Under-the-Hill."

"He's a very prominent, well-known and well-respected businessman," Julienne said. "And I think it's a very good sign. Maybe we're starting to regain some respectability. But I cannot for the life of me imagine how we're to properly receive him. What are we going to do? Gather around that dismal dining room table?"

"Properly receiving him will be for us to welcome him, make him feel at home, and begin to get to know him," Aunt Leah said firmly. "And the table in the ballroom will be fine for that."

"But that's not the most important question by far," Julienne said with obvious distress.

"Then what is?" Carley asked. She had been following the conversation with great interest.

Impatiently Juliennne replied, "You're going to have to learn, Carley, the most important question of all for a lady: What am I going to wear?"

THAT DIFFICULT PROBLEM WAS smoothly and efficiently taken care of by Robbie. She and all the ladies visited the stateroom where their trunks were stored; they had decided not to drag them back down to the cargo deck, where they were in the crews' way anyway. All of them found the dresses they wanted to wear, the appropriate petticoats and underthings, their jewelry, accessories for their hair. Robbie even knew where their almost-forgotten hoop skirts were, all of them flattened and encased in two bedsheets and hung up on the wall. When Lyle Dennison arrived that afternoon, Roseann, Leah, and Julienne were all dressed in lovely summer muslin at-home dresses, with wide flounced skirts and dainty shawls. Carley was in a green-and-blue striped dress with blue satin ribbons in her pigtails, and she looked as pretty and fresh as the spring flowers.

They had a family meeting with Darcy, who had agreed to meet Dennison at the gangplank and bring him in to introduce him to his family. Julienne was a little surprised that Darcy didn't dress in his best clothes to receive their important visitor; he wore a plain white linen shirt, creased black trousers, and his boots were shined. When Julienne asked him where his coat, tie, and waistcoat were, he replied, "It's too hot for all that folderol, Jules. Besides, I'm going to pay my respects and then go back to work. I don't want to sit in this stuffy ballroom drinking tea."

Since Darcy had gotten interested in piloting, he had seemed to truly have changed. Before, when he worked, he seemed to be merely acting out of guilt, and was also somewhat cowed by Dallas Bronte. But now he was eager and interested in every valve, lever, piston, and bolt on the *River Queen*.

At exactly three o'clock—the fashionable time for what was called "morning calls"—Lyle Dennison appeared on horseback at the *River Queen*'s berth. Dismounting from a prancing black stallion, he came forward immediately to Darcy, his hand extended. They shook hands and spoke for a few moments, while Jesse took Dennison's horse and led him to a hitching post by the boardwalk. Still talking, Darcy and Dennison boarded the boat, and

Julienne and Carley hurried to their seats. They had been watching out the window.

They came into the ballroom, where the ladies were indeed seated around the dining table. He betrayed no sign of surprise or censure at their shabby, and rather odd "parlor," merely bowing deeply as Darcy began the long recitations required by formal introductions.

Julienne studied Dennison avidly, though she kept her expression coolly polite. He was a big man. Right at six feet tall and thickly muscled, his body was bulky, like a bare-knuckle boxer. He had hair so black it seemed to glint blue. His features were rugged, with a prominent nose, an iron jaw, and very sharp dark eyes under thick black brows. His dress was impeccable, a three-piece cream broad-cloth suit with a matching cream silk low-crowned hat. A fine gold watch chain hung suspended from his waistcoat pocket at exactly the right arc. The only other accessory he wore was a large square-cut diamond pinky ring.

When Darcy introduced them, Dennison took her hand and bowed over, looking straight into her eyes with an intense, appreciative gaze from his glinting dark eyes. It nonplussed her for a moment, for she had almost forgotten what it was like to be in this social situation, meeting an attractive new man who so obviously appreciated her good looks. But she quickly recovered and greeted him warmly.

When Darcy introduced him to Carley, she stuck out her hand and he made a very courtly bow over it. "Miss Carley, it is my great honor to meet you. I see that all of the ladies in this family share the same beauty."

"Thank you, Mr. Dennison," she said politely, but then she squirmed a little and said, "Julienne said you own the *Columbia Lady*. Could I come see it sometime, please?"

Roseann whispered, "No, dear."

But with a good will Dennison smiled at her, then included everyone else as he said, "Miss Carley must be a mind reader. I had hoped that you would all join me on the *Lady* for dinner, perhaps on Friday night? Would that fit into your social calendar, Miss Carley?"

Carley giggled and answered, "I don't have a social calendar yet, Mr. Dennison. I only just turned eleven."

"It won't be long before you'll need one," he said with assurance. "As pretty as you are, I'm sure it will be a full one, too."

"That's good of you, Dennison," Darcy said, "but of course my sister didn't intend to wrangle an invitation from you." In spite of his words, his eagerness to visit the *Columbia Lady* was evident. Even though he had been at the Moak's party, all he had seen that night was the grand ballroom and the card room. Now he wanted to see the firebox and the engine room and especially the wheelhouse.

"No, no, I assure you, I intended to extend this invitation for dinner on Friday night," Dennison assured him. "Of course I realize that it is short notice, and also on short acquaintance. But I hope you'll indulge me and accept the invitation."

"We will need to speak with our pilot, Mr. Bronte, to find out if the *River Queen* will be here or not," Roseann said. "But if we are in town, we would love to dine with you on your lovely boat, Mr. Dennison."

"Very good," he said warmly, glancing at Julienne, who smiled warmly at him.

Roseann urged him to sit down and asked if he would prefer tea or fresh lemonade. He chose lemonade, and so did Darcy, who sat down with him. Immediately he began asking questions about the *Columbia Lady.* He asked about her boilers, about her engine, her running times, her freight capacity, and on and on. Julienne had been a little surprised that Darcy had stayed, after his assertion that he didn't want to sit around with them for a social call. But then, when she realized that he was talking about his new favorite topic—piloting steamboats—she understood.

None of the ladies were perturbed that Darcy monopolized their guest. Even Carley understood that when men were present, their conversation always took precedence, and under no circumstances were they to be interrupted. She and the ladies sipped lemonade and observed Lyle Dennison and listened.

After awhile, Lyle asked Darcy to give him a tour of the *River Queen.* Her mother and aunt looked pleased, and Carley begged to come, promising to be quiet. The three of them left, with Julienne cringing inside. Now looking at the *River Queen* through Lyle Dennison's dark penetrating eyes, she was so embarrassed she could have happily sunk through the floor.

"What an interesting gentleman," Roseann said happily. "Although I have gotten over our lack of social life—mostly—I am looking forward to dining out again. And, Julienne, he's so handsome! Well, not handsome. Striking, perhaps I should say."

"Yes, he does make an impression," Julienne agreed.

As if she were talking to herself, Aunt Leah murmured, "He has a certain air about him—no, that's not right. Something about him, his presence. He's not crude, not at all, but I sense a certain aggressiveness in him, a sort of dangerous edge."

"I don't understand, Leah," Roseann said plaintively. "He has such elegant manners, and he's so kind to Carley. I can't believe he could be *dangerous*."

Julienne thought, *I can*. Without realizing it, her lips turned upward in a small private smile.

CHAPTER SIXTEEN

Two weeks later, on a sweltering July afternoon, the *River Queen* docked at her berth to unload her latest return load from New Orleans, an entire steamboat full of foodstuffs: tinned sardines, peaches, cherries, dried peaches, apples and currants, salt beef, flour, coffee, tea, sugar, rice, casks of vinegar, and many other things. The shipment was going to Rumble and Wensel Groceries and Provisions, the biggest general store in Natchez-Under-the-Hill. It was the first time they had shipped with the *River Queen*.

As soon as they docked, Rumble and Wensel wagons started lining up at the *Queen*. Dallas, seeing that the unloading was in good hands, went straight to the store and collected the *River Queen*'s pay. After that he went down to the Blue Moon Saloon.

"Hello, Dallas, quick trip this time, eh?" Otto said with surprise.

"Yeah, I'm trying to make them quick and clean. The *River Queen*'s getting a reputation on the river, and I mean to keep it up."

Otto nodded and asked, "So, you a drinking man today?"

"Yeah, I got the mulligrubs. Give me a whiskey."

As he poured it, Otto said in a low voice, "Well, I don't think you're going to be cheered up too much in here this evening." He glanced around nervously.

Dallas turned to see four men slouched at a table in the corner, playing poker. He recognized them, though he only knew one of them by name, a short, stout, grim-faced German by the name of Ritter Kahn. All of them were wearing guns, and Kahn always carried a wooden walking stick with a brass head. It was rumored that he had it drilled out and filled with lead shot.

Dallas turned back around, took a sip of his drink, and shrugged. "New Big Bosses? I've seen 'em around. Look just as ugly and dumb as the old Big Bosses to me." The Big Bosses were the ruling gang on Natchez-Under-the-Hill, running the protection rackets and supposedly "policing" the boardwalk.

Otto dropped his voice even lower. "Well, they're my big bosses now. Someone bought the Blue Moon, we don't know who, but Kahn runs the Moon now. He's a rough one, he'll crack a man over the head for just looking funny. Thing about it is, those apes he runs with, they're all the time pulling guns and shooting up the place, even if it's just a couple of the river boys in a fistfight. Seems like it's meaner in here than it was before, even with their 'protection.'"

"Who bought the Moon?" Bronte asked.

"Dunno. Only Kahn and his boys know, I guess, and they're not saying. But Kahn came in with the title, it's all legal and aboveboard, I guess. Old Man Snedeker is about eighty years old, guess he thought it was time to retire." Snedeker, the owner of the Blue Moon, lived in a shack right behind the saloon, and as far as Dallas knew, never set foot in the place.

Men started coming in and demanding drinks, and Dallas took a look around. He could see bulletholes in the walls and ceilings, an old dark smoky mirror on one wall was gone, the big gaudy painting of a red-haired woman reclining, scantily clothed, had bulletholes in it and hung crookedly. The Blue Moon Saloon had boasted two front windows, a luxury that only a couple of other saloons had in Natchez-Under-the-Hill, and now one of them had a star-shaped hole in it and had been boarded over. The men that came in carefully avoided the table where Ritter Kahn and his men sat.

Otto came back to pour Dallas another whiskey, and Dallas asked, "Is Lulie with a customer?"

"Yeah, she should be down any time now," he answered. "Think it was a half-hour fellow."

Dallas sipped his drink very slowly. Though he had been spending much more time in the Blue Moon in the last few weeks, he hadn't been drinking very much. After that night when he had met Rev Brown, he had decided that he was getting too old to drink like a fool kid. *Funny how much worse the hangovers are when you get older. Just isn't worth it any more.*

At the back of the saloon, in the half-dark, he saw Lulie coming down the stairs. She saw him and weaved between the crowd slowly, her head down. When she reached him she looked down at the bar and said in a jocular tone, "Buy me a drink, mister?"

Dallas frowned, reached over, and tipped her face up to look at him squarely. Lulie's right eye was swollen shut, a huge lump that was turning lurid blue. His face darkened dangerously.

Quickly she laid her hand on his arm. "Dallas, please don't make a big to-do. It'll only get you hurt, maybe shot, and I'll get in trouble."

"Who did this to you?" he said between gritted teeth.

She shrugged. "A customer, said I was too skinny, and he was gonna get his money back, but he took it out on me first. But it don't make any difference, Dallas. You see Minnie Mae over there? Wearing that red scarf wrapped all up around her neck? It's because she's got fingerprints on her neck. She almost died, choking to death, and it was one of Kahn's boys. And look at DeeDee. Both arms covered in bruises. Her back is too. And that was Kahn himself. Said he caught her stealing drinks."

Dallas signaled Otto and said, "Give us both a double." Otto, with a furtive look, turned his back to pour the drinks and then brought two full shot glasses to them. Quickly Dallas picked up Lulie's glass and slid his own over to her. With a furtive glance up at him, she emptied the glass quickly. Dallas sipped her drink. It was lukewarm unsweetened tea.

Otto muttered, "Sorry, Dallas. House rules now, and I got no desire to get beat with that stick." He quickly turned away.

Dully Lulie said, "We gotta buy our own drinks now."

Dallas tightened his mouth, and the next time Otto came by, he said, "I want Lulie for the night, Otto. And give me one of the real rooms, not the half-hour closets. And I want a bottle of whiskey, one of those you got back there that hasn't been opened."

Otto swallowed hard and said, "That's gonna be ten dollars, Dallas. Three for Lulie, two for the room, and five for the bottle."

Without comment Dallas threw a ten-dollar bill down. It was more than he made in two weeks working on the *Queen*. Otto handed him a bottle and two shot glasses, and a key. "Room 12. Best we got, the one with the formal parlor," he said with disgust.

THEY WENT UP TO Room 12. The luxurious appointments of this expensive two-dollar room was that the cot had sheets on it instead of just a bare mattress, and it had a pillow. The "formal parlor" consisted of a round scarred table and two rickety straight-back chairs underneath a single grimy window. Without speaking, Lulie and Dallas sat down, and Dallas poured them both a drink. Lulie tossed hers back, and Dallas poured her another. She managed a smile. "Thanks, Dallas. I don't know why you take such good care of me. I don't deserve it."

Staring at her black eye with anger, he muttered, "No one deserves that, Lulie. And you're a nice girl in a bad place. I wish I could help you more. Get you out of this stinking mudhole."

Lulie took a sip of her whiskey and sighed deeply. "Ain't no place any better," she said. "What I hear is that the Bon Ton, the Silver Street Palace, and even the Rip 'Em Up are all run by Kahn and his men now, so all those girls are going through the same thing. And Dallas, I ain't no nice girl. Even if you could get me outta here, settle me someplace somehow, I'd be back in the nearest saloon in a day or two. If I had any money, I'd spend it on whiskey. When I ran outta money, I'd go back to work."

Dallas nodded sadly. "Yeah, I see what you mean, Lulie. It's the way of this old world, isn't it? It's just that this is the first time I've seen the saloons let the girls get hurt. Seems to me like that kind of thing's not good for business."

"Damaging the merchandise?" Lulie said dryly. "I dunno. Kahn and his men don't seem to think it matters. And I gotta admit, I haven't seen business fall off none. Saloons in Natchez-Under-the-Hill are busy all the time." She gave him a searching look. "You look down, Dallas, and I don't think it's all 'cause of my shiner. You been hanging around here a lot lately. What happened to your fancy lady owner? She didn't kick you off the boat, did she?"

"No, business is good, she's got no reason to fire me," he said moodily. "She's just been busy lately, with some of her top-drawer friends. One, at least, that she thinks is top-drawer."

"A man?" Lulie guessed shrewdly.

"Yeah. Man named Lyle Dennison, just moved to Natchez from New Orleans about a month ago. Big muckety-muck, bought the *Columbia Lady*. He owned one of the biggest slave markets in New Orleans, and word is on the river that he's bought into the Forks of the Road, and he's planning on doubling the traffic this year." The notorious Forks of the Road slave market in Natchez was one of the biggest and most profitable markets in the Cotton South.

"Hard for me to care much about slaves," Lulie said carelessly. "I know you don't hold with it much, but then again you're fool enough to think you can save someone like me. Anyways, so your lady is steppin' out with this Dennison?"

"Yeah, just about every night we're in town," he answered, staring down at his drink, slowly revolving the glass between thumb and forefinger. "He's got all the women charmed right up to their hairpins, and Darcy, too, because he's like a kid, he loves that big palace Dennison owns." Taking a drink, he went on, "I don't wanna talk about it any more, Lulie. I think I'll just go on back to the *Queen* and sack out."

Lulie dropped her gaze and muttered, "Okay, Dallas. Whatever you want."

He rose, adjusting his gun belt. He had taken to wearing a belt with bullet loops and a holster when he was going to be in Natchez-Under-the-Hill after dark. He started to say good-bye to Lulie, but then he noticed her drooping shoulders and dropped head. "C'mon, Lulie, give me a big good-bye hug, girl. You've got the room for the night, you can maybe get a good night's sleep. Tomorrow I'll come early and take you to the Bread and Boar and get you some food. You look like a scarecrow."

Still she sat, her head down, and merely shook her head. A thought dawned on Dallas, and he said grimly, "If I leave, you're going to lose the room, aren't you. Kahn will make you go back to work, and he'll sell the room again."

"Yeah," she said quietly. "He's not stupid, he's sharp and sly. When he sees you leave, he'll come get me."

Temper flared in Dallas, but at the same time he knew the situation was hopeless. What was he going to do? Many of the saloons did the same thing, although the Blue Moon never had, and that was one reason he liked it. He could go down and confront Kahn, but all that would do is likely cause a fight, and from what Otto said it might even cause a big gunfight. And he couldn't win, anyway. Brutal men like Ritter Kahn roamed the streets by the dozens. Whatever happened, Lulie would be in the same situation afterwards as she was now.

"Aw, forget about all of 'em," he said with forced cheer, shedding his coat and sitting back down. "Ma'am, would you buy me a drink?"

Lulie looked up and smiled.

THAT NIGHT LYLE DENNISON took Julienne to the King Cotton Theater, the finest playhouse in Natchez. He had a box, and they were the only two in it, though it was large enough for a dozen chairs. A British company was performing *Hamlet*, and Julienne enjoyed it immensely. At the intermission she said, "You know, Lyle, you're going to be the talk of the town, escorting a woman like me that has fallen so far in status and reputation. Everyone is watching us instead of the play."

Julienne had seen many of their old "friends," including the Moaks, who had a box on the other side of the theater. They had all frigidly nodded to one another, and then the Moaks pretended to watch the play, though they kept whispering among themselves and furtively glancing toward Dennison's box. With great amusement, Julienne saw Archibald Leggett hovering over Susanna Moak.

Motioning for an attendant to bring them champagne, Lyle said easily, "Julienne, we've been seeing each other for two weeks now. You know me. I'm not one of those pretend blue-bloods with their skinny noses stuck up in the air. I came from nothing, and I made something of myself, and I've found that money talks. Even to would-be aristocrats. I don't care a wooden nickel for what they think." With a shark's smile, he raised his champagne glass toward another box where two elderly ladies were talking and staring at them.

After the play Lyle took her to the Red Velvet Restaurant, a pretentious upper-class eatery that lived up to its name, for every chair was covered in red velvet, and the curtains that separated the small private tables were heavy crimson draperies with gold tassels. It was scandalous for Julienne to be dining with him in one of those intimate little corners alone, but she no longer cared. This was the second time she had been out with Lyle without a chaperone. He had taken her family out, of course, to dine on the *Columbia Lady* twice, on a picnic, to dine at the grand home he had just bought, and to the Main Street Playhouse to see *Rip Van Winkle*, which Carley had loved. After two weeks he had asked the family to accompany him to a party at the town square. The city sponsored it, and it included fireworks, dancing, a barbecue, and fiery political speeches. By now Roseann and Aunt Leah were well aware that Lyle's polite attentions were because of his obvious attraction to Julienne, and they had allowed her to go alone with him. Two nights later he had taken her to dinner at a friend's home, a family named Tisdale that had also just moved to Natchez from New Orleans. Francis Tisdale was a distant cousin of Lyle's, and he had just gotten his captain's license, so the conversation was lively and interesting to Julienne.

Now, safely hidden from prying eyes in the restaurant in their booth, Lyle slid his arm around the back of the loveseat they were seated on and asked, "Lobster is the Red Velvet's specialty, I hear. Would you like to have lobster for dinner?"

"I've never had lobster," Julienne admitted. "I would like to try it."

Lyle ordered lobster for her and prime tenderloin for himself. When she tasted her dinner she said, "I do like it, very much. I'm a little surprised, because I'm heartily sick of anything to do with fish."

"Supposed to show good breeding to like lobster," Lyle grinned. "I don't like it and you do, which I think shows that it might be true."

"Nonsense," Julienne scoffed. "If there's one thing I've learned, it's that good manners and gallantry have nothing to do with birthright. And besides, you like Shakespeare, and that's not exactly the kind of thing that the common people care for."

"I don't like Shakespeare," he said, pouring more champagne into her crystal wineglass. "I only wanted to go because I knew you do."

"That's nice of you, Lyle," she said softly.

"Not really, I'm not just being nice. I like you a lot, Julienne. You're smart and you're funny and you're a beautiful woman. Spending time with you has been one of my greatest pleasures the last few weeks."

Julienne smiled at him. "I've enjoyed your company too, Lyle, very much. I know you must think it's because you're obviously wealthy, and I'm obviously not. But I really do like you too, Lyle."

He shrugged. "I meet women all the time that are moneygrubbers. You're not, I could see that from the first time I met you. But, Julienne, I have to ask you, since you brought it up. I understand about what happened after your father died, but now that you've got the *River Queen* running again and making a profit, why don't you invest in her and get her fixed up to carry passengers? Even with your family living on board, you've still got, what, twenty staterooms? And the dining room could be fixed up, and you could have musicians and dancing in there too."

"I would love to do that," Julienne said harshly, "especially I would love to fix up our staterooms, they're like—well, you've seen the empty ones. Ours aren't much better. But it doesn't matter, because the bank won't loan me any money."

"Which bank?" Lyle asked.

"Planter's, and Preston Gates has been a friend of the family for years. But the Board of Directors has not. I've talked to Mr. Gates about it, but even though I didn't have a figure in mind, he said there was no use in even getting estimates for fixing up the *Queen*. Without my father, the bank feels that loaning money to the Ashby family is too great a risk."

Lyle nodded. "I do some business with Planter's, and I know Gates. If he says it, it's true."

"I know, I trust him. At first, when my father died, I didn't. I thought he was a vulture. But I've learned that he's really a good friend, and he's done all he can to help us. He even told me that if he had the money, he'd make a private loan to us. But he's not able to do that."

"Well, then," Lyle said slowly, "why don't you ask me?"

"What?" Julienne said, startled. "Ask you what?"

"For the money. I could loan it to you. After all, we were just talking about what good friends we are. That's the kind of thing that friends do, they help each other out."

She stared at him, bemused. "I never thought of such a thing, Lyle."

"No, I know you haven't. But if I had realized your situation, I would have suggested it before. I do this a lot, you know, it's just a business investment. I invest in all kinds of enterprises. For you, the *River Queen* would be the security just like at the bank, only I'd charge you a lower rate of interest. Just business, see?"

For a moment Julienne couldn't think clearly, because every alarm in her mind started blaring when she thought of taking money from a man. But the way he had explained it was not like he was giving her money in return for any "favors." As he had said, it was a simple business transaction.

She tried to speak, and then finally all she could say was, "Wouldn't that be an imposition?"

"I have eleven notes out right now, Julienne. Four of them are to my friends, the rest are businessmen, all of them are secured, and I'm making money on the interest. I'd be happy to help you in this way. I think the *River Queen* would be a solid investment."

"I don't know," she said hesitantly. "I don't even have any idea how much money it would take to refit the *Queen*."

They were sitting very close together, and now Lyle took her hand. "Tell you what," he said warmly. "Why don't you tell me what you've got in mind, and that'll give me a better idea of how much money you're going to need."

Bright hope began to glimmer in her mind, with visions of the *River Queen* painted and trimmed in gingerbread-work, of nicely-appointed staterooms with brass beds and fine satiny sheets, of marble-topped dressing tables and velvet curtains, of a dining room with glowing wood floors and paneling, of dancing in a satin dress in the ballroom lit by crystal chandeliers. Her eyes sparkled, and she began to talk.

They talked for an hour in the restaurant, and then all the way back to the *Queen* in his fine glassed landau. As always, he walked her on board, but instead of politely tipping his hat and bowing good-night at the end of the landing stages, he took her arm and walked her up the stairs to the double doors leading into the ballroom. He put his hands on her waist and turned her to him. "Why don't you come to my house tomorrow morning? I'll draw up the papers, and by tomorrow afternoon I can have workmen already starting on the *Queen*. I'll bet you I can get her done and back on the river in a week."

She hesitated. For an unescorted woman to go to a man's house was unheard of, except for prostitutes. She thought about asking Aunt Leah to accompany her, but uneasily she thought that her aunt would not approve of Lyle loaning them money. Her aunt was always very polite to him, but Julienne sensed that she really didn't care much for him, or at least that she didn't trust him. And she couldn't possibly ask her mother to come with her, for Roseann would flitter and flutter and the entire thing would make her so nervous she would probably end up in tears.

He watched the emotions flitting across her face knowingly. Coolly he said, "I know that Bronte has been something like a business partner to you, even though he's just your pilot. You can bring him if you're uncomfortable coming to my home."

"No!" she said vehemently. "And I—it's not that I don't want to come to your home, Lyle, it's just that—oh, forget it! I'm a businesswoman, after all, and it's just business. What time shall I call?"

He grinned, his brown-black eyes glinting. "At your convenience, ma'am. Normal business hours begin at eight o'clock."

"I'll be there at eight o'clock, then."

She knew that he was going to kiss her. He put his hands at her hips, swayed her against him, and kissed her full and heavy on the lips. He did it well, and she knew that he was a man that had known women. She didn't care, she was acutely aware of the full masculine force of his personality, and she was drawn to him. She eagerly returned his passionate kiss and managed to utterly crush any tiny hints of doubt or regret or shame rising in her mind.

Lyle Dennison was going to give her back her life.

CHAPTER SEVENTEEN

Julienne stood on the Texas deck, watching the Blue Moon Saloon. After she had returned from Lyle's house that morning, she had steeled herself and gone looking for Dallas Bronte. She had decided to tell him that she had taken out a loan from Lyle Dennison first of all, even before she told her family. She knew she was going to have a fight on her hands. Dallas detested Lyle Dennison, though he would never tell Julienne why. They hadn't been nearly as close since she had been seeing Lyle, and Julienne told herself that she didn't care.

But she cared now, because she had made Caesar tell her where Dallas was. He had spent the night at the Blue Moon. Though she knew he had been spending time there when they were home, this was the first time he had stayed all night there since he had come on board the *River Queen*.

He finally came out, blinking in the sun and pulling his hat down over his eyes. As he walked to the *River Queen*, Julienne saw that at least he wasn't drunk, he was striding solidly, his shoulders squared. As he crossed the gangplank, he glanced up at her and imperiously she waved for him to come up.

When he reached the Texas deck, she said, "I need to talk to you, please. Would you come in and sit down with me for a few minutes?"

"Sure," he said with surprise. It was the first time in a long time she had sought him out.

They went into the ballroom and sat at the dining table. She crossed her hands on the table, frowned, and seemed not to know how to begin.

Dallas said lazily, "You're all prettied up. Little early to be stepping out with Dennison, isn't it?" It was barely eleven o'clock in the morning.

"I haven't been stepping out with him," Julienne retorted sharply. "It's a little early to be drinking in the Blue Moon, isn't it?"

"I haven't been drinking this morning," he said quickly, but he dropped his eyes.

"You smell like you've been drinking for a week," Julienne said with open disgust. "And you stink like cheap perfume. But I don't care about that. I'm glad you brought up Lyle Dennison, because that's who I want to talk to you about."

His head came up alertly, and he repeated, "Dennison? What about him?"

Julienne shifted in her chair a bit and she began fidgeting, rubbing her fingers together restlessly. "You know I've always wanted to fix the *Queen* up so we can start having passengers, and a dining room and dancing."

"Yes, I know," he said cautiously. "And I've told you that'll happen one day, but it's going to take awhile before we can establish a reputation so the bank will loan you the money."

"Lyle's loaning me the money," Julienne said defiantly. "He says the *Queen* would be a good investment for him."

"What!" Dallas almost shouted. "Have you lost your mind, woman, to even consider that?"

Julienne swallowed hard and managed to make her voice even and firm. "I'm not just considering it, I've already done it. This morning I signed the papers."

Dallas jumped up, knocking the chair over so hard it skittered across the floor. After pacing back and forth several times, his face working, he turned back to her.

"How much?" he asked, his voice rising.

"A lot, but we can pay it back easy," she said quickly. "The payments are only ninety-four dollars a month."

"How much?" he repeated loudly.

"T-ten thousand dollars," Julienne answered. This time she couldn't keep her voice from faltering.

His head dropped and he took a deep breath. He stayed that way, standing still with his arms at his sides, his head down, breathing hard. Julienne knew he was trying to control his temper. After what seemed like a long time he looked up at her, and his face was as darkly set as she had ever seen it.

"Ten thousand dollars," he said in a dead tone. "Julienne, you could build a whole new steamer from the keel up, twice as big as the *River Queen*, fully outfitted."

"I don't have to use all the money," she argued. "It's been deposited in our bank account. Lyle just said he wanted to make sure I had plenty. I can make the payments as long as I want, and he said that in a few months the *Queen* will make enough money to completely pay off whatever monies I've used, and the loan will be paid off."

"Uh-huh. And so, who's managing this refit? Who's getting the estimates from the carpenters, the painters, the metalworkers, the glassmen, all the vendors? Who's getting the extra crew you'll need, and who's buying the extra safety equipment you have to have when you carry passengers, and the permits? Who's hiring the cooks and servants you'll have to have?"

"Lyle can take care of all of that," she said disdainfully. "He's already done lots of work on the *Columbia Lady*, and he's got contacts in all kinds of businesses, and he's got craftsmen of all kinds working for him on different enterprises. He says he can probably get the *Queen* renovated and back on the river in a week or ten days."

"Yeah, he's got contacts all right," Dallas growled. "And a lot of investments, including a bunch of saloons and gambling halls and brothels in Natchez-Under-the-Hill. He tell you about those business ventures, Miss Ashby?"

Her face paled for a moment, but then she resumed her defiant gaze. "I'm sure Planter's Bank does business with those kinds of places, but you wouldn't say a word if I was getting the loan from them."

"Oh yes I would. If you're so taken with Dennison that you want to make excuses for him, fine. I'll leave him out of it. But haven't you learned anything, Julienne, from losing your house and plantation? If you take out a loan against the *River Queen*, then you don't own her any more. You might lose her. Didn't that ever enter your mind?"

"No, it didn't! Lyle's a friend, and we're going to be able to pay him back whatever money we use for the *Queen* in a few months. He would never take the *River Queen* away from me!"

"She's not just yours. She belongs to your family. Did you talk to them about this?"

Julienne's face worked, and now she, too, jumped out of her chair and came to stand in front of him, scowling. "You seem to be forgetting something. You're not in my family. You are the pilot of the steamer that my family owns. You have no right to ask me any questions about my family!"

"So you didn't tell them," he said tightly. "And you're exactly right, ma'am, about you and your family. I just work for the Ashbys. But even though you're as blind as a bat, I can see it coming. As of today everyone on this boat's working for Lyle Dennison. And I'm not going to work for him. I don't care if I have to go back to being a roughneck."

"Well, I guess that means you'll be leaving then!" Julienne shouted angrily.

"I guess so!" he shouted back. "And one last thing, *Miss Ashby.* I was working for you and your family to help you, and you helped me too. But you're not going to find another pilot on this earth that's going to work for seventy cents a day. You're looking at three or four hundred dollars a month to replace me. Maybe that ten thousand dollars you borrowed isn't so much money after all!"

He stalked through the doors, and Julienne knew he was going to his stateroom to get his things.

She was so angry that for a few moments she was glad he was leaving. Throwing herself back into one of the cheap slat chairs, she thought with vicious triumph, *Soon I'll be sitting on a heavy padded chair covered in velvet. Blue, maybe . . .*

But after awhile of gloating, she began to think of Dallas's words, and for the first time she let some of those faint voices of doubt finally filter through to her conscious mind. *Three hundred dollars a month for a pilot? And just the payment on the loan another hundred dollars? That's four hundred dollars a month I just committed to, and that doesn't include anything else at all!*

She started feeling slightly panicky, but with an iron will she forced herself to be calm. How many times in the last months had she said to herself, *I can't do this! I won't do this!* but then she did do whatever it was, whether cleaning the sanitary rooms or eating oxtail soup. She could do this, and she would do this. Even without Dallas Bronte.

Her heart sinking, she realized the plain truth.

As of today she no longer had Dallas, and she no longer had a choice.

DALLAS PACKED HIS FEW belongings and left the *Queen*. He didn't say anything to any of the crew or to the rest of the family. This action of Julienne's had been like getting hit in the face. Once he had actually been hit in the stomach so hard it had knocked the breath out of him, and that's what he had felt like when Julienne had told him of this disaster.

He went back over to the Blue Moon, and with one look at his face Otto poured him a double. Dallas took it, downed it, and grunted, "Another."

While he was pouring it, Lulie came up, wearing the same grubby green dress she'd worn the day and night before. It was soiled, and the black lace around the neck was torn. She had lost weight, and one shoulder of the limp fabric kept slipping off. "Back so soon, Dallas?" she asked.

"Yeah," he said shortly. "And I don't want to talk about it. Otto, give me back the room for the night, and another bottle of the real stuff. Lulie, I don't want to be rude, but I just want to be alone for awhile."

"No, no, Dallas, you go on, I just now got down here. I need to work, earn some money," she said quickly, then added in a low, slightly ashamed voice, "and I could use a drink." Lulie had drunk the entire bottle of whiskey last night, except for two shots that Dallas had had.

"Give us both a drink, Otto," he said quietly. Ritter Kahn wasn't there, but two dusty-looking hard-faced men with guns were sitting in the corner, their boots propped up on the tables, watching.

Otto poured Lulie's fake shot and Dallas's real one, Dallas turned his back and traded them swiftly. Lulie downed hers, and sighing, Dallas tossed back the tasteless tea as if it were the best smooth whiskey. "I'll come back down later tonight," Dallas said to her. "I'm just gonna take a while and think."

"Okay," she said lightly, kissing him on the cheek. "Goodness knows I can't help you do that."

"Want a bottle?" Otto asked.

"No, maybe tonight," he answered and went upstairs, back to Room 12. The empty bottle and two shot glasses were still on the table. The cot's sheets were mussed, where Lulie had slept, and the pillow was still on the floor where Dallas had slept. He had told Julienne the absolute truth. To him Lulie was something like a little sister.

He ached all over from sleeping on the floor, so he tossed the pillow up onto the cot, took off his jacket, gunbelt, and boots, and laid down. It was sweltering in the room, and it stank of whiskey and sweat and just plain old dirt and grime, and Dallas thought he would never go to sleep. *I'll just lay here for awhile and figure out what to do,* he thought grimly. *I thought I'd never find myself in this position again, holed up in a fleabitten room with no job. I should know by now that you can't count on a soul on this earth. I was a fool to think I'd ever be anything but a servant to Julienne, I mean to the Ashbys,* he mentally corrected himself. Their conversation played over and over again in his mind until he was actually physically tired from the mental exertion. And so he finally let himself drift off into an uneasy doze.

Gunshots!

Without even blinking Dallas jumped up, put on his gunbelt and boots, and ran downstairs. He had heard three gunshots, a pause, and then two more. Now men were yelling and women were screaming. It was chaos when he reached the saloon.

He scanned the room, his sharp eyes taking in everything: a dead roughneck, another wounded, Ritter Kahn and one of his men standing holding smoking guns, a line of bottles broken along the wall, Otto peeking up from where he knelt behind the bar. And then he found Lulie. Two of the other girls were knelt over her, lying on the floor. A big black stain was creeping over her stomach. Dallas went to her, scooped her up in his arms, and ran down the boardwalk.

A few doors down in the next alley was a stairway up to an office above a gambling hall. Dallas took the stairs two at a time and kicked open the door. A small, stooped, gray-haired man with spectacles looked up from a book, startled. He stood up and grimly said, "This way." He led Dallas to a room with two cots in it. Gently Dallas laid Lulie down. Her eyes were closed and her face was so white that he thought she might already be dead. The bloodstain on her stomach had spread around to her back, and Dallas's sleeves were red with blood.

"Is she dead?" he demanded harshly.

The man bent over her and put his hand on her chest and his ear to her mouth. "Not yet," he said grimly. "But I doubt I got time to get that bullet out. She's probably going to die before I can get started good."

Dallas nodded numbly. "Do you think she'll wake up, Doc?" Everyone called him "Doc Needles," because no one knew his real name, or if he was a real doctor. But he tended most of the victims of gunshots and knife fights and beatings in Natchez-Under-the-Hill.

"Got no way of knowing," he said. "She might, before she goes. Sometimes they do, sometimes they don't. What do you want me to do?"

"I guess just let me stay with her. Would you leave me some morphine just in case she wakes up?"

"You can stay here, but it's gonna cost you ten cents," he said carelessly. "Morphine's gonna cost, depending on how much you give her."

Dallas gave him a fifty-cent piece and Doc Needles added in a more kindly tone, "If she wakes up she's not gonna be able to swaller. I'll fix up a shot. You just call me if you need me to give it to her."

Dallas nodded, still staring down at her, watching the very slight, slow rise and fall of her chest.

Doc set a chair behind him, and wordlessly Dallas sat down, took Lulie's hand, and began to wait. Silently Doc went back into his office, closing the door behind him.

Dallas didn't know how many minutes it was before Lulie stirred. Her one eye opened—the other one was still black and blue and swollen shut—and she whispered, "Is that you, Dallas?"

"Yeah, it's me."

"I'm scared, Dallas! I'm going to die!"

Dallas had the impulse to try to offer her some hope, but something kept him from that. Doc Needles had been so certain and the shadow of death was already on Lulie's face. He could not think of a single thing to say, and finally he said, "I wish I could help you, Lulie."

"I'm going to die," Lulie repeated. Her eyes were filled with dark shadows. She said, "I can't face God, not after what I've done. Tell me what to do, Dallas. How can I get right with God?"

No question had ever caught Dallas Bronte with such force. He knew well what to tell the dying woman. His own grandfather had been a Methodist pastor, and Dallas had spent much time with him. Finally he remembered a day when he had gone with his grandfather to make calls. They had gone to a house where a man was dying, and very clearly Dallas remembered the man had asked his grandfather almost identically the question that Lulie had asked him. *I'm going to die, Pastor. What can I do to get right with God?*

"Tell me, Dallas," she groaned, "I can't die. I'd go straight to hell."

At that moment Dallas Bronte wished with all of his heart that he was a man of God, but he was not. He knew, however, the right thing for Lulie to do, just as he knew the right thing that he himself should have done years ago. He held both of her hands and said, "You've got to do two things, Lulie. You've got to tell God you're a sinner."

"Oh, Dallas, He knows that."

"I guess He does, but that's what the Bible says. If we confess our sins, He's faithful and just to forgive us our sins."

"Does the Bible say that really?"

"It really does."

"I can do that. What's the other thing?"

"You have to ask Him to save you in the name of Jesus. Jesus died on the cross for you and for me and for all sinners."

"And that's all I have to do? I've always believed in Jesus. I just didn't obey Him."

"That's the way you get saved." Dallas felt like an absolute hypocrite! When he himself had known for years how to become a Christian but had run from that very thing. Now he saw the dying woman had turned her eyes up to him, and she whispered, "I can do that, Dallas. Will you pray for me?"

"Sure I will, Lulie." Dallas bowed his head still feeling like an absolute hypocrite he prayed for the girl. Even as he prayed, he heard her whispering a prayer, and when finally he said, "Amen," he said, "Did you tell the Lord that you sinned against Him?"

"Yes, I did."

"And did you ask Him to save you in the Name of Jesus?"

"I did that, Dallas. Is there anything else?"

"No," Dallas hesitated and then said, "There was a thief on the cross next to Him, Lulie, when Jesus was being executed. That thief looked over at Jesus, and he did what you just did. He said, 'Lord, remember me,' which was what you said to God."

"What happened?"

"Jesus looked at him while He Himself was dying, and He said, 'This day thou shalt be with me in paradise.'" The old words came easily, for he had heard his grandfather preach many a sermon using that verse. He looked down and saw that Lulie was nodding, but her eyes were fluttering, and finally closed. He sat still, watching her, holding her hands.

Finally her chest rose, fell, and she didn't breathe again.

Dallas mumbled sorrowfully, "I'm no good, Lord, but I think You heard this woman's prayer." He got up and left. He knew then what he had to do. It was something that he had put off for years.

CHAPTER EIGHTEEN

Dallas, along with his horse, made his way slowly along the pathway that hugged the Mississippi River. It was late afternoon, and the clouds were rolling up carrying with them a hint of rain, or so it seemed to him. A sound caught his attention, and he stopped and turned to face the river where he saw a side-wheeler appear around the bend. He watched it and recognized it almost at once as the *Julia Tavers*. He knew it was named by the owner Henry Tavers after his wife had died after a brief marriage. He knew that Tavers had spent the rest of his life alone and had never really gotten over her death. He had heard a man once who knew Tavers well say, "On his death bed the last thing he said was, 'Now, I'm going to be with Julia again.'"

Still thinking about this, Dallas was startled when a huge frog suddenly croaked and made a tremendous jump, hitting the water with a plunking sound and disappearing in the brown current. Dallas smiled briefly. "You don't have any worries, frog. I'm not trying to catch you. Never did like frog's legs anyway."

Fifty yards farther down the pathway he stopped, sat down on a fallen tree, and for a moment became as still as a statue. He had been alone for most of the week that he had been at his camp. He had built a lean-to on a piece of high ground, stashed his grub and the feed for his horse there, but had actually spent little time except to sleep. Every day he had gotten up with the sun, cooked a breakfast, then started walking along the bank or following trails through the timber. The first two days he had walked hurriedly, taking long strides as if he had a schedule to follow, but then he had realized that this was not doing what he had come for. He made his mind up, and the next day after breakfast, he went to the river and for six solid hours had sat on a log, soaking up the sounds of the river and from the woods. He had come to this isolated spot to try to find some meaning for his life, and for him that meant finding the God that his grandfather had preached and believed in.

Slow going were those first days of silence and stillness, but he had found himself with a discipline he had not known he possessed. Most of his life had been a time of activity, sometimes a furious period of work that occupied him completely. Now as Dallas sat quietly watching the Mississippi roll toward the south, he realized that he had learned one thing that his grandfather had drilled into him when he was just a boy. *Get alone, away from folks, boy. Find a place and learn to be still, and if you wait long enough, God will find you!*

He thought of the days that had gone by, seeming to move more slowly all the time in some mysterious way. During this period he had waited for God to speak, but nothing had happened. It was not as though he expected a literal voice to come down out of the heavens or for God to speak to him as He spoke to Moses, but he had to have *something*. At times during this period he wanted to run away, to get back to the world of action, of people, but he had doggedly stuck it out and still he sat there as the minutes passed him by.

A light rain began to fall, but he paid no heed to the tiny drops, little more than a mist. Finally when it stopped, he got up and made his way back through the cane break that bordered the river. When he arrived at his camp, he dug out the canvas sack he used to store his food and discovered that it was practically empty. He had eaten most of the food that he had brought with him, and when he looked farther he discovered he had run out of feed for his horse. For a moment he hesitated, then decided to go to the small town he had passed a week ago and buy some supplies.

Straightening up, he walked over to the horse that he had hobbled and slapped her on the shoulder. "Got to eat and so do you, Rosie." The grazing was pretty good around his camp, but the mare had gone through the grain he had brought. He saddled up quickly, mounted, and rode toward the south. He kept Rosie at an even trot, for she was short-legged and chubby, built to haul a cart, not really a saddle horse. He didn't mind. Patting her neck with affection, his mind went back to what had become practically an obsession with him. *Where are You, Lord? I don't know how to find You—but I am not giving up!*

A WEATHER-BEATEN SIGN LEANING askance on a skinny pole proclaimed the name as Bennettville. A smile came to Dallas's face, and he murmured, "That sign is in about the same bad shape as the whole town."

Indeed, Bennettville was nothing to write home about. It had one main street though there were several side streets and some alleyways. He passed by a blacksmith's shop, a lawyer's office, a post office. He finally drew up in front of a sign that read simply, "General Store." Stepping out of the saddle, Bronte grabbed the two empty feed sacks he had brought for supplies and moved through the doorway. He saw at once that it was the typical small general store, with both sides of the narrow building lined with shelves containing groceries, medicine, some hardware, and rolls of textiles. Across the back was a counter with a pair of scales and a roll of paper. There were barrels with pickles and crackers, and the smell of spices was in the air.

"Help you, friend?" The speaker was a heavy-set man with a full head of brown hair and a neat beard to match. He was chewing on a twig of some sort and shifted it to different positions as he spoke. "You just barely caught me. I'm closing early."

"Need a few things," Bronte said and called out the items he needed. The clerk moved quickly, and when Bronte had finished he began totaling the items on a small tablet. He said firmly, "You owe me nine dollars and fifty-three cents."

Handing the money over, Bronte asked, "Closing pretty early, aren't you?"

"Why, we got us a fine revival meeting going on at the church." He put out his hand, smiling and said, "I'm Davis Williams, one of the deacons. Didn't get your name."

"Dallas Bronte."

"Mmm. Don't know of any Brontes in this part of the world."

"No, I don't have any people here. Or anywhere else, for that matter, that I know of."

"You staying in town tonight?"

"No, I'm camped out on the river."

"Doing a little fishing? Some hunting maybe?"

"A little fishing. Mostly just soaking in the silence and enjoying being out of the crowd."

"A man needs to do that sometimes. Well, Mr. Bronte, you'd do well to come to the meeting tonight. A fine evangelist we got! Best I ever heard! You'd be right welcome."

Ordinarily Bronte would have put the invitation aside instantly, but right now he felt an impulse that this was something he needed to do. It was the first indication of any sort of sign or pressure from what might be the Lord, so he said, "Well, maybe I will, sir. My grandfather was a Methodist preacher."

"I know you're proud of him. Tell you what, Mr. Bronte, my wife always cooks enough for ten people. So I have to eat leftovers most of the time. Let me close up here, and you and me will go get some of her cooking."

"Oh, that would be an imposition."

"Not at all! Not at all!" Williams said. "She loves to cook. She loves to feed me and so you wait right here."

It took only a few minutes for the owner to close the store down, and then the two started down the street. "The house is right down the street. You better bring your horse. You can keep her in the barn in case it starts raining."

Williams kept up a steady flow of warm conversation all the way down to his house, and Dallas's sense of embarrassment at imposing disappeared. *I could use a good home-cooked meal. And maybe the preacher will give me a little push in God's direction.*

Dallas felt uncomfortable as he entered the church, which was crowded. "I think I'll just take this one seat back here, Deacon."

"You better come up front where you can hear good."

"Oh, my hearing's fine." He smiled at Williams and sat down. Williams looked around and said, "Folks, this is Mr. Dallas Bronte. Make him welcome."

As soon as the deacon left, those sitting close to Dallas spoke to him. A couple of the men extended their hands, those that could reach him. He shook them and then sat back on the bare straight-backed pew.

They arrived about on time, for a tall, lanky man with a mournful face but a beautiful tenor voice said, "Folks, we are going to sing the Holy Spirit into this meeting. So, put your heart right in it while we praise the Lord."

They all stood to sing, and Dallas was surprised to recognize most of the songs that followed. He had heard them over and over again as a young boy attending his grandfather's services, but he had no idea he could still remember the words after all these years. The congregation was untrained musically, but they had enthusiasm and there was a good spirit in the place. It was a crude church with home-made benches, people wearing working clothes, but Dallas felt at ease here.

Finally the service was over, and the song leader said, "Folks, let me introduce you to our evangelist, Reverend Cletus Calloway."

Reverend Calloway stepped up to the lectern. He was holding a Bible in his hand, but he did not open it. He stood looking out over the congregation, and Dallas saw that he was a middle-aged man, trim, with neatly-combed hair and a pair of gray eyes that had a direct look in them that Dallas had seen in some strong-willed men. He was wiry, but Dallas could see that he had the hands of a working man. His voice was clear, and to Dallas's relief he did not shout or scream at his congregation. He smiled pleasantly and said a few words by way of welcoming visitors and thanking the church for having him.

He said in a firm voice, "If you will turn in your Bibles to the Gospel of Luke, the eighth chapter, beginning at the forty-third verse, I will read the text." Dallas noted, however, that he didn't open his Bible but simply began to quote.

> *And a woman having an issue of blood twelve years, which had spent all her living upon physicians, neither could be healed of any, came behind him and touched the border of His garment: and immediately her issue of blood staunched. And Jesus said, Who touched me? When all denied, Peter and they that were with him said, Master, the multitude throng thee and press thee,*

and sayest thou, Who touched me? And Jesus said, Somebody hath touched me: for I perceive that virtue has gone out of me. And when the woman saw that she was not hid she came trembling, and falling down before him, she declared unto him before all the people for what cause she had touched him, and how she was healed immediately. And he said unto her, Daughter, be of good comfort: thy faith hath made thee whole; go in peace.

Reverend Calloway continued, "We have this same incident set forth in Mark's Gospel, the fifth chapter, which adds several elements not given in Luke. For one thing it says she had had the issue of blood twelve years, that she had suffered many things of the physicians and had spent all that she had and was not better but worse."

Looking calmly over the congregation he said, "I suppose most of you may know the penalty that was imposed on people in this woman's day who had her malady. There's a terrible chapter in the book of Leviticus. Any woman like this was unclean. Everything she sat upon, all who touched her shared in the defilement. So in addition to her continual weakness, she was made to feel herself nothing but an outcast. This must have destroyed this poor woman's spirit and brought great loneliness to her."

He paused for a moment then smiled. "This is what I call a wayside miracle. It didn't occur in a church. There were no officials present. Jesus was on His way to heal somebody else. But on the way this woman, this much afflicted woman who had literally been dying for twelve years, decided somehow to come to Him."

Dallas leaned forward, for the minister was a good speaker and Dallas found himself caught up with the story.

"I think she was a woman of great determination. She knew this disease was going to take her life. I think she said to herself, 'If there is any possibility of getting rid of this sickness, no matter what it costs me, I'm going to do it.'"

Then the minister looked out and said, "There may be someone in this building tonight who says I'm a lost soul, but if a lost soul can be saved, if guilt can be washed away, it will be done. Even if you have a hard heart, you can press on until God does something." This statement struck Dallas hard for he felt it described his case exactly. He listened as the preacher went on speaking about the woman who had decided to risk everything in order to gain the blessing that she wanted from Jesus.

"And this woman," the minister continued, "adopted the likeliest means she could think of. The Scripture says she had been to physicians until she had spent all of her money. She went to gentlemen who were supposed to understand the signs of medicine, but she found no relief. No doubt she tried men who were educated. In fact, she probably met some who claimed they could heal her complaint. 'Follow my orders and you will be restored,' they might have told her. But it was all in vain, no one could help her. No one but Jesus Christ.

"Perhaps someone here tonight has tried everything and nothing has worked, but I stand before you right now to say that the Jesus that this woman touched, who healed her instantly, is the same Christ. He has risen from the dead, He is seated at the right hand of God, and He is calling to everyone. 'Let them that heareth come.' So, no matter what you have tried or what you have done or not done, if you feel in your soul and in your spirit something tonight, a yearning for God, I have it in my heart that God has brought you to this place so that you can reach out and touch the garment of Jesus."

The words seemed to penetrate Dallas, and he slumped down and dropped his head, unable to look at those about him.

"You have tried to save yourself by prayers, and your prayers have probably turned your thoughts upon your sin and you've become wretched. You have been trying to feel good and to do good, but the efforts made you feel how far you are from the goodness you desire. In the fruit of your efforts you have suffered all the more, but you are no better off."

The minister then lifted his eyes just as Dallas looked up, and the two seemed to be the only men in that room. The evangelist said, "And now perhaps, dear friend, you are saying what can I do? What shall I do? I will tell you. You can do nothing except what this woman ultimately did. You are without strength, without merit, without power, and God grant that you may look to the glorious Christ before this service is over."

The sermon went on and Dallas felt weak. The words of the evangelist were like bullets that struck against him! It was as if the man had eyes that could see through flesh and blood and right into his heart.

Finally the evangelist said, "Look at what this woman did at last. Weaker and weaker she had become. She hears of Jesus of Nazareth, a man sent of God who is healing sick folks of all sorts. She puts the stories together and then she says, 'Oh, I will go to Him. I have no money, but if I can only touch the border of His garment I'll be made whole.'" The preacher threw his head back and his voice sounded like a trumpet. "Oh what a glorious, wonderful thing that was! Splendid faith. My dear friend, I do not know your heart. I wish I could come and save you personally. Try Jesus Christ. Trust Him and see if He will not save you. Every other door is shut to you, but I beg you to exercise courage, born of desperation. May God's Holy Spirit help you to thrust out your fingers, reach out and touch Jesus. Say 'Yes, I freely accept Christ. By God's grace I will have Him to be my only hope.'

"After all," the evangelist continued, "this was the simplest thing she could do. Touch Jesus. All of the operations performed on her had perhaps been intricate, but all this was so simple. It's always simple when a man or a woman finally gets into their head that there's really nothing they can do. I'm sure she thought, *People will say it's foolish that touching a robe could get anybody healed, but I will go no matter if they laugh, no matter if they shove me aside. I'm going to put my trust in Jesus."*

By this time Dallas felt weaker than he ever had in his life. His heart seemed to be beating like a drum. He could hear the words of the preacher but beyond that he could hear something else. It was not a voice, not a vocalization, but an impulse. It was as if someone was echoing an amen to all that the preacher said, and then he heard the preacher say, "You may say tomorrow may be more convenient. No, if God is dealing with your heart tonight, it may be for the last time. He stands at the door and knocks. Now it's your turn to move toward Him, to put your trust in the Lord Jesus. When you have done this you will be saved, just as she was healed. 'He that believeth in Him hath everlasting life.' Do not leave this place tonight without knowing God. If you will just simply say, 'Yes, Lord Jesus, I will be whatever You want me to be.' Confess your sins and call out to God, then the great transaction will be done. By the living God I do implore you trust the living Redeemer. As I shall meet you all face-to-face before the judgment seat of Christ, I do beseech you. Put out the finger of faith and trust the Lord Jesus who is so fully worthy to be trusted."

Dallas heard the preacher say something else, then he was aware that everyone was standing. When he got to his feet he felt weak as if his legs would not hold him, and when he lifted his head his eyes met those of the evangelist whose gaze was fixed steadfastly on him. He heard him say, "Come and touch Jesus right now or be forever lost."

Dallas suddenly stepped out of the pew, pushing against those that were ahead of him. He stumbled forward, and when he got to the front, Reverend Calloway saw the tears running down Dallas's face. Dallas was shocked by this, for he was not a crying man. The evangelist said, "Brother, let's both kneel here and we'll pray. And I will stand beside you as you reach out and touch the robe of Jesus just as that poor woman did."

THE SERVICE WAS OVER. Many had come to shake hands with Dallas, who felt slightly stunned, but he knew something important, something real, had happened to him. When the last of the crowd had left, Williams came and said, "I'm proud of you, Mr. Bronte. God's done a work. I can see that." He hesitated and then said, "We're having a baptismal service tomorrow. There will be fourteen. I'd like for you to make number fifteen. Would you come and join us?"

Dallas felt a sense of resistance to stand forth and go through a ceremony that he never could see as meaningful, but something within him said, *Yes, you must go.* He said, "I sure can, Deacon."

"Fine! Fine! Now you come along. You're going to spend the night with us. We'll have time to talk about these things."

Later that night, after Dallas had gone to the room that Deacon Williams put him in, he sat down on the bed, his head still whirling. But persistently his very heart told him, *Now, at last I have done one right thing.* He well knew that he was different. He had no idea about how to go about serving God so he got on his knees and said, "God, You know I'm not worthy of anything, but I thank You for leading me to this place and for bringing me into the kingdom of God. Now, help me and guide me." And as he prayed, he knew for the first time in his life that God wasn't somewhere far off. He was right in Dallas's own heart.

CHAPTER NINETEEN

For eight days the *River Queen* had been a floating chaos, it seemed to Julienne. Dozens of men swarmed everywhere, breaking out all the windows to replace them, tearing off paneling, tearing up the ballroom floor, hammering, sawing, nailing, painting, drilling, banging, shouting, and above all, cursing. Lyle had sent a man to oversee the refit, a coarse, squat man with a heavy German accent named Ritter Kahn. Kahn ruled the workers not with an iron hand but with a heavy stick that he doled out blows with constantly. Julienne had asked him to completely redo her mother's stateroom first, and for a day and a half they had huddled up on the hurricane deck, trying to stay away from the workmen. But their profane shouts and orders rang out continuously, and the family gave up on trying to shield Carley.

She herself was very subdued and stayed with her mother and Aunt Leah at all times. Darcy stayed with the workmen, trying to keep up with what they were doing and trying to keep Kahn from abusing them, but Ritter Kahn paid no attention to him at all. And neither did the workmen, because Darcy didn't hit them.

The next day the painters were finishing up on the last detail work, and the bills started coming to Julienne. That night she sat in her stateroom, which was now outfitted just as she had envisioned, with a brass bed and a soft mattress, two fluffy pillows, and immaculate white sheets. She had a gas lamp at the new table, which was fitted in the corner, with drawers on one side and a tiny desk on the other, with a velvet-covered stool. The drapes for her brand-new window were blue velvet, with a white satin cord. But all of that was forgotten as she began to sort through all of the bills for the fixtures, the windows, the mirrors, the beds, the paneling, the new flooring, the bed linens, the tables and chairs for the dining room, and many more things that Julienne wasn't even sure of what they were. And the worst was the cost of the workmen. Quickly thumbing through the pages and adding the labor costs up in her head, she estimated almost two thousand dollars for that alone. All together she was looking at a pile of bills that amounted to almost eight thousand dollars.

Dropping the papers, she held her head in her hands. She had let Lyle make all the decisions about the renovations. He had said he was going to get this company to do such-and-such, that father and son to paint so-and-so, this vendor for the brass, and on and on. It had all sounded so good to Julienne, both to think of how beautiful the *Queen* was going to be, and especially the fact that she didn't have to figure out all of the complex tasks herself. After Dallas Bronte had left, she had unquestioningly— even gladly—put all her trust in Lyle Dennison.

But the enormity of the cost was like a heavy weight pressing down on her shoulders. Somehow she had been thinking that perhaps they would come up with a beautiful new steamer, ready for passengers and dancing in the ballroom, for about two thousand dollars. Why had she thought that? Had Lyle said that? She didn't know.

Julienne felt as if she had been in some sort of numbing fog since Dallas Bronte had left. She had never realized how much she leaned on him, she and her whole family. He had been the bulwark that had kept them going, that they depended on, that they knew would help them no matter what happened. A great chasm opened up in Julienne, and with it was an almost physical pain, when she started to think about how much she missed him.

"No!" she said aloud, and sat upright. He was gone, she was in business with Lyle now, and she knew that Lyle cared for her.

At least that's what she told herself. Wearily deciding she would ask Lyle to go over the accounts when he called the next day, she readied herself for bed. Robbie had laid out her nightclothes, and she quickly washed up and put them on. Lying wide awake, she thought, as she had bleakly thought so many times since Dallas had left, *I have no choice.* The thought gave her no comfort, and she had terrible nightmares of drowning. It was the first time she'd had such dreams since after she and Dallas had been in the wreck of the *Missouri Dream.*

Robbie brought her breakfast, and Julienne picked at it. She didn't have much appetite. Soon Robbie returned to help her dress, for since the men had started working on the *River Queen,* and Lyle came to the boat every single day, Julienne always wore her good clothes, at-home receiving dresses or afternoon promenade dresses. She had had to forego the hoop skirt, though. She had tried it the first day and she had found that everywhere she went she was subject to getting paint on it, or wood glue, or caught on a nail or a piece of lumber. One man, lumbering behind her with an enormous crate on his shoulder, had accidentally stepped on her skirt and her hoop skirt had come very close to coming untied and falling down. Julienne had fled, but not before she heard Ritter Kahn cursing the man and three solid whacks from his stick.

Lyle called at about two o'clock, and she met him in the ballroom. He was dressed finely, as always, with a tan satin vest, a gleaming white shirt, and a dark brown chocolate-colored frock coat. "Have you met the new servants yet?" That morning six Negros, two women and four men, had come to the boat, telling Caesar and Libby that they were the new servants. The women were cooks and maids, and the men were going to serve as servants to the male passengers and as waiters at meals.

"Yes, I have met them," Julienne said, frowning. "You know, we don't have slaves on the boat, Lyle. Caesar and Libby have been free for more than five years now."

He laughed, a manly guffaw that normally Julienne found attractive. Today she found it rather uncouth. "Julienne, my dear, that just shows that you're not a very good businesswoman. You never pay for labor if you can afford to buy a slave. They belong to me, and I'm loaning them to you. That way, they're free, to you. And so you won't have to use my money to pay them."

He had been saying things such as that, and they made Julienne uneasy. She had thought that once she put up her steamboat as security for a loan, the money she got would be *her* money. But Lyle kept talking about *his* money, and somehow it made Julienne feel cheapened, as if she had indeed been bought and was being paid for.

He didn't seem to notice her discomfort, for he took her arm and said, "Let's go down to the main deck. I want to introduce you to your new crew."

"But I don't want a new crew," Julienne protested. "I want the old one."

"You can keep the three men you have, Julienne. But of course you must have always known that three men is not a crew, it's three slaves. To run this boat right you have to have at least six crewmen, three firemen, a first and second mate, three engineers, two pilots, and a captain."

"That many!" Julienne blurted out. "But why?"

As if he were explaining to a rather dull child, he said slowly, "Because that way you can run twenty-four hours a day. Three eight-hour shifts for the engine room and firebox, two twelve-hour shifts for the pilots. No passenger boat can afford to stop every twelve hours for a pilot to rest."

"Oh, I see," Julienne said uncertainly. "I suppose that they are all going to cost a great deal of money?"

"Don't worry about it, we'll talk about it later." They had reached the main deck, where a group of men stood just inside the main cargo doors. When Julienne and Lyle walked up, they turned and removed their hats and bowed.

Lyle said, "Gentlemen? Please welcome Miss Ashby, she's come to visit her new crew." Turning to Julienne, he said, "I have a surprise for you. Of course you remember Mr. Tisdale. Well, he's going to be your new captain."

Julienne remembered his cousin from when they had dined at his home. He was a man of about forty, nice-looking in a feminine sort of way. He had blond hair, blue eyes, and a thin blond mustache. He had a very subservient air toward his cousin. Nervously he bowed over her hand and mumbled civilities.

Lyle continued, "And of course you already know Mr. Kahn. He's your new first mate."

"Yes, I know him," Julienne said icily. "And the *River Queen* already has a first mate, Lyle. Your pardon, of course, Mr. Kahn."

"Of course," he muttered, with a small mocking bow. His cruel features mirrored a sort of condescending amusement.

"I understand, Julienne, but Mr. Kahn has a lot of experience supervising work crews. It really doesn't matter what type of crew it is, as long as a man can manage them well."

Julienne turned to look up at him, her dark eyes stormy. "Lyle, Ring Macklin is the first mate of the *River Queen*. That's all there is to it."

"All right, Julienne," he said with a forced smile, and then he introduced her to Nathan Killingsworth. "He's our first pilot. He was second on the *Columbia Lady*, but I've promoted him."

He was a severe-looking man, about five-ten, slender and wiry. He had nondescript brown hair, but his eyes were a cold gray. Unsmiling, he bent over Julienne's hand and said, "Pleasure, ma'am."

"Mr. Killingsworth, my brother had started to learn the river with Dal—with our last pilot. I hope you'll continue to teach him, he seems to have a knack for it, and—"

He interrupted her impatiently. "I don't take cub pilots, Miss Ashby. They're just a nuisance."

"It's her brother, he's an owner," Lyle said in a warning tone. "You'll take him."

Killingsworth looked icily angry, but he merely said, "Sure, Mr. Dennison. You're the boss."

With outrage Julienne was thinking, *No, I'm the boss*, but before she could frame anything to say, Lyle was taking her arm and leading her back up the steps to the Texas deck again. "You don't need to meet the roughnecks," Lyle said. "Your second pilot won't be here until tomorrow. But I've got very good news, Julienne. I've already got the *River Queen* a load to New Orleans. We've got all of the staterooms filled, a full cargo, and thirty deck passages."

"Really, Lyle?" Julienne said now excited. "When do we leave?"

"August 1. In three days."

"Oh, that's wonderful, Lyle!" she said happily. "So soon!"

They reached the doors leading to the stateroom hall, and Lyle turned to her. "Of course, you do know, Julienne, that you're going to have to pay the captain and the pilots their salary for the month ahead, not after the month is over. That's customary."

"Oh," Julienne said doubtfully. "And—how much, exactly, are we paying the pilots and the captain? No more than the 'customary' amount, I hope."

"No, we got them at the going rates. Two hundred dollars for the captain and three hundred fifty for the pilots."

"Nine hundred dollars!" Julienne blurted out. "But—" She started to object, but she couldn't think of anything to object to. Dallas had told her a long time ago that pilots were commanding between three and four hundred dollars a month. She had no idea what captains made—in truth, she didn't even know what captains *did* except mingle with passengers—so she could hardly object to anything that Lyle told her.

"Don't worry, I've got the money," he said to Julienne reassuringly. He took her hand and squeezed it, and Julienne thought that he might have actually tried to kiss her, right there in broad daylight, except there were still men in the ballroom painting the window frames. "I wish we could go out tonight, but I'm afraid I have a previous engagement. I'll see you tomorrow, then?"

"Yes. Yes, tomorrow," she said in some confusion. He left, and she fled to her room. As she thought over the last eight days, and the things that had happened, and some of the things that Lyle had said, and Ritter Kahn and Nathan Killingsworth, and the slaves that the *River Queen* now had, dark and frightening thoughts began to grow in her mind. Moving very slowly, as if she were an elderly woman, she opened the bottom drawer of the little chest and took out a sheaf of papers, folded into thirds. It was her contract with Lyle Dennison.

She skimmed over the first page, which she had already read, when she signed the contract. But she had not read the entire thing; Lyle had told her that it was eleven pages of legalese, and that the payments were going to be ninety-four dollars and forty-two cents per month. As she read, she realized with a shock that the term of the contract was for ten years. She would have to pay one hundred dollars a month for ten years to pay this loan off? With dread she kept reading, and on the very last page, she drew in a ragged breath and let it out in a moan.

Rising, she stumbled to her bedside and fell to her knees, burying her face in her crossed arms. "Oh, Lord God, what have I done? How could I have been so blind? Oh, please forgive me, Lord! Right now that's all I care about. You are all I have, only You are faithful and true, and I think I really know it and believe it this time. Whatever happens, if we lose the *Queen*, if I never see Dallas again, if by my stupidity I've lost everything for my family and we are desolate, I will cling only to You." Julienne prayed for long hours and finally fell into bed and slept better than she had slept for weeks.

DARCY LOOKED DOWN AT the palms of his hands. He had worked blisters on them but finally they had gone away, and he had the beginning of calluses. He had never done manual labor before, and he didn't much care for it now. But he had learned a lot about steamboats, and now he was seriously considering becoming a pilot. And he knew good pilots knew a lot about engines, so he still came down to watch Rev work, and he even pitched in sometimes. Today they had two new pilots that Rev was breaking in, showing them all the features of the *River Queen's*

engine, cooing over it as if it were a cute kitten.
The two new engineers, both gruff men, one of
about thirty and one of about forty, said very little,
but it was plain they were interested. They began
talking about some of the new parts that Lyle
Dennison had ordered, and Rev came over to talk
to Darcy.

"They don't seem to be quite as helplessly in love
with that engine as you are, Rev," he joked.

"Ah, they seem like good engineers. Neither one
of them knows the Lord, though. I'm going to have
to do some heavy praying for them," he said airily.

"Yeah, put in a request to the Big Man Upstairs
for me, too, would you? Ask him to smite Ritter
Kahn down dead," Darcy said sarcastically.

"He's not a godly man, that's for sure and certain.
He really lays out on these new black crewmen,
and I don't like that one bit. Doubt the Lord does
either, though it's not my place to go asking Him to
up and kill somebody dead."

"I know, I know," Darcy rasped. "Just joking.
Sort of."

Just then they heard shouting up in the boiler
room, and both Darcy and Rev hurried up to see
what was going on.

One of the blacks who was hauling wood from
the deck into the firebox stood cowering, while
Kahn was yelling in his face. "You're as slow as a
half-dead mule, boy! When your fireman calls for
wood, you get up and move!" Suddenly he reached
out and struck him with his fist. The black man was

small, and his head flew backwards, the cut on his eyebrow gushing scarlet blood.

"Please don't do that, Mr. Kahn," Jesse protested. "I ain't needin' that wood in split seconds, I give 'em plenty of notice 'fore it's time to load her up."

Darcy said angrily, "You don't have to hit these men, Kahn. They'll work without getting beaten every time they turn around."

"You keep your mouth shut, girlie boy, you may be an Ashby but you got no business down here. As you for you, Fire-boy, I don't need any help to run this crew."

Jesse had gone to kneel by the man and look at his eye. "This here's a bad cut, Mr. Ashby. I think it's going to need a stitch or two."

Kahn pulled the stick that he carried at his side out of his belt, swung it and struck Jesse across his broad back. The blow of the leaded weapon drove Jesse to the deck. "You got no word to say to nobody but me down here, boy!" he snarled. He raised the stick again.

Coolly Darcy reached out and picked up a shovel. He swung it as he would a baseball bat and it hit Kahn squarely in the back of the head. He collapsed instantly, dropping his stick.

"That made a funny *thunk*," Rev observed. "*Whanged* almost like his head was made outta rock."

"I thought it sounded more like a *whang*, like hitting an iron skillet," Darcy said.

They went to help Jesse up, who protested that he was fine. "Good, if you're sure you're okay," Darcy said. "Take this man to Doc Needles to get sewed up, will you, Jesse? Here's some money."

They stood up and looked around. All of the new crewmen were blacks, and they stared at Kahn's prone figure with fear on every face. With a disgusted grunt Darcy reached down and picked up Kahn's stick, walked through the cargo area out to the main deck, and tossed the stick into the river. Returning, he and Rev stared down at Kahn solemnly.

"Think he's hurt bad?" Rev asked.

"I don't know, and don't much care. I'd hate for him to die right here in our firebox, though. Trash up the place."

Julienne came running in then. She had seen Jesse taking the bleeding man up to the boardwalk. "What's happened, Darcy? Oh," she said when she saw Kahn lying face down on the floor. "What happened to him?"

"I hit him. With a shovel," Darcy said helpfully.

Julienne studied him. "Well, he's not dead. I can hear him snorting. What's he doing down here anyway? I told Lyle that Ring is the first mate, and we didn't need Kahn here."

"I don't know," Darcy said. "I'm so used to seeing him walking around beating people, it just slipped my mind to ask his exact position."

Rev shrugged. "I don't know. He's never come in the engine room and hit anybody."

One of the crewmen spoke up in a frightened whisper, "Mr. Ashby, suh?"

Darcy turned. The young man that spoke was stout, and looked like he was about fourteen years old. "Yes? I'm sorry, I don't know your name."

"I'm Tommy, suh. Mr. Kahn, there, he tole us that Mr. Dennison made him crew chief. I didn't know what that means, except that he must be our boss."

"Are you a slave, Tommy?" Julienne asked abruptly.

"No, ma'am, I works on the river, have for five years now, most always hauling wood for the firemen. And I ain't never heard of no crew chief on no steamer." He was growing more confident since he had Darcy's and Julienne's interest.

"That's because there's no such thing," Rev said dryly. "First mate is boss of the crew, that's what a first mate is."

"Then he's fired. Again," Julienne said with spirit.

He started twitching, then moving, then groaning. He turned over and sat up, rubbing the back of his head. "Who hit me!" he roared.

"I did. And you're fired. Again," Darcy said. "Get off this boat right now, and don't come back."

He scrambled to his feet. "You can't do that!" he said, his slablike face turning scarlet.

"Oh yes I can, and so can my sister. Now we've both fired you, Kahn. You leave right now, or I'm going to have you arrested. By the real police, I mean."

Cursing under his breath, he walked slowly to the door. Abruptly he turned and demanded, "Give me my stick!"

Darcy shrugged. "I tossed it in the river. I suggest you throw yourself off the boat to look for it."

Kahn's eyes narrowed and he said in a menacing undertone, "You've got no idea what you're in for, Ashby. You're going to pay for this." He made a crude mock bow to Julienne. "Be seeing you soon, Miss Ashby."

"What did he mean by that?" Darcy asked Julienne. "That didn't sound good at all."

"I'm not sure," she said uncertainly.

Rev said soberly, "Nothing good about that man that I can see. I'm going to pray hard for your protection, Miss Julienne. I'm thinking you may need it."

KAHN WENT STRAIGHT TO Lyle Dennison. He told the story, and he was still in a rage. "I'm not putting up with that Ashby pup! Kicking me off that floating pile of junk!"

Lyle shrugged. "Forget Ashby and the *River Queen*, Kahn, you've got other things to do."

"I got unfinished business on the *Queen*," he muttered.

Lyle pulled a cigar out, put it in his lips, and then lit it with a match. He puffed some blue smoke in the air and said, "Don't worry about it, Kahn. If you're stuck on working the crew on the *River Queen*, just give it a little time. Then I'll put you back on her."

Kahn looked confused. "All this money you put in her? But you didn't buy her, did you?"

"Not really," he answered lazily. "At least, not yet."

The truth was that Lyle really was more attracted to Julienne Ashby than any woman he had ever met. He even cared for her, in his own way. He respected her because he knew she was untouched, and that only increased his desire to possess her. But he had no intention of marrying her.

Lyle Dennison was a cunning man. He had figured it all out, within moments after he had offered Julienne a loan and he saw that she would take it. The bills he had submitted to her were, in reality, just under two thousand dollars. With the new crew wages and salaries, she was going to owe him at least nine thousand dollars. And Lyle had taken very great care to talk and explain continuously to Julienne as she signed the contract, and it had worked. She had never seen the $9,000 balloon payment due in three months. On October 19, 1855, Lyle Dennison would own the *River Queen*. He was sure that Julienne would come "under his protection," as they so delicately put it in England, before she would let her family be thrown out on the street. And Lyle Dennison was a man that would do that, literally, without a second thought.

Now he continued, "You don't really need to know the details, Kahn. All you have to know is—" he took another puff and blew smoke out in a long stream—"at the end of the story, I'm going to get the boat, and I'm going to get the girl. And you can do whatever you want on the *River Queen*, and I can do whatever I want with the girl. And then we'll both be very, very happy."

Chapter Twenty

It was early afternoon when Dallas Bronte came back to Natchez-Under-the-Hill. Slowly he walked down the boardwalk. When he passed the Blue Moon Saloon, he heard the tinkling of the tinny piano and someone singing off-key inside. A sadness gripped him as he thought of how Lulie had died and a poignant wish formed in him. *If I'd only known then, Lord, what I know now, maybe I could have helped her more.* But that was past and gone so he put it behind him.

When he came to Inman & Sons, he went in and Mr. Inman greeted him in a friendly manner. "Do you know when the *River Queen* is due back, Mr. Inman?"

He answered, "She's due in today. She's carrying a load from New Orleans for me. I know when you were piloting her, she wasn't late. Don't know about this new pilot, it's her first haul since she's been all fixed up."

"Thank you, sir," he said courteously, and left. He walked down to Rumble and Wensel Groceries and Provisions, went in, and said hello to Mr. Rumble and Mr. Wensel, and some other acquaintances who welcomed him back warmly. No one asked him any questions, and he knew that the story about Lyle Dennison and Julienne Ashby going into partnership together would be all over the river, and they could guess the rest. He bought a sarsaparilla, went outside, and took a seat in one of the straight chairs that river men often sat on to watch the steamers come in and out.

He didn't have to wait long. The *River Queen* came steaming in, shining in the sun, steam whistle blaring. She looked beautiful, like a brand-new boat. She was painted an immaculate white, all of the railings were new, with intricate gingerbread designs atop. Thin red stripes were painted all along her decks, and the paddle wheel was painted a bright cheery red. Her old stacks had been replaced with newer, higher ones, and were topped with ironwork that looked like crowns. *River Queen* was proudly painted on her side in crimson intricate script.

He watched her pull in with a critical eye. The pilot was showing off, bringing her in too fast, making the firemen pile on a big draw of steam to make the sudden reverse required to bring her to a stop. He watched the new crew lower the landing stages, with Ring shouting out crisp orders. Passengers came filing out, well-dressed men and women who headed straight up the street to the harbormaster's office to await carriages and buggies. After that the deck passengers came out, workingmen and women with children, dressed in poor clothing. They mostly started to walk up Silver Street.

The two pilots hurried down the outside stairwells. Dallas recognized one of them, Nathan Killingsworth. He was known to be a good pilot but he did run boats hard. The other pilot was a young man that Dallas didn't know. Both of them headed directly for the Blue Moon Saloon.

After the passengers were gone, wagons started pulling up to her gangplanks, and the crew and drivers started unloading. Dallas was a little surprised that the *River Queen* was carrying a load of liquor, cases and cases of it. But then again, he realized, Lyle Dennison was probably arranging their loads for them. Somehow he didn't think that Aunt Leah, or even Roseann Ashby, would care much for hauling a ton of liquor to Natchez-Under-the-Hill.

Dallas watched and waited, but none of the Ashbys came out on deck or left the boat. Once the unloading was done, the new crew left, but he saw that Rev, Jesse, and Ring were still on the boat. Dallas stood up, picked up his knapsack, and went down to the *River Queen*'s berth. He walked up the landing stage, and heard Ring and Jesse talking in the boiler room, but he really wanted to see the Ashbys first. He climbed the stairs to the Texas deck and went into the ballroom. Inside the double doors, he stopped in amazement.

Crystal chandeliers had been lit, even though there were no passengers on the boat. He savored the rich glow of the walnut paneling, the almost luminescent floor of blond ironwood polished to a high degree, and the painted frames of the windows that lined each wall, admitting the last feeble golden gleams of the sun. The room was filled with round dining tables with white tablecloths, and chairs padded in sky-blue velvet.

He was still standing there, staring around, when he heard his name called. He saw Carley running full-speed, so fast that her pigtails seemed to stretch out behind her. She was laughing, and he dropped his bundle, stooped down, and grabbed her. He tossed her high in the air, caught her and then hugged her.

"Dallas, you came back!" she said in her high, little-girl's voice. "Skillygalee, you were gone forever!"

"New word, huh? I like it. Where is everybody?"

"They're coming, we're about to have dinner. You're going to eat with us, aren't you? And move back into the captain's cabin, he's such a little ponce, I wish he'd go away and you'd be captain. And pilot. Okay? You'll stay, won't you, please, please, Dallas?"

"Where'd you hear the word *ponce*?" he demanded, but her answer was lost as Roseann and Leah came in, talking quietly. When they saw Dallas, they both stopped and stared at him in surprise. Then they hurried to meet him, and to his surprise both women insisted on kissing him on the cheek in the midst of their warm greetings. They both started asking questions at once, almost as imperiously as Carley had.

Finally Leah said, "Roseann, let's stop gibbering like two pecking hens at Mr. Bronte, we'll scare him off again. Please, Mr. Bronte, won't you join us for dinner? It should be—"

Julienne came through the door, halted in mid-stride, her eyes widening. She and Dallas stared at each other for a few moments. Then she picked up her skirts, ran, and threw herself into his arms. In shock Dallas clasped her to him. Julienne tried to say something, but instead she just burst into tears.

"Skillygalee," Carley said in amazement.

Roseann and Leah glanced at each other, and Leah said, "Perhaps we'd better . . ."

"Yes, of course," Roseann said quickly. "Come along, Carley."

"But I want to listen to what Julienne and Dallas are going to say!" she complained.

Roseann took her hand and said, "Yes, dear, so do I. But it wouldn't be polite, so let's go to my stateroom and we can have our dinner there."

". . . AND so I got saved that night, and baptized the next morning," Dallas said quietly. "And I stayed with the Williamses for two nights, but I kept on remembering what my grandfather had told me, about getting off by myself, being completely alone without distractions, to really seek the Lord. So I went back to my old camp, and stayed there, and read the Bible, and prayed. Wandered around a lot, just thinking about things."

"What made you decide to come back?" Julienne asked.

He hesitated, then shook his head a little. "Funny how I've never thought I was a dishonest man, but I don't tell the truth all the time. Sometimes it's hard to just say what you mean, tell people what you really want." He looked straight into her eyes and said, "I feel like the Lord was telling me to come back. I feel like He wanted me to come back to the *River Queen*. And I hope I can get my old job back again."

Julienne laughed, a delightful sound that made Dallas grin. "I've heard you better be careful what you pray for. I'm offering you a job as pilot of the *River Queen*, Dallas. Hope you're ready for what you're getting into."

He started to answer, but just then Robbie slipped through the door and came to their table. They looked up, and she curtsied prettily. "I'll just clear, if you're finished, Mr. Bronte, Miss Ashby."

"Hm? Oh, yes, thank you, Robbie," Julienne said.

Actually, Robbie had served them dinner and dessert and coffee, but they had been so absorbed in talking that neither of them had noticed her at all. Now, as she gathered up their empty pie plates, she said softly, "Welcome back, Mr. Bronte. We all hope you'll stay for awhile."

"I plan to," he said happily. "Thanks, Robbie. You know, you look real pretty. Have you done something to your hair?"

She blushed and said, "No, sir, except I just quit winding it up so tight, it was giving me headaches. That's all." Her hair was done in a soft figure-eight chignon, and she had let some soft short curls escape around her face. She disappeared back through the galley door.

Julienne blurted out, "I saw you kiss her."

"What?" Dallas said blankly.

"Kiss. Robbie. The first night she was here."

"Oh, that! I had forgotten about that. But I didn't kiss her, she kissed me, to tell me thank you. Girl hasn't said half a dozen words to me since, except for 'Yes, Mr. Bronte' and 'No, Mr. Bronte.'"

"You forgot? How could you forget?" Julienne demanded.

"Because it didn't mean anything," Dallas said gravely. "She'd had a real bad time, she was scared, and I think I'm the first man she ever met that had a truthful kind word for her. She thanked me, and I guess I thought about it for a few days, but it didn't take long to realize that she's just a kid. I'm not interested in kids. And she's not interested in me."

Julienne listened, unmoving. Then she relaxed and said, "No, she's not, Dallas. She's in love with Revelation Brown. That's why she's letting herself look pretty again."

"She is? How's Rev taking it?"

"He's scared to death," she answered, her dark eyes sparkling. "But he'll live. It's his own fault. He started taking her to church, and she got saved, and then they had lots to talk about, and there you are."

"Good ol' Rev," he said affectionately. "He deserves a good woman. I'll be glad when I can tell him about me finding the Lord. You'll probably be able to hear him whoop up in Natchez. But I don't want to talk to the crew yet, Julienne. Now that I've told you about me, I want to know everything about you and the *River Queen*. If you want to talk to me, I mean," he added quickly.

"Oh, Dallas, it's an answer to prayer," she said. "I'm so ashamed, but I want to tell you everything. Don't worry, I don't expect you to rescue me again. I just want so much to talk to you, like we used to."

"I want that too," he said warmly. "I've missed you, Julienne." He reached out his hand, and after a moment she put her hand in his, and they kept holding hands as they talked.

"I've missed you too, Dallas. Oh, you're not going to believe how stupid, how wrong, how—"

"Don't do that," he interrupted her. "Whatever mistakes you've made, or whatever wrongs you've done, have you asked the Lord to forgive you for them?"

"Yes, I have," she said firmly. "And He has."

"Then you're forgiven, and He's forgotten. What's past is past, and what's done is done. All we have to do now is ask Him how to go on from this day, now. So please just tell me about the situation, without blaming yourself, and then we'll figure out what to do."

Greatly comforted, Julienne started talking. She told him about the loan, and how happy she'd been to get it, and how she had felt. Then she told him about the exorbitant expenses, and she saw his face darken, but she kept on talking in a smooth, relaxed manner. She explained about the night she had realized that Lyle had been using her and lying to her, and about how she had finally read the contract and found out about the balloon payment due in October. "It's impossible that we would be able to come up with $9,000 by then," she said with the first sign of unhappiness.

"With God all things are possible," Dallas quoted. "My grandfather used to quote that so much it stopped meaning a thing to me. But it means everything to me now. It's true, Julienne. I believe that the Lord will give us a way to get out of this predicament."

"I don't know," Julienne said softly, clutching his hand harder. "I really have gotten over feeling like God is going to punish me for what I've done. But I also know that sometimes people sin, and God forgives them, but there are still consequences. God will not make you pay for your sins, but this world will. It's still possible that by October Lyle Dennison will own this boat, and he'll kick me and my family right out onto that muddy street out there."

"You do understand, don't you, Julienne, that that's not what he's planning? No, he'll make you an offer so that you and your family will be taken care of," Dallas said harshly.

Julienne sighed deeply. "I didn't understand anything about that part of it, you know. Now I do, because I've talked to Darcy. He's the only one I've told about this. He's been helping me, Dallas. I'm so proud of him." She gave him a wry smile. "He explained to me about what Lyle was going to do when the payment comes due. Then he told me that he'd challenge him to a duel, shoot him dead like the skunk he is, and all our troubles would be over with."

Dallas smiled back at her reassuringly. "I don't believe it'll come to that. What you say is true about the consequences of sin, Julienne. But many times we can humbly ask the Lord to deliver us from evil, and He will. I'm going to believe that He will make all of this right, for your family, for the *River Queen*, for Rev and Robbie and all of us who care about you and your family."

Julienne leaned closer to him and asked, "And what about us, Dallas? Will the Lord make it right for us?"

"I don't know the answer to that right now, Julienne," he said honestly. "Do you?"

"No," she said, "I have my wishes, and my dreams, but I don't truly know His will right now."

Dallas grinned. "Maybe saying just the plain truth isn't as hard as I thought it was."

"I'm simply astounded to discover how smart you've become in the last few weeks," Julienne teased him.

"Ain't I?" Then he grew serious, and he went on, "Okay, Boss, I accept your job offer. And I know that means we've got about ten thousand more things to talk about. But I have a suggestion first."

"What's that?"

"Would you pray with me, Julienne?" he asked simply.

She smiled at him, bowed her head, and said, "Dearest Lord Jesus, thank You so much that Dallas has come home."

LYLE DENNISON SHOWED UP at the *Queen* the next day at two o'clock, as always. He was surprised—and not pleasantly by any means—to see Dallas Bronte come forward to stop him at the foot of the gangplank. Julienne and Darcy followed him.

"What do you think you're doing here, Bronte?" he demanded roughly.

"I work here. What do you think you're doing here?" Dallas retorted.

Dennison's mouth twisted, and he spoke over Dallas's shoulder. "Julienne, what do you think you're doing? He's nothing but a lowdown drunk river rat! You've got two good pilots! Unless he's just roughnecking for you," he sneered.

"I'm standing right in front of you, Dennison, you got anything to say about me, you say it to me," Dallas said.

Ignoring him, Dennison said, "Julienne? You owe me an explanation."

"No, Lyle, all I owe you is nine thousand dollars," she said dryly.

"And you're going to get it, too, in just a couple of weeks," Dallas said evenly. "In the meantime, you're not welcome on this boat. Just leave this family alone, Dennison. From now on."

"Not welcome on this boat! I'll have you know I paid for all the shiny new toys on this boat! I'll come on board her any time I please!" he shouted, his craggy face turning red.

"You did not pay for anything, Dennison," Darcy said in his usual lazy, bored tone. "My sister did, with money that you loaned her, and put into her bank account. At that time it became her money. She could have taken it out and made a bonfire with it, and it wouldn't have been any of your business. Just like the *Queen* isn't any of your business, Dennison. I'm not as polite as Mr. Bronte, so I'm telling you to get your foot off of my sister's gangplank, go get on that horse, and let us see your backside for the last time!"

Dennison stood unmoving, his foot planted solidly on the gangplank. "I'll ruin you, Bronte. This boat will never get one crumb of freight again, and not a single soul will set foot in a stateroom."

"Wrong," Dallas said succinctly. "I've been busy this morning. Miss Ashby gave me the shipping schedule you gave her, and I've already been around to all the agents and shippers and confirmed our freight. As for passengers, if they cancel, we'll get more. Easy pickings in summertime for a fine boat like the *River Queen*."

As Dallas talked, Dennison's face got uglier and uglier. "Well, you have been busy scuttling around, haven't you, River Rat? Had your first drink yet this morning?"

"It's afternoon," Julienne said with disdain. "And those insults to Mr. Bronte are real old news, and frankly, you're boring me. Please leave. Now."

"All right, I'll leave now," he grunted, "but I'll be back, right here, at eight o'clock in the morning on October 19. If you don't hand me nine thousand dollars right then, the *River Queen* will be my boat. And you and your fine family, and especially you, Mr. Bronte, will be kicked right out into the street."

"I told you," Dallas said with exaggerated patience, "you're going to have your nine thousand dollars the first week of September, Dennison."

He laughed, a brittle sound. "Where are you going to get that kind of money? No one in his right mind would loan any of you nine thousand dollars!"

"You did," Dallas said mildly. "But that's beside the point. Go check Inman & Sons office, Dennison. They were just putting up the handbills when I was there. There's going to be a steamer race the first of September, and the winning purse is ten thousand dollars. And the *River Queen* is going to win it."

CHAPTER TWENTY-ONE

Despite the still-scorching weather, New Orleans had turned out on September 1 to watch the beginning of the Great Race. If she was known for anything, the Crescent City was famous for being able to celebrate. People came from all over the United States and even from other countries to wander the sections of New Orleans that offered everything for the tourists.

A platform had been built on the wharf, decked out with bunting and with flags flying high overhead. A hot fast breeze whipped them, and they snapped and popped while beneath them the mayor of New Orleans and the governor of Louisiana gave pompous speeches ringing with patriotic phrases.

Bands had been playing, and there had been dancing in the streets, and bets were being made on every corner on the winner of the Great Race. The newspapers had taken up the drama of it all, and not just in the South, but all over the country.

From their position in the pilothouse of the *Queen*, Dallas and Julienne watched the festivities and people coming and going on board the other ships in the race. Julienne said, "The whole country is talking about this race, Dallas."

"They sure are. Even people that don't normally gamble are getting in on this action. Some people are betting their last dime on the winner."

She turned to him and studied him for a moment and then asked, "Dallas, is there any chance that we can win this race? I mean, all of these other ships are bigger than the *Queen*."

"The bigger the better," Dallas smiled. He reached out and took her hand. "Bigger doesn't mean faster. They have bigger engines, but then they've got a lot more weight for those engines to push."

"But some of them are side-wheelers. They've got two paddle wheels. Doesn't that mean they can go faster?"

"Not really. The paddle wheels on those side-wheelers are very narrow. Single paddle wheels on the back of the stern are three times as large as those."

"Then why do they have them on the side?"

"It makes the ship more maneuverable. You can back one and turn the other forward and make a sharp turn. But that doesn't give you an advantage in a straight-out full-on race."

Dallas pulled out his watch and said, "Only thirty minutes before the race starts. I need to go down and talk to Jesse and Rev and Ring. You want to come with me? Or you want to go stay with your family?"

"I'm coming with you," she decided.

They went down to the boiler room, where the crew were busy hauling firewood and loading it into the furnaces, getting the boilers up to a heavy steam. Jesse was directing them and studying the gauges.

"All set, Jesse?" Dallas asked.

"Yes, sir. Got four whole cases of that rich pine."

"Good, Jesse, that's really good. He turned, walked over to a wooden case, picked up a small piece, and handed it to Julienne. "See this? Smell of it."

She took the chunk of wood he handed her and said, "It smells strong, like turpentine."

"Well, that's about what it is. Your hands are probably sticky now."

She handed the wood back and asked, "Yes, they are. What is it?"

"Well, most of the time we use hardwood as fuel on these boats. It burns longer, and you don't have to stop as often for wood. Besides, it's easier to get than this kind of wood. We call this rich pine. I can remember when I was a boy my folks would send me out to collect it. You don't need any paper or anything to start it. Look." He pulled a match out of his pocket, struck it on one of the boilers, and held it under the piece of wood. Almost at once it began to glow and then burst into flame, and he dropped it into the furnace. "It's like a torch. It's full of turpentine, and you know how that stuff burns."

"Why is that better than hardwood?"

"It burns quick and it burns hot. If you stay up in the pilothouse with me," Dallas said, "you'll hear me call for quick steam. Rich pine will blaze up and get that water in the boiler to boiling almost at once. More steam, faster engine, faster paddle wheel, win the race," he said. He was excited, his dark eyes alight, his face alive with enthusiasm.

Julienne couldn't help but smile at him. "Then why doesn't everyone use it?"

"It's tricky stuff. It burns quicker, so you have to stop more often for wood. And it's not like chopping down an oak tree. You have to hunt for rich pine."

They went back to the engine room, where Rev and Ring were checking and double-checking the engine. "You know she's in perfect shape, Rev, it's pretty much up to her now. If we'll just keep her all steamed up and happy, she'll come through for us, all right. Ring, you keep a sharp eye out on Rev and Jesse and the crew. Anything happens, any little thing, you let me know, all right?"

"Sure, Captain Dallas," Ring said playfully. Darcy had happily fired Francis Tisdale, and they hadn't bothered to hire another captain. All of them had been calling Dallas the captain.

"Well, the Lord be with us," Rev said, grinning. "I've been saying my prayers. I usually don't pray over sporting events, but this is different. I believe you've been taken in usury, ma'am, and it's only righteous that the usurer get his due and not a penny more."

"Thank you, Rev. That's kind of you," Julienne said with some confusion. When they left she asked Dallas, "What did that mean?"

"I dunno. But if it made Rev pray for us to win, then I'm all for it."

He took her hand again as they walked up the stairs. "Are you sure you want me in the wheelhouse, Dallas?" Julienne asked. "Are you sure I won't be a distraction?"

He grinned. "I'm sure I want you in the wheelhouse, and I'm sure you'll be a distraction. A welcome one."

They went into the pilothouse and waited. Dallas took his stance behind the wheel, resting his hands on it like he had done thousands of times before. He savored the feel of it, the growl of the engine just beneath them. He could feel the *River Queen* straining to go.

A cannon sounded, and immediately Dallas ran the backing bell. The *Queen* backed up obediently, and just at the right moment he rang the forward bell, and she surged forward.

There were six boats in the race, and all of them battled to get away from the wharf, the side-wheelers turning neatly and the stern-wheelers backing and filling, as the *Queen* did. But still, in mere minutes they were all six heading up north.

"Why don't you try to get in front of them all, Dallas?"

"Going to be a little bit tight here. Six boats this close together, it's too easy to have a collision. Happens a lot, even when you're not racing."

He spoke prophetically for just ahead of them the *Oscar McCoy* was rammed by the *Lady Gay*. The *McCoy* was left behind leaking, the captain shaking his fist at the *Lady Gay* as she trundled by him.

"And so there are five," Dallas murmured. He rang the bell twice, his and Jesse's private signal for "open her up," and she began to gain speed. Dallas nodded with satisfaction. "I see the *Columbia Lady* running for the front of the pack. It's two hundred sixty-eight miles from New Orleans to Natchez. We'll let 'em slug it out for awhile and then we'll pass them."

JULIENNE WAS ENJOYING THE race. The boats were scattered out now. Two were almost out of sight, the slower ones. "They'll never make it, they've already fallen too far behind," Dallas observed. "Looks like it's us, the *Lady Gay*, the *Princess of Orleans*, and the *Columbia Lady*'s still in front."

Darcy came up to join them. "Do you think we can catch her, Dallas?"

"Oh, sure. She's going to have to stop for wood soon, probably at Baton Rouge. That's when we'll make our move."

"What move?" Julienne asked curiously.

"We have a plan, Miss Julienne," Dallas said jovially. "But you're just going to have to wait and see what it is."

Sure enough, when they reached the port of Baton Rouge, all three of the other boats slowed, then turned into the port. "Going for wood, just like you said, Dallas," Darcy said with satisfaction.

"Aren't we going to have to stop for wood?" Julienne asked.

"We're going to do it a little bit different," Dallas said. "You'll see."

They kept steaming along at full speed, until Baton Rouge was far behind them. Finally Dallas said under his breath, "Right on time."

He slowed the ship down, guiding it carefully in a ruler-straight line. Darcy stood at the starboard window, watching, and he said, "You've got it, Dallas. You want me to go down and help?"

"No, you take the wheel. I'll go see about it," Dallas said, and as soon as Darcy stepped up he ran out of the pilothouse.

Julienne had been sitting on the lazy bench, and she hopped up to stare out the right window. She saw a barge, loaded with wood, that was shoved off from shore and was being poled along by a number of strong-looking men. Dallas appeared on the side of the main deck, along with the fire crew. Jesse threw the barge a line and then the crew pulled it alongside. At once the crew in the wood boat began throwing chunks of wood on board, which was grabbed and stacked by the members of the crew. The *River Queen* never did stop, and Dallas was back in just a few minutes. "I'll take her back now, Darcy. You did fine. You know this part of the river is tricky, but in a couple of hours you know we'll be past Point 142 and there's about two hours worth of straight easy steaming, and then I'm going to let you take over. You ready for it?"

"You're not leaving me alone, are you?" he asked anxiously.

"'Course not. But I am going to need to sit down on that nice fat new lazy bench and rest and eat something."

"Okay, if you're sure," Darcy said doubtfully.

"Darcy, I would never let you touch that wheel if I wasn't sure of you," he said quietly.

Darcy looked satisfied. "I'm going down to the engine room, see how everything's going. I'll be back about eight o'clock."

After he left Julienne said, "That was a neat trick, with the wood barge, Captain Dallas."

"That was my secret," Dallas said with a grin. "What Rev and Jesse did was set up those fellows at that point on the river. All we had to do was slow down and pull up beside them in the stream and tow 'em upstream while we unloaded the wood. Never had to stop, and now we've got enough wood to get us all the way to Natchez. It'll take the *Columbia* a couple of hours to load up enough wood for that monster. And that, Miss Ashby, is how we're going to win this race."

DARCY CAME UP AT eight, and Dallas gave him the wheel. Robbie brought up a tray, and he and Julienne sat on the lazy bench and ate biscuits and bacon and drank hot tea. When they finished, Dallas laid his head back on the bench and closed his eyes. He and Julienne were holding hands and she sat contentedly in the dark wheelhouse, watching him sleep.

Once she asked quietly, "Darcy, are you nervous?"

He didn't answer for a moment, then he answered in a very low voice so as not to disturb Dallas, "I started to make a joke like I always do. But right now I don't feel like joking. I'm not nervous, not at all. I think maybe it's partly because Dallas believes in me, and partly because I asked Rev to pray for me before I came up here. Now, Jules, don't go thinking I'm going to get all crazy like you and Rev and now Dallas. I just figured it couldn't hurt."

"Okay," she said solemnly. "I won't go thinking you're going to get all crazy." She looked back at Dallas and saw a small smile steal across his lips.

After about an hour and a half, Dallas took over again. Darcy nodded to him in a businesslike way after handing the wheel over to him and left the pilothouse. Julienne went down to the galley, made a pot of strong coffee, and took it up to the pilot-house. She stood by Dallas and held his cup. Every once in a while he'd grab it and take a quick sip. He never looked away from the river.

When he finished, Julienne said, "I think I'll just lie down on the lazy bench for awhile and rest, Dallas."

"Sure you don't want to go to your stateroom and take a good nap?"

"No, I'd rather stay here," she answered.

"Good," he said quietly. "I'm glad."

She had no more than laid down when she heard a loud WHANG and then the engine started sounding *ker-THUNK, ker-THUNK, ker-THUNK!* She jumped up, and Dallas ordered, "Go to the speaking tube, and shout down there and ask what's happening. She's pulling to one side, I can't let go for even a minute."

Frantically Julienne ran to the big tube, rang the bell stridently, and yelled, "Ring? What's happened?"

It was a few seconds before Ring's voice echoed up through the tube. "Rev says we threw the reach rod. He's working on it now."

Even before Dallas could speak, Julienne asked, "Can he fix it?"

They heard Ring's garbled voice as he stepped away from the tube. Then he answered, "Yeah, he's got a spare. But we're gonna have to stop, Dallas. Rev says if we keep going we'll kick out the pitman arm."

"That's bad, isn't it," Julienne said.

"Yeah, that would stop us dead in the water," Dallas answered shortly. He was fighting the wheel, standing on a port-side spoke, for the *Queen* was hitching over to the starboard side. She was slowing, though. "Hang the bells," he grunted. "Yell down there and tell Ring to shut her down so we'll just slow to a stop."

But before Julienne could relay the instructions Ring shouted up, "We're shutting her down, Dallas. Rev says we have to. Should be drifting to a full stop in just a few minutes."

"If I can keep her from grounding out," he said. He was pushing the wheel with all his strength and putting his full weight on one foot on the spoke. Julienne came and climbed up onto the wheel, standing on the spoke right above the one his foot was on. Very slowly the *Queen* drifted away from the dangerously near starboard shore. It seemed like a very long time to Julienne, but actually it was less than a minute that they were out in the middle of the river again. "Step off," Dallas said tersely, and she jumped off the wheel. He managed to do a slight correction, the wheel seeming to turn more easily in his hand. Darcy came running in, and Dallas said, "Kingpin's up. Hold her steady." Then he ran out of the pilothouse.

As the *Queen* wallowed powerless in the water, Darcy kept one hand on the wheel, merely correcting the slight play. The kingpin, the one wrapped in stout leather twine, was pointing straight up, which meant that the rudder was perfectly straight.

Julienne asked, "What happened, Darcy?"

He shrugged, "I don't know, Jules. I was down there in the engine room. I heard what you heard. We threw some rod, and it got everything out of whack."

"Do you have any idea how long it's going to take Rev to fix it?" she asked anxiously.

"Not a clue. But I know this: Rev's probably one of the best engineers on the river, and Dallas Bronte is almost as good. Between the two of them, they'll get it fixed as soon as is humanly possible."

"Dallas? An engineer? I didn't know that."

"He doesn't talk about it much. Rev told me, that's the only way I know. I guess Dallas likes piloting so much that he'd hate to be an engineer. But Dallas Bronte is a real smart man, Jules. You did know that, didn't you?"

"Oh, yes," she said firmly. "I do know that."

They decided not to go down to the engine room, because they knew they would only be in the way. They stood there together, silent and worrying. Then ahead they saw a faint glow and realized it was a light behind them. They looked back, and they saw the sky-high four-decker *Columbia Lady*, every light on the boat lit, speeding towards them. As they watched, she pulled close to the *River Queen*, much too close for safety. But apparently it was just so Lyle Dennison could step out of the pilothouse, stand on the hurricane deck, and shout to the *River Queen* a full two stories beneath him.

"You be careful with her, Julienne! You're never going to beat me now, so she's my ship!"

"Idiot," Darcy said with disgust. "No river man ever calls a steamer a 'ship.' It's like telling someone that your horse is a moose. Two different things, and only morons don't know the difference."

"I wonder if he's right, though," Julienne said worriedly. "We're about four hours out of Natchez, right?"

"Yeah, but don't worry, Jules," Darcy said confidently. "After all, we know that Rev is praying hard for that reach rod right now."

It was about an hour before they could tell that the firemen were building up the steam again. A few minutes later Dallas came back into the wheelhouse. "Thank the Lord for Rev and his obsession with having an extra everything, right down to the last screw. We're going to get the *Queen* back in the race right now." The engines started up, with the old familiar rhythmic *chunk, chunk, chunk* sound.

Dallas took the wheel and said to Darcy, "I just told Jesse to give her everything she's got, and when Rev's ready he's going to holler up at me."

"Everything she's got," Darcy repeated. "What does that mean?"

"Cap the safety valve and use as little water as possible."

Darcy asked hesitantly, "Yeah, that's gonna give us speed, and quickly, but isn't that how boilers blow up?"

"Sometimes," Dallas answered tightly. "I'm praying, Rev's praying, Jesse's praying, Julienne, you pray. Might not be a bad time for you to start, Darcy."

"Don't think so," he said in his old breezy voice. "I'm just going to go down and say 'me, too' to everything Rev says." He walked out.

Dallas grinned. "He's gonna pray. Thank the Lord, we're rolling already!" The *River Queen* had started to move, and she was already picking up speed within the first few revolutions of her paddle wheel.

Julienne wondered how Dallas could smile. She was so deathly worried now that they would lose the race, and all of her old terrible fears came rushing back. "You know that the *Columbia Lady* passed us about an hour ago," she said dispiritedly.

"Yeah, I know. Jesse went out on deck to see her, and he heard what Dennison yelled at you." He couldn't turn to look at her, but he hesitated a minute as if he were searching her face. "Julienne, you're not scared, are you?"

"Yes, I am. Aren't you?"

"No, I'm not scared. God isn't the author of fear, He's our Comforter. Just trust in Him, Julienne. Don't trust in the *River Queen*, or Rev's prayers, or even me. Just trust Him, and no matter what happens, you're going to be blessed, because you're a child of the King."

JESSE WAS PILING ON the steam, even Julienne could tell. They seemed to be flying instead of steaming with a paddle wheel. The acrid smell from the rich pine invaded the pilothouse.

Once Ring called up and said, "Captain, the boilers are getting red. Jesse's worried."

"Tell Jesse I trust him. He knows those boilers like Rev knows that engine. Tell him to keep adding water, a little at a time. He'll know how much and when."

It was only thirty minutes after this that Dallas suddenly exclaimed, "Look, Julienne, there's the *Columbia Lady*. We've got a chance."

"How far to Natchez?"

"Just a couple of hours. I think we can beat her." As they drew slowly nearer to the big steamer, Dallas grunted, "She's making black smoke."

"What does that mean?" Julienne asked.

"It means," Dallas answered, "that they're putting in rich pine just like we are. I'd bet that Dennison is capping his safety valve too."

They followed her doggedly, and sometimes Julienne thought they were gaining on her, and sometimes she thought they were falling farther behind. The *River Queen* seemed to be straining, like a live thing. The heat from the boiler room was heating up even the pilothouse, two decks up. Ring's gravelly voice sounded up the tube again.

"Dallas, Jesse says this is it. She's running hot as the nether regions."

"Ask him can he keep it up for just about another hour," Dallas ordered Julienne.

"Dallas wants another hour," Julienne yelled, "and I do too. And so do you."

"I think we're both gonna blow our fool selfs up," Ring said grumpily but faintly as he turned away from the speaking tube.

Julienne stared at the *Columbia Lady* so hard her eyes and temples started to hurt. Dallas, of course, kept his sharp gaze straight ahead always. Finally Julienne whispered, "We're gaining on her, aren't we, Dallas? We are, aren't we?"

"Yeah, Julienne, we are. I really think that if Jesse and Rev can keep it up, we'll nose in front of her before we get to Natchez," he said firmly.

Just ahead was a sharp bend in the river, and when the *Columbia Lady* reached it she completely disappeared. Tensely they searched the darkness ahead.

In about two minutes they saw what seemed to be a white cloud rising from the water, immediately followed by a loud explosion that shook the *River Queen*.

"Oh, no, no," Julienne said faintly.

"Her boilers burst for sure," Dallas said grimly. He reached up and rang the big bell, pulling the cord hard, so the continual deep gongs sounded urgent.

Immediately Ring shouted up, "What is it, Dallas?"

Julienne answered, "The *Columbia Lady*'s boilers burst, Dallas is pretty sure. He says full steam ahead until you hear the backing bell, then pull her up hard. Get some fire buckets and the fire crew ready!"

Dallas guided the *Queen* around the bend, and Julienne gasped. The beautiful steamer's nose was down, her pilothouse and the front half of her decks blown to splinters. She was on fire, and people were jumping overboard. Almost without thinking Julienne prayed, *Thank You, Lord, that it's not wintertime.* She remembered the icy cold down to her bones in that water the night she and Dallas had wrecked.

Dallas rang the backing bell, and at once they felt the paddle wheels stop, then groaning, start turning in reverse to stop the *Queen*. Dallas was busy maneuvering the wheel, so Julienne said, "I'm going on down to the main deck, Dallas."

"Go on. Be careful. Send Darcy up here, I can swim better than him."

"I will." She ran down the stairs and found Darcy, already sitting down on the deck and taking off his boots. "Go up and take the wheel, Darcy. Dallas is a strong swimmer, he'll be able to help more than you will."

Rebellion crossed his face, but then he pulled his boot back on and ran up the stairs.

The next few hours were a nightmare. Some of the passengers and crew had been blown into the river, killed instantly by the explosion. Others were drowning in the water. Dallas, Rev, Jesse, and Ring jumped in again and again, dragging people to the *River Queen*. Julienne and Caesar and Libby worked on the deck, helping to bring them up, while Roseann, Leah, and Robbie, took them into the now-empty ballroom, laid them down, and covered them with whatever they could find: sheets, tablecloths, towels, stored canvas pieces, their own bedlinens.

Julienne looked up and saw that Lyle Dennison had swum to the *Queen* by himself, and Caesar and Libby were helping to haul him aboard. She had thought that Lyle had been killed, because the pilothouse was nothing but a burning pile of splintered wood. But then she realized that Lyle wouldn't have stayed in the wheelhouse for long. He must have been in some other part of the boat. Julienne forgot all of her bitterness and anger toward him at that moment. She was glad he hadn't been killed.

"I'm all right, I don't need any help," he was saying irritably to Caesar and Libby. "Unless you can find me a drink."

"They're passing out brandy in the ballroom," Caesar said kindly.

Dallas, who was between dives to look for survivors, walked up to face him squarely.

Dennison stared at him, then muttered, "Well, you've won, Bronte."

"Not the way I wanted to. I'm sorry you lost the *Columbia Lady*, Dennison. I truly am."

"So am I. And the *River Queen*. But regardless of how it happened, you beat me, Bronte. And I can take my beatings like a man." He stuck out his hand.

Dallas shook it. "Takes a big man to lose gracefully. I wish you well, Dennison."

He nodded with a sort of dignity. Dallas turned and started searching the water for more survivors.

As Lyle walked past Julienne he said quietly, "Congratulations, Miss Ashby."

"Thank you, Lyle," she said warmly.

He went in the ballroom and, being very familiar with the *River Queen*, walked between the people lying on the floor straight back to what he had planned to be the gentlemen's salon. Already there was a fully-stocked bar, locked away in a small storage closet. He doubted that the Ashbys even knew of it. He pulled out an expensive bottle of brandy and took a long gurgling swig of it. "So I lost the *Columbia Lady* and the *Queen*," he murmured to himself, "and I lost the girl. Too bad for me. I can build more boats. But I don't think I'll ever get another girl like her."

THE *STATE OF CAROLINA* had come out of Natchez and reached the wreck about half an hour after it happened. They doubled up the rescues, helped to bring on the dead, and soon both she and the *River Queen* were back in Natchez. Even though it was almost 2 a.m., people had been waiting up, crowded all up and down Silver Street, the wharves, and the boardwalk, waiting for the winner. When the two boats came in with their tragic news, word spread quickly. Soon wagons, buggies, and carriages were lined up to take the injured to hospitals or hotels and the dead to the city morgue.

The mayor of Natchez, Big Jim Scanlon, came to the *River Queen* and said, "You won, Mr. Bronte."

"Not the way I'd like to have won," Dallas said. "It's always a shame to see a fine ship go down."

"It is, it's a shame and a waste and a tragedy that some have lost their lives. But come on with me, Mr. Bronte. We're going through with this ceremony."

Going through the ceremony meant going up to the platform that had been built, and the mayor made a speech, then handed Dallas a box. "Here's the prize, but I want to say you won more than the race. I've been hearing how you stopped and saved all the passengers you could. I honor you for it."

That was all the ceremony. There was too much tragedy to celebrate.

It was about four a.m. before things died down enough for Dallas to return to the *River Queen*. Julienne sat on deck in her rocking chair, waiting for him. He went to lean on the railing, as he had done so many times before, and she joined him.

Roseann, Leah, and Carley were all still up in Roseann's stateroom. Caesar, Libby, and Robbie were working in the galley. A delicious aroma of bacon came floating out on the deck. "Nobody's sleepy, and everybody's hungry," Julienne said lightly.

"I didn't realize until I smelled that bacon that I'm starving," Dallas agreed. "It has been one long, hard night."

"You know," Julienne said slowly, "I think that this was a great and mighty thing that the Lord gave us. Not winning the race and winning the money, but helping those people, the survivors. That was a great and mighty thing."

"I think you're right."

The two stood in easy silence for awhile. Then abruptly Julienne turned to him and said, "I think I'd like to get married." She said it as calmly as if she had said, "I'd like to have a drink of water."

Dallas stared at her and then began to grin. "When would you like that?"

"Mm, I don't know. Tomorrow, maybe?"

"Anybody in mind for the groom?"

She reached up, put her arms around his neck, pulled his head down and kissed him. "You're the candidate in the lead right now."

They kissed again, a long lingering kiss full of promise to both of them. Finally Dallas lifted his head and said, "I don't even know what exactly you're expecting from a husband."

"Oh, don't worry, I wrote down a list. Here it is." She reached into her pocket, pulled out a soggy piece of paper, and handed it to him.

He looked at it and said, "Julienne, this is a very important document, and I can't read it at all. So now what do we do?"

She laid her head against his broad chest and then said, "I'll tell you what it said. It said the man I marry must love me with all his heart and must never leave me."

He lifted her chin and said somberly, "Julienne Ashby, I love you with all my heart. I have for a long time, and I thank the Lord that I can tell you now. I promise you, I'll never leave you. I promise you I'll do my best to be a good husband, and a good friend, to you for all of our lives."

"Finally, finally, the man I've been longing for all my life. Thank You, Lord."

Dallas said, "Amen."